HTML
Professional Projects

John W. Gosney

Premier
Press™

The Premier Press logo and related trade dress are trademarks of Premier Press and may not be used without written permission.

Microsoft FrontPage XP, Microsoft SQL Server 2000, and Notepad are either trademarks or registered trademarks of Microsoft Corporation in the United States and/or other countries.

All other trademarks are the property of their respective owners.

Important: Premier Press cannot provide software support. Please contact the appropriate software manufacturer's technical support line or Web site for assistance.

Premier Press and the author have attempted throughout this book to distinguish proprietary trademarks from descriptive terms by following the capitalization style used by the manufacturer.

Information contained in this book has been obtained by Premier Press from sources believed to be reliable. However, because of the possibility of human or mechanical error by our sources, Premier Press, or others, the Publisher does not guarantee the accuracy, adequacy, or completeness of any information and is not responsible for any errors or omissions or the results obtained from use of such information. Readers should be particularly aware of the fact that the Internet is an ever-changing entity. Some facts may have changed since this book went to press.

ISBN: 1-59200-055-X

Library of Congress Catalog Card Number: 2003101213

Printed in the United States of America

04 05 06 07 08 BH 10 9 8 7 6 5 4 3 2 1

Premier Press, a division of Course Technology
25 Thomson Place
Boston, MA 02210

SVP, Retail Strategic Market Group:
Andy Shafran

Publisher:
Stacy L. Hiquet

Senior Marketing Manager:
Sarah O'Donnell

Marketing Manager:
Heather Hurley

Manager of Editorial Services:
Heather Talbot

Acquisitions Editor:
Todd Jensen

Associate Marketing Manager:
Kristin Eisenzopf

Project Editor:
Jenny Davidson

Technical Reviewer:
Brian Lich

Retail Market Coordinator:
Sarah Dubois

Copy Editor:
Cathleen Snyder

Interior Layout:
Bill Hartman

Cover Designer:
Mike Tanamachi

Indexer:
Kelly Talbot

Proofreader:
Kim Benbow

HTML
Professional Projects

For Melissa, Genna, Jackson, and George.
I love you all very much!

Acknowledgments

While I may be the only person with his name on the cover, a book of this size and scope is most definitely the work of several people, and those people deserve some very well-earned acknowledgment.

Todd Jensen, acquisitions editor extraordinaire, retained his patience (and great sense of humor) as the book evolved over various deadlines and life interventions (including a little life intervention of his own—congratulations, Todd, on becoming a father for a second time).

Brian Lich, technical editor, continues to prove himself an absolute professional and trusted friend. Aside from always answering my silly questions with tact (that is, not laughing directly at me for asking such questions in the first place), Brian is a virtual cornucopia of knowledge; there is very little, if anything, he doesn't know about computers and technology in general. Having Brian's skill applied to this project has made it a better book several times over.

Special thanks are in order to Cathleen Snyder, copy editor, and Jenny Davidson, project editor. They (along with Brian) ensured the accuracy of this book's content to a level that is beyond my comprehension; the three of them caught so many of my mistakes—technical, grammatical, or otherwise—I couldn't imagine working on a project like this without them. Best of all, they are all incredibly funny and generally just plain cool people to work with. Can an author ask for anything more? An extra special nod to Jenny, who had to track this project over the inevitable content and structure revisions and keep everything coordinated and moving forward. Jenny, I owe you one.

I'd also like to thank Dr. Chris Miller of the Indiana University School of Dentistry, who always encourages me to explore and develop my professional interests—I could not have completed this project (or several others) without his mentorship and support. Thanks as well to Stacy Hiquet of Premier Press for continuing to present project opportunities. Stacy, it is always a pleasure to work with you! Thanks as well to Donald Fagen, Walter Becker, and Robert

Zimmerman, as without their special creative talents this book would have been a lot less fun to work on (you need good music as you write, and these guys provided it over long hours of sitting at the computer).

Finally, and as always, I'd like to give very special thanks to my family for always supporting and encouraging me while I worked on this and other projects. You make everything worthwhile, and I love you all very, very much.

John Gosney
August, 2003

About the Author

John W. Gosney is currently the Director of Information Technology for the Indiana University School of Dentistry, as well as an instructor for the university on the Indianapolis campus. He also has worked within the pharmaceutical industry as both a technical writer and Web/systems application developer. His professional writing credits include several industry analysis/market research reports on different aspects of technology, including reports on artificial intelligence, emerging trends in electronic delivery of entertainment, and commercial applications of artificial sense technologies. Additionally, he has published seven titles with Premier Press, including *JavaScript Professional Projects* (w/Paul A. Hatcher), *ASP Programming for the Absolute Beginner,* and *Web-Enable Your Small Business In a Weekend.* Mr. Gosney holds a B.A. from Purdue University and an M.A. from Butler University.

Contents at a Glance

Contents

Chapter 6   Creating and Manipulating Tables 99

Chapter 7   Integrating HTML Frames and Advanced Formatting 117

Chapter 26   Creating a SQL Server 2000 Database 533

Introduction

You're standing in the bookstore, wondering what to think of all the computer books, let alone all the books on HTML or Web design in general. Maybe you are a seasoned IT professional without much Web experience, and you're looking for a no-nonsense, direct approach to a specific topic. Or perhaps your area of interest is not information technology, but you're looking to take your particular topic to the Web by building a Web site for your small business, school, or nonprofit organization. Or maybe you have any one of the many other good reasons to build a Web site. Whatever the case, you are holding this book in your hands because you have a desire to work with HTML and, as a result, the Web.

Compared to even a few years ago, it is a good time to be jumping into the HTML arena. Despite the relatively recent "dot com" bust, the Web is still a vital mechanism for delivering information and doing business. Indeed, many businesses—having learned from the failures of the dot coms—are taking the best of the Web and integrating it with their internal processes to build exciting and productive methods of doing business. Large-scale CRM (*Customer Relationship Management*) applications and enterprise-level productivity suites are leveraging the power of the Web to bring real-time information to customers, field sales personnel, and inside business units. The result is the delivery of information on demand, along with users' growing expectations of such delivery. Another result is information representative of larger, inclusive processes (in other words, a snapshot of a company's functioning across various departments).

Maybe your interest in HTML isn't quite that advanced; perhaps you are looking to build a functional, easy-to-use Web site for your nonprofit small business or school. If that is the case, then have no fear; this book is relevant for you, too. Because no matter what type of information you are looking to empower via the Web, some basic design principles apply to every Web site. This book will highlight those principles by focusing on the tools used to deliver them (hyperlinks, forms, tables, frames, cascading style sheets, and so on). Moreover, the projects in this book will highlight the practical application of these tools and design principles across a variety of different applications, from nonprofit Web sites to small business Web sites.

So are you ready to jump into the exciting world of HTML and the Web? If so, then you won't be disappointed with this book.

Structure of the Book

As I mentioned, the focus of this book is on building real-world applications, or "professional projects." How will these projects be presented, and what can you expect to learn as they relate to HTML? Each project in Part II will be divided into four sections.

- **Project Introduction**. The first chapter in each of the project sections will serve as a general outline for the specific information delivery requirements that will be utilized in the project. Each Web site has its own information delivery requirements (different subject matter, different target audience, and so on). To aid in the general technical implementation, this first chapter in each section will reference specific chapters from Part I so you can review the essential application foundations as necessary.

- **Identifying Process Goals**. For successful Web design, it is essential that you have a solid understanding of the actual process and procedures that have driven the development of the Web site in the first place! This critical element is often overlooked in books on nearly all computer- or technology-related topics. Often the all-important pre-design issues are not even considered. All successful projects (computer-related or not!) begin with a well-designed plan, complete with clear objectives and a defined procedure for post-implementation concerns (in other words, change-control procedures). That said, this section of each project will consider the project's specific needs (addressed in the first chapter of each project) and how they will be implemented. Put simply, this chapter will map out the Web site and consider the encompassing functionality of the entire site. To help you develop this plan, each project will be presented as a fictitious case study containing a description of the major players and issues facing the Web design team.

- **Addressing Customer Usability Issues**. Having a good plan is only part of the overall Web design puzzle. Another critical element is ensuring that your Web solution will actually meet the specific requirements of your users or customers. While the word "customer" will take on different connotations in each of the projects, the central concerns—regardless of the type of Web site you are constructing—remain the same: Will the final Web site be something that is intuitive *and* functional to use? These chapters in each of the projects will look at this all-important question, and will serve as a vital link between how you plan the Web solution and how it is implemented via the actual HTML.

- **Building the Solution**. These chapters will focus on the actual solution and will contain all source code, explanations, and references to related HTML topics. However, in addition to just presenting the application code, these chapters will also include extensive analysis as to how the solution is an actual fulfillment of the requirements set forth in the preceding chapters. In short, these chapters will ensure that you see the application's design and implementation as a *complete* solution.

In summary, this book has been written from a holistic, total application solution perspective. Although you'll be presented with the basic HTML tool set in Part I, the real focus is on the project case studies and practical, viable examples of how to best plan and design Web sites specific to your own unique organization.

What Are the Project Case Studies?

So what project case studies will you be presented with? Four case studies/ projects will be developed in this book; a brief description of each follows.

- **The Small Business Web Site**. A locally owned music store wants to build a Web presence that communicates to the local community the terrific variety of titles they stock and provides general information about store hours, location, and so on. Moreover, the store wants to build a foundation to allow business transactions to be conducted online sometime in the future.

- **The Nonprofit Web Site**. A local school wants to build a Web site to enhance its community outreach programs (such as PTA) and provide a homework forum where students can check in and get assignments on a daily basis; moreover, they want the site to utilize a "portal" design that can provide a comprehensive overview of the entire educational process, with different "views" of that process depending on the user type (parent, teacher, or student).

- **Building a Web Site with an HTML Editor Application**. Although this book will focus on hand coding your HTML (which is, by the way, the best way to learn), you will find that after a while, a good HTML editor can make quick work of some of the more mundane tasks associated with Web design. The third project in this book will look at Microsoft FrontPage XP, a leading HTML editor. To evaluate the application, you will explore the tool set from Part I using FrontPage, so you can see how it automates the creation (and editing) of HTML code, as well as allowing you to bring advanced functionality to your Web design.

- **Integrating a Database with HTML.** The final project in Part II will highlight the extended power and functionality that integrating a database can bring to your HTML and overall Web site design. For this project, you will get an introduction to Microsoft SQL Server 2000, a leading database package that you can use to allow for the construction of dynamic, data-driven Web sites. In addition to learning how to Web-enable your database, you will also learn the basics of structured query language (SQL), which allows you to access and manipulate your data based on specific search parameters; in this project, you will see how a database can further enhance the small business Web site by—among other things—allowing customers to search (via the Web site) current store inventory.

Conventions Used in This Book

There are several special conventions used in this book to aid your understanding.

 TIP

Tips provide helpful shortcuts and tricks to assist you with the topic at hand.

 NOTE

Notes provide additional information about the product or technology being discussed.

CAUTION

Cautions provide you with warnings of potential pitfalls and problems you might encounter along the way.

SIDEBAR

Sidebars contain additional information that is not directly relevant to the chapter, but which you might find interesting or helpful during your learning process.

PART I

HTML Essentials

As you will discover in this book, effective Web design is both a technical and business process challenge. That is, you can have the most technically precise site, but if it doesn't facilitate a real business process need (whatever that business or process might be), it will be less than successful. However, there is no denying that you must understand the underlying technical structure of a Web site, and that structure is otherwise known as HTML. In the chapters that comprise Part I, you will learn the essential techniques of working with HTML by studying and applying all of the classic markup tags. You will also learn to work with one of the most exciting and powerful innovations to be brought to "classic" HTML: cascading style sheets (CSS). In addition, you will be introduced to the additional functionality of integrating scripts into your HTML, as well as working with an HTML editor application (Microsoft FrontPage XP).

Chapter 1

**HTML and the
World Wide Web
Consortium: Past,
Present, and
Future**

Regardless of whether you have any previous experience with HTML and Web design—from creating simple pages with a Web editing tool to implementing more advanced projects—you should understand the administrative infrastructure of HTML and many related Web technologies. Specifically, this involves the World Wide Web Consortium (W3C for short), the administrative body that dictates many of the standards for Web technologies, including HTML.

Rather than being a history lesson on the origins of HTML, this chapter will focus on the active projects (both within the W3C and otherwise) that are shaping the current and future direction of HTML. Like everything else in this arena, it is imperative that you have a firm understanding of not only the current state of a given technology, but also the initiatives that will influence the future look, feel, implementation, and functionality of that technology. That is what this chapter is all about.

 TIP

You might be wondering why the future of HTML is the first chapter of the book; after all, wouldn't this chapter make better sense as an appendix? Although that argument is valid for many technologies, the Web moves fast—very fast—compared to even the breakneck speed of the IT industry in general. Given the project-oriented nature of this book, a key component of project planning is anticipating for future developments. So when you work with the Web in any capacity, it is imperative that you think ahead so you aren't taken by surprise by the technology or by a process or procedure you might later want to facilitate using the technology.

An Overview of the World Wide Web Consortium

Consisting of more than 430 member organizations worldwide, the W3C is committed to developing the Web to its full potential by making technical recommendations and, in the process, by developing protocols with the aim of producing a common, functional infrastructure for true interoperability across all facets of the Web. A collaborative effort, the W3C is hosted by MIT/LCS (*Massachusetts Institute of Technology Laboratory for Computer Science*), ERCIM (*European Research Consortium in Informatics and Mathematics*), and Keio University, Japan. In addition to these, other support organizations including CERN (*European Organization for Nuclear Research*) and DARPA (*U.S. Defense Advanced Research Project Agency*) contribute to the hosting and support of W3C. Figure 1.1 highlights all of the information available at the W3C Web site.

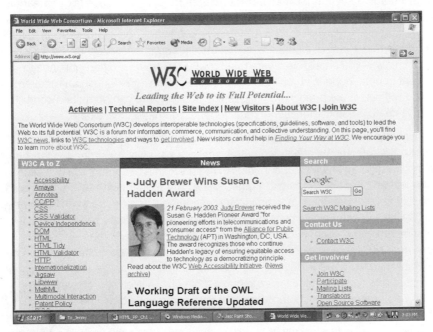

FIGURE 1.1 *The W3C Web site provides a wealth of information about not only the current projects and initiatives under development, but also the history and development of the Web.*

NOTE

Visit the W3C on the Web at http://www.w3c.org. In addition to current news updates on developing projects, you can view a complete background of the organization, links to member organizations, and fascinating historical archives and documents related to the Web's history and evolution. Check it out!

IS BASIC HTML AN OUTDATED TECHNOLOGY?

So why should you care about the W3C and its activities? Well, most importantly, you should realize that the basic HTML that is described and illustrated in this book is a somewhat old technology.

Now, this potentially loaded statement needs some clarification. (After all, if you've plunked down hard-earned money for this book, you want to be sure the technology you are reading about is worth your time.) The term *old technology* is not meant to imply that HTML will be written off anytime soon; after all, it is the foundation code of the Web, and—as you will read in a moment—a primary goal of the W3C is to foster the development of new technologies that build on present successes. However—and this is critical—you should be aware that basic HTML means different things to different people, depending on—and this is also critical—the functional requirements. As you will see in the project chapters of this book, HTML can be quite a complicated beast depending on the functional requirements you need to facilitate.

For example, compare the functional requirements of a corporate intranet site to the functional requirements of an elementary school's Web site (described in this book). Both utilize HTML; however, the functional requirements of each of the two sites are quite different. For the corporate intranet, sales data presented to field sales reps is probably an amalgamation of various internal company factors, such as inventory, availability, and competitive pricing. However, for the elementary school site, the data might be just the product of one person, such as a teacher who has placed a homework assignment on the Web site. The final product of both examples can be accomplished via basic HTML; that is, the information—whatever it is—is neatly formatted and placed within, for example, a table on the Web site. However, the underlying processes that determined that data—in other words, the functional requirements—are quite different. More than likely, a corporate intranet will involve underlying business processes that are more complex than the underlying processes for an elementary school Web site. (Well, maybe… !)

So, to bring this full circle, what does this have to do with HTML being a potentially outdated technology? Again, the basic HTML of yesteryear (just a few years ago!) might not be sufficient to get the job done if the functional requirements of your organization are complex. For example, your Web site might require database integration so customers can search inventory, place orders, and so on. This type of functionality moves beyond basic HTML. To accomplish this, you might want to integrate a Web scripting language (such as Microsoft's Active Server Pages) with your basic HTML to allow your Web site to talk to an underlying database server.

However, it is important to realize that no matter what the complexity of your final Web site, the underlying processes and functional requirements must take precedence. So regardless of whether your site utilizes basic HTML or advanced scripting languages, the focus must remain on more than just the technology. As you will see in the project chapters of this book, there are really four major components of developing your Web site.

◆ **Assessing the HTML needs**. What exactly do you want to Web enable? This is a critical first step in any Web/HTML enterprise, regardless of the scope or size of the project.

◆ **Developing an implementation plan**. You need to give as much time (if not more) to planning your technology implementation as you devote to the actual technology work itself. Indeed, if you plan well, the actual coding should be gravy, and the end result should be a useful, functional Web site.

◆ **Building the solution**. This step is self-explanatory, but again, keep in mind the ever-critical planning and assessment stages.

◆ **Administering the application**. You build a Web site, but how will you use it and how will you address future requirements? Change control and long-term administration are critical, often overlooked steps.

So is basic HTML an outdated technology? The vast majority of the time, the answer to that question is no—if you plan, assess, implement, and administer your solution with foresight, patience, and skill. But if you jump into a technology solution (Web-based or otherwise) and respond in a knee-jerk fashion to new requirements, no technology—no matter its age or capabilities—will save you from a bad experience. Food for thought as you begin your own HTML professional projects.

In addition to its hundreds of member organizations, the W3C also has specific sub-groups charged with specific goals.

- ◆ **The W3C Team** includes more than 60 worldwide researchers and engineers who spearhead the technical work of the W3C and generally manage the operations of the consortium. The majority of the Team's work is conducted at MIT/LCS, ERCIM, and Keio University.

- ◆ **The W3C Technical Architecture Group** was created in 2001 to provide general direction on the technical aspects of the Web. It consists of five elected and three appointed participants. The Group conducts all of its work via a public mailing list and makes larger recommendations through the W3C.

- ◆ **The W3C Advisory Board** was created in 1998 to provide general strategy and advice to the larger team. The Board has no decision-making authority; however, it proposes changes in the W3C process to the Advisory Committee.

The Mission of the W3C

Clearly, the worldwide scope of the W3C—with member organizations and offices located throughout the world—demands that the Consortium have a well-defined focus if it is to succeed and help develop the Web to its full potential.

Fortunately, this is indeed the case; the mission and vision of the W3C are clearly defined. Although the Consortium's mission and vision are described in more specific detail on their Web site (and in various supporting documents), their own seven-point summary serves as a neat capstone to the organization's central goals.

1. **Providing universal access**. With the growing popularity (and functionality) of access devices such as Web-enabled cell phones and PDAs, it seems that people want access to the Web regardless of their location. As a result of this increasing push for Web access on demand, the W3C has a primary goal to not only encourage this (universal) access initiative, but also to help ensure that you have equal access to the Web and the information it contains, regardless of what access device you are using, where you are physically located, what culture you belong to, or even your physical or mental ability.

2. **Enhancing the meaning of information**. This book was written specifically for "human consumption"; in other words, it was written in a language that was intended for human beings to read and understand. But what if the information contained in this book could be manipulated so that computers—free of human interaction—could understand it too, and in turn present the findings of their "reading" for quicker manipulation? This is the goal of the W3C's push toward the "semantic Web" and the additional languages—RDF, XML, and so on—being developed to aid in this process. The idea is to make it easier to exchange and manipulate information in potentially faster and more efficient ways than just using plain text. (In the process, this will aid in the primary goal of universal access.)

3. **Developing trust and confidence in the Web**. In addition to universal access and better ways to manipulate information, the Web must be an instrument in which people can trust and have confidence. This includes taking responsibility for what you publish to the Web, as well as having confidence in the information you retrieve (and potentially rely on in various critical ways). The W3C sees this trust and confidence issue as critical to the future development of the Web as an information exchange medium, and is thus involved in various initiatives (such as XML signatures and annotation mechanisms) that will help to deliver this trust. Think of this in terms of the W3C being analogous to a car manufacturer and a driver of a car as the Web developer. While the carmaker ultimately can't determine how their product is driven, they still feel it is their responsibility (rightly so) to produce a product with strong safety devices and that people can trust. Similarly, the mission of the W3C is to help develop a product—the Web—that, because of its very design and tools with which it is manipulated (HTML, XML, and so on), "drivers" (for example, Web developers and general users) have a product they can trust.

4. **Achieving inherent interoperability**. Certainly one of the major—if not *the* major—promises of the Web is that it seeks to deliver a universal information access mechanism. If this universal access is to be realized, then interoperability must be achieved in terms of the software and hardware that power the Web and allow access to the information it

contains. The W3C is a vendor-neutral organization; as such, it seeks to promote interoperability across technologies through industry consensus and the open exchange of ideas.

5. **Nurturing a structure that supports change**. As I mentioned at the beginning of this chapter, if you are going to work with the Web in any capacity, you need to expect and indeed welcome change. A few years ago it would have been impossible to predict the changes in how the Web functions and in the functionality it is asked to support across all facets of global communication. That said, the W3C has a central goal: to develop an evolving Web that can adapt to change quickly without losing its functional base.

6. **Focusing on decentralization**. The Web was created as a communication mechanism free of a central point of failure. In other words, if one location was knocked out (for example, in the case of a nuclear attack—remember, the Internet was first developed under this Cold War mentality), a message could simply be rerouted to another location where it could be passed along its delivery path. This decentralization not only adds to the functionality of the Web, but it also increases security because the entire network is not dependent on just one or two locations.

7. **Developing new multimedia**. Perhaps the most exciting feature of the Web in terms of delivering on the promises of universal access and interoperability is the continuing development of multimedia tools for information access. The W3C actively supports the development of what they call the "Cooler Web" to help support these multimedia tools and the new levels of functionality that they can bring to information access.

W3C Activities and Recommendations

Clearly, the goals listed in the previous section are ambitious, to say the least. Yet the W3C has been very successful in meeting the challenges of these goals, and they have a strong foundation to continue to meet the challenges these goals will present in the future.

In addressing these goals, the W3C bases much of its activity on the work of specific working, interest, and coordination groups. These groups consist of representatives from member organizations, the W3C Team, and outside experts. To help develop the work of these groups to the highest efficiency and potential, the activities of the W3C are divided into four major domains.

1. **Architecture Domain**. This domain develops the underlying technologies and infrastructure of the Web.

2. **Information Domain**. This domain focuses on the interoperability and accessibility goals and works with all facets of the tools of interaction (such as formats and languages) to help deliver this promise of interoperability and accessibility.

3. **Technology and Society Domain**. With the development of specialty areas of cyber-law and other professional categories that focus on the impact and influence of the Web on various areas of business and society, there exists a strong need to develop standards revolving around social, legal, and public policy issues and concerns that are affected by (and that, in turn, affect) the Web. This domain seeks to address these issues to ensure the technical developments of the Web remain in harmony with administrative and procedural requirements across local, state, federal, and global bureaucratic arenas.

4. **Web Accessibility Initiative (WAI)**. Just as the name implies, this domain works to ensure that the benefits of the Web remain accessible to all people, regardless of mental or physical disabilities. From research and development to education and outreach, the WAI domain seeks to guarantee that the Web remains a viable and accessible communication tool for everyone.

 NOTE

All of the W3C's activities, goals, and mission statements are available in much greater detail at http://www.w3c.org/consortium.

With all of this organization, individual working teams, groups, and domains, what has the W3C accomplished since its inception? In a word: much! The W3C has published more than 40 recommendations across all facets of the Web, from functionality perspectives to technology protocols and requirements. In the process, it has upheld its primary goal to build on the existing success and foundation of today's technology to help lead the way to the most exciting, functional, viable, and efficient Web of tomorrow.

Communicating and Participating with the W3C

Although you don't need to be involved with the W3C to work with HTML, it should be clear from the discussion thus far that it's advantageous to participate in the ongoing development of the Web (including HTML) that the W3C facilitates.

That said, Table 1.1 provides an overview of the various ways you can become involved with the W3C, from direct membership to becoming involved in newsgroups. Figure 1.2 highlights an example of the sense of "community spirit" the W3C wants to facilitate among developers by providing information on open-source releases.

Table 1.1 W3C Organizational and Participation Units

Topic	URL
W3C membership	http://www.w3.org/Consortium/Prospectus/Joining
General public participation in W3C	http://www.w3.org/Consortium/Public
Mailing lists	http://www.w3.org/Mail
Translations (English is the official working language of the W3C; this link provides information for translation services for W3C documents and other materials.)	http://www.w3.org/Consortium/Translation
Open source software	http://www.w3.org/Status

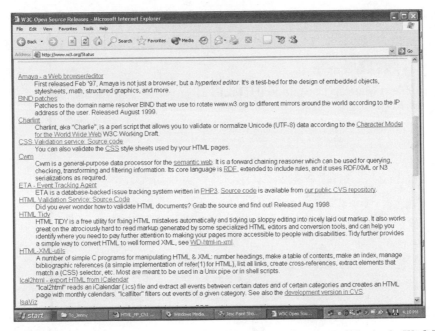

FIGURE 1.2 *A listing of just a few of the open-source releases accessible via the W3C Web site*

The W3C and HTML (and Where HTML Is Headed)

Keeping in step with the mission and goals of the W3C, HTML continues to be an evolving technology. Indeed, since the early days of the Web, HTML has seen some major changes in both its infrastructure and its implementation. Given the explosive growth of the Web in general and the tremendous (did someone say infinite?) range of applications that are being Web enabled, HTML has needed to keep pace with these changes to deliver on its goal to be a primary vehicle for the successful implementation of all of the Web's promises.

Along the way, the W3C has presented various recommendations and related initiatives and work on HTML and HTML-related standards. From early tag standards to the now recent pairing and collaboration with HXTML, there is much you should be aware of in terms of how HTML has developed and how that development has been spearheaded by the W3C in many cases. Figure 1.3 shows the W3C home page, which is always being updated to reflect new information on both the Web itself and the people who help shape it.

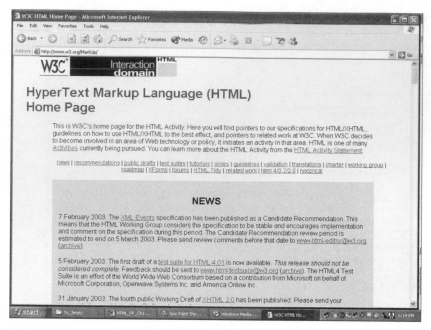

FIGURE 1.3 *The HTML home page on the W3C Web site.*

The history of HTML has gone through four basic iterations over the past several years. They are

- ◆ **HTML 2.0**. The early standards for HTML contained many of the core features still seen in today's version of the language.

- ◆ **HTML 3.2**. The first W3C recommendation for HTML, this version added popular features such as support for superscript, subscript, tables, and so on. It also provided backward compatibility for HTML 2.0.

- ◆ **HTML 4.0**. This was an early gold standard for HTML, and it is the version to which most early HTML programmers took hold. However, HTML 4.01 has since superseded HTML 4.0.

NOTE

You can still read the W3C specifications for each of the HTML versions listed here on the W3C Web site. In addition to being historically interesting, you can see how different functionalities changed from one version to another and how such functionality was accounted for to ensure backward compatibility with earlier versions of HTML whenever possible. Backward compatibility is an important point, and certainly one to keep in mind as you develop your own Web sites and anticipate the omnipresent push toward future needs and developments.

As I noted earlier in this chapter, you don't have to be involved with the W3C (or even visit its Web site on a regular basis) to produce strong Web sites. However, in the exploding, ever-changing arena that is the World Wide Web, regular visits to the W3C can keep you abreast of changes that are coming down the technology pike and present you with vendor-neutral overviews and technology specifications.

 NOTE

For the latest updates to W3C HTML activity, visit http://www.w3.org/MarkUp/Activity.

WHY WORRY ABOUT THE VENDOR-NEUTRAL STANCE OF THE W3C?

Back in the early days of the Web (1997–1998!), browser compatibility was a much greater issue than it is now. Specifically, if you were designing Web pages, you had to be very aware of how your site might look (and function) if it were viewed in Microsoft Internet Explorer versus Netscape Navigator, for example. Although some differences were minor, there were other major differences in how the browsers interpreted HTML and related scripts (such as JavaScript). In the worst-case scenarios (and there were many of them), critical site functionality wouldn't... well... function if it were viewed in a different browser than the one for which the site was designed. To make things more complicated, vendors would disregard HTML standards (for example, those recommended by the W3C) and build additional HTML functionality into their browser applications. Although some of this functionality was impressive, it presented a serious roadblock to the W3C's universal interoperability goal (and the larger philosophy of the Web in general). Thus the browser wars began, and they are still fought today.

Fortunately, the W3C continues to take a vendor-neutral stance. Although you might not be able to completely escape the long reach of some of the vendor-specific requirements of your development environment (in other words, if you are in a Microsoft environment, you tend to play by Microsoft's rules), you can still go a long way toward making your life easier—and making your site accessible to the greatest number of potential visitors—by avoiding as much vendor-specific functionality as possible, and by sticking to the universal recommendations set forth by the W3C (not just their HTML recommendations, but recommendations for all Web-related technologies).

Figures 1.4 through 1.7 illustrate some vendor-specific issues. In each comparison, there are significant display problems either because of backward-compatibility issues in the site design (in other words, it wasn't designed for older browsers) or due to vendor-specific functionality only accessible in a specific browser.

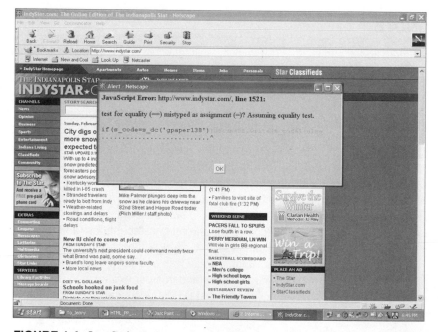

FIGURE 1.4 *JavaScript errors prevent the newspaper Web site from being viewed in its entirety using Netscape Navigator 4.04.*

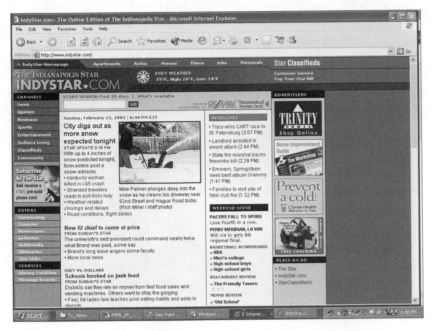

FIGURE 1.5 *The same site viewed with Microsoft Internet Explorer 6.0.*

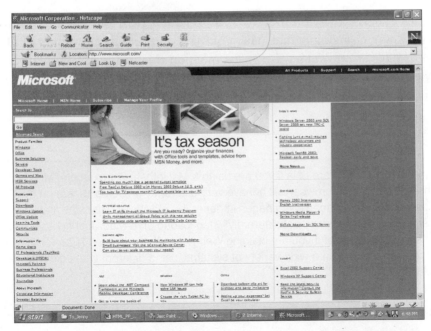

FIGURE 1.6 *Viewing the Microsoft Web site with an older version of Netscape Navigator. Note the fuzzy appearance of the text and the lack of functionality (in other words, the drop-down menu) shown in Figure 1.7.*

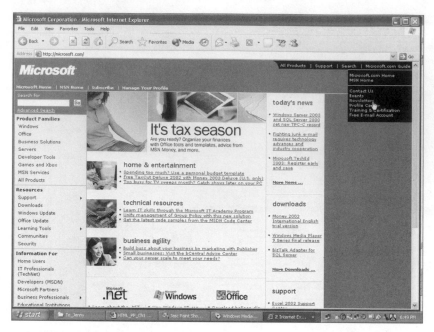

FIGURE 1.7 *The Microsoft Web site viewed with Internet Explorer 6.0.*

Current HTML activity on the W3C site is rich, varied, and again indicative of the Web's ever-changing nature. Much of the recent activity surrounds XHTML (*Extensible Hypertext Markup Language*; more on this in a bit); however, you can also view recent updates to other critical issues such as accessibility guidelines for the visually impaired or otherwise physically challenged.

 CAUTION

Another issue to be aware of is if you are using a Macintosh. For example, Microsoft's Internet Explorer Web browser will behave very differently (in some cases) on a PC as compared to a Mac. Indeed, Web pages in general—and the functionality they contain—may both look and act differently when loaded on a Mac. Just another issue you need to be aware of if you are building Web pages that will need to be (or that you want to be) accessed on a wide variety of systems, using different types of Web browser applications.

TIP

Although writing your HTML to be as vendor-neutral as possible is a great idea, there are other accessibility issues you should consider as well. Certainly, one of the most important issues is designing your site so it is as accessible as possible to the visually impaired or otherwise physically challenged. The W3C has published some recommended guidelines for making your site accessible in this regard. You can view these guidelines—as well as general accessibility guidelines—at http://www.w3.org/WAI/Resources/#gl.

What else can you find about recent W3C activity regarding HTML? The following is a short overview of some of the projects the W3C is currently working on; you can learn more about these projects by visiting the W3C site.

♦ **XML.** Defined as the universal format for structured documents and data on the Web, XML moves beyond HTML in that it allows for more precise placement and manipulation of data on Web pages.

♦ **CSS (*Cascading Style Sheets*).** In the old days, if you wanted to change the visual layout of a page (fonts, margins, and so on), you had to perform a lot of tedious, line-by-line code changes. With style sheets, you can set these attributes universally for your Web pages, and then quickly change them if you need to. I will cover style sheets extensively in Chapters 9 and 10 as well as within the project chapters.

♦ **DOM (*Document Object Model*).** DOM is an evolving method for adding dynamic effects to Web pages that is independent of specific languages or computer platforms (thus furthering many of the goals discussed earlier, including accessibility, interoperability, and the "Cooler Web"). You will explore this topic in more detail in the project chapters of this book.

♦ **Internationalization.** The Web is a worldwide entity, and thus should not be structured to present data in only one language. HTML 4.0 and 4.0.1 allow for the transmission and manipulation of various language sets, furthering the accessibility and ease of use of Web content across the electronic language barriers that previously existed.

◆ **Accessibility**. People with visual or other disabilities should not be prevented from taking part in the rich, developing arena that is the Web. The W3C and many other organizations (including hardware and software manufacturers) are making a dedicated push to ensure that the Web is accessible by everyone.

◆ **XForms**. This evolving technology seeks to add a tremendous amount of new functionality to typical HTML forms. You can read more about XForm development on the W3C site (see Figure 1.8).

◆ **Representation of mathematics on the Web**. Remember your high school or college calculus class and all the formulas and mathematical functions? It often was hard enough to write those neatly, let alone type them! (Ah, type… the old days are certainly behind us, aren't they?) The W3C is working on an XML application called MathML that seeks to ease both the presentation and interpretation of mathematical expressions on the Web.

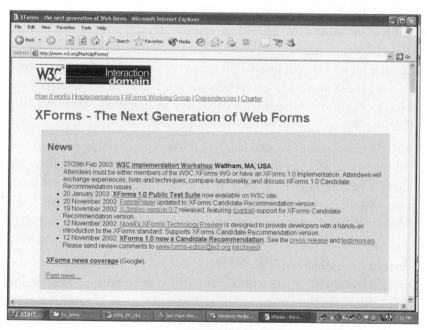

FIGURE 1.8 *The XForms section of the W3C site. Note the W3C domain (the Interaction Domain) to which this work belongs. I described the domains and general organizational structure of the W3C earlier in this chapter.*

Moving toward XHTML

HTML is an evolving technology—so much so that it will probably evolve itself out of existence. Now don't panic: All technology—even widely successful technology such as HTML—moves on to greener pastures. The key to this transition—as this book will stress continually—is planning for that inevitable transition to make it as smooth as possible.

XHTML is the planned successor to HTML. The current W3C recommendation is XHTML 1.0; additional recommendations are currently under development (see Figure 1.9).

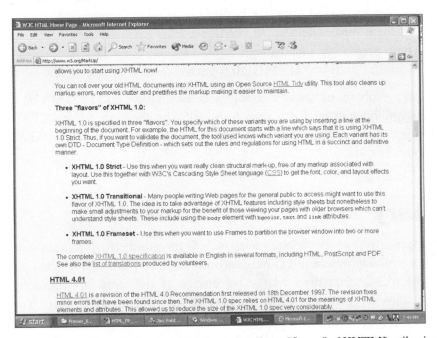

FIGURE 1.9 *Note the description of the three different "flavors" of XHTML, allowing an upgrade path of your choice from HTML 4.0.1 to XHTML 1.0.*

Because XHTML 1.0 utilizes the feature set of HTML 4.0 (and 4.0.1), with some general modification you can use it in existing browsers.

Why should you be interested in XHTML? Consider the following:

◆ As with any technology, there will always be new ways to manipulate data. This seems like an obvious point, but it is especially critical in regard to the Web, given that Web sites are often the front-end interfaces to many larger data manipulation processes and technologies (such as database integration with Web sites). A goal of XHTML is to be modular, so that new data manipulation techniques and agents can be integrated more easily into existing Web structures.

◆ With the continuing popularity of portable devices (such as Pads and cell phones) or otherwise non-traditional Web accessibility devices, there is a growing need for a standardized method of presenting Web content to these various devices. XHTML presents a new level of interoperability in presenting Web content across various access devices. Indeed, the working draft of XHTML 2.0 is geared toward these portable devices.

Again, the evolving nature of technology is inevitable, and HTML is no exception. As you move through this book (especially the chapters in Part I), I'll be sure to point out the emerging XHTML standards and feature sets that complement traditional HTML.

Summary

This short introductory chapter's purpose was threefold—first, to familiarize you with the evolving nature of HTML; second, to make you aware of the organization (the W3C) that does a large percentage of the work in suggesting how HTML should evolve; and third, to stress that functionality requirements can and do dictate the different utilizations of HTML across different Web sites (such as a corporate intranet versus an elementary school Web site).

The remaining chapters in Part I will focus specifically on the various attributes and features of HTML, and will show—where appropriate—their XHTML successors. Additionally, the chapters will provide links to W3C and other resources that might help you better understand or work with the particular features being described. For example, there is a tremendous amount of information regarding cascading style sheets (discussed in Chapters 9 and 10 and on the W3C Web site, including documentation and open-source applications that help you work with them.

Chapter 2

**Manipulating
and Formatting
HTML Text**

There's a reason why some people are described as artistic; moreover, there's a reason why the more talented ones make a nice salary—having the talent and natural artistic ability to be a good (or great) designer is not easy.

I am not one of those artistic people; however, I am frequently asked to play the role of designer when working with technology. And, if I'm guessing correctly, you are asked (or soon will be asked) to play that same role. Indeed, those of us working within technology fields are asked to wear many hats that often are outside our direct area of expertise and experience.

The interesting (and frustrating) thing about HTML is that it is not by design a feature-rich tool set for manipulating graphics. Indeed, the very opposite is true; in its original (and, for the most part, subsequent) incarnations, HTML was designed for very simple text markup, not for exact or otherwise sophisticated graphic design. Still, many people think of HTML as a graphics tool. Although the Web is by nature a communication medium that invites the utilization of graphics, tweaking HTML to fit your graphical presentation requirements can be a challenge.

However, there are some things you can do to strengthen your work. Using tables, frames, and other goodies in the HTML tool bag, you can actually create some pretty sharp-looking Web pages. This chapter will focus on some of the most basic (but critical) design issues by looking at a variety of basic text-formatting techniques.

HTML Terminology Overview

Terminology is probably not the right word to use in this context; however, there are some general terms and definitions that you should be aware of when working with HTML.

If you've done much work on the Web (and if you're reading this book, I'm sure that you have), then you are already familiar with the material in the following sections. However, I will refer to these terms—tags, attributes, and absolute/relative URLs—throughout the book, so take a moment to verify that you understand these concepts.

DOES CAPITALIZATION MAKE A DIFFERENCE?

Should you capitalize your HTML code? Technically, it doesn't make a difference: `<A HREF="WWW.YAHOO.COM">` will work just as well as `<a href="www.yahoo.com">`.

However, there are some things to consider. First is the issue of readability. When you go back to look at long chunks of code, lowercase can be easier on the eyes.

Second—and directly related to the preceding point—is consistency. If you mix and match capitalization within your code, it can be harder to troubleshoot and can open the door to coding errors.

Finally, capitalization *does* make a difference in other programming languages (such as XML), so again, consistency is the name of the game so you will have good habits when you move to other Web technologies, programming languages, and so on.

Tags and Attributes

An HTML tag is indicated by opening (<) and closing (>) brackets. Each tag contains various attributes, depending on the tag used. Look at the following sample HTML code:

```
<font face="Arial" size="3">This is an example of text.</font>
```

What are the tag and attribute(s) in this HTML?

◆ The tag in this example is the `<font>` tag. Notice the closing `</font>` tag as well. This tag will affect everything between the opening and closing `<font>` tags. (In this case, the text "This is an example of text." would be affected.)

◆ The attributes of the `<font>` tag are, in this case, the font face (which is set to Arial) and the font size (3, or 12-point text). Note that in many instances in HTML there is a numerical reference—especially with text formatting—to the usual "point" reference in text.

TIP

As you will see in Chapters 9 and 10 when cascading style sheets (CSS) are discussed, many of the traditional formatting tags in HTML have been deprecated in favor of using style sheets; however, the original tags are still quite valid and—especially if you are new to HTML—worth understanding if for nothing else to further appreciate the power and functionality of CSS.

Here's another example:

```
<font face="Arial" size="3"><a href="http://www.yahoo.com">Click here to go
to Yahoo!</a></font>
```

◆ This example uses two different tags. The first, as you saw just a moment ago, is the `<font>` tag. The second is the `<a href>` tag, which is used to set a hyperlink.

◆ The attributes of the two tags should be apparent. In the case of the `<font>` tag, the attributes are the same as in the previous example (Arial font, size 3). For the `<a href>` tag, the attribute is the URL of the hyperlink (in this case, http://www.yahoo.com). Note that with the `<a href>` tag, the inclusion of the actual URL (in this case, http://www.yahoo.com) and all text that subsequently follows up until the closing `</a>` tag is what will be presented on the Web page as the actual hyperlink. You will learn all about working with hyperlinks in Chapter 5, "Understanding Hyperlinks."

This code listing is also an example of nested tags, or the process of placing more than one tag within another tag(s). While you can't nest all tags (as you'll see when you work with HTML tables), the important thing is to keep an eye on the order in which you open and close your tags. For example, look at the following two lines of code:

```
<a href="http://www.yahoo.com">Click here to go to yahoo.com</a> -- I think
you will find it a useful site.
<a href="http://www.yahoo.com">Click here to go to yahoo.com -- I think you
will find it a useful site.</a>
```

Although the two lines of code appear very similar, note that in the first one, the closing </a> tag is placed in a different location than in the second example. As you can see in Figure 2.1, this has a major effect—the text that comprises the hyperlink is different due to the placement of the closing </a> tag.

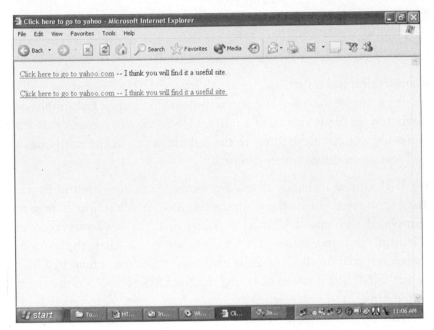

FIGURE 2.1 *Watch how you place your closing tags so that you achieve the desired text formatting or other HTML effect.*

Put simply, depending on the tag and its specific attributes, you need to be aware of different formatting issues, which will be discussed in this chapter and throughout the book.

Absolute and Relative URLs

The URL (*Uniform Resource Locator*) is a major building block of the Web. For this discussion, you need to be aware of the difference between absolute and relative URLs and how each one can affect your HTML coding.

In an *absolute URL*, the address includes the entire file location (including the server name). A *relative URL* only shows the file name relative to the current location.

For example:

```
http://www.someweb.com/somefolder/somefolder_2/somefile.html
somefile.html
/somefolder_2/somefile.html
../somefolder_2/somefile.html
```

The first line here is an absolute URL; it shows the entire path (including the server name) to the file (in this case, somefile.html).

The second, third, and fourth listings are all relative URLs; they show a URL that is relative to a current location. What exactly does that mean? Put simply, depending on where your file is stored, in a relative URL you can assume that the location of the file will vary depending on the full file path. (In the third line of code, the "../" represents the complete file path.)

Relative URLs come in handy if you are moving your files around because you don't have to worry about hard coding the full path, which might change anyway. For example, if you have a URL that points to http://www.serverA.com/folder_A/file.html and you move it to a new server, so that the path is now http://www.serverB.com/folder_A/file.html, you could use a relative URL when making the initial link. Instead of typing the full URL, you could use the relative URL ../file.html; in this case, when you move from server A to server B (as indicated in the different URLs), the link to your file (file.html) remains active.

However, if you had typed the *absolute* URL (in other words, the full path name), you would have to retype it for the link to your file.html file to remain the same.

You will learn more about these issues in Chapter 5. For now, keep in mind that generally speaking, relative URLs are easier to work with because you only have to remember the actual name of the file (or perhaps the folder it is retained in), rather than the entire URL path.

 CAUTION

While you will again see more discussion of this in Chapter 5, be forewarned that depending on the type of Web server that is hosting your site, relative paths may not function. There is really no harm in always including the absolute path, other than you might have to type a few extra characters (that is, you include the full file path instead of the abbreviated relative URL).

General HTML Page Layout Tags

Every HTML page will (or should) have some basic tags.

◆ `<HEAD>`. Think of this tag as the container for all of the general layout information for your page. Within the `<HEAD>` and `</HEAD>` tags, you will find general information about your page. (As you will learn later, some of this information is useful in identifying your page to search engines.) Note, however, that except for the title, none of the information contained within the `<HEAD>` tag will be displayed to your viewers.

◆ `<TITLE>`. This is where you assign the all-important title to your Web page. It's easy to overlook this tag, so you should be careful that you don't; the title of a page will appear at the top of the browser window, and is thus an important navigation element to let visitors to your Web site know where they are.

◆ `<BODY>`. This is where most of your HTML code is placed; as such, it corresponds to the body of your Web page content.

 TIP

Many HTML editors, such as FrontPage or HomeSite, will present you with a basic Web page template when you select File, New. The `<HTML>`, `<HEAD>`, `<TITLE>`, and `<BODY>` opening and closing tags are presented within this template (see the following code listing). Take advantage of this template to remind yourself to include these important tags within your document (in other words, don't delete them)!

In the following code, you can see a document template that is often produced by default in HTML editors. This template outlines the use of the primary HTML tags.

```
<html>

<head>
<meta http-equiv="Content-Type" content="text/html; charset=windows-1252">
<meta name="GENERATOR" content="Microsoft FrontPage 4.0">
```

```
<meta name="ProgId" content="FrontPage.Editor.Document">
<title>New Page 1</title>
</head>

<body>
</body>

</html>
```

This example was produced using Microsoft FrontPage. (Note the FrontPage-specific <META> tags, which I will discuss later.) This template presents all of the major document tags (both opening and closing) and also a default page title. When you create your own pages, don't forget to include these tags, and be sure to title your page (using the <TITLE> tag)—hopefully something more descriptive than "New Page 1."

Utilizing the <META> Tag

<META> tags are quite useful in providing information about the contents of your page so it can be picked up and properly indexed by various search engines.

The previous code listing was generated using Microsoft FrontPage, which inserted some default <META> tag information in the opening page template. More than likely, you'll want to tweak these <META> tags so they are more illustrative of the content that actually exists on your page. Examine the following code listing to see in greater detail how the <META> tags have been utilized.

```
<meta name="keywords" CONTENT="rock music, 1970s, popular culture, Steely Dan">
<meta name="description" CONTENT="A retrospective analysis of the rock group Steely Dan">
<meta name="author" CONTENT="Bill Lee">
<meta name="generator" CONTENT="Microsoft FrontPage 4.0">
```

GETTING "PICKED UP" ON THE WEB

Having a Web site is one thing, but actually getting people to visit it is something else entirely. While the usual suspects are clearly important here (that is, good design, good content… basically, having something that people are in fact interested in), Web surfers won't know how great your site is unless they can find it!

How Web sites get categorized and turn up on various search engines and portals (for example, Yahoo!) is a difficult issue and can depend on a variety of factors. (How big is your organization? What content are you expressing on your site?) However, the skillful use of <META> tags can enhance your ability to be "picked up" by a Web search. Consider the example listed here: this site would have a good chance of being found if a user typed in "Rock Music," "1970s", "Popular Culture," and/or "Steely Dan."

Also, another important issue is trying to determine how users will search for your site. On a recent drive home from work, I heard an advertisement for an otolaryngology (that's an "ear, nose, and throat" doctor to you and me) practice. They included their Web site in the advertisement. It isn't hard to imagine that many users might incorrectly spell "otolaryngology," so in the <META> tag of the site, it wouldn't be surprising if the designers considered different common misspellings of this word, not to mention including more common phrases such as "ENT" or even the individual terms "ear," "nose," and "throat."

So, as you move into publishing your site and thinking about how interested folks are going to find it, the <META> tag becomes more critical. While there is no guarantee your site will be picked up by every search (or even several searches), having well-defined <META> tags can certainly help your cause.

The Text Alignment Attribute

HTML includes an `align` attribute that allows you to do some basic text alignment in your Web pages. As with everything else, the best way to see this attribute in action is to look at a code example.

```
<p align="left">This text is left aligned.</p>
<p align="center">This text is center aligned.</p>
<p align="right">This text is right aligned.</p>
```

Pretty simple, right? Figure 2.2 shows how this looks in a Web browser.

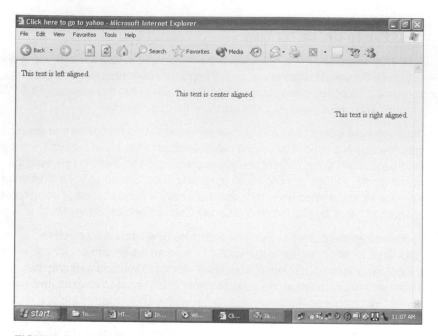

FIGURE 2.2 *HTML allows for basic left, center, and right alignment.*

 TIP

The ⟨p⟩ tag simply puts a paragraph break between each line.

Style sheets and DHTML (*Dynamic HTML*) allow for more exact placement of text on your Web page. You will explore both of these issues in later chapters of Part I.

Basic Font Manipulation Techniques

To begin your study of text formatting, take a look at Figure 2.3. As you can see, there are various text-formatting issues at work here, including the type of font, the size of the font, and various formatting features (such as underlined text).

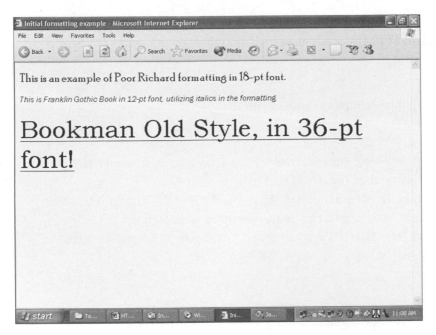

FIGURE 2.3 *A variety of text formatting features have been applied in this example, probably to a confusing effect—if this were in fact a real Web page!*

 NOTE

For the examples in this (and subsequent) chapters, I have used Microsoft FrontPage as my HTML editor of choice. However, to help you better understand the actual HTML structure, I have listed the code generated by FrontPage. While I would be a liar if I said I still hand-coded all my HTML, I do suggest you try your hand at coding your own HTML prior to becoming overly dependent on an HTML editor application. While these tools can (and should) save you lots of time, it is worth your effort to initially work with a simple text editor such as Notepad as you code and experiment with your initial HTML pages. Doing so will help you understand what you can and can't do with HTML. Note, however, that you will learn more about FrontPage in Chapter 12, "Working with an HTML Editor," as well as the third project of Part II.

The following code listing shows how this formatting is presented within the standard HTML layout tags, such as <HTML>, <BODY>, and <TITLE>.

```
<html>
<head>
<title>Initial formatting example </title>
</head>
<body>
<p><font face="Poor Richard" size="5">This is an example of Poor Richard
formatting in 18-pt font.</font></p>
<p><i><font face="Franklin Gothic Book" size="3">This is Franklin Gothic Book in
12-pt font, utilizing italics in the formatting.</font></i></p>
<p><font face="Bookman Old Style" size="7"><u>Bookman Old Style, in 36-pt
font!</u></font></p>
</body>
</html>
```

While this code example is fairly straightforward, I want to point out a few things with regard to basic text formatting.

◆ The font is set by the <FONT> tag. In this example, the font is set by declaring its name in quotes (for example, "Poor Richard").

◆ The size of the font is set in a similar fashion; however, note the difference in how this is indicated in the size attribute of the <FONT> tag. Although the last line of text reads "36-pt," the size attribute is set to 7. In HTML, valid size attributes are 1–7, which in turn correspond to point size (which is used in HTML editors and word processing applications).

◆ Other formatting, such as italics (<i>) and underlining (<u>), can be set before or after the <FONT> tag attributes. However, for ease of reading and troubleshooting your HTML code, it's a good idea to get into the habit of formatting your code the same way—you'll definitely thank yourself later when you have to read through hundreds of lines of HTML to find what you're looking for!

CAUTION

HTML can be maddeningly difficult to troubleshoot because the placement of an opening or closing tag—depending on other formatting attributes you have set on the page—can alter the appearance of your text and be difficult to find. That said, it really is a good idea to get in the habit of "clean coding" by always placing your formatting tags (and all others, for that matter) in the same order.

TIP

Many of these formatting tags have been deprecated in HTML 4.0, or the functionality they present can be facilitated through the use of style sheets. (See Chapters 9 and 10 for more information on this.) However, you can obviously still use these tags, and they can come in handy for quick formatting and Web page design issues.

Bolding Text

You can bold text to make it, well, bold—or to otherwise draw attention to it. In Figure 2.4, several different sections of text have been bolded to show various effects.

As you can see in Figure 2.4, the bolding is a bit distracting and doesn't seem to follow any logical order—different words are bolded, many of which don't seem to warrant any special formatting. If you look at the code listing for this page, you can see how the <b> tag has been utilized.

```
<html>
<head>
<title>Working with the bold tag</title>
</head>
<body>

<p><b>March 31, 2003</b></p>
<p><b>Mr. Bill Lee</b></p>
<p><b>c/o Katy Lied Products</b></p>
<p><b>1234 South Fagan Street</b></p>
<p><b>Indianapolis, IN 46201</b></p>
```

```
<p>Dear Mr. Lee,</p>
<p>This is to <b>inform </b>you that <b>you are not going to believe </b>the <b>offer
</b>we have in <b>store </b>for you.  If you call us <b>right</b> now, we
can <b>give YOU THE </b>details.</p>
<p><b>THANK YOU,</b></p>
<p>Customer <b>SERVICE DEPARTMENT</b></p>


</body>
</html>
```

◆ TIP

You will see   in several code listings throughout this book. It simply refers to a character space in the actual text. If you are using an HTML editor such as FrontPage and you hit the space bar on your keyboard, the corresponding   will be inserted in the HTML to reflect the space.

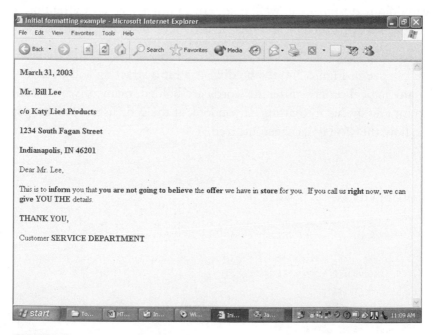

FIGURE 2.4 *Use text bolding carefully to highlight only the areas of your text to which you want to draw attention.*

What's going on with this HTML? Well, not much… at least in terms of good, effective formatting. The <b> tag has certainly been overused. But in addition to that, notice how confusing this code is to read. Not only are the bold tags haphazardly placed throughout the text, but the use of capitalization also makes both the HTML and what appears on the actual Web page difficult to read.

In the next section, in which you will look at the <u> underlining tag, notice how this messy formatting has been cleaned up, improving the text presentation and making the HTML much easier to read.

Underlining Text

You can use underlined text as effectively (if not more so) than bold text. Look at Figure 2.5 to determine which you think is a more attention-grabbing format.

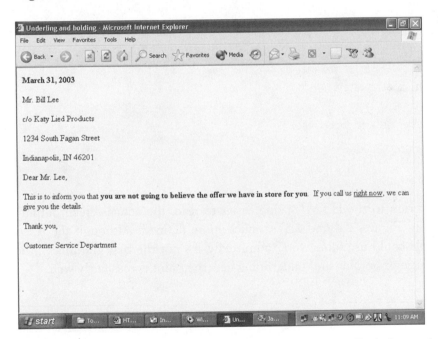

FIGURE 2.5 *You can use bolding and underlining individually or collectively to make sure your text gets the attention it deserves.*

Notice how much easier the following code sample is to read, compared to the previous one.

```
<html>

<head>
<title>Working with underling and bolding</title>
</head>
<body>

<p><b>March 31, 2003</b></p>
<p>Mr. Bill Lee</p>
<p>c/o Katy Lied Products</p>
<p>1234 South Fagan Street</p>
<p>Indianapolis, IN 46201</p>
<p>Dear Mr. Lee,</p>
<p>This is to inform you that <b> you are not going to believe the offer we have in store
for you</b>.  If you call us <u> right now</u>, we
can give you the details.</p>
<p>Thank you,
<p>Customer Service Department</p>

</body>
</html>
```

In addition to the HTML being easier to read, the actual screen output (compared in Figures 2.4 and 2.5) is much more defined. Although the text in this example could use some work (admittedly, it's not the best grammar!), the clear, single use of bolding and underlining gets the point across fairly well.

 CAUTION

Be careful you don't use too much underlining in your Web pages. As you will see in Chapter 5, hyperlinks are associated with underlined text. If you have a lot of underlined text on your page, readers might think words are hyperlinks when in reality they are just underlined.

Italicizing Text

The final basic text-formatting technique is italics, which are set using the `<i>` tag and are illustrated in Figure 2.6

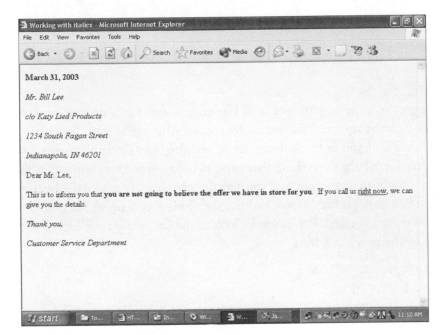

FIGURE 2.6 *Italics are the final basic text-formatting technique within HTML.*

Again, the use of italics has been kept consistent and not mixed with other formatting. This helps to create a clean, formatted look that is not too busy. In this example, the use of italics also helps to draw attention to the letter's heading.

```
<html>

<head>
<title>Working with italics </title>
</head>
<body>

<p><b>March 31, 2003</b></p>
<p><i>Mr. Bill Lee</i></p>
<p><i>c/o Katy Lied Products</i></p>
<p><i>1234 South Fagan Street</i></p>
<p><i>Indianapolis, IN 46201</i></p>
```

```
<p>Dear Mr. Lee,</p>
<p>This is to inform you that <b> you are not going to believe the offer we have
in store for you</b>.  If you call us <u> right now</u>, we
can give you the details.</p>
<p><i>Thank you,</i>
<p><i>Customer Service Department</i></p>

</body>
</html>
```

Although this code is getting a little busier, it is still fairly easy to read. A good way to clean it up even further is to remove the extraneous formatting tags. Remember that you only need one set of opening and closing tags for a specific formatting attribute; everything that appears between the two will retain that formatting. So in this example, you can put the opening `<i>` tag at the beginning of the first line you want italicized, and put the closing `</i>` tag at the end of the last line you want italicized. For example, look at the following code listing and compare it to the previous listing.

```
<p><b>March 31, 2003</b></p>
<p><i>Mr. Bill Lee</p>
<p>c/o Katy Lied Products</p>
<p>1234 South Fagan Street</p>
<p>Indianapolis, IN 46201</i></p>
```

As you can see here, the extraneous `<i>` tags have been removed; however, everything that appears between the opening and closing `<i>` tags retains the italicized formatting. This makes the code easier to read and (by default) troubleshoot because the coding is generally less busy.

 NOTE

Again, more than likely you will be using an HTML editor to do your initial coding and subsequent editing. The code listings provided so far are the product of Microsoft FrontPage, and thus FrontPage automatically put in the line-by-line formatting (such as the opening and closing `<i>` tags around each line). In reality, this probably won't be a big issue because you'll be using an HTML editor to do your work. Still, it is a valuable and telling comment on how busy the editors can make your code, often unbeknownst to you! You'll really see this later when you start looking at more advanced HTML functionality, such as tables and frames.

Advanced Text Formatting

Although the word "advanced" is probably a bit of a misnomer in the context of this chapter (admittedly, this is basic—yet important—stuff), basic HTML offers other formatting options that allow for more sophisticated text markup. I will discuss superscript, subscript, bulleted and numbered lists, and the manipulation of font colors in the following sections.

Superscript and Subscript

Presenting superscript and subscript on your Web pages is easy.

◆ The ⟨sup⟩ tag is used for superscript. Anything you place between the opening ⟨sup⟩ and closing ⟨/sup⟩ tags will have superscript formatting applied to it.

◆ The ⟨sub⟩ tag is used for subscript. Anything you place between the opening ⟨sub⟩ and closing ⟨/sub⟩ tags will have subscript formatting applied.

The following code listing provides a quick example of these tags.

```
You might want to use a superscript to make a reference to a footnote. <sup>1</sup>

You might want to use a subscript in order to <sub> highlight a hyperlink, such as <a
href="http://www.someplace.com">here</a>.</sub>
```

Figure 2.7 highlights how superscript and subscript appear on a Web page.

 NOTE

The W3C is currently working on a standard for the presentation of scientific notation on Web pages. You can find more information on this topic at http://www.w3.org/TR/html401/struct/text.html#h-9.2.3

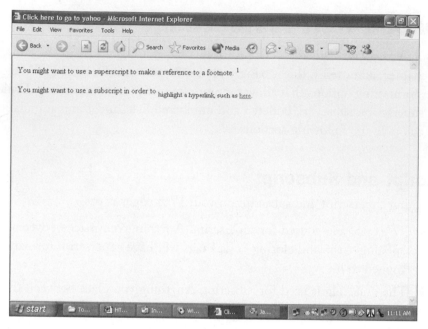

FIGURE 2.7 *An example of the* <sub> *and* <sup> *tags in action.*

Bulleted and Numbered Lists

Bulleted and numbered lists are probably the most common advanced text formatting that you will find on a Web page. Although they are a bit more complicated to use than some of the other tags you have seen in this chapter, they are still quite easy once you get the hang of them.

Take a look at the following code, which illustrates the use of both bulleted and numbered list formatting.

```
<p>The following are all good things to have for a picnic:</p>
<ul>
  <li>Plastic utensils</li>
  <li>A picnic basket</li>
  <li>Bug repellant</li>
  <li>A blanket</li>
  <li>A nice bottle of wine</li>
</ul>
```

```
<p>The following are the top five great things about summer:</p>
<ol>
  <li>Going swimming</li>
  <li>The smell of freshly-cut grass</li>
  <li>The Fourth of July</li>
  <li>Vacations!</li>
  <li>Going to see a baseball game</li>
</ol>
```

Figure 2.8 shows the result of this code in a Web browser.

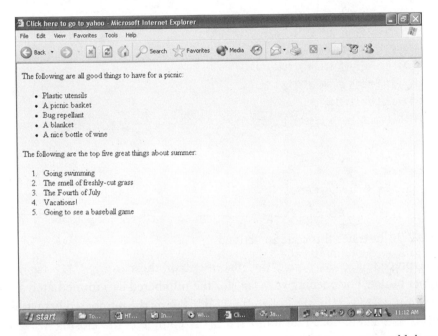

FIGURE 2.8 *Bulleted and numbered lists can draw attention to your text and help neatly format your Web page content.*

By this point in the chapter, you can probably figure out the tag scheme for bulleted and numbered lists, but just in case you need a hint:

◆ For bulleted lists, you use the opening `<ul>` and closing `</ul>` tags. Then, you surround each item you want to individually bullet with opening `<li>` and closing `</li>` tags.

◆ Numbered lists are very similar, except that you use opening `<ol>` and closing `</ol>` tags to denote them. However, just like the bulleted list, you use opening `<li>` and closing `</li>` tags to individually number each item.

You might want to nest a numbered list within a bulleted list or vice versa. This is easily accomplished by specifying the placement of your opening and closing `<ul>` and `<ol>` tags, respectively. For example, take a look at the following code listing.

```
<p>The four seasons of the year, with the top five things about each season:</p>
<ul>
  <li>Spring</li>
  <li>Summer
    <ol>
      <li>Going swimming</li>
      <li>The smell of freshly-cut grass</li>
      <li>The Fourth of July</li>
      <li>Vacations!</li>
      <li>Going to see a baseball game</li>
    </ol>
  </li>
  <li>Fall</li>
  <li>Winter</li>
</ul>
```

Figure 2.9 illustrates this code in action.

In the preceding code, notice the placement of the closing `</li>` tag for the Summer bullet. The opening `<ol>` tag (for the numbered list) immediately follows the opening `<li>` tag (for the bulleted list). This nests the numbered list within the bulleted list. Then, once the numbered list is complete, the closing `</ol>` tag is immediately followed by the closing `</li>` tag, so that the next bulleted item (in this case, "Fall") will not appear as an item of the numbered list.

 TIP

You might be wondering whether an HTML editor would make this type of formatting easier. If you think the answer is yes, you are absolutely right! However, it is helpful to learn how to code by hand so you can use an editor to its full advantage. Even though such applications generate code automatically, you often need to go into that generated code and tweak it to your liking.

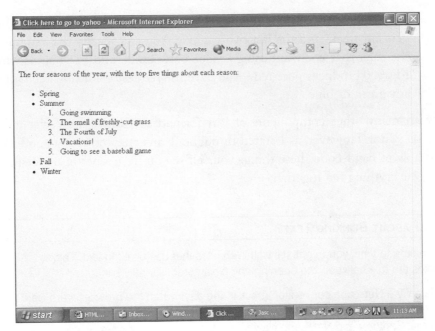

FIGURE 2.9 *You can easily nest numbered and bulleted lists to achieve more effective text formatting.*

Manipulating Font Colors

You can easily manipulate text color via the color attribute of the `<font>` tag. You can set the attribute to one of two values.

◆ You can literally use the name of a color. In this case, you can set the color to one of sixteen defined colors, such as `<font color="Red">`.

◆ You can use the hexadecimal value of the color, which allows you to select from literally hundreds of color combinations. Each color has a hexadecimal value; by tweaking this value, you can tweak the color. For example, the hexadecimal for basic red is FF0000. However, a slightly lighter shade of red is FF3118. In your HTML code, you use these hexadecimal values in the `color` attribute. For example, to use the hexadecimal for red, you would type `<font color="#FF0000">`, where the "#" preceding the number indicates that you are using a hexadecimal value. The hexadecimal number is split into three colors—red, green, and blue—where the first two numbers of the hex are red, the next two numbers are green, and the last two are blue. You can specify the amount of the color that you want using a value between 00 and FF. That is why FF0000 produces pure red—you have the reddest color possible without any green or blue.

As with many other components of text formatting, things are easier with an HTML editor. However, as I stated throughout this chapter, it is a good idea to learn how to hand-code these things yourself so you have a better understanding of how everything fits together.

WHAT ABOUT BLINKING TEXT?

From time to time, you might still visit Web sites that use blinking text. The `<blink>` tag makes the text between the opening and closing tags literally blink.

Originally a Netscape convention (back in the days when the browser wars were more contentious and there were serious differences between browsers such as Microsoft Internet Explorer and Netscape Navigator), the use of blinking text was seen in some ways as a mark of defiance against the Microsoft juggernaut. Why was this the case? Simple: Internet Explorer did not support blinking text.

But as with all things rebellious (if you want to put it that way), blinking text got old really fast. Today, it is generally considered bad design (both aesthetically and functionally) to use blinking text. If you really want to draw attention to a specific section of content, a better choice is more reserved (yet no less effective) means of text formatting, such as attractive fonts and other formatting techniques mentioned in this chapter.

So beware of blinking text and, when you can, avoid using it in your Web pages.

Summary

The purpose of this chapter was to provide you with the obligatory overview of basic HTML formatting and to ensure your familiarity with some standard terminology. I covered basic formatting techniques, both in a Web page and in the invisible (but no less important) page structure and header tags, such as <META> tags and the <head> and <title> tags. You also looked at some of the more advanced basic text-formatting options, including bulleted and numbered lists, superscripts, and subscripts.

While it is critical that you understand the basic concepts, the other underlying goal of this chapter was to give you a firsthand look at, quite frankly, how rudimentary (boring?) HTML coding can be. By "boring," I don't mean the end result—exciting and functional Web pages—but rather the repetitive processes that are involved in getting the text to look the way you want. Once you have an idea of how these basic tags function, you will probably never hand-code them again; instead, you'll rely on the power and convenience of an HTML editor such as FrontPage. Still, it is a great idea to understand the tags and attributes so you can customize or tweak the code that these editing applications automatically produce.

Chapter 3

Placing and Manipulating Images

The Web is a visual medium, so knowing how to work with and manipulate images and graphics is important for developing attractive Web sites and presenting your content in the most exciting, effective manner possible. This chapter will look at the structural issues of how to integrate images and graphics into your Web pages. You will learn to work with the `<img>` tag, which is the primary method of inserting images into your pages. You will also learn how to format your images and smoothly integrate them with the rest of your content. (In other words, you'll learn how to wrap text around an image.) This chapter and Chapter 4, "Working with Page Layout," should give you all the information you need to professionally manipulate images and graphics on your Web pages.

 NOTE

When I say that this chapter will focus on the structural issues of working with images, I mean that you will learn the underlying image-manipulation and formatting tags, and you will be introduced to tips and strategies for how best to work with both. However, this chapter is not about image design and/or creation. There are literally hundreds (if not thousands!) of quality image-creation applications available, many of which are shareware or available for a nominal fee on the Web. Moreover, many programs include images and other artwork or graphics that you can work with on your own. (This chapter will use as its example a graphic taken from the Microsoft Clip Art collection, which is included in the Office suite.)

Working with the `<img>` Tag

The `<img>` tag and its attributes contain most of what you need to know in terms of basic image manipulation. That said, this chapter will focus on the exploration and discussion of this tag, and how you can utilize it most effectively.

The following code listing illustrates the use of the `<img>` tag in a simple Web page, shown in Figure 3.1.

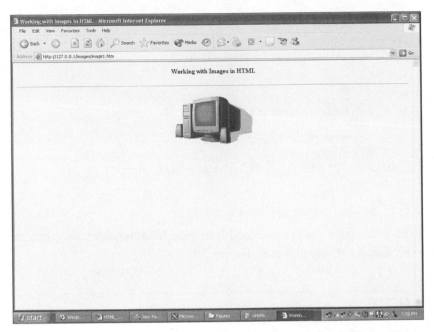

FIGURE 3.1 *You should become very familiar with the* <img> *tag and its attributes to effectively work with images on your Web pages.*

 NOTE

If you want to follow along with the code examples in this chapter, you can replace the sample graphic image with an image you might have stored on your system. The discussion of the code listing will tell you how to replace the image source in the listing (and all subsequent code listings in the chapter) with an image of your own.

1. Within the Intepub folder on your computer, create a new folder called Images.

2. Open your text editor, create a page, and save it as Image1.htm in your new Images folder.

3. Locate an image of some type on your computer and save it in your newly created Images folder.

4. Enter the following code as you see it here. However, within the <img> tag for the src (source) attribute, change the name of the file to the name of the image you just placed into the Images folder.

```
<html>
<head>
<title>Working with Images in HTML</title>
</head>
<body>
<p align="center"><b>Working with Images in HTML</b></p>
<hr>
<p align="center">
<img border="0" src="/j0285750.wmf" width="192" height="118">
</body>
</html>
```

5. Save the page. When you load it in your Web browser, your image will be displayed, much like in Figure 3.1.

 NOTE

The shadow effect in the graphic in Figure 3.1 is part of the image itself; it is not a special effect of any `<img>` tag attribute.

I want to examine the use of the `<img>` tag in the preceding code listing to make sure you understand its basic operation as well as some of the attributes that I used with it.

◆ **Border.** You can create a line border around an image by setting the `border` attribute to greater than 0. Figure 3.2 illustrates the page created in the code listing, except this time the `border` attribute is set to 3 instead of 0.

◆ **Src.** Short for *source*, this attribute lets your page know where to look for the actual image file. In the case of the example code listing, the image is stored in the same Images folder as the page that calls the image (Image1.htm).

◆ **Width** and **Height.** These attributes are self-explanatory. They are assigned values in pixels. Figure 3.3 shows the page created in the code listing again, except this time the `width` attribute is set to 300 and the `height` attribute is set to 400.

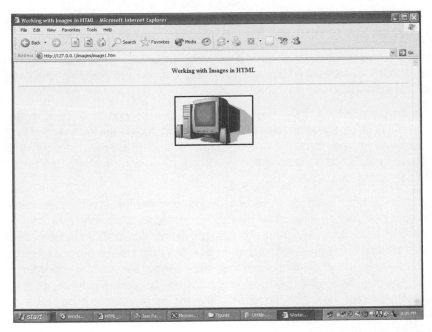

FIGURE 3.2 *Set the border attribute to give your image a lined border. The higher the number, the darker and more pronounced the border will be around the image.*

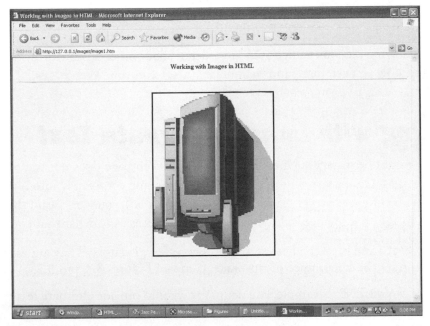

FIGURE 3.3 *You should be cautious about changing the size attributes of an image because it can lead to distortion, as shown in this figure.*

TO WAIT OR NOT TO WAIT FOR IMAGES TO LOAD: THAT IS THE QUESTION

I'm sure you've surfed the Web and come across pages that take literally forever to load in your Web browser because of an excessive amount of images on the page and/or images that are very large.

While the prevalence of high-speed Web access is certainly growing (cable modems, DSL, and so on), the vast majority of home users still access the Web via dial-up modems. As you read through this chapter (and whenever you consider your HTML work), you need to keep the speed issue in mind so you don't frustrate visitors with Web pages that load slowly.

This issue becomes even more critical when you consider that some visitors might view your Web pages via handheld devices (or any device other than a typical desktop or laptop computer). Although this type of user demands an entirely different level of thought about your Web design—a level of thought that is beyond the scope of this book—the number of images and their sizes on your site really takes center stage. An image being displayed on a very small screen can wreak havoc on your overall Web design, not to mention the fact that the image will load even slower on devices with very small screens, such as handheld devices.

Long (but important) story short: Keep the issue of load time in mind when you design your pages so you don't cause visitors to grow impatient and leave your Web site before the first page is even completely loaded into their Web browsers.

The following sections will go into more detail about other attributes of the `<img>` tag and how you can place and manipulate images on your Web pages.

Working with Image Alternate Text

There might be instances when a visitor to your Web page does not want to display images. Or, if a visitor stops the page from loading completely into his or her browser (or if for whatever reason the page doesn't load), you won't want the usual blank image spot to appear, leaving the visitor clueless as to what that content is supposed to represent.

To illustrate the importance of this issue, compare Figures 3.4 and 3.5.

As you can see in this example, you definitely want to provide alternate text in case your images don't load. However, you can also use this alternate text to give additional information about the image being displayed.

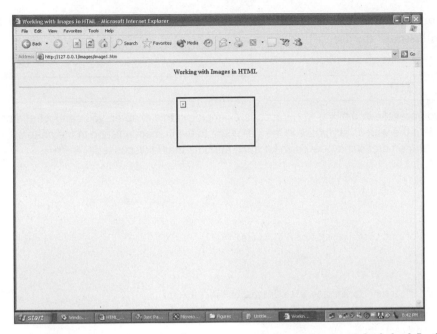

FIGURE 3.4 *Imagine that for whatever reason, the image doesn't completely load. In this figure, the visitor would have no idea what type of image (or content) is supposed to be represented by the blank spot.*

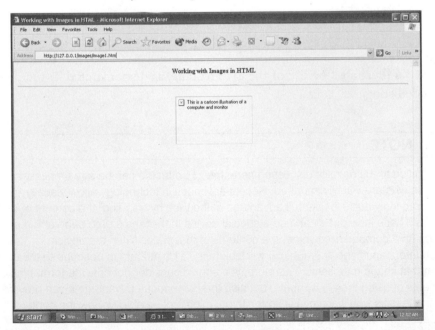

FIGURE 3.5 *Again, the image doesn't load, but thanks to the alternate text, the visitor at least has some idea of what the missing image is supposed to represent.*

All of this is done using the `alt` attribute of the `<img>` tag. The following code listing illustrates the use of this attribute.

TIP

If you are following along with the code examples in this chapter, you can just add or update the various attributes in the `<img>` tag to the first code listing in the chapter, rather than creating a new page for each attribute that is discussed.

```
<html>
<head>
<title>Working with Images in HTML</title>
</head>
<body>
<p align="center"><b>Working with Images in HTML</b></p>
<hr>
<p align="center">
<img border="0" alt="We sell this computer, as well as all accessories, hardware and
software. Take time to explore our site and all we have to offer!" src="/j0285750.wmf"
width="192" height="118">
</body>
</html>
```

Figure 3.6 illustrates the use of the `alt` attribute, as demonstrated in the preceding code listing.

NOTE

In addition to the benefits discussed here, the `alt` attribute can be a real necessity for visitors who are visually impaired. Recent advances in technology allow visually impaired individuals to take full advantage of the Web by "reading" the content of Web pages. These individuals can use a special device that scans a Web page and then reads (in a computerized voice) the contents of that page. When the device encounters an image or graphic, it will look to the `alt` attribute to describe to the user what that image represents. Therefore, you should consider not only the formatting benefits of using the `alt` attribute, but also the tremendous advantage it can provide for those folks who want to visit your site but might not be able to view the content because of a vision handicap.

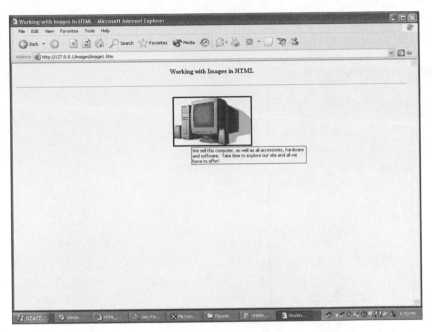

FIGURE 3.6 *You can provide valuable supplementary information about the image, your page, your Web site, or your entire organization via skillful and creative use of the* alt *attribute.*

Strategies for Loading Images Quickly

As I've mentioned a few times in this chapter, users will quickly grow impatient if they have to wait very long for your Web pages to load. Often, a page that has too many graphics (or a single large graphic) will cause visitors to leave in favor of another page that loads more quickly and efficiently.

There are several ways you can avoid having this fate befall your Web site, ranging from simply scaling down the size of your images (via the width and height attributes) to creating thumbnail links to larger images. The following sections will discuss these issues and show you how to best implement them in your pages.

Changing the Width and Height of an Image

As you saw in Figure 3.3, you can use the width and height attributes of the <img> tag to change the size of your image. A good way to experiment with different width and height attributes is to get your image information directly from your

Web browser. Figure 3.7 illustrates image information being displayed in Internet Explorer.

FIGURE 3.7 *You can quickly view an image's properties in a Web browser.*

To view the Properties dialog box in Internet Explorer, follow these steps:

1. When the page loads, right-click on the image.
2. From the menu that appears, select Properties. The Properties dialog box shown in Figure 3.7 will appear. Note how the image width and height attributes are the same as those set in the <img> tag.

 TIP

Don't overlook the image file size information, also shown in Figure 3.7. In this example, the file size is 5,186 bytes, or just a little over 5K. Such an image would load very quickly even via a slower dial-up connection.

Experimenting with the width and height attributes is a great way to decrease the load time of your Web pages. However, keep in mind the image distortion that can occur (refer back to Figure 3.3). You might find that a better way of dealing with multiple or large images is to provide thumbnail links that load the larger image when clicked. This just happens to be the subject of the next section, so let's move on to that discussion.

Creating Thumbnail Links to Images

I'm sure you have visited many Web pages where multiple images are displayed in smaller form so you can click on an image to display a larger version of it. These smaller images are known as *thumbnails*, and they are a terrific way of presenting all your visual content in a manner that allows for much faster loading of your images.

Take a look at the following code listing, which highlights the use of a thumbnail for the computer graphic I have used throughout this chapter.

```
<html>
<head>
<title>Working with Images in HTML</title>
</head>
<body>
<p align="center"><b>Working with Images in HTML</b></p>
<hr>
<p align="center"><a href="j0285750.gif">
<img border="2" alt="We sell this computer, as well as all accessories, hardware and
software. Take time to explore our site and all we have to offer!"
src="/j0285750_small.gif" width="100" height="61"</a></p>
</body>
</html>
```

If you look at the `<img>` tag in this code listing, you will notice a few things that allow for the use of a thumbnail version of the image:

◆ First, there is the use of the `<a href>` tag prior to the `<img>` tag. The `<a href>` tag is used to create hyperlinks, which you will learn more about in Chapter 5, "Understanding Hyperlinks." In essence, the `<a href>` tag and its corresponding `</a>` closing tag allow you to point to a file that will load in the Web browser when the hyperlink is clicked (in this case, when the smaller thumbnail image is clicked).

◆ Within the `<img>` tag, notice how the width and height attributes are different than in previous code listings—both values are smaller. Also notice how the src attribute is now pointing to a different file. This file is the smaller, thumbnail version of the larger graphic. Put simply, there are now two images—the thumbnail, which first appears when the page is loaded, and the full-blown image, which is linked via the `<a href>` tag.

Figures 3.8 and 3.9 illustrate the use of a thumbnail. These pages represent the preceding code listing as it would look when loaded in a Web browser.

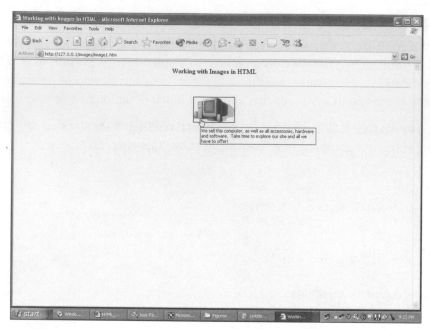

FIGURE 3.8 *When the page first loads, the thumbnail image is loaded. When the mouse pointer passes over the image it turns into a hand, indicating that the figure is a hyperlink.*

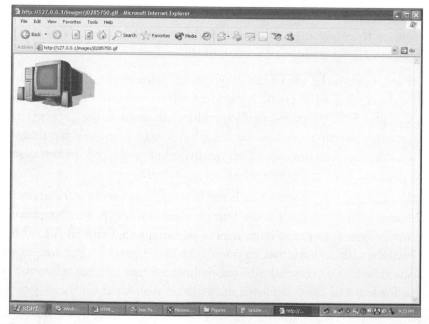

FIGURE 3.9 *When the thumbnail is clicked, the figure to which it points (in this case, the image of the computer with its original* height *and* width *attributes) appears on screen.*

In reality, the use of thumbnails involves two images (one thumbnail image and one larger, complete image), as well as the `<a href>` tag to turn the thumbnail into a hyperlink to the complete image. Again, you will learn more about hyperlinks in Chapter 5.

Using Low- and High-Resolution Images

A somewhat nefarious method of capturing readers' attention while they wait patiently for an image to load is through the skillful use of the low- and high-resolution attributes of the `<img>` tag.

The following code listing highlights how you can use a combination of two such images, and how each can correspond to a low and high resolution.

```
<html>
<head>
<title>Working with Images in HTML</title>
</head>
<body>
<p align="center"><b>Working with Images in HTML</b></p>
<hr>
<p align="center">
<img border="0" src="/j0285750.wmf" width="400" height="600" lowsrc="j0285750_low.wmf"
width="50" height="100">
</body>
</html>
```

Not unlike the discussion of thumbnails, the preceding code listing works with two images—one high-resolution and the other low-resolution. The neat thing about the `lowsrc` attribute is that this image will load quickly first (because it is lower resolution and the actual file size is not as large). Then the higher-resolution image will load over it. The benefit of this is that instead of seeing the empty placeholder shown in Figure 3.4, the reader's attention is captured by the low-resolution image, giving him or her an idea of the image that will soon load in high resolution. The idea is that if readers see the image—even in rough format—their curiosity will be piqued and they will wait until your higher-resolution images and the rest of your Web page content load into their browsers.

TIP

Remember, this effect is achieved through the use of two separate images, one captured (for example) in lower resolution, in black and white (versus color), and so on.

Image and Text Formatting

It's one thing to have exciting images on your Web page, but it's another thing altogether to have them neatly integrated into the rest of your content. Compare Figures 3.10 and 3.11 and see whether you can tell a difference between how the image and surrounding text integrate (or don't integrate) with each other in terms of page layout.

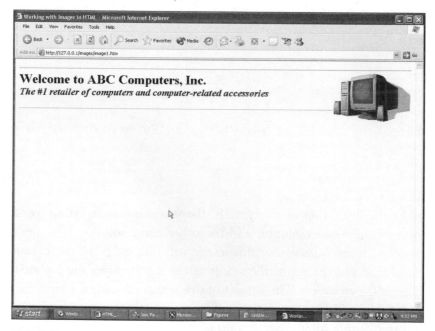

FIGURE 3.10 *By wrapping the text around the graphic, you achieve a neat, integrated appearance between the image and the supporting text.*

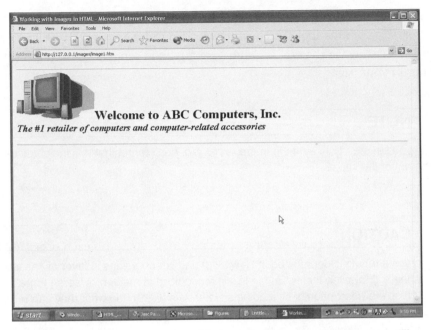

FIGURE 3.11 *This doesn't look horrible, but it lacks the clean layout shown in Figure 3.10.*

You can easily wrap text around an image (as shown in Figure 3.10) using the `align` attribute within the `<img>` tag. The following code listing illustrates the HTML behind Figure 3.10.

```
<html>
<head>
<title>Working with Images in HTML</title>
</head>
<body>
<hr>
<img border="0" src="j0285750.gif" width="192" height="118" align="right">
<b>
<font size="6">Welcome to ABC Computers, Inc.<br> </font>
<i><font size="5">The #1 retailer of computers and
computer-related accessories</font></i></b></p>
<hr>
</body>
</html>
```

As you can see in the `<img>` tag, the `align` attribute is set to `right`. (It can be `left`, `right`, or `center`.) This allows the text to wrap around the image. By utilizing some simple formatting via the `<i>`, `<b>`, and `<hr>` tags, you can add some very neat formatting to your pages.

NOTE

When you set the `align` attribute in the `<img>` tag, don't forget that this indicates the alignment of the image.

CAUTION

The `align` attribute is deprecated in HTML 4.0 and later versions in favor of cascading style sheets. (However, the `align` tag is still recognized in major browsers.) For a more complete description of cascading style sheets (CSS) and what they can bring to your Web design, see Chapters 9 and 10, which provide an introduction to cascading style sheets.

By combining different `align` attributes, you can do some pretty nifty layout tricks with your Web content. Figure 3.12 shows an example of how you can use two figures with different `align` attributes to create some impressive layout effects on your pages.

The following code listing illustrates the HTML behind Figure 3.12. In reality, the only special formatting is for the two images; one has the `align` attribute set to `left`, and the other has it set to `right`.

```
<html>
<head>
<title>Working with Images in HTML</title>
</head>
<body>
<hr>
<img border="0" src="j0285750.gif" width="192" height="118" align="right">
<b><font size="6">
Welcome to ABC Computers, Inc.
<br></font>
```

```
<i><font size="5">The #1 retailer of computers and
computer-related accessories</font></i></b></p>
<hr>
<img border="0" align="left" src="j0195384.gif" width="189" height="193"></p>
<font size="5">Your computer is supposed to be your trusted workhorse, a useful
tool that can help bring your best ideas to fruition and allow you to enjoy all
the fruits of your labor.</font></p>
<img border="0" align="right" src="j0294350[1]1.gif" width="191" height="175"></p>
<font size="5">But as with all things mechanical, your computer can break down
or suffer problems that can put a serious crimp into your best efforts to get
that report on your boss' desk before quitting time. It's times like these
when time becomes a real premium, and when you need answers to computer
questions quickly, and from experts that you can trust.</font></p>
<hr>
</body>
</html>
```

Take some time now to experiment with the `align` attribute and discover how you can use it effectively in combination with your text.

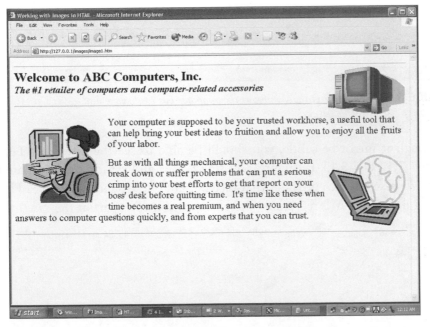

FIGURE 3.12 *By mixing and matching images with different `align` attributes, you can create some attractive layout effects on your Web pages.*

Adding Space around an Image

You can use the hspace and vspace attributes of the <img> tag to add a nice buffer zone between your images and the text that surrounds them. Compare Figure 3.13 to Figure 3.12 to see how figure spacing can alter the appearance of your images and text.

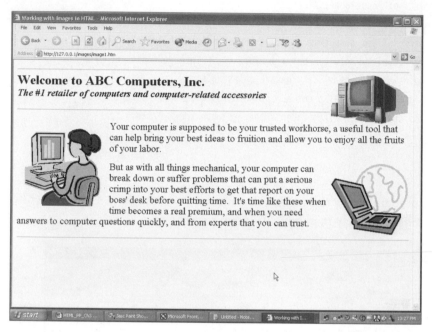

FIGURE 3.13 *The image of the woman at the computer has the* hspace *and* vspace *attributes set to 20 pixels each.*

Although it might be subtle, you should be able to see the difference between Figures 3.12 and 3.13. In Figure 3.13, the hspace and vspace attributes are both set to 20 pixels, which provides that nice buffer zone around the image. The following line of HTML represents these two attributes as part of the <img> tag:

```
<img border="0" hspace="20" vspace="20" align="left" src="j0195384.gif" width="189"
height="193">
```

Manipulating Images in an HTML Editor

As you will see throughout the chapters of Part I, you can work with HTML using a simple text editor like Notepad. (And as you learn HTML, using a simple text editor is a good idea to ensure that you have a firm understanding of the tags, their attributes, and how they all function.) However, you will probably want to move on to an HTML editor because it makes such quick work of the more mundane and tedious aspects of working with HTML, as well as bringing additional functionality to your Web design.

Working with images is certainly a good reason for putting the power of such an application to work for you. This section will briefly describe the image-manipulation tools available in Microsoft FrontPage. (I will formally introduce FrontPage in Chapter 12, "Working with an HTML Editor," and you will get to see it in action in the third project of Part II.)

TIP

If you have FrontPage, open it now to follow along with what I present here. Note that I am using FrontPage XP; however, recent previous versions of the application will possess the same functionality you see here.

Figure 3.14 shows the Image1.htm page opened in FrontPage, with the Pictures toolbar also visible.

I won't go through all of the functionality of this toolbar, but you should take note of some of the functionality that is presented in FrontPage in terms of working with images:

◆ **Auto Thumbnail.** The Auto Thumbnail feature is particularly useful for automatically creating smaller thumbnail versions of the image in question. When you select an image and click on this button, FrontPage automatically creates a smaller version of the image (by adjusting the `height` and `width` attributes of the `<img>` tag) and a hyperlink `<a href>` attribute.

◆ **Rotate/Flip buttons.** These buttons are useful for adjusting the appearance of your images with regard to their orientation on the page. Figure 3.15 highlights an image on the Image1.htm page that has been both rotated and flipped in FrontPage.

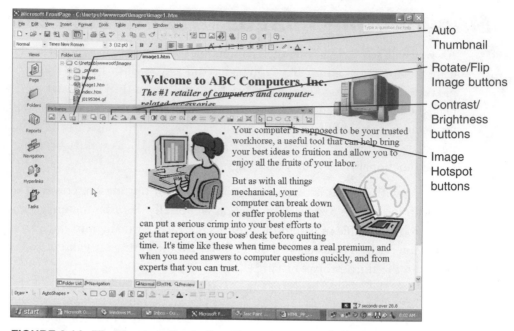

Auto
Thumbnail

Rotate/Flip
Image buttons

Contrast/
Brightness
buttons

Image
Hotspot
buttons

FIGURE 3.14 *The Pictures toolbar in FrontPage can make quick work of your basic image-manipulation needs for a Web page.*

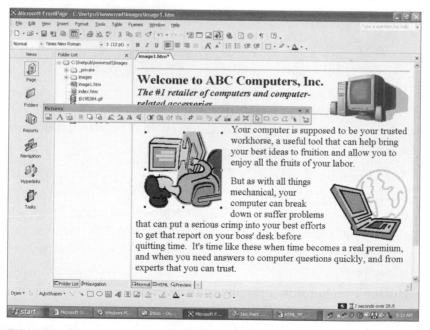

FIGURE 3.15 *Using the FrontPage Flip and Rotate buttons on the Pictures toolbar, you can quickly change the orientation of your images.*

- ◆ **Contrast/Brightness buttons.** These are also self-explanatory. Although they are not as powerful as the same functionality in a graphics-manipulation application (such as Photoshop or Paint Shop Pro), they are still useful for quick and dirty image editing in FrontPage.
- ◆ **Image Hotspot buttons.** As you will learn in Chapter 5, you can turn your images into hyperlinks. You can also divide your image into specific sections so that each section is its own link. This is known as an image map, and you can use the Image Hotspot buttons on the Pictures toolbar to quickly define these specific sections of your image and set their hyperlink properties (such as the address of the file or page to which you are linking).

Help with Image Creation

There are people who were born with pencils in hand, and then there are the graphically challenged. Somewhere in between lie the majority of us—and our abilities to create useful images and graphics for our Web pages.

Although this chapter (or book, for that matter) does not discuss actual image creation, there are several excellent resources you can turn to depending on the type of image creation and manipulation application you are using. The following are all great titles published by Premier Press or Muska & Lipman that can assist you with Adobe Photoshop, an industry-recognized tool for creating and manipulating images and graphics of all types:

- ◆ *Adobe Photoshop 7 Creative Workshop* by Premier Press
- ◆ *Photoshop 7 Type Effects* by Muska & Lipman
- ◆ *Photoshop 7 Image Effects* by Muska & Lipman
- ◆ *Adobe Web Pack: Photoshop 7, LiveMotion 2, and GoLive 6* by Muska & Lipman
- ◆ *Adobe Photoshop 6 Digital Darkroom* by Premier Press
- ◆ *Adobe Photoshop 7 Fast & Easy* by Premier Press

Summary

This chapter introduced you to the essentials of image placement and manipulation in HTML. Now you should be familiar with the `<img>` tag and its various attributes, including the following:

- border
- src
- align
- vspace
- hspace
- width
- height
- lowsrc

You also learned how to work with the `<a href>` tag (which you'll learn more about in Chapter 5) to create thumbnail images you can link to larger higher-resolution images. Also in this chapter, you were presented with tips and techniques for making your images (and pages) load faster and neatly integrating your images and text for a smooth layout. Finally, you were shown how you can quickly and easily insert and manipulate images by working with an HTML editor such as Microsoft FrontPage.

Chapter 4

**Working with
Page Layout**

You can think of your page layout as the design template for your Web pages and overall Web site. (Indeed, I will use the word *template* repeatedly in this chapter, as well as when I begin talking about more advanced page-layout control.) As an example, determining the background color of a page or using an image watermark are both important design considerations. This becomes even more of an issue when you work with more advanced HTML, such as framesets (which you'll learn about in Chapter 7, "Integrating HTML Frames and Advanced Formatting"), because you want to ensure that all of your frames load with a consistent look and feel.

However, in addition to these larger layout issues, some more basic HTML formatting issues also affect page layout, such as:

◆ Using the text alignment tags to center and right- or left-justify information

◆ Setting margins

◆ Creating line breaks or other dividers for your Web content

◆ Working with block quotes or applying special layout formatting to passages of text

All of these issues will affect page layout. Considered along with the information presented to you in Chapter 2, as well as the other content-formatting chapters of Part I, you should have enough information to bring your Web content to life in the most exciting fashion possible.

 CAUTION

If you haven't already guessed, getting your Web content to look just right takes some time. Given differences in browser types, screen resolution, and so on, a page can look one way on Bob's computer but appear completely different on Sally's. That said, you need to test and experiment with your page layout to determine the best presentation of your material.

An Early Discussion of Cascading Style Sheets (CSS)

Imagine that you wrote a very long report for your company, and within the report you constantly referred to a product by its abbreviation, Product ABG. However, you wrote this report late at night, and the next day, just minutes before you are set to present the final report to your boss, you realize the product abbreviation is not ABG, but AGB. The abbreviation is listed nearly a hundred times in your report. How will you have time to go through and change each instance of the term?

If you are using a word processing application (and who doesn't, right?), you simply do a find and replace and you are done in seconds. Cascading style sheets (CSS) allow you the same flexibility within your Web pages. However, CSS doesn't just give you the ability to do a quick find and replace; rather, they allow you to set certain formatting parameters up front so you don't have to worry about specifically formatting each and every HTML tag in your document.

If this sounds like a great idea, it is. Prior to CSS, there were many proprietary HTML tags developed by competing companies (specifically Microsoft and Netscape) to allow for special text placement and formatting. Indeed, this chapter could have been longer if I had explained some of the proprietary tags for specific browsers. However, there is really no need for this; why bother with just addressing one browser type (or worse, doubling your HTML coding by accounting for different browser types) when you can use CSS and be done with it?

You'll see CSS explained in more detail and put to use in the project chapters of Part II. However, as you move through this and other formatting chapters in Part I, keep CSS in mind. Although the general HTML tags are still valid and can be used effectively, implementing style sheets in your pages can save you time and make your pages easier to edit (a major issue when you're dealing with complex pages).

Page Background Layout Issues

Establishing page-background formatting is one of the easiest yet most effective ways to make your Web pages more attractive and visually appealing. By setting a background color or doing something more advanced, such as using an image as a background (or as a watermarked image), you can really make your content come alive with a neatly designed background layout scheme.

To begin, first create a new folder within your Inetpub directory.

1. Within your Inetpub directory, create a new folder and call it Layout.
2. Open your text editor and create a new page called background.htm.
3. Save this page within your new Layout folder.
4. In the background.htm page you just created, enter the following code exactly as you see it here:

```
<html>
<head>
<title>Working with Page Layout</title>
</head>
<body bgcolor="#008000">
<p align="center"><font color="#FFFF00">
<b>Welcome to the ABC Store</b></font></p>
<p align="center"><font color="#FFFF00">
<i>Your one-stop-shop for all your computer needs!</i></font></p>
</body>
</html>
```

5. Save this page again, and then open it in your Web browser. It should appear similar to Figure 4.1.

TIP

Take time to carefully review your Web pages when you change the background and font colors. That way, you can ensure that everything is visible and you don't have a color conflict. This would include (critically) the colors you assign to your hyperlinks. For example, if you set your page to a blue background and you don't change the default color of your hyperlinks (which are blue prior to being clicked), they might get washed out or rendered invisible, which obviously would not be a good thing. You will learn how to set the colors of your hyperlinks (that is, the color they appear prior to, during, and after they are clicked) in Chapter 5, "Understanding Hyperlinks."

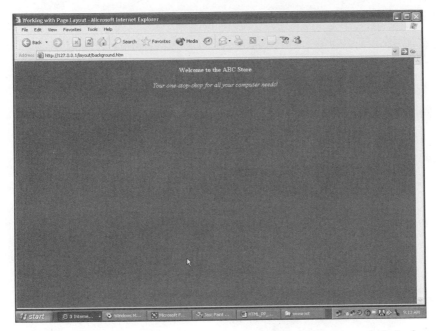

FIGURE 4.1 *Setting the background color can have a major impact on the look of your Web page.*

The background color is set via the `<body>` tag, through the use of the `bgcolor` attribute. In this example, the background color is set to green (`bg color="#008000"`), and the font color of the text is set to yellow (`font color="#FFFF00"`) so it will show up clearly.

Setting a Background Image

Although simply changing the background color of a page can be effective, you can achieve some far more dramatic effects by utilizing a background image on your Web pages. Figure 4.2 illustrates the use of a background image on the same background.htm page you created earlier.

The following code listing illustrates the use of a background image, as shown in Figure 4.2. If you want to enter this code, replace the existing code for background.htm with what you see here. As you saw in the examples in Chapter 3, simply replace the name of the image being used with the name of an image that is stored on your computer. (Don't forget to use the correct file path as well.)

```html
<html>
<head>
<title>Working with Page Layout</title>
</head>
<body background="BD18187_.gif">
<p align="center"></p>
<table border="1" style="border-collapse: collapse" bordercolor="#111111" width="100%">
  <tr>
    <td width="100%" bgcolor="#008000">
    <p align="center"><font size="7">Welcome to ABC Computers</font></td>
  </tr>
</table>
</body>
</html>
```

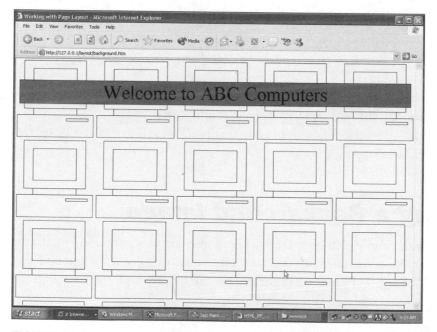

FIGURE 4.2 *Using a background image can be an easy and effective way to liven up your content presentation.*

As you can see in this listing, the `background` attribute is set to a specific image rather than a color. And, as you can see in Figure 4.2, the image repeats itself throughout the background of the page. Note that the text is placed within a table; you will learn more about how to do this in Chapter 6, "Creating and Manipulating Tables." (I placed the text within a table to show you a simple example of how you can use table formatting to place your text.)

 NOTE

All of the issues involving image size and load time (which you learned about in Chapter 3) still apply when you work with background images.

Figure 4.2 is really just for demonstration purposes; the image really takes over the page, even though it is set to a background. The best background images are those that are made into watermarks (in other words, images that are transparent and set to grayscale so the text and other material on the page can sit on top of them without the underlying image taking over the visual presentation).

Aligning Text on the Page

As you saw in Chapters 2 and 3, you can perform some simple text alignment using three attributes.

- The `center` attribute aligns everything to the center of the page. The text in the table in Figure 4.2 uses the `center` attribute.
- The `right` attribute aligns content to the right. Figure 4.3 illustrates this attribute in action.
- The `left` attribute aligns content to (surprise!) the left.

Clearly, there isn't much to these three attributes; however, when used in conjunction with other layout features such as wrapping text around an image, their power becomes more apparent. Keep an eye out for best practices in aligning material on your pages without distracting from the content.

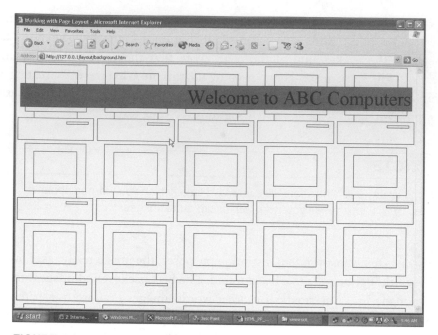

FIGURE 4.3 *Even a simple formatting change can have a major effect on how your Web content appears.*

Working with Margins

Working with margins is difficult (that is, if you aren't using style sheets) because the Netscape and Microsoft browsers support margins in different ways.

However, take a look at Figures 4.4 and 4.5 to see how changing the margins can affect your page layout.

To set the margins in Internet Explorer, use `leftmargin="`*number*`"` and `topmargin="`*number*`"`. For example

```
<body leftmargin="150" topmargin="50">
```

This sets the left margin to 150 pixels and the top margin to 50 pixels.

To set the margins in Netscape, use `marginwidth="`*number*`"` and `marginheight="`*number*`"`. For example

```
<body marginwdith="150" marginheight="50">
```

This sets the left margin to 150 pixels and the top margin to 50 pixels.

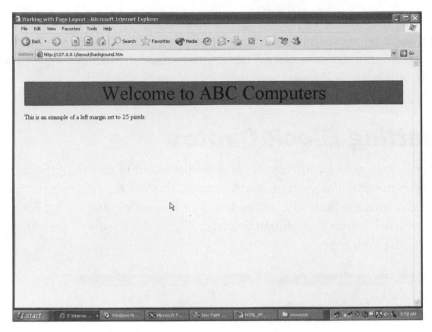

FIGURE 4.4 *A left margin set to 25 pixels.*

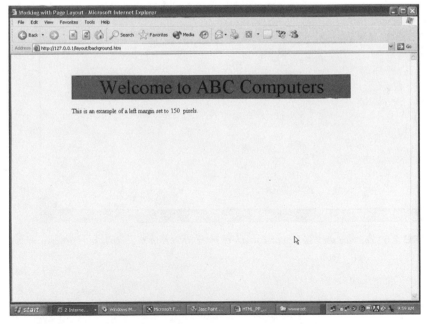

FIGURE 4.5 *A left margin set to 150 pixels.*

Note that you can use the margin tags together or individually (as shown in Figure 4.5; there is no top margin set in that figure). In a nutshell, the potential for conflicting layouts makes the margin tags a good candidate for replacement via style sheets, which you will learn more about in Chapters 9 and 10.

Formatting Block Quotes

You will often need to differentiate sections (or *blocks*) of text from the surrounding Web content. There are many ways to do this (such as placing the text in a table, changing the font color and general font formatting, and so on), but you can also use block quotes to highlight your text. Figure 4.6 illustrates the use of block quotes on a Web page.

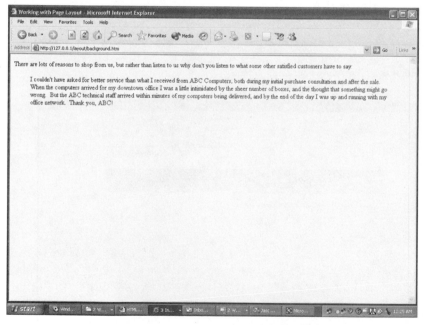

FIGURE 4.6 *You can use block quotes to draw more attention to specific sections of your content.*

Block quoting is done via the `<blockquote>` tag. You simply place the tag in front of the text you want to block quote, and then use the closing `</blockquote>` tag when you are finished. The following code listing, which was used to produce Figure 4.6, illustrates the use of this tag.

```
<html>
<head>
<title>Working with Page Layout</title>
</head>
<body>
<p>There are lots of reasons to shop from us, but rather than listen to us why
don't you listen to what some other satisfied customers have to say:</p>
<p>
<blockquote>
I couldn't have asked for better service than what I received from ABC
Computers, both during my initial purchase consultation and after the sale. 
When the computers arrived for my downtown office I was a little intimidated by
the sheer number of boxes, and the thought that something might go wrong. 
But the ABC technical staff arrived within minutes of my computers being
delivered, and by the end of the day I was up and running with my office
network.  Thank you, ABC!
</blockquote>
</body>
</html>
```

Summary

This short chapter introduced you to some additional formatting options available within HTML. Although there are some you will use quite often, such as the `background` tag, most of what I presented here is deprecated in HTML 4.0 and can be better achieved using CSS, which you will learn about in Chapters 9 and 10. The other major point to take away from this chapter is that when you are dealing with any special formatting on your Web pages, you should factor in additional time to test and tweak the look of your content to account for variations in your own opinion, discrepancies in the browser being used to view your Web pages, screen resolution, and other issues that are beyond your control but that will affect how your content is displayed.

Chapter 5

**Understanding
Hyperlinks**

Hyperlinks are the bread and butter functionality of the Web because they allow the very concept of the Web—that is, the interactive association of documents—to be a reality. However, despite their ease of use (which I will show you in this relatively short chapter), the effective and intelligent use of hyperlinks is a different manner. Put simply, there is a certain art to the effective placement of hyperlinks because you have to consider issues such as:

◆ Where in my Web page or document do I need to include hyperlinks?

◆ How many hyperlinks are appropriate or necessary on my Web page?

◆ How can I use hyperlinks as a navigation tool within my Web site?

◆ In what ways can I use hyperlinks to guide users through my Web site without presenting my content in a forced manner? (In other words, how do I avoid giving the impression that there is only one pathway of discovery in my Web site?)

These questions really aren't technology issues. (If you learn one hyperlink, you learn them all!) Rather, they are really process and design issues, which I will discuss further in the project chapters of Part II. However, you still need to understand the attributes of the `<a href>` tag (the primary HTML tag used to develop hyperlinks) and the layout possibilities for hyperlinks (for example, image maps) to effectively address these process and design issues.

Working with the `<a href>` Tag

To link one Web page to another, you need to utilize the `<a href>` tag. Create a new Web folder and page so you can follow along with the example exercises presented in this chapter.

1. In your Inetpub folder on your computer, create a folder and call it Links.

2. Open your text editor and create a new page called LinkTest.htm. Save it in this Links folder. For this illustration, either resave this page (also in your Links folder) as LinkTest2.htm, or just create another page (howev-

er you like) and save that page as LinkTest2.htm. It doesn't have to be anything complicated—just so you can have a page to "link to" for this example.

In your LinkTest.htm page, type the following code exactly as you see it here:

```
<html>
<head>
<title>Sample Hyperlink Page</title>
</head>
<body>
<p><a href="LinkTest2.htm">Click here to link to my other sample page</a>.</p>
<p>Click <a href="LinkTest2.htm">here</a> to link to my other sample page.</p>
</body>
</html>
```

Save this page and load it into your Web browser. It should look like Figure 5.1.

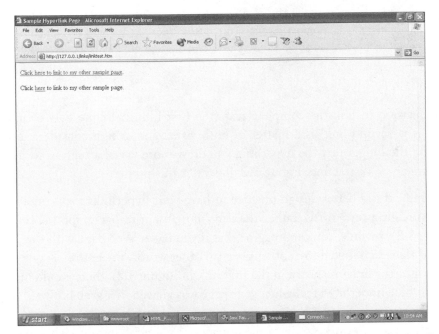

FIGURE 5.1 *Two examples of hyperlinks, illustrating the visual difference between linking one word and an entire sentence.*

The `<a href>` tag is simple to use; however, take note of the following points to make sure you understand how the tag is employed in this particular listing.

◆ Basically, to create a hyperlink as in the preceding code, you place the opening `<a href>` tag before the first character where you want your hyperlink to begin. Before the closing `>` of this tag, you insert (in quotes) the address of the page to which you want to link. In this example, the name of the page (which you also created earlier in this chapter) is LinkTest2.htm.

◆ Place the closing `</a>` tag after the final character where you want your hyperlink to end. Note that in the preceding code listing, the first hyperlink is the entire sentence, whereas the second hyperlink is only on the word "here."

 NOTE

Notice that the address of the hyperlinked page in the preceding code listing consists of just the file name. However, you must include the full address (such as http://www.yahoo.com) in some situations. I'll talk more about this issue later in the chapter.

The decision to link the complete text (the first link in Figure 5.1) or just one word (the second link) is a matter of both visual and design considerations. By making the longer text the hyperlink, you draw more visual attention to it; however, it can be distracting. Figure 5.2 illustrates this point.

Generally, it is a better design practice to have your hyperlinks focus on a particular word or a few words, rather than making an entire paragraph (as shown in Figure 5.2) the link. You can imagine that if you had a Web page with three paragraphs that each linked to another page (in other words, the entire paragraph was made into the link, as shown in the first link in Figure 5.2), there would be nothing but blue underlined text when your page was viewed in a Web browser! Again, I'll talk more about the design and process issues of hyperlinks in the project chapters, but for now keep the visual impact of Figure 5.2 in mind when you need to place a hyperlink on your page.

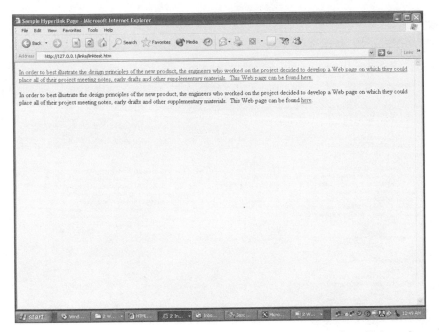

FIGURE 5.2 *The portion of your text that you decide to make the hyperlink can have a significant visual impact.*

Creating Hyperlinks within the Same Web Page

When you need to have a link to content within the same page, you can utilize anchors (otherwise known as *bookmarks*) to allow your users to quickly jump from one section of text to another.

The text in Figure 5.3 is Article I of the Constitution of the United States. Notice the links at the top of the page to Section 4 and Section 8. These links arc bookmarks to the specific sections (in this case, 4 and 8) of Article I. When readers click on these links, they are taken to that specific section of the text, as shown in Figure 5.4.

How do you create these bookmarks? Examine the following code listing, which illustrates the use of bookmarks as they appear in Figures 5.3 and 5.4.

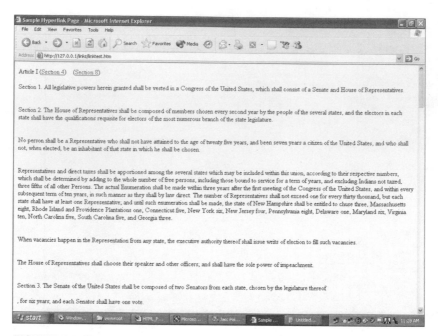

FIGURE 5.3 *Bookmarks placed at the top of a long document...*

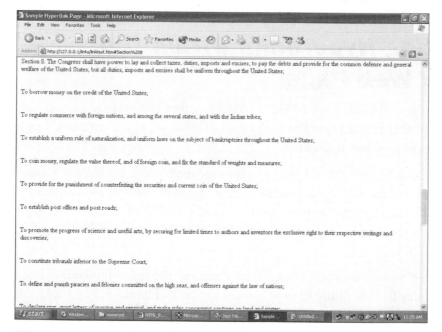

FIGURE 5.4 *...can allow readers to quickly jump to a specific section of text within the document.*

TIP

If you want to follow along with the example here and work with an electronic version of the U.S. Constitution, you can find the entire contents of the document online at http://www.law.cornell.edu/constitution/constitution.overview.html.

```
<p>Article I (<a href="#Section 4">Section 4</a>)    (<a href="#Section
8">Section 8</a>)<br>
<br>
Section 1. All legislative powers herein granted shall be vested in a Congress
of the United States, which shall consist of a Senate and House of
Representatives. <br>
```

This code listing highlights the two bookmark links at the top of the page. All that is different in the `<a href>` tag is the use of the # sign before the name of the section of the text to which the bookmark is pointing.

Now take a look at the section of the document to which the two bookmark links actually point. The following code listing highlights the bookmark for Section 4 of Article I of the Constitution.

```
<br>
<a name="Section 4">Section 4</a>. The times, places and manner of holding
elections for Senators and Representatives, shall be prescribed in each state by
the legislature thereof; but the Congress may at any time by law make or alter
such regulations, except as to the places of choosing Senators.
<br>
```

Notice in the preceding code listing that the actual bookmark is identified by the `<a name>` tag. Similar to how the `<a href>` tag is used, you simply assign the bookmark a name and place it in quotes inside the opening `<a name>` tag. Then—just like for a hyperlink—you place the closing `</a>` tag after the last character of the desired bookmark text. In this code listing, the actual bookmark is the text "Section 4."

Bookmarks are a great way to provide quick navigation within a document. However, you might find that after users click on a link to a bookmark and read the associated text in that section, you want them to be able to quickly jump back to the top of the document. In this case, it is a good idea to place a "return to top" bookmark after each bookmark. Figure 5.5 illustrates this point.

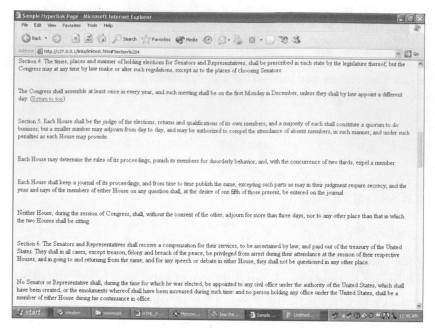

FIGURE 5.5 *A "return to top" bookmark can be a useful navigation feature in a long document.*

 TIP

You can name the bookmark whatever you want when you define it in the `<a name>` tag. However, it is a good idea to name it something indicative of the text to which it points, which will make it easier to remember. In fact, if the actual text isn't too lengthy, you can give the bookmark the same name as the text, which is what I did in the preceding code listing (for example, "Section 4" and "Section 8").

In the case of Figure 5.5, when readers click on the "Return to top" link, they are actually clicking on a bookmark that returns them to the top of the document. The following code listing illustrates this point.

```
<a name="Section 4">Section 4</a>. The times, places and manner of holding
elections for Senators and Representatives, shall be prescribed in each state by
the legislature thereof; but the Congress may at any time by law make or alter
such regulations, except as to the places of choosing Senators. <br>
<br>
```

```
The Congress shall assemble at least once in every year, and such meeting shall
be on the first Monday in December, unless they shall by law appoint a different
day. (<a href="#Article I">Return to top</a>)
```

As you can see in the last sentence, the link "Return to top" points to the book-mark named Article 1 (`<a href="#Article I">`). In this case, the Article I book-mark is simply the first text that appears on the page, so this link really does return the reader to the top!

Absolute and Relative URLs

As you know, URL is short for *Uniform Resource Locator*, and there are two basic kinds of URLs.

◆ **Absolute.** A URL is absolute if it contains a protocol, a server name, and a full directory path. For example, http://www.abc.com/catalog/products.htm is an absolute URL because it contains all three of these items. http is the protocol, abc.com is the server name, and /catalog/products.htm constitutes the directory path.

◆ **Relative.** A URL is relative if it only contains the directory path. For example, the URL/catalog/products.htm is relative because it doesn't contain the rest of the path listed in the example for the absolute URL.

When do you use either type of URL? Imagine you have several documents under one folder, such as:

```
/Products
     ProductA.htm
     ProductB.htm
     ProductC.htm
     ProductD.htm
     ProductE.htm
```

Imagine that this is a Web folder directory on a server named ABC, so a link to the ProductA.htm document would consist of http://www.abc.com/Products/ProductA.htm.

Now imagine you have a Web page that lists all of the products, and each product has a hyperlink to one of the pages in the preceding list. Such a page might look like the following code listing.

```
<html>
<head>
<title>Absolute URL Example</title>
</head>
<body
<p>Welcome to our store.  Click one of the following links for more
information on that product:</p>
<ul>
  <li><a href="http://www.abc.com/products/productA.htm">Product A</a></li>
  <li><a href="http://www.abc.com/products/productB.htm">Product B</a></li>
  <li><a href="http://www.abc.com/products/productC.htm">Product C</a></li>
  <li><a href="http://www.abc.com/products/productD.htm">Product D</a></li>
  <li><a href="http://www.abc.com/products/productE.htm">Product E</a></li>
</ul>
```

Technically, there is nothing wrong with this code. Each hyperlink is defined and uses an absolute URL. However, compare this listing to the following code listing, which utilizes relative URLs.

```
<html>
<head>
<title>Relative URL Example </title>
</head>
<body
<p>Welcome to our store.  Click one of the following links for more
information on that product:</p>
<ul>
  <li><a href="../products/productA.htm">Product A</a></li>
  <li><a href="../products/productB.htm">Product B</a></li>
  <li><a href="../products/productC.htm">Product C</a></li>
  <li><a href="../products/productD.htm">Product D</a></li>
  <li><a href="../products/productE.htm">Product E</a></li>
</ul>
```

As you can see, the `<a href>` tag has been considerably shortened by simply using the relative URL path to each page link. This is useful—and a better idea in this example—because all the product files (productA.htm, productB.htm, and so on) reside in the same folder, so there is no need to use the entire URL.

Creating Image Maps

Image maps are a great way to add visual quality to your hyperlinks because you can turn the images (such as graphics and pictures) on your Web page into links. Moreover, you can divide the images into specific sections so each section is its own hyperlink. This process is known as creating an image map.

Figure 5.6 illustrates a simple graphic that is being used as an image map. In this graphic, each of the four squares is a link to a different page. You can see how the status bar in the browser window (see the callout on Figure 5.6) changes between Figures 5.6 and 5.7, as the mouse pointer is moved over different parts of the image.

Technically, image maps are easy to create. All you do is define the coordinates of the area for each specific link. However, defining the coordinates by hand is very, very tedious (if not impossible). Fortunately, there are countless applications that create image maps available for download on the Web (most for free). Moreover, when you work with FrontPage XP in Chapter 12, "Working with an HTML Editor," you will see yet another compelling reason to work with an HTML editor: FrontPage has automated tools for creating your image maps.

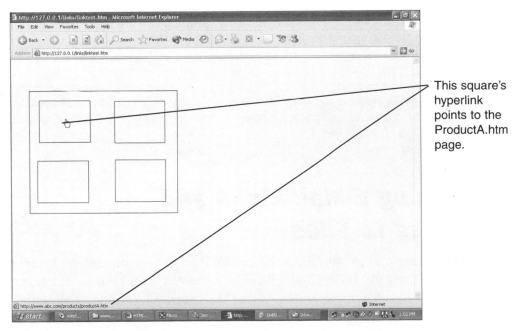

This square's hyperlink points to the ProductA.htm page.

FIGURE 5.6 *Each of the four separate squares is a hyperlink to a specific file.*

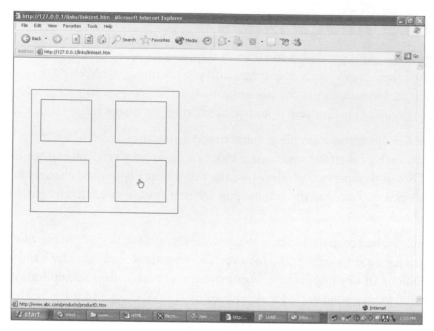

FIGURE 5.7 *This square links to the ProductD.htm page.*

For now, be aware that this functionality is possible. You will also create image maps for the Web sites you create in the projects in Part II.

 TIP

Many HTML editors can automate the task of image map creation. You'll see how this can be done via FrontPage in Chapter 12, "Working with an HTML Editor" as well as in the third project of Part II.

Creating E-Mail Links and Linking to Files

In addition to creating links between Web pages, you can also use hyperlinks for e-mail and file linking. You utilize the `<a href>` tag for both tasks, but instead of providing a link to the corresponding Web page, you provide a link to the e-mail address or file.

◆ **Linking to an e-mail address.** Simply replace the Web page link in the `<a href>` tag with the appropriate e-mail address. When clicked, `<a href="jdoe@abc.com">Send an e-mail to Joe</a>` would open up the user's e-mail program and automatically address the e-mail to jdoe@abc.com.

◆ **Linking to a file.** Within the `<a href>` tag, list the path to the file, making sure to add the file extension to the end of the link. For example, `<a href="http://www.abc.com/products/catalog/spring_03.doc">Click, here for the Spring 2003 catalog</a>` would link to the Word document spring_03. (You know it is a Microsoft Word document because it has a .doc extension.)

Formatting Hyperlinks

The default color for hyperlinked text is blue; however, you might want to change this to make the hyperlinks have a strong visual fit in your site's overall design scheme. The following code snippet highlights how you can change the color of hyperlinks that haven't yet been clicked, as well as those that have already been visited.

NOTE

Already-visited links are those that the user has previously clicked. Instead of bright blue, they are usually a light purple to indicate that they have already been clicked.

```
<body link="Red" alink="Yellow" vlink="green">
```

As this code snippet illustrates, you set the colors of your hyperlinks within the `<body>` tag of your Web page. There are three specific color-formatting attributes you can set:

◆ `link.` This sets the color of links that have yet to be visited. In the example above, the links will appear in red.

◆ `alink.` This attribute sets the color of the link when the user clicks on it. In this example, that color is yellow.

◆ `vlink.` Finally, the `vlink` attribute sets the color of links that have already been visited. This color has been set to green in this example.

TIP

If you want your hyperlinks to be a uniform color regardless of their status, set all three of the color attributes to the same color.

Creating Keyboard Shortcuts for Hyperlinks

The demands of your Web page might call for you to set keyboard shortcuts for some of the functionality. This is a particularly interesting feature with hyperlinks if those links are serving as navigation tools for your site. For example, imagine you are designing an online billing system for a small company. On the main menu page for the system, there are hyperlinks to accounts payable, accounts receivable, and inventory. Given that users will visit these links frequently, you can set keyboard shortcuts. That way, when the page with the links is loaded into a Web browser, the user can use the keyboard shortcuts to move between associated pages, instead of clicking on the hyperlinks.

To bring this functionality to your Web pages, you can add the accesskey attribute to your <a href> tag. The following code snippet provides an example of this.

```
<a href="acntspayable.htm" accesskey=a>Accounts Payable</a>
```

In this example, the hyperlink to the page acntspayable.htm has been assigned the shortcut key of "a." When the page that contains this hyperlink loads in the browser, the user can either click on the link or use the keyboard shortcut to follow the link.

Although this is useful functionality, there are a few issues you should keep in mind.

◆ In Windows, users hold down the Alt key and press the associated shortcut key to use keyboard shortcuts.

◆ Keyboard shortcuts can cause strange things to happen in pages that utilize framesets, so you shouldn't use keyboard shortcuts in such pages.

◆ Most important, a keyboard shortcut you assign might override a keyboard shortcut of the browser itself. You need to keep this in mind when assigning your shortcuts so you don't override the useful functionality of the browser shortcuts. (Users might be very familiar with these browser shortcuts and like to use them, in which case they would be quite annoyed that the familiar shortcut key doesn't work they way they are used to.)

◆ Keyboard shortcuts should work on a Macintosh as well; however, instead of using the Alt key, use the Ctrl key. But, the new Mac Web browser application (Safari) does not recognize the accesskey attribute.

Utilizing Hyperlinks in Frame Pages

The use of hyperlinks in a frameset brings different challenges and functionality. For example, you might want to have a list of hyperlinks in one frame that point to content that loads in another frame. I will fully explain this functionality, along with the specific HTML tags and attributes that allow it, in Chapter 7, "Integrating HTML Frames and Advanced Formatting."

Summary

This chapter provided you with a brief yet comprehensive overview of the general functionality of hyperlinks. You learned how to link from one page to another via the `<a href>` tag, as well as how to set links (bookmarks) in a page. Moreover, this chapter defined absolute versus relative URLs. It also discussed the use of image maps to bring a visual component to your hyperlinks by integrating them with graphics and pictures. You also learned how to link to files and create e-mail links. Finally, you learned some basic hyperlink formatting, including how to create keyboard shortcuts for hyperlinks and how to change the colors of the links that appear on your Web pages.

Chapter 6

*Creating and
Manipulating
Tables*

The tags that govern the creation and formatting of tables are without a doubt some of the most useful, all-purpose HTML tags available. With just a little bit of imagination, you can use tables to bring all kinds of formatting power to your Web pages. Indeed, you won't spend much time working with HTML before you need to work with tables.

There is good and bad news about working with tables, however. The good news is that like most HTML tags, the tags that you use to work with tables are not complicated. The basic tags (`<table>`, `<tr>`, and `<td>`) are easy to learn. Moreover, the attributes for these tags, which include table-formatting attributes such as border and cell width, are also not difficult to learn.

So what's the bad news about tables? Depending on your table's complexity in terms of the number of columns and rows, its formatting, other special HTML elements you might have included, and so forth, the HTML code behind the table can grow quite complex... and it can grow very quickly. As you will see in this chapter, it doesn't take a very large table to produce a mess of HTML. That said, working with tables can be reason enough to move to an HTML editor (such as Microsoft FrontPage) because it makes easy work out of creating and formatting tables.

Still, this chapter will not assume you are using an editor; I will assume you might be working with a simple text editor such as Notepad. Even if this is the case, you can accomplish all your table design and formatting goals—it just might be a bit more tedious for you!

Table Basics

I want to begin by designing a relatively simply table.

1. Within your Inetpub folder, create a new folder called Tables.

2. Open your text editor and create a new page called FirstTable.htm. Save this page in your newly created Tables folder.

3. On your FirstTable.htm page, enter the following HTML exactly as it appears here:

```
<html>
<head>
<title>Working with Tables</title>
</head>
<body>
<table border="2" bordercolor="#FF0000" width="100%" cellpadding="2"
bordercolorlight="#008000" bordercolordark="#008000">
  <tr>
    <td width="50%">1</td>
    <td width="50%">2</td>
  </tr>
  <tr>
    <td width="50%">3</td>
    <td width="50%">4</td>
  </tr>
</table>
</body>
</html>
```

4. Save the page again and open it in your Web browser. Your screen
should appear similar to Figure 6.1.

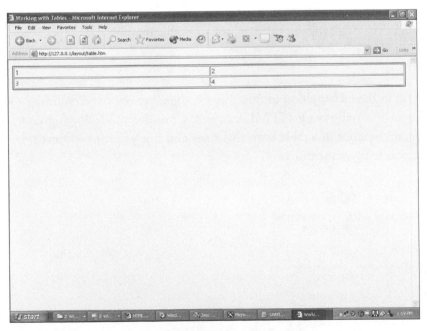

FIGURE 6.1 *A simple table with some specific properties set.*

As an introduction to table tags and formatting, take some time now to go through the following items:

◆ First, the table is created using the `<table>` tag.

◆ Next, specific attributes of the table are set, such as the border width, the border color, the light and dark border colors, and the cell padding value. (I will discuss all of these attributes later in this chapter.)

◆ Next, the row (`<tr>`) and column (`<td>`) tags are utilized. Between the opening and closing `<tr>` tags, you see two sets of opening and closing `<td>` tags. You can read this as one row (the `<tr>` tag) and two columns (the `<td>` tag sets) before the closing `</tr>` tag. Because this is repeated, you can tell by looking at the HTML that this table consists of two rows and two columns.

◆ Finally, the table completion is denoted in the HTML with the closing `</table>` tag.

TIP

Confused about `bordercolor`, `bordercolorlight`, and `bordercolordark`? You might want to just ignore them, as they are specific to Internet Explorer only (that is, they will only work in IE). If, however, you want this kind of exact control over your table color attributes, you might enjoy using them, but remember that only users with IE will be able to see your border color handy work.

As I said in the introduction to this chapter, the more rows and columns you have, the larger the underlying HTML can get. Consider the following code listing, which corresponds to a table with five rows and five columns. (Don't type this in unless you really want to!)

```
<html>
<head>
<title>Working with Tables</title>
</head>
<body>
<table border="1" width="100%">
  <tr>
    <td width="10%"> </td>
    <td width="10%"> </td>
    <td width="10%"> </td>
```

```
  <td width="10%"> </td>
  <td width="10%"> </td>
  <td width="10%"> </td>
  <td width="10%"> </td>
  <td width="10%"> </td>
  <td width="10%"> </td>
  <td width="10%"> </td>
</tr>
<tr>
  <td width="10%"> </td>
  <td width="10%"> </td>
  <td width="10%"> </td>
  <td width="10%"> </td>
  <td width="10%"> </td>
  <td width="10%"> </td>
  <td width="10%"> </td>
  <td width="10%"> </td>
  <td width="10%"> </td>
</tr>
<tr>
  <td width="10%"> </td>
  <td width="10%"> </td>
  <td width="10%"> </td>
  <td width="10%"> </td>
  <td width="10%"> </td>
  <td width="10%"> </td>
  <td width="10%"> </td>
  <td width="10%"> </td>
  <td width="10%"> </td>
</tr>
<tr>
  <td width="10%"> </td>
  <td width="10%"> </td>
  <td width="10%"> </td>
  <td width="10%"> </td>
  <td width="10%"> </td>
  <td width="10%"> </td>
  <td width="10%"> </td>
  <td width="10%"> </td>
```

```
  <td width="10%"> </td>
  <td width="10%"> </td>
 </tr>
 <tr>
  <td width="10%"> </td>
  <td width="10%"> </td>
  <td width="10%"> </td>
  <td width="10%"> </td>
  <td width="10%"> </td>
  <td width="10%"> </td>
  <td width="10%"> </td>
  <td width="10%"> </td>
  <td width="10%"> </td>
  <td width="10%"> </td>
 </tr>
</table>
</body>
</html>
```

As you can see, table HTML can get quite lengthy, not to mention complex. In this listing, there are no special attributes added to the table (such as border color), nor are there any text or other HTML elements (such as form elements). You can imagine how tedious it would be to create or edit such a table in a regular text editor such as Notepad.

That said, take a look at Figures 6.2 and 6.3, which illustrate the table creation tool in Microsoft FrontPage.

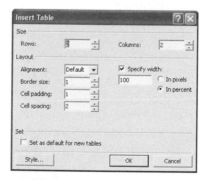

FIGURE 6.2 *The first step in creating a table in FrontPage.*

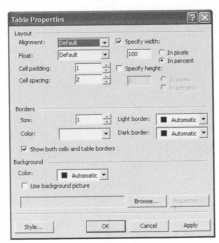

FIGURE 6.3 *When the table is created, FrontPage gives you easy access to setting the specific attributes of the table.*

FrontPage is by no means the only HTML editing tool; however, I want to bring the great functionality of this tool to your attention now, in case you are not familiar with it. In addition to helping you with the more mundane HTML tasks (such as table creation), the better editing tools give you total Web site control functionality. Enough said about this for now; I'll introduce FrontPage in more detail in Chapter 12, "Working with an HTML Editor" and in the third project of Part II.

Configuring Specific Table Attributes

As you saw in the code examples in the previous section, you can set several table attributes, including border color and width, cell width, and so on. The following sections will detail each of these attributes.

Setting Borders

As with all HTML borders, a table border helps to distinguish your table from the surrounding text. Figures 6.4 and 6.5 show two examples of table borders to give you an idea of the differences that are possible when you set the border to different values.

Table borders are set using the border attribute, as shown in the following code example:

```
<table border="5" width="100%">
```

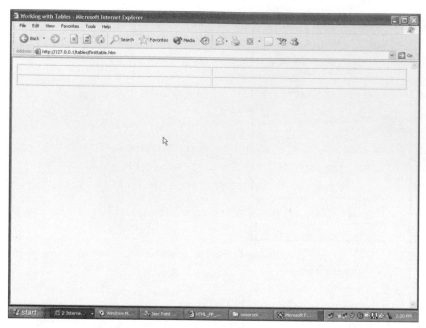

FIGURE 6.4 *A simple table with a border value of 1.*

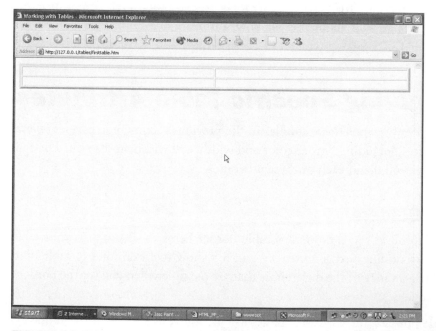

FIGURE 6.5 *The same table with a border value of 5.*

An interesting trick—especially when you are using tables to format large sections of text—is to set the border to 0. The lines for the borders will disappear, of course, but you still get all the advantages of the neat table formatting. You'll see this technique utilized throughout the project chapters in Part II.

Setting Table Width

If you look at the code snippet in the previous section, as well as the longer listings earlier in the chapter, you will notice that the table `width` attribute is always set to 100%. This means that the table will span the length of the screen.

This might be okay if you are working with a very large table, but usually you want your tables to take up only a small portion of your total screen real estate. In those cases, you will need to adjust your table width.

Figure 6.6 illustrates the same table shown in Figure 6.5, except the width has been set to 50%.

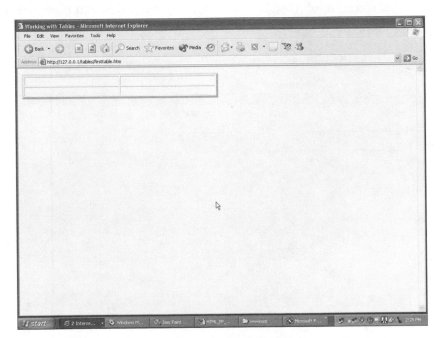

FIGURE 6.6 *Changing the width of your table can alter its overall appearance, as you will see in the figures later in this section.*

Setting the table width is easy. Simply change it to a percentage by using the width attribute, as shown here:

```
<table border="5" width="50%">
```

You can also set the table width in pixels rather than as a percentage, which can give you greater control over the exact width of your table. To use pixels, simply remove the % from the width attribute so you are assigning the width value a numeric value (which translates to pixels).

Changing table width can have a significant impact on the content contained in your table. For example, take a look at the difference in appearance between Figures 6.7 and 6.8. In Figure 6.7 the width has been set to 100%, whereas in Figure 6.8 the width has been reduced to 50%.

As with all things HTML, it is best to experiment with different values and layouts when you are working with table width (and all other table attributes). Also keep in mind that the table might display differently depending on the visitor's browser type, screen resolution, and other issues over which you have little control in your design.

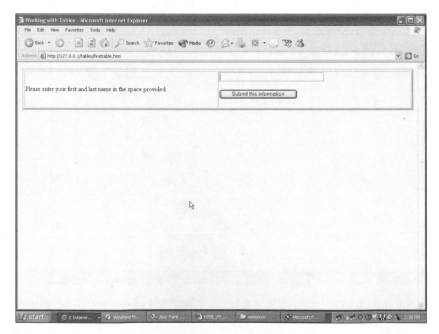

FIGURE 6.7 *Leaving the table width set to the default 100% can lead to some very uneven formatting on your pages.*

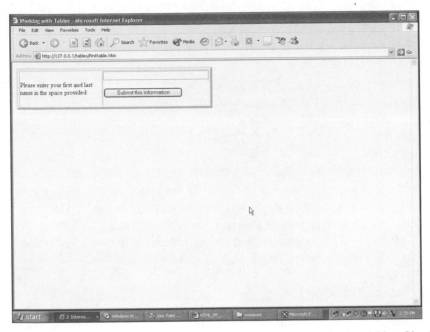

FIGURE 6.8 *Adjusting the table width to fit your table content is a better idea. Clearly this table has a neater appearance than the one in Figure 6.7.*

Integrating Text with Tables

As you saw in Chapter 3, you can have text wrap around tables just as you can with images on your Web pages.

By using the same `align` attribute and setting its value to either center, left, or right, you can integrate your tables more neatly into the flow of text in your page.

Go ahead and experiment with some of this table-text integration.

1. If it's not already open, go ahead and open the FirstTable.htm page you created at the beginning of this chapter.

2. Delete any existing HTML and enter the following code as you see it here:

```
<html>
<head>
<title>Working with Tables</title>
</head>
<body>
<table border="3" width="50%" align="right">
```

```
<tr>
  <td width="50%">User's First Name:</td>
  <td width="50%">Robert</td>
</tr>
<tr>
  <td width="50%">User's Last Name:</td>
  <td width="50%">Smith</td>
</tr>
</table>
<p>When integrating tables into your text, it is important to have them
formatted properly; however, it is equally important to place them on your
page so that they appear to be neatly integrated with the other elements
that are being displayed on your page. In this example, I have created an
example table and aligned it to the right, so that this text wraps around
it and gives a natural, integrated appearance.</p>
</body>
</html>
```

3. Save the page and load it in your Web browser. Your screen should appear similar to Figure 6.9.

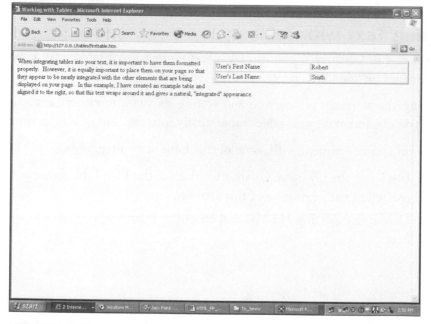

FIGURE 6.9 *You can use the* align *attribute to give your tables a neater, more integrated appearance on your page.*

You might try experimenting with the `align` attribute to see how it affects the appearance of your table. You can also use the `align` attribute to format the appearance of individual table cell contents. I will discuss that topic a bit later in this chapter.

Cell Spacing and Cell Padding

In addition to adjusting the parameters of the table shell, you will want to be able to control the formatting of the individual table cells. There are several attributes that allow you to do so, including the `cellspacing` and `cellpadding` attributes.

Figure 6.10 highlights a simple table that has these two attributes set greater than their default values of 1.

The cell spacing and cell padding attributes for the top table are shown here:

```
<table border="3" width="50%" cellspacing="3" cellpadding="5">
```

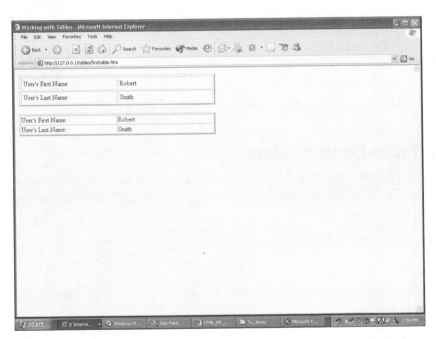

FIGURE 6.10 *The cell spacing and padding in the top table are set to 1; in the bottom table, the two values are set to 3 and 5, respectively.*

Spanning Cells across Columns and Rows

There will be instances when you need to span more than the cell width in order to fit all of the content into the cell. In cases like this, you can adjust the colspan or rowspan attributes.

The following code listing highlights a table with a cell that has its colspan attribute set to 3 (so that it spans three columns).

```
<table border="1" width="50%">
  <tr>
    <td width="50%" colspan="3">This is an example of a cell that spans three
    columns.</td>
  </tr>
  <tr>
    <td width="50%">2</td>
    <td width="50%">3</td>
  </tr>
  <tr>
    <td width="50%">4</td>
    <td width="50%">5</td>
  </tr>
</table>
```

Figure 6.11 shows this code as it would look in a Web browser.

Setting Table Border Colors

You can set a variety of color options for the table shell and the individual cells. If you are using Internet Explorer, you can adjust the actual table border using the following two attributes:

◆ bordercolordark
◆ bordercolorlight

The following code sample illustrates how you can set these two attributes within the <table> tag.

```
<table border="1" width="100%" bordercolorlight="#FF0000" bordercolordark="#000080"
bordercolor="#FFFF00">
```

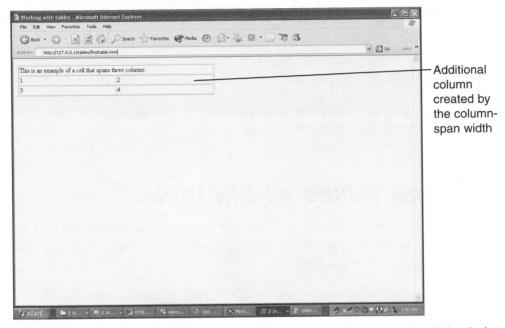

FIGURE 6.11 *The upper-left cell has a column span width set to 3; you can see the additional column at the far right side of the table.*

CAUTION

Remember, this feature is only supported in Internet Explorer.

Changing Cell Color and Using Background Images

You can change the background color of a cell using the `bgcolor` attribute, with which you are already familiar. Simply utilize this attribute within the `<table>` tag, and then set the value to the color of your choosing.

The following code snippet illustrates this technique:

```
<td bgcolor="#FFFFFF">
```

You can also insert a background image into a cell (or cells) by using the `background` attribute, with which you are also familiar. Assign the `background` attribute the location of the image you want to use. For example

```
<td background="/Tables/TestImage.gif">
```

In this example, the image named TestImage.gif would be set as the background image for the specific cell.

TIP

Note that you can apply both of these attributes to the table in general; simply add and set their values within the `<table>` tag.

Nesting Tables within Tables

There is nothing that says you can't nest a table within another table. This technique can come in handy for advanced formatting requirements. Figure 6.12 highlights two nested tables.

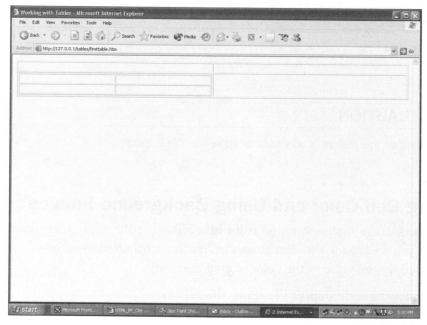

FIGURE 6.12 *The cell in the lower-left corner has a table nested in it.*

To nest a table within another, all you have to do is create another instance of the <table> tag in the cell in which you want to nest the table. The following code listing represents the HTML behind Figure 6.12.

```
<html>
<head>
<title>Working with Tables</title>
</head>
<body>
<table border="1" width="100%">
  <tr>
    <td width="50%"> </td>
    <td width="50%"> </td>
  </tr>
  <tr>
    <td width="50%">
    <table border="1" width="100%">
      <tr>
        <td width="50%"> </td>
        <td width="50%"> </td>
      </tr>
      <tr>
        <td width="50%"> </td>
        <td width="50%"> </td>
      </tr>
    </table>
    </td>
    <td width="50%"> </td>
  </tr>
</table>
</body>
```

Again, note the two instances of the <table> tag. In theory, you could have an infinite number of nested tables; however, if this starts to become a reality, you might reconsider the initial design scheme for your content and create something that is easier to manage.

TIP

When you start nesting tables, configuring specific table attributes, and adding content, it really becomes tedious to use a simple text editor. Again, everyone has their own preferences, but working with tables is reason enough to start using an HTML editor application, in my opinion.

TIP

You can use tables in interesting ways with HTML forms, in terms of overall functionality and content presentation. You'll learn more about this in Chapter 8, "Utilizing Forms for Dynamic Web Pages."

Summary

This chapter introduced you to working with HTML tables. You learned the basic table tags, including `<table>`, `<tr>`, and `<td>`, as well as several specific attributes you can apply to a table to get better control over width, borders, colors, cell spacing, background colors and images, and other general formatting issues. You also learned how to integrate text and tables by wrapping the text around the table. Perhaps most important, you got a firsthand glimpse of how using an HTML editor can really speed up the more mundane and tedious HTML tasks, such as creating tables. This is especially helpful as the tables become complex and include lots of formatting or when you nest one table inside another.

Chapter 7

Integrating HTML Frames and Advanced Formatting

Initially a Netscape convention, Web pages that utilize frames have become nearly the de facto standard for presenting complex information. The benefits of working with frames are many (as you will see in this chapter). After you get some basic design principles clear, frames are very easy to build and customize, even with a simple text editor like Notepad.

This chapter will explore the basic HTML behind frames and point out specific types of framesets that you might want to consider based on how you want to present your content. This chapter will take a form-follows-function approach because your frame design will vary depending on how you want to guide visitors through the content on your site.

 NOTE

There was a time when frames were a Web novelty, and only a small percentage of Web browsers supported them. Although it is still probably a good idea to keep this in mind when building Web pages that utilize frames, you can (and should) feel safe in assuming that the vast majority of the visitors to your site will have Web browsers that allow them to view frames.

Understanding Frameset Terminology

Although frames are not overly complicated, there is some terminology that you should understand. The best way to learn this terminology is to actually build a simple frameset, and then work backward through each HTML tag so you understand what it does.

1. In the Inetpub folder on your computer, create a folder and call it Frames.

2. Open your text editor and type the following code exactly as you see it here:

```
<html>
<head>
<title>HTML PP Frames</title>
</head>
```

```
<frameset cols="150,*">
  <frame name="contents" target="main" src="FrameTest_Left.htm">
  <frame name="main" src="FrameTest_Right.htm">
  <noframes>
  <body>
  <p>This page uses frames, but your browser doesn't support them.</p>
  </body>
  </noframes>
</frameset>
</html>
```

3. After you've typed the code, save it in your Frames folder as FrameTest.htm.

Now I want to go through this code to highlight some of the major things that are happening.

◆ First, you haven't created a frame page with this code. Rather, all you've done is created the frame container, so to speak. If you look at the code, you will see that it references two additional Web pages—FrameTest_Left.htm and FrameTest_Right.htm. As you will see momentarily, these Web pages will plug into the frame container created by this code.

◆ Speaking of those two additional pages, you will notice that within the line of code where they are first listed, they are each given a name: FrameTest_Left is given the name contents and FrameTest_Right is given the name main. This will make sense when you see this particular frameset displayed in a Web browser, as shown in Figure 7.1.

◆ Finally, notice the specific HTML tags that mention frames in this code:

   ◆ `<frameset>` and `</frameset>`. These tags denote the section of your HTML that will utilize frames.

   ◆ `<noframes>` and `</noframes>`. These tags, included within the `<frameset>` tags, will display alternate content if the visitor's Web browser is not able to display frames. In the preceding code, the text that will appear for these browsers is simply, "This page uses frames, but your browser doesn't support them."

Figure 7.1 illustrates what this frameset will look like when it's loaded into a browser capable of working with frames.

FrameTest_Left.htm   FrameTest_Right.htm

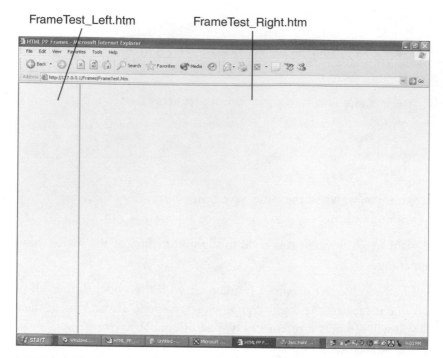

FIGURE 7.1 *A very basic frame page. Notice the vertical divider that separates the two pages that make up the frameset (FrameTest_Left.htm and FrameTest_Right.htm).*

To display the frameset on your computer, you also need to create the two pages that make up the frameset. I just used blank pages in Figure 7.1, but to make things more interesting, create those two pages now.

First create the FrameTest_Left.htm page.

1. Open your text editor.

2. Type in the following code:

```
<html>
<head>
<title>FrameTest_Left </title>
<base target="main">
</head>
<body>
<b> Welcome to the frames test!</b>
<hr>
This is the contents frame.
</body>
</html>
```

3. Save this page as FrameTest_Left.htm and save it to the Frames folder you created at the beginning of this chapter.

4. Next type the following code:

```
<html>
<head>
<title>FrameTest_Right </title>
</head>
<body>
<hr>
<p align="center"><font size="7"><b>This is the Main Frame!</b></font></p>
<hr>
<p align="center">(You can have hyperlinks in the contents frame that point to
this frame)</p>
</body>
</html>
```

5. Save this page into your Frames folder as FrameTest_Right.htm.

6. Now reload the FrameTest.htm page in your Web browser. It should look like Figure 7.2.

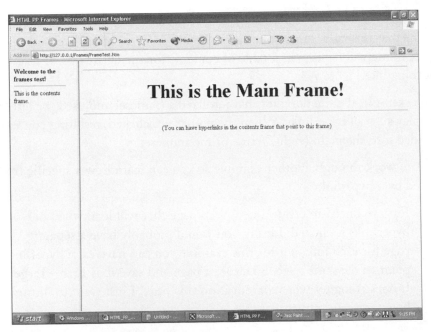

FIGURE 7.2 *Adding some additional text makes it is easier to see the two frames that make up this particular frameset.*

Congratulations, you've built your first frameset! As I noted at the beginning of the chapter, the basic structure of a frameset is easy; however, there are many specific options you can set and a variety of ways you can divide your frames. (In other words, you are not limited to that vertical bar, nor are you limited to just two frames.) I will devote the rest of this chapter to looking at all these configuration options and how (and when) you can best use them.

NOTE

As I mentioned at the beginning of the chapter, most browsers are now capable of working with frames. However, if you want to provide extensive information within the `<noframes>` and `</noframes>` tags, you are certainly not limited to the standard "This page uses frames, but your browser doesn't support them." Still, before you put a lot of time into providing alternate content for frame-challenged visitors to your site, you should remember that most visitors will be able to display your frames with no problem.

Targeting Specific Frames with Hyperlinks

Imagine that the basic frameset design in Figure 7.2 is an actual Web site and that the left frame will be used as a table of contents for the entire site. It might look something like Figure 7.3.

In this example, the site designers have utilized a frameset and used the left frame to display a list of hyperlinks. When these links are clicked, resulting content will be loaded into the main (right) frame of the frameset.

I want to work through another example so you can learn how a specific frame is targeted by a hyperlink.

1. First you need to create a new Web page that will load when one of the hyperlinks is clicked. Ideally, you would probably have a separate Web page for each link, but for this example you can have each hyperlink point to the same page. So create a page and save it as FrameTarget.htm. It doesn't matter what content is on this page; I just want to illustrate how targeting frames works.

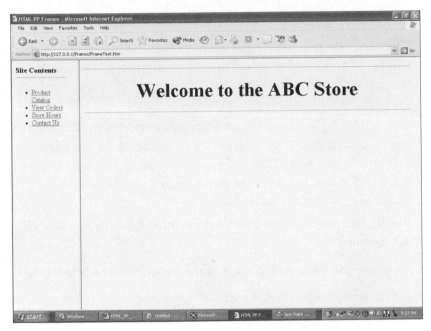

FIGURE 7.3 *The imaginatively titled ABC Store, utilizing the left frame to display hyperlinks that will point to the main (right) frame.*

2. Type the following code into your text editor:

```
<html>
<head>
<title>FrameTest_Left</title>
<base target="main">
</head>
<body>
<font size="4"><b>Site Contents</b></font><hr>
<ul>
    <li><a target="main" href="FrameTarget.htm">Product Catalog</a></li>
    <li><a target="main" href="FrameTarget.htm">View Orders</a></li>
    <li><a target="main" href="FrameTarget.htm">Store Hours</a></li>
    <li><a target="main" href="FrameTarget.htm">Contact Us</a></li>
</ul>
</body>
</html>
```

3. Save this page as FrameTest_Left.htm (which will replace the page you created earlier in the chapter).

This page has some additional frame-specific HTML tags.

◆ The `<base target="main">` tag indicates that the hyperlinks on this page will point to the frame named `main` in the frameset. If you refer back to the first code listing in this chapter, you can see that the `main` frame was associated with FrameTest_Right.htm.

◆ The hyperlinks on this page are fairly straightforward, with the exception of adding the `<a target="main">` parameter. Like the `<base target="main">` tag, this additional parameter simply indicates that the links will point to and load into the frame named `main` (again, the FrameTest_Right.htm page).

◆ Finally, this page utilizes a bulleted list format, which you learned about in Chapter 2.

Figure 7.4 shows the frameset after one of the hyperlinks has been clicked.

You might be wondering whether you can target the same frame in which the hyperlinks are placed. The answer to that is yes. As shown in the preceding code listing, instead of having `<a target="main" href="FrameTest.htm">`, you would change `<a target="main">` to `<a target="contents" href="FrameTet.htm">`.

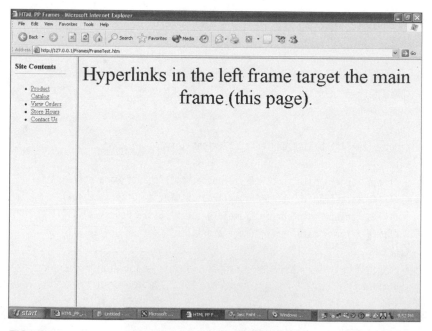

FIGURE 7.4 *When a hyperlink is clicked, its associated page is loaded in the main frame.*

In the FrameTest_Left.htm page that you re-created in the preceding code listing, change the first hyperlink so it points to the contents page. Remember from your frameset structure (the first code listing in this chapter), the `contents` frame is associated with FrameTest_Left.htm. If you make this change, save the page, and then reload theFrameTest.htm page into your browser. Click on the first hyperlink, and your screen will look like Figure 7.5.

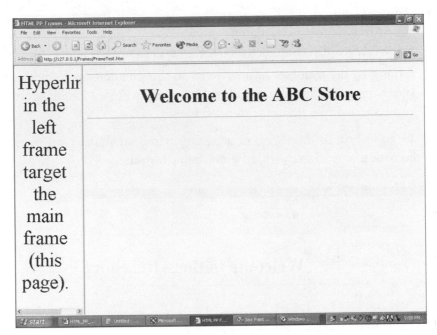

FIGURE 7.5 *You can target the same frame in which your hyperlinks are placed.*

Obviously in this simple example, there is no benefit to targeting the same frame in which the hyperlinks are placed. (And because of the frame divider, you cannot see all of the content that loads.) However, there will be times when you want to do this targeting, which will be illustrated later in this chapter.

TIP

You can also target hyperlinks within frames to a specific location. For example, you can have a hyperlink open a new window. You'll learn more about this concept later in the chapter, when I discuss the different types of frame layouts you can use.

Configuring Specific Frame Parameters

Now that you understand basic frame terminology and how to target specific frames with hyperlinks, you've mastered 90 percent of working with frames. Everything else you do with frames in terms of the actual HTML revolves around the following two issues:

◆ **Adjusting frame-specific parameters.** From adjusting frame width to preventing visitors from resizing the frameset when it loads in their browsers, you can configure several frame-design parameters.

◆ **Changing the frameset layout.** So far in this chapter, the frame examples have utilized a basic frameset. However, as Figure 7.6 illustrates, you can have multiple frames within a frameset.

I want to go on with a discussion of adjusting frame attributes, and then move into a discussion of working with different frame layouts.

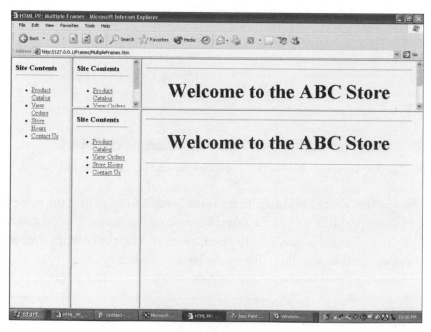

FIGURE 7.6 *Although you can technically have as many frames as you want, the more you add the busier (and more confusing) your frameset layout becomes.*

NOTE

Figure 7.6 should serve as both a warning and a guide to what is possible with frames. It's a warning because you can see how confusing multiple frames can be. But on the other hand, it hints at some very exciting content presentation opportunities that are available with frames if they are used correctly. (This figure is not an example of these exciting content presentation opportunities, but you get the idea!)

Adjusting Frame Borders

As you saw in Figure 7.5, not all of the content is visible because the frame border is not wide enough to accommodate it. In situations like this, you need to consider adjusting the frame border to ensure that all of your content is visible.

The border width is set in the frameset container page (see the first code listing in this chapter). In that example, the border was set to 150 pixels. Follow these steps to adjust it:

1. Open the FrameTest.htm page in your text editor.
2. Change the value from 150 to 300.
3. Save the page and reload it into your Web browser. Your screen will look like Figure 7.7.
4. Click on the first link, which should still be targeting the same frame (FrameTest_Left.htm). Comparing Figure 7.8 to 7.5, all of the content is now visible thanks to the widening of the frame border.

Some other important factors to keep in mind when working with frame borders:

◆ You can change the color of the frame border by adding the Bordercolor=[*color*] attribute in the opening frameset tag. For example, if you wanted to change the frame border to red in the first code listing in this chapter, you would use the following line:

```
<frameset bordercolor="red" cols="300,*">
```

◆ To make a frame border invisible, you can set the frame border and frame spacing attributes to 0. For example, if you wanted to make the frame borders invisible in the first code listing in this chapter, you would use the following line:

```
<frameset cols="300,*" framespacing="0" border="0" frameborder="0">
```

Figure 7.9 illustrates this borderless frame. Note that setting the border to 0 doesn't remove your frames; it simply removes the border.

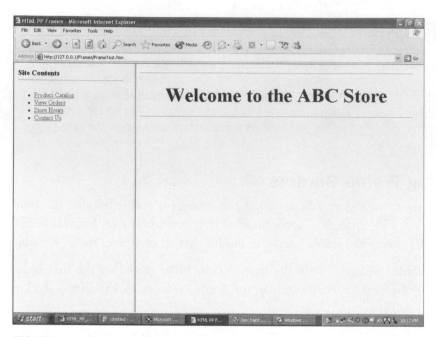

FIGURE 7.7 *Widening the frame border to ensure that all content can be displayed.*

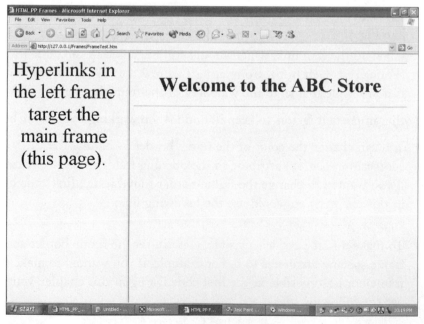

FIGURE 7.8 *You might want to experiment with the frame border width so it displays all your content but doesn't leave too much white space or distort the formatting of your individual pages that load into the specific frames.*

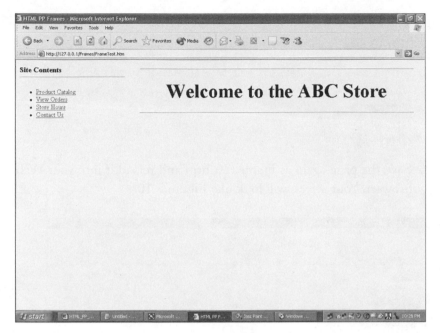

FIGURE 7.9 *Removing borders can have interesting effects in terms of how your framesets (and related content) appear.*

You can do some additional formatting with borders, as you will see when you work with different frame layouts later in this chapter.

Adjusting Frame Margins

In both Netscape Navigator and Internet Explorer, frame margins are set to a default value so that the content begins slightly down and to the right. However, by adjusting the frame margins, you can change how the content initially loads.

1. Open the FrameTest.htm page in your text editor.

2. Add the `marginwidth` attribute and its associated values, as you see in the following code listing:

```
<html>
<head>
<title>HTML PP Frames</title>
</head>
<frameset cols="300,*">
<frame name="contents" target="main" src="FrameTest_Left.htm" marginwidth=50
marginheight=25>
```

```
<frame name="main" src="FrameTest_Right.htm" marginwidth=100 marginheight=150>
<noframes>
<body>
<p>This page uses frames, but your browser doesn't support them.</p>
</body>
</noframes>
</frameset>
</html>
```

3. Save the page again as FrameTest.htm and reload it into your Web browser. Your screen will look like Figure 7.10.

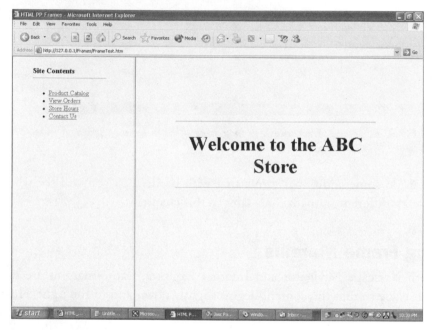

FIGURE 7.10 *Adjusting the margins will result in different text placement.*

Showing or Hiding Scroll Bars

Another basic frame attribute is whether or not you want to show scroll bars. As you saw in the messy frame layout in Figure 7.6, scroll bars appeared because there was more content in the frame than could be displayed on the screen, and scroll bars were necessary to allow visitors to move up or down through the content.

However, depending on your layout design, you might not want scroll bars to be presented. In that case, you simply adjust the scrolling attribute. For example, if you didn't want scroll bars to appear in any of the frames in the first code listing in this chapter, you would simply set the scrolling attribute to no for each frame, as shown in the following code listing:

```
<html>
<head>
<title>HTML PP Frames</title>
</head>
<frameset cols="150,*">
  <frame name="contents" target="main" src="TestFrame_Left.htm" scrolling=no>
  <frame name="main" src="TestFrame_Right.htm" scrolling=no>
  <noframes>
  <body>
  <p>This page uses frames, but your browser doesn't support them.</p>
  </body>
  </noframes>
</frameset>
</html>
```

 NOTE

Scroll bars only appear if you have content that exceeds the size of the frame. There wasn't enough content to generate scroll bars in the first example in this chapter, so they wouldn't have appeared even if you had set the scrolling attribute to yes.

Preventing Frame Resizing

The final basic frame attribute is to determine whether you want to allow visitors to resize your frames.

Why should you care about this attribute? You can (and will) put a lot of effort into how your content is presented on your Web pages. Often the neatest presentation of this content will require you to carefully adjust the border and margin attributes of your frames. If you allow visitors to resize the frames on their own, it can seriously detract from the most effective presentation of your content.

You can prevent visitors from resizing your frames by including the `noresize` attribute within the `<frame>` tag proper. The following code listing shows an example of this:

```
<html>
<head>
<title>HTML PP Frames</title>
</head>
<frameset cols="150,*">
  <frame name="contents" target="main" src="FrameTestLeft.htm" noresize scrolling=no>
  <frame name="main" src="FrameTestRight.htm" scrolling=no>
  <noframes>
  <body>
  <p>This page uses frames, but your browser doesn't support them.</p>
  </body>
  </noframes>
</frameset>
</html>
```

In this example, you will notice that the `contents` frame doesn't allow for scrolling or resizing; the `main` frame also does not allow scrolling, but it doesn't prevent users from resizing the frame. The important thing to note about this is that you can specify the specific attributes you want each respective frame to possess.

Manipulating Frameset Configurations

The figures in this chapter have thus far illustrated a basic frameset that resembles a table of contents—that is, you have a left frame that more than likely contains hyperlinks that target the right frame.

However, this is by no means the only type of frameset configuration at your disposal. In fact, as you saw in Figure 7.6, you can nest and divide framesets within other framesets for all kinds of interesting presentations.

In this section, I want to show you some examples of common framesets you might want to consider if your Web site design calls for frames.

TIP

As you will see in Chapter 12, "Working with an HTML Editor," and the third project in Part II (covered in Chapters 21 through 24), working with an HTML editor such as Microsoft FrontPage can make quick work of the more tedious aspects of working with and configuring frames. In FrontPage, as in many HTML editors, there are several frame page templates that automatically create all of the configurations I'm going to discuss in this section.

The Banner and Contents Configuration

In this widely-used frameset configuration, you are given the same table of contents frame you've seen in the figures thus far. However, you are also given a banner frame on which you can place information. Figure 7.11 illustrates this configuration.

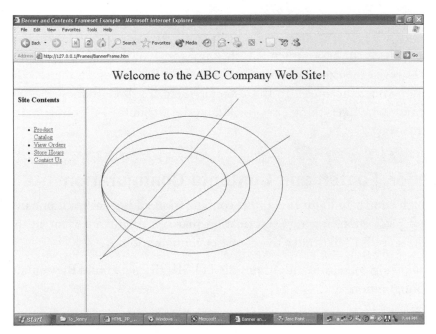

FIGURE 7.11 *The banner and contents configuration.*

The frameset code for this configuration follows:

```
<html>
<head>
<title>Banner and Contents Frameset Example</title>
</head>
<frameset rows="64,*">
<frame name="banner" scrolling="no" noresize target="contents" src="Banner_Top.htm">
<frameset cols="176,*">
<frame name="contents" target="main" src="Banner_Left.htm">
<frame name="main" src="Banner_Right.htm">
</frameset>
<noframes>
<body>
<p>This page uses frames, but your browser doesn't support them.</p>
</body>
</noframes>
</frameset>
</html>
```

As you will see, the basic structure is the same for all of these configuration examples. However, the names of the frames will differ depending on the specific configuration you want to use. In this example there are three frames—banner, contents, and main. Everything else—including the attributes—is configured exactly the same way.

The Header, Footer, and Contents Configuration

Although similar to Figure 7.11, this configuration adds a footer frame in which you can place supplementary information that you might not want in the main frame. Figure 7.12 illustrates this frameset configuration.

The following code listing illustrates the HTML that will build the container for this configuration.

```
<html>
<head>
<title>Header, Footer and Contents Frameset</title>
</head>
<frameset rows="64,*,64">
```

```
<frame name="top" scrolling="no" noresize target="contents" src="Header_Top.htm">
<frameset cols="189,*">
<frame name="contents" target="main" src="Header_Left.htm">
<frame name="main" src="Header_Right.htm">
</frameset>
<frame name="bottom" scrolling="no" noresize target="contents" src="Header_Bottom.htm">
<noframes>
<body>
<p>This page uses frames, but your browser doesn't support them.</p>
</body>
</noframes>
</frameset>
</html>
```

Again, notice the names given to each frame (top, contents, main, and bottom), which tell the Web browser how to display the frames.

Figure 7.13 illustrates the target of the Product A hyperlink. The visitor has clicked on this link, and new content has been loaded into the footer frame.

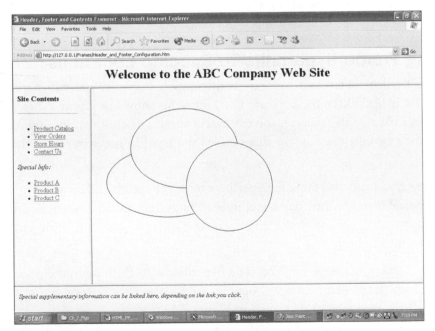

FIGURE 7.12 *Use the footer frame to place additional, perhaps supplementary, information.*

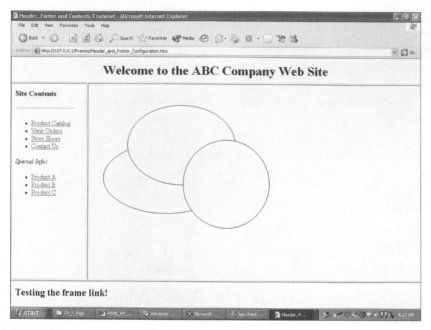

FIGURE 7.13 *Allowing content to be loaded into a footer frame is a good way to present information, but not have it overwhelm the main "content" frame.*

Targeting Frame Hyperlinks to Specific Locations

In the header, footer, and contents configuration example, you will notice that there are hyperlinks in the contents (left) frame (as shown in Figure 7.12). As you learned earlier in the chapter, you can target specific frames within a frameset so that, for example, the links in this content frame will open content in the main frame.

However, you can also include hyperlinks to target specific locations within your frameset. There are four basic methods of targeting specific locations within a frameset, and all are accomplished by setting the TARGET attribute (with which you are already familiar).

- ◆ **TARGET=_blank.** When you set a hyperlink with this target, the page to which the link points will open in a new, blank window on top of the existing frameset, as shown in Figure 7.14.

- ◆ **TARGET=_self.** Use this attribute if you want to have the hyperlink point to the same frame that contains the link. As you saw in Figure 7.5, this will achieve the same result as if you linked to the name of the frame that contains the hyperlink.

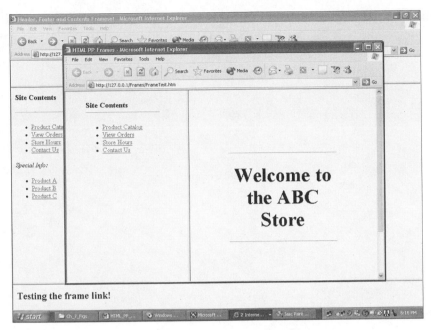

FIGURE 7.14 *Utilizing the* TARGET=_blank *attribute to open the content in a new window. In this case, the link pointed to the FrameTest.htm frameset you created earlier in the chapter.*

◆ TARGET=_top. By utilizing this attribute, you will open the content completely outside of the frameset, in a new window. Unlike in Figure 7.14, this will not open a new browser window; rather, it will open the content independent of the frameset that contains the link. Put simply, using this type of target will take your content completely out of the parent frameset.

◆ TARGET=_parent. This attribute is nearly identical to the TARGET=_top attribute except when you are using nested framesets. (More on this later in the chapter.)

Top-Down Hierarchy Configuration

The last specific example of frameset configuration I want to show you is the top-down hierarchy configuration. Figure 7.15 illustrates what this looks like when loaded in a Web browser.

This is also an example of a frameset configuration where you need to put much care and thought into your final design; otherwise, you will end up with a very

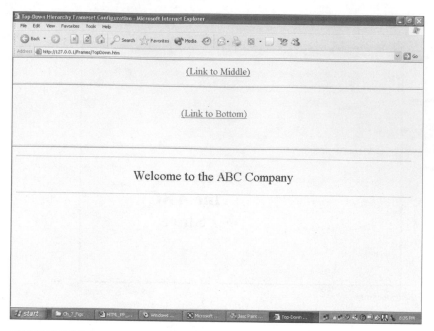

FIGURE 7.15 *Use hyperlinks at the top to change content in the middle, and use hyperlinks in the middle to change content at the bottom.*

confusing Web site. For example, if you click on the top link, information will load into the middle frame, replacing the link that is currently there. Figure 7.16 highlights this.

 NOTE

You could have your visitors use the navigation buttons on their browser to move back and forth between hyperlinks. That way, if they clicked the top link and were presented with Figure 7.16, they could click the Back button in their Web browser to once again be presented with the initial frameset (see Figure 7.15). Thus, they would once again have the links in each frame viewable. But this isn't really the most intuitive navigation scheme. Once again, use caution when designing this and all other framesets to ensure that you present information in the most efficient manner possible.

One advantage to this type of configuration is that you have more direct horizontal screen real estate. For example, in Figure 7.17, the hyperlink in the middle frame has been clicked, resulting in the FrameTest.htm frameset being loaded into the bottom frame. Compared to Figure 7.6, this figure isn't nearly as confusing.

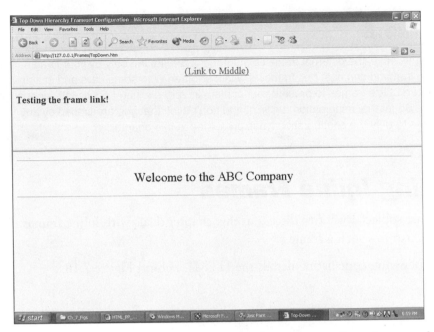

FIGURE 7.16 *You must use caution when using the top-down configuration so you don't overwrite important hyperlinks or other critical information.*

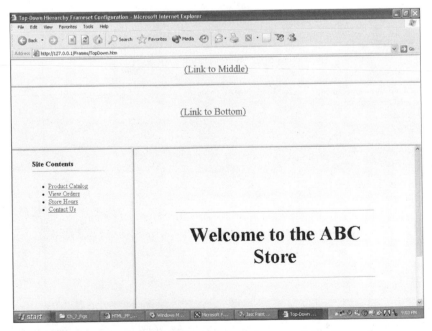

FIGURE 7.17 *You can load a different frameset into an existing frameset.*

NOTE

In many ways, the different frame configurations are limited only by your imagination, given that you can nest one frameset within another. With some care and imagination, you can utilize frames to present your content in very exciting and visually appealing ways. So let that imagination run wild, and don't think that you are limited by any means to only the configuration types presented in this chapter.

Creating Inline Frames

The last subject I want to discuss in this chapter deals with inline frames. Figure 7.18 illustrates such a frame.

The following code listing details the HTML behind Figure 7.18.

```
<html>
<head>
<title>Welcome to the ABC Company</title>
</head>
```

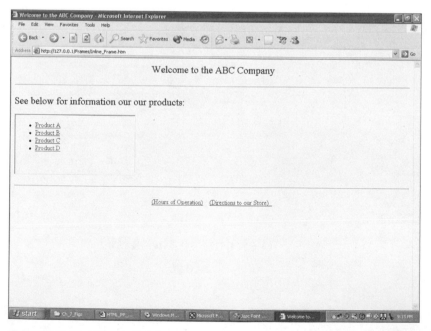

FIGURE 7.18 *Using inline frames can allow you to utilize the functionality of frames while giving your pages a frame-free appearance.*

```
<body>
<p align="center"><font size="5">Welcome to the ABC Company</font></p>
<hr>
<p align="left"><font size="5">See below for information on our products:</font></p>
<p align="left"><iframe name="I1" src="Inline_Frame_A.htm">
Your browser does not support inline frames or is currently configured not to display
inline frames.
</iframe></p>
<hr>
<p align="center"><a href="http://www.someabccompanylink.com ">(Hours of
Operation)</a><p>
<a href="http://www.someabccompanylink.com">(Directions to our Store)</a></p>
</body>
</html>
```

Some general things to note about this code:

◆ The inline frame is noted by the `<iframe>` tag, which is similar to the regular `<frame>` tag in that you identify a source page to load (in this case, the page called Inline_Frame_A.htm—see the following code listing).

◆ Although it is not shown in this particular code, you can set all of the same attributes for inline frames as you can for regular frames (such as `frameborder`, `scrolling`, and so on).

◆ Although inline frames are fairly standard, they were originally a Microsoft convention, so older versions of the Netscape Web browser, for example, might not support them. You might want to take more care in including "Your browser does not support inline frames" than you did with the text for browsers that don't support regular frames.

The following code listing illustrates the source page that is linked to the inline frame in the preceding code listing.

```
<html>
<head>
<title>Example of inline frame </title>
</head>
<body>
<ul>
  <li><a target="_self" href="ABC.htm">Product A</a></li>
  <li><a target="_blank" href="ABC.htm">Product B</a></li>
  <li><a target="_self" href="ABC.htm">Product C</a></li>
  <li><a href="ABC.htm">Product D</a></li>
```

```
</ul>
</body>
</html>
```

Note that the specific targeting you learned in the previous section is also used in this page. Figure 7.19 illustrates what happens when the second link (Product B, as shown in Figure 7.18) is clicked. Because this hyperlink utilizes the `target="_blank"` attribute, the content that is associated with the link opens in a new window.

 NOTE

All of the projects in Part II will utilize frames in their design, so you'll have ample opportunity to see how you can use frames in real-world Web sites. Moreover, when you work through the FrontPage project (in Chapters 21 through 24), you will see how all of this frame HTML can be automated and made much easier using the FrontPage templates and other design tools.

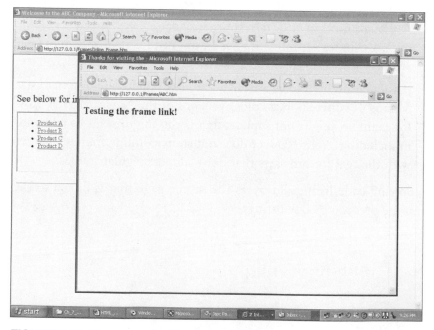

FIGURE 7.19 *You can work with all the same attributes (including setting specific hyperlink targets) for inline frames as you can for regular frames.*

Summary

This chapter introduced you to the wonderful world of HTML frames and gave you an overview of the various attributes and configurations that are possible with them. You were first introduced to basic frame terminology, and then you became familiar with the general frameset, including how frames are named and source pages are identified. You then worked with some general frame attributes and learned how to target individual frames (and/or specific locations) via the use of hyperlinks and the `target` attribute. Finally, you were introduced to inline frames, which originally were viewable only in Internet Explorer. As you move through the projects in Part II of the book, you will see frames utilized in a variety of ways to present content for everything from a small business Web site to a secondary school site.

Chapter 8

**Utilizing Forms
for Dynamic
Web Pages**

Well-designed forms are a cornerstone of any effective Web site because they are the central tools for capturing information from your visitors. Whether it is a general customer-feedback form or a specialized form in the online store section of your Web site, you need a way to interact with your visitors, and forms are generally the way that it is done.

As you learned in Chapter 7, there are a great deal of special configuration and customization attributes you can use to deal with forms, including attributes to control the general appearance of the form and its specific elements (such as radio buttons and text boxes). You'll work with all of these issues in this chapter.

CAUTION

Before you begin this chapter, you need to realize that form design is only part of the puzzle. The other critical half is how you will process the form information you collect. In other words, when a site visitor provides you with information via the form and clicks on the submit button, what technology will come into play so you can get your hands on that information? This can be a complicated issue depending on the type of form processing you employ, the type of Web server you have access to, and how you want to receive and manipulate the information you collect. Chapter 11, "Integrating Scripts and Other Advanced Functionality," will address this issue of form processing to some degree, and you will also see it in the FrontPage project of Part II.

Form Basics

The basic HTML form tag is simply `<form>`. The following code listing is a simple example of how to place a form on your Web page.

```
<html>
<head>
<title>Simple Form Example</title>
</head>
<body>
<form method="POST" action="FormProcessing.asp">
```

```
<p>What is your first name: <input type="text" name="FirstName" size="30"></p>
<p>What is your last name: <input type="text" name="LastName" size="30"></p>
<p><input type="submit" value="Click here to submit the form" name="Submit"></p>
</form>
</body>
</html>
```

When you save this code as a Web page and load it into a browser, it will look like Figure 8.1.

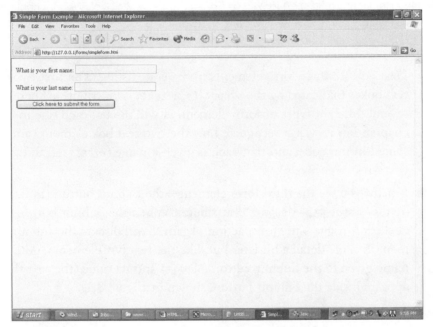

FIGURE 8.1 *A simple form that collects two pieces of information from visitors.*

I want to go through this code and point out several key components of the form, all of which will be discussed in detail in this chapter:

◆ After the usual opening header HTML (for example, `<head>`, `<title>`, and `<body>` tags), you insert the `<form>` tag. There are two important things to note about the attributes within the `<form>` tag:

◆ First is the `method` attribute. Put simply, this tells the server that will process the form how to process the data. `POST` and `GET` are the most commonly used method attributes; `POST` is used to post the form on the page, and `GET` is later used to retrieve information from the form.

◆ Second is the ⟨action⟩ attribute. Similar conceptually to a hyperlink, the value assigned to this attribute is literally used as a pointer to instruct the form where to go with its data when the Submit button is clicked. In the preceding code listing, the form will be sent to the file FormProcessing.asp.

 NOTE

The file extension .asp is short for *Active Server Pages*, a Microsoft Web technology that I will discuss in this chapter and other parts of this book.

◆ Next you see three form elements in the code listing. The first two are text boxes (indicated by the ⟨input type=text...⟩ attribute). There are several different types of form elements; I will discuss each one in this chapter. For now, just recognize how the two text box elements are presented in this code, and that each is given a name (FirstName and LastName, respectively).

◆ Finally, you see the third form element—the Submit button (indicated by the ⟨input type="submit"⟩ attribute). When the Submit button is clicked, it triggers the form action. Again, I will discuss the submit element in more detail a bit later but, like the text box elements, note the name given to the Submit button (Submit) and its value (the text that appears inside the Submit button, shown in Figure 8.1).

This typical form contains all the necessary attributes to present a form on a Web page. The remainder of this chapter will focus on how this form and other more complex forms are built, customized, and processed.

Understanding Form Elements

In the previous example, you saw two different form elements—a text box and a Submit button. However, there are many different types of form elements, and each has its own specific attributes and ability to be customized. The following sections will look at each of these elements and give you an opportunity to work with them in an actual Web page.

To best demonstrate these different elements, you should follow along and create them in a Web page. Take some time now to set up a Web page by following these instructions:

1. In your Inetpub folder on your computer, create a folder called Forms.

2. Open your text editor, create a blank page, and save it in your Forms folder as FormTest.htm.

3. On the page, type the following code exactly as you see it listed:

```
<html>
<head>
<title>Simple Form Example</title>
</head>
<body>
<form method="POST" action="FormProcess.asp">
</form>
</body>
</html>
```

4. Save the page and keep it open in your text editor because you are going to be working with it in the following sections.

Text Boxes

As you saw in Figure 8.1, you can use a text box to gather narrative information (either text or numerical data). Generally, a text box is used to gather short pieces of information, such as a person's name and address. A text area element (which I'll discuss a bit later) is used to gather more extensive input, such as a customer's opinion on a specific issue.

The text box element has the following attributes available for configuration:

◆ **Name.** Every form element needs a name so you can readily identify each one when the form is processed.

◆ **Initial value.** If you don't want your text box to appear empty when the form loads, you can specify a value that will appear inside the box.

◆ **Width in characters.** This attribute specifies the width of the text box. This is an important attribute to consider depending on the type of information you will be gathering. Although the information will scroll as the user types if it exceeds the length of the text box, it is a good practice—and more visually pleasing—to set the text box length wide enough to accept all the information without scrolling.

◆ **Tab order.** An issue for all the elements in your form, this indicates (along with the other elements in the form) the order in which the specific element will become active when the Tab key is pressed. (I'll discuss tab order in more detail later in this chapter.)

◆ **Password field.** Imagine that you want a text box to capture a visitor's credit card number. You can set the `password` attribute to `yes` so that as visitors enter their information into the text box, asterisks will appear rather than the actual number. Figure 8.2 illustrates the use of the `password` attribute in a text box.

On the FormTest.htm page you created at the beginning of this chapter, enter the following code after the opening `<form>` tag:

```
Enter your first and last name here:
<input name="UserName" size="40" value="(Enter Your Name)" tabindex="1"></p>
```

You just created a text box called `UserName`. You gave the text box a width of 40 characters and set an initial value of `"(Enter Your Name)"` to appear in the box. Finally, you set the tab index (order) to 1, indicating that this will be the first of

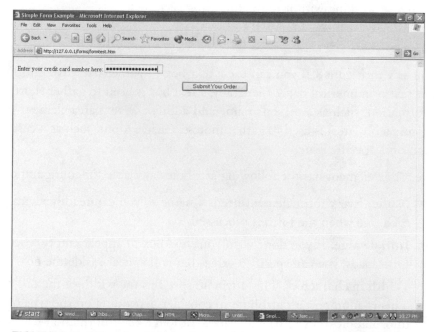

FIGURE 8.2 *Although specific numbers are being typed, only asterisks appear in this credit card number field.*

all the form fields that will appear on this form to be made active when users press the Tab key on their keyboards.

Text box elements are very basic, so I want to move on to the next form element.

 NOTE

As you work through each of the following sections on form elements, you will add to your FormTest.htm page. When you're done, you will have a Web page that includes each of the form elements, so just keep adding to the page as you move through the following sections.

Text Areas

Like the text box element, text area elements are used to gather narrative information from users. However, they are designed to capture more extensive information.

The text area element has the same properties as the text box element, except it does not have a password option. Also, in addition to the width property, the text area element also allows you to set the number of lines, which will determine the height of the form element.

On the FormTest.htm page you created at the beginning of this chapter, enter the following code after the `</p>` tag that ended the preceding code listing:

```
Enter a brief description of yourself here:</p>
<textarea rows="10" name="UserDescription" cols="40" tabindex="2">
</textarea></p>
```

Save the FormTest.htm page and load it into your Web browser. Your screen should look like Figure 8.3.

You've now created a text area element named `UserDescription`. You gave it a width of 40 characters and a height (via the value assigned to the `row` attribute) of 10. The tab index (order) is 2. Finally, you chose not to give it a default value because you have not provided any text for the `value` property, like you did in the text box code listing.

Now you can add some check box elements to your form.

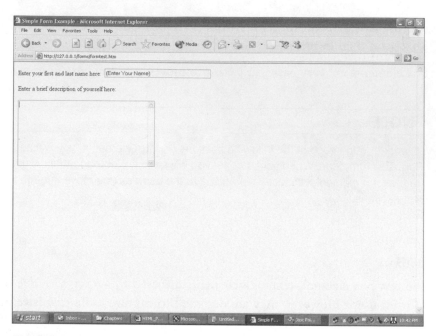

FIGURE 8.3 *You now have a text box and a text area element on your form.*

Check Boxes

I'm sure you've taken countless surveys with sections that say, "Check all answers that apply." The check box element is the HTML equivalent of those.

The check box element has the following attributes:

- ◆ **Name.** This is the name you want to assign to the form element.
- ◆ **Value.** You can think of a check box as being on (checked) or off (unchecked). In fact, for the value attribute, you can literally assign the value as on or off. However, most designers will give this a number or a short text value to indicate whether or not the box has been checked. Assigning a number can be advantageous because you can perform calculations (for example, if you run a script on the form results) to determine how many people responded to a specific question in a certain way.

Go ahead and create some check boxes on your ever-growing test form. Enter the following code in your FormTest.htm page, right after the code that produced the text area element:

```
I enjoy the following sports:</p>
Basketball: <input type="checkbox" name="Basketball" value="1"
tabindex="3">   
Football: <input type="checkbox" name="Football" value="2"
tabindex="4">   
NASCAR: <input type="checkbox" name="Nascar" value="3" tabindex="5">   
Soccer: <input type="checkbox" name="Soccer" value="4" tabindex="6"></p>
```

Your FormTest.htm page should now look like Figure 8.4 when you load it into a Web browser.

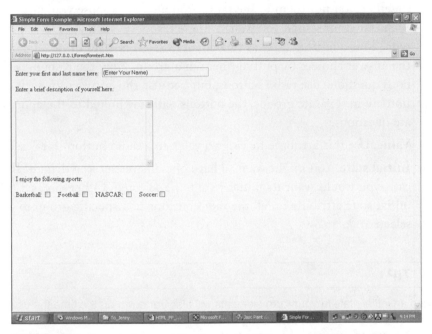

FIGURE 8.4 *Four check boxes. Note that you can select more than one check box.*

 NOTE

The   you see in the code listing is equivalent to one tab. This puts some space between each of the check boxes. Refer back to Chapters 2 and 4 for more information on text formatting and layout.

Radio (Option) Buttons

There will be times when you want to present a choice of answers on your form, but you only want the user to respond with one answer. This is where radio buttons come into play.

Radio buttons utilize the following attributes:

◆ **Group name.** Assume you have a question for which you only want a single response, such as "What is your gender?" For this question, you have two possible answers—male or female. To link your answer choices together, you put them in the same group. Now suppose you have another question for which you want a single response, such as "Do you have a pet?" This question also has two possible answers—yes or no. Again, link the answer choices by putting them in a group. Now the responses for both questions use radio buttons, but because the answers for each question are in separate groups, the buttons will stay linked to the appropriate questions.

◆ **Value.** Use this attribute to assign a value to a radio button if it is selected.

◆ **Initial state.** You might want to have one answer set as a default. In that case, you would want its initial state to be selected. Otherwise, set the initial state attribute on all the radio buttons in a specific group to not selected.

TIP

Having an initial state in your form elements will also cut down on the time the user spends on the form (always something to aspire to) as well as make the form, in general, easier to navigate and understand.

Add the following code to your FormTest.htm page. This code will create two radio buttons as part of a question that asks users to indicate their gender.

```
<p align="left">My gender is:</p>
<p align="left">Male:<input type="radio" value="M" checked name="Gender"
tabindex="7">   
Female: <input type="radio" name="Gender" value="F" tabindex="8"></p>
```

Your FormTest.htm page should now look like Figure 8.5.

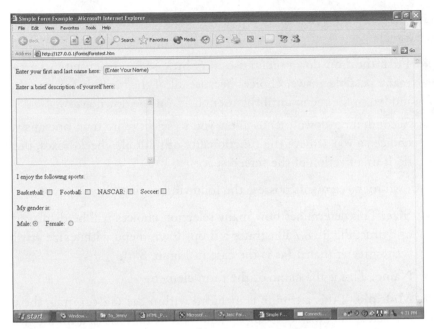

FIGURE 8.5 *Unlike check boxes, you can select only one radio button per group.*

Note that in the preceding code listing, the `checked name="Gender"` attribute is included for the first radio button, but it is not for the second button. Including this attribute with the male choice indicates that this radio button is selected by default.

Drop-Down Menus

Theoretically, you could accomplish the same functionality of a drop-down menu using check boxes or radio buttons; however, there is a major caveat with that statement. Imagine you have a question on a form that asks users to select the state in which they live. If you tried to do this with radio buttons, you would need 50 of them, which wouldn't look good on your page or be very user-friendly. Or suppose you wanted to ask users how many different states they have lived in over the course of their lives. In this case, you could use check boxes. (You couldn't use radio buttons because many users would have lived in more than one state, and you'd want them to be able to select multiple options.)

In both cases, a drop-down menu is clearly the best answer because it achieves two primary goals.

◆ First, the drop-down menu uses very little screen real estate to present many possible answer choices because all of the possible selections are hidden in the menu until the user clicks on the down arrow.

◆ Second, drop-down menus allow you to select more than one answer choice so you achieve the functionality of multiple check boxes, but you do it in a fraction of the screen space.

Drop-down menu elements possess the following attributes:

◆ **Size.** This determines how many selection choices will be displayed at one time. Figure 8.7 illustrates a drop-down menu with a size attribute set to greater than 1 (as is the case in Figure 8.6).

◆ **Name.** This is the name of the form element.

◆ **Multiple.** If this attribute is included within the <select> tag, the user can select multiple choices. (I'll talk more about this in a moment.)

◆ **Option value.** As with all form elements, use this attribute to assign a value to a selection choice.

As with all of the other form elements, take time now to add a drop-down menu to your FormTest.htm page by entering the following code exactly as it appears:

```
<p> What is your age range: <select size="1" name="Age" tabindex="9" >
<option value="1">less than 18</option>
<option value="2">18-25</option>
<option value="3">26-38</option>
<option value="4">39-50</option>
<option value="4">51-65</option>
<option value="6">greater than 65</option>
</select>
</p>
```

Your FormTest.htm page should now look like Figure 8.6

Figure 8.7 shows the same drop-down menu, but with the size attribute set to 5. Increasing the value of the size attribute allows the various answer options to be visible.

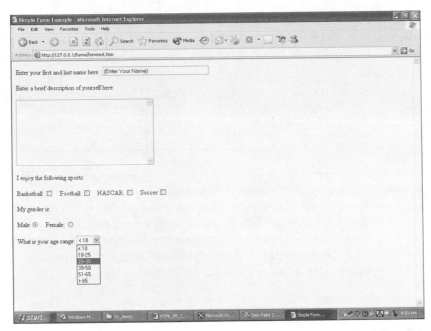

FIGURE 8.6 *The drop-down menu as it appears when selected, showing all possible answer selections.*

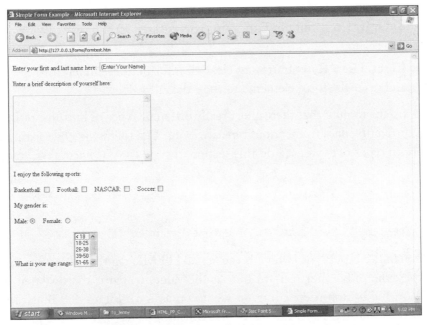

FIGURE 8.7 *Increase the size attribute so the various options in the drop-down menu are visible.*

You will notice that in the preceding code listing, the ⟨select⟩ tag contains the attribute multiple. As I mentioned, this allows users to select more than one answer from the drop-down menu. Although this would not be applicable for the particular question illustrated in Figures 8.6 and 8.7, it would be very applicable if the question asked the user to select the different U.S. states in which he or she has lived.

TIP

As with many form elements, the value you assign to a particular option might seem to have little to do with the actual option. For example, in the preceding code listing, the options reflect specific age ranges but the values assigned to those options are 1, 2, 3, and so on. In many cases, answers to form questions are inserted into a database, and working with simple numbers that correspond to values is easier and more practical than inserting the actual option (such as "less than 18").

Push Buttons

The final form element I want to discuss is the push button. There are two basic button types:

◆ **Submit.** Use a Submit button to (you guessed it) submit your form for processing.

◆ **Reset.** Use a Reset button to clear all information entered into the form and reset the form elements to their default values.

It's important to note that there aren't really different types of buttons; rather, you assign different values to the input type attribute. The following code listing illustrates both types of buttons. Add this section of code to your FormTest.htm page.

```
<p>
<input type="submit" value="Submit Your Answers!" name="Submit" tabindex="10" >
<p>
<input type="reset" value="Reset form" name="Reset" tabindex="11" >
```

Other than the input type (which is the actual HTML tag that identifies the button type), the only other real attribute is the value, which is the text that is displayed on the button (depending on what you assign). Figure 8.8 illustrates the two buttons that were added to the FormTest.htm page.

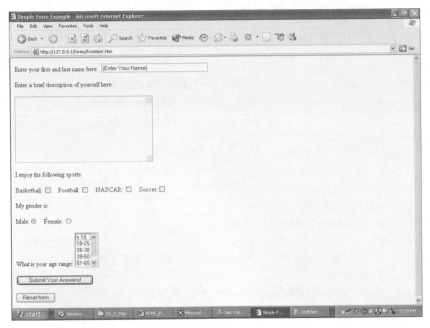

FIGURE 8.8 *Two different types of buttons, differentiated by the value assigned to the input type attribute.*

FormTest.htm HTML Review

At this point, your FormTest.htm page should include all of the form elements discussed thus far in the book. Review your page HTML against the following code listing before you move on to the next section in this chapter.

```
<html>
<head>
<title>Simple Form Example</title>
</head>
<body>
<form method="POST" action="FormProcessing.asp">
Enter your first and last name here: 
<input name="UserName" size="40" value="(Enter Your Name)" tabindex="1"></p>
<p align="left">Enter a brief description of yourself here: </p>
<textarea rows="10" name="UserDescription" cols="40" tabindex="2"></textarea></p>
I enjoy the following sports:</p>
Basketball: <input type="checkbox" name="Basketball" value="1"
tabindex="3">   
Football: <input type="checkbox" name="Football" value="2"
```

```
tabindex="4">   
NASCAR: <input type="checkbox" name="Nascar" value="3" tabindex="5">   
Soccer:<input type="checkbox" name="Soccer" value="4" tabindex="6"></p>
My gender is:</p>
Male:<input type="radio" value="M" checked name="Gender" tabindex="7">   
Female: <input type="radio" name="Gender" value="F" tabindex="8"></p>
What is your age range: <select size="5" name="Age" tabindex="9">
   <option value="1">less than 18</option>
   <option value="2">18-25</option>
   <option value="3">26-38</option>
   <option value="4">39-50</option>
   <option value="4">51-65</option>
   <option value="6">greater than 65</option>
   </select></p>
<input type="submit" value="Submit Your Answers!" name="Submit" tabindex="10" >
<p>
<input type="reset" value="Reset form" name="Reset"tabindex="11" >
</form>
</body>
</html>
```

Working with Hidden Form Fields

Sometimes you will want to pass data in a form that you don't want your visitors to see—either for simplicity or convenience or because they really don't need to be bothered with seeing it. For example, if you are working with a product order form, you might need to pass special inventory instructions in your form so that the information is included as the form gets processed.

Hidden form fields are a great way to pass such information without the user knowing it. The following code listing will add two hidden fields to your form. (You should add this code to your FormTest.htm page, right after the reset button element and before the closing </form> tag.)

```
<input type="hidden" name="Month" value="July">
<input type="hidden" name="Year" value="2003">
```

Save these additional lines of code to your FormTest.htm page. Again, because these are hidden form fields, they will not be displayed on screen. However, when the form is submitted, it will include two additional fields (Month and Year) that can be processed because they contain the values July and 2003, respectively.

CAUTION

Although hidden form fields don't display on the screen, you can ascertain their presence by looking at the page source in a Web browser, as illustrated in Figure 8.9. That said, don't use hidden form fields to contain sensitive information such as credit card numbers and user passwords because they are definitely not a secure mechanism for passing this kind of information.

```
formtest[1] - Notepad
File  Edit  Format  View  Help
<p align="left">Enter a brief description of yourself here: </p>
<p align="left">
<textarea rows="10" name="UserDescription" cols="40" tabindex="2"></textarea></p>
<p align="left">I enjoy the following sports:</p>
<p align="left">Basketball:
<input type="checkbox" name="Basketball" value="1" tabindex="3">   
Football: <input type="checkbox" name="Football" value="ON" tabindex="4"> &nbs
NASCAR: <input type="checkbox" name="Nascar" value="ON" tabindex="5">  &n
Soccer:<input type="checkbox" name="Soccer" value="ON" tabindex="6"></p>
<p align="left">My gender is:</p>
<p align="left">Male:<input type="radio" value="M" checked name="Gender" tabindex=":
Female: <input type="radio" name="Gender" value="F" tabindex="8"></p>
<p align="left">what is your age range:
<select size="5" name="Age" tabindex="9">
<option value="1">&lt; 18</option>
<option value="2">18-25</option>
<option value="3">26-38</option>
<option value="4">39-50</option>
<option value="4">51-65</option>
<option value="6">> 65</option>
</select></p>
<p align="left">
<input type="submit" value="Submit Your Answers!" name="Submit"></p>
<input type="reset" value="Reset form" name="Reset">
<input type="hidden" name="Month" value="July">
<input type="hidden" name="Year" value="2003">
</form>
</body>
</html>
```

FIGURE 8.9 *Use caution when utilizing hidden form fields because they can be seen in the page source code.*

Basic Form Formatting Techniques

Knowing how to place your form elements on the page is one thing, but organizing them so your form looks good and is easy to use is another key component.

Fortunately there are some easy formatting techniques you can utilize in your forms to achieve both of these goals. This section will discuss those techniques and how you can improve both the form (no pun intended!) and the function of your FormTest.htm page.

Grouping Form Elements Using the <fieldset> Tag

Often you will have form fields that seek to gather information about the same subject. For example, you might be building a form for a healthcare agency, and you might have several boxes that correspond to different medical conditions that patients need to check if they are affected by the ailment. Using the `<fieldset>` tag, you can put a nice border around all these check boxes and label this section of the form to make it easier to work with and understand.

Figure 8.10 illustrates the use of the `<fieldset>` tag by adding it to your FormTest.htm page. Notice how the radio button and drop-down menu elements are now grouped together and titled "Demographic Information."

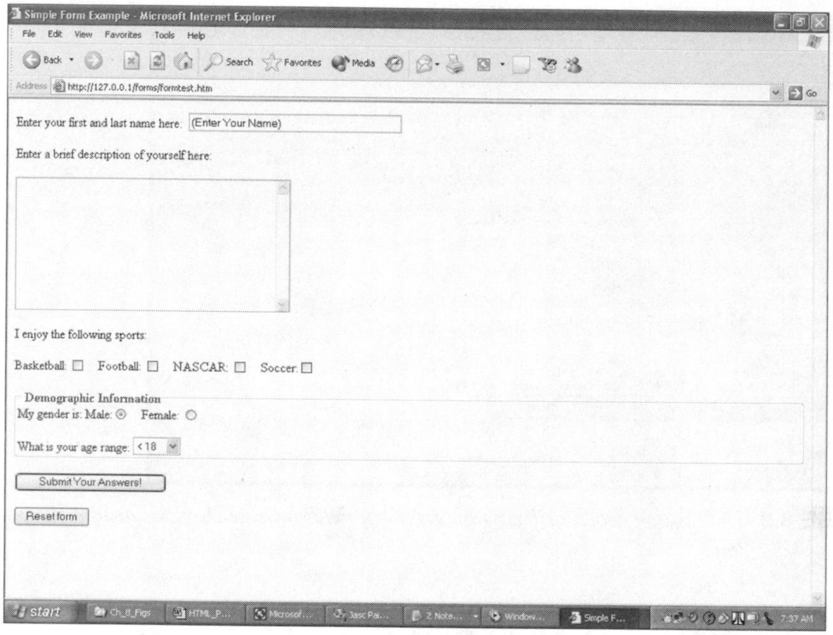

FIGURE 8.10 *Use the `<fieldset>` tag to neatly group and organize your related form fields.*

To achieve this result, adjust the following section of code (changed code is in bold) in your FormTest.htm page so that it appears like the following code listing.

```
<html>
<head>
<title>Simple Form Example</title>
</head>
<body>
<form method="POST" action="--WEBBOT-SELF--">
  Enter your first and last name here: 
  <input name="UserName" size="40" value="(Enter Your Name)" tabindex="1"></p>
```

```
<p align="left">Enter a brief description of yourself here: </p>
<p align="left">
<textarea rows="10" name="UserDescription" cols="40" tabindex="2"></textarea></p>
<p align="left">I enjoy the following sports:</p>
<p align="left">Basketball:
<input type="checkbox" name="Basketball" value="1" tabindex="3">   
Football: <input type="checkbox" name="Football" value="2"
tabindex="4">   
NASCAR: <input type="checkbox" name="Nascar" value="3" tabindex="5">   
Soccer:<input type="checkbox" name="Soccer" value="4" tabindex="6"></p>
<fieldset align=left>
<legend><b>Demographic Information </b></legend>
My gender is: Male:<input type="radio" value="M" checked name="Gender"
tabindex="7">   
Female: <input type="radio" name="Gender" value="F" tabindex="8"><p>What is your age
range:
<select size="1" name="Age" tabindex="9">
<option value="1">&lt; 18</option>
<option value="2">18-25</option>
<option value="3">26-38</option>
<option value="4">39-50</option>
<option value="4">51-65</option>
<option value="6">> 65</option>
</select></p>
</fieldset><p align="left">
<input type="submit" value="Submit Your Answers!" name="Submit"></p>
<input type="reset" value="Reset form" name="Reset">
<input type="hidden" name="Month" value="July">
<input type="hidden" name="Year" value="2003">
</form>
</body>
</html>
```

The `<fieldset>` tag has two basic attributes:

◆ **Align.** This is an optional attribute—it will default to left align. However, you can set the value of the attribute to left, middle, or right to align the legend (title) of your grouping.

◆ **Legend.** This is the title of your grouping. In the preceding code listing (and in Figure 8.10), the legend is set to Demographic Information.

Formatting Frames with Tables

You can greatly improve the look of your forms if you use tables to neatly group and organize your form elements. You can utilize all the table-formatting techniques you learned in Chapter 6 and simply add the form elements to the individual table cells.

Figure 8.11 illustrates your FormTest.htm page once again, but this time tables have been used to organize the form. Compare this to the other figures in this chapter. Clearly, Figure 8.11 is more attractive and would be easier to work with because it is more neatly formatted.

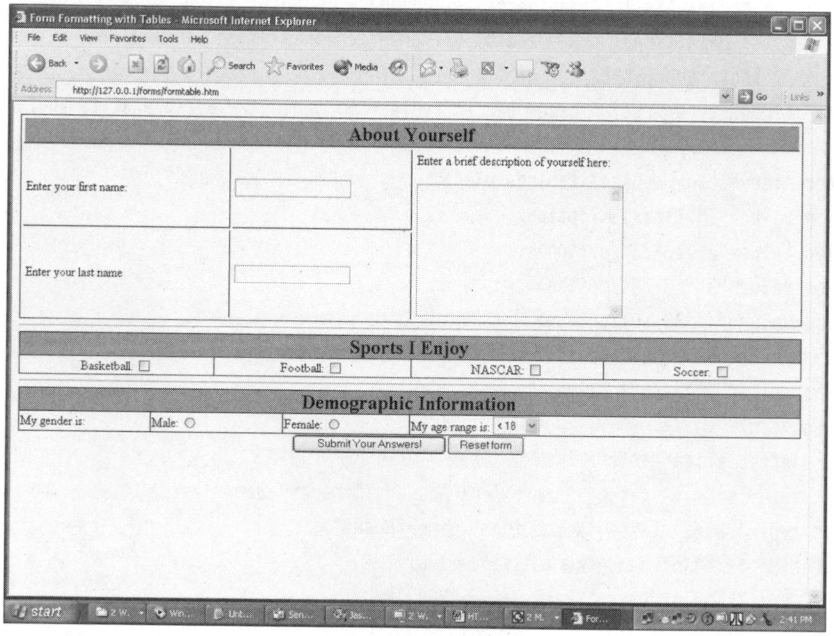

FIGURE 8.11 *The formatting that is possible with tables is limited only to your imagination and how you want to present your information.*

The following code listing highlights the inclusion of the table formatting. You can create a new page in your text editor, enter this code, and save it as FormTable.htm. Feel free to change the table formatting and experiment with the form elements using the skills you learned in Chapter 6 and this chapter.

```
<html>
<head>
<title>Form Formatting with Tables</title>
</head>
```

```html
<body>
<form>
<table border="1" style="border-collapse: collapse" bordercolor="#111111" width="100%"
cellpadding="2" cellspacing="4">
<tr>
<td width="22%" colspan="3" bgcolor="#FF0000">
<p align="center"><font size="5"><b>About Yourself</b></font></td>
</tr>
<tr>
<td width="6%">Enter your first name:</td>
<td width="5%"><input type="text" name="FirstName" size="20" tabindex="1"></td>
<td width="11%" rowspan="2">Enter a brief description of yourself here:<p>
<textarea rows="10" name="UserDescription" cols="30" tabindex="3"></textarea></td>
</tr>
<tr>
<td width="6%">Enter your last name</td>
<td width="5%"><input type="text" name="LastName" size="20" tabindex="2"></td>
</tr>
</table>
<hr>
<table border="1" style="border-collapse: collapse" bordercolor="#111111" width="100%">
<tr>
<td width="100%" bgcolor="#FF0000" colspan="4">
<p align="center"><font size="5"><b>Sports I Enjoy </b></font></td>
</tr>
<tr>
<td width="25%" align="center">Basketball:
<input type="checkbox" name="Basketball" value="1" tabindex="4"></td>
<td width="25%" align="center">Football:
<input type="checkbox" name="Football" value="2" tabindex="5"></td>
<td width="25%" align="center">NASCAR:
<input type="checkbox" name="NASCAR" value="3" tabindex="6"></td>
<td width="25%" align="center">Soccer:
<input type="checkbox" name="Soccer" value="4" tabindex="7"></td>
</tr>
</table>
<hr>
<table border="1" style="border-collapse: collapse" bordercolor="#111111" width="100%">
<tr>
<td width="100%" bgcolor="#FF0000" colspan="4">
<p align="center"><font size="5"><b>Demographic Information</b></font></td>
```

```
</tr>
<tr>
<td width="17%">My gender is: </td>
<td width="17%">Male:
<input type="radio" value="M" name="Gender" tabindex="8"></td>
<td width="16%">Female:
<input type="radio" name="Gender" value="F" tabindex="9"></td>
<td width="50%">My age range is:
<select size="1" name="Age" tabindex="10">
<option value="1">&lt; 18</option>
<option value="2">18-25</option>
<option value="3">26-38</option>
<option value="4">39-50</option>
<option value="4">51-65</option>
<option value="6">> 65</option>
</select></td>
</tr>
</table>
<input type="submit" value="Submit Your Answers!" name="Submit" tabindex="11"><input
type="reset" value="Reset form" name="Rest" tabindex="12"></p>
<input type="hidden" name="Month" value="July">
<input type="hidden" name="Year" value="2003">
</form>
</body>
</html>
```

Disabling and Securing Form Fields

You might have a form that is in a constant state of flux in terms of how it is used and that it contains fields you might not always want to be accessible by the user. However, to save yourself time later when you need the fields again, you don't want to delete them from your form.

In cases such as this, you can disable the specified form fields. They will still appear on the form, but they won't be accessible to the user. The following code listing again highlights the FormTest.htm page; this time with the text area field disabled.

```
Enter a brief description of yourself here:</p>
<textarea rows="10" name="UserDescription" cols="40" tabindex="2" disabled>
</textarea></p>
```

Not much to say about this topic except that you can disable any form element by adding the `disabled` attribute (as shown in the preceding code snippet) to the specific form element tag.

The other issue that I need to discuss here, however, is how you keep a form element from being changed. As you develop your pages, there will be times when you will collect information from a user, and then redisplay that information in an update form at a later date. (In other words, you allow the user to come back later and modify information.) However, there might be instances when you don't want the user to change some of the information he or she initially entered.

Another example of this issue would be when you want the same default information to be entered on every form. In this case, you could create a regular form field and set the default (initial) value to whatever this information might be.

You can use the `readonly` attribute to accomplish both these goals. The following code listing highlights this attribute with the same text area form element that was used in the preceding code listing.

```
Enter a brief description of yourself here:</p>
<textarea rows="10" name="UserDescription" cols="40" tabindex="2" readonly>
</textarea></p>
```

Figure 8.12 highlights the `readonly` functionality. The text displayed in the text area field cannot be changed and will be submitted for every user who completes the form.

A Note on Form Processing

As I mentioned at the beginning of this chapter, knowing how to develop a form with the different form elements and formatting is important; however, knowing how to process the information entered into the form is critical.

There are many different ways to process a form, but all of them involve some type of scripting language that goes beyond the limits of straight HTML. Although many of these scripting languages aren't difficult to learn, and many HTML editors such as Microsoft FrontPage (which you'll work with later in this book) can automate this scripting, a discussion of the scripting languages goes beyond the scope of this chapter.

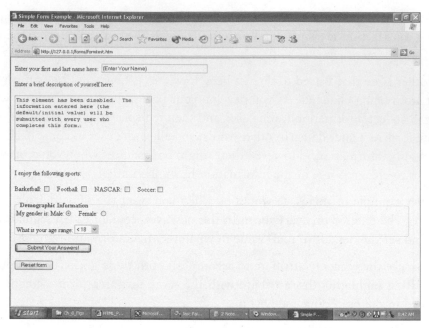

FIGURE 8.12 *Using the* readonly *attribute, you can set default information or prevent informa-tion contained within a form field from being changed.*

Still, as you've worked through this chapter, I'm sure you've noticed the action attribute of the forms, as shown here:

```
<form method="POST" action="FormProcessing.asp">
```

The value assigned to the action attribute is the page that will actually perform the form processing (in this case, FormProcessing.asp). Although I haven't discussed this page yet, you will return to the FormTest.htm page in Chapter 11, "Integrating Scripts and Other Advanced Functionality," where you will get an introduction to form processing via the use of Microsoft Active Server Pages. (This is what the .asp file extension is short for.) The important thing to note now is that form processing is possible without knowing much advanced programming. However—and this is an important caveat—form processing (including the use of Active Server Pages) requires special configuration on the actual Web server, for which different issues must be addressed.

The bottom line on form processing is that before you begin developing forms, make sure you know the type of Web server infrastructure that will host your Web site and what options are available to you for form processing.

TIP

Regardless of the type of form processing available on your Web server, there are countless sample processing scripts (written in a variety of languages) available for download from the Web. If you are coming to this book for information on HTML design and implementation, but you are not necessarily interested in form processing and scripting, you can look to such scripts to give you the functionality you need without having to learn a programming language.

NOTE

Working with forms is often inherently linked to working with databases because you will often want to store the information you gather from the form in a database for later manipulation. Again, this is an advanced subject, like form processing itself. However, you will see examples of how you can perform this database integration using an HTML editor in Chapter 11 and in the third and fourth projects of this book. These projects discuss in detail working with an HTML editor (FrontPage XP) and a database application (Microsoft SQL Server), respectively.

Summary

This chapter presented you with all the basic information you need to start developing your own forms. You learned to work with all the essential types of form elements, from text boxes to drop-down menus. You also learned how to set the specific attributes for each element. In addition, you were introduced to formatting your forms and making them more attractive and easier to use. Finally, you learned about form processing and what it involves, including the ability to integrate form data with databases. I will give you further instruction on both these topics in later chapters of this book.

Chapter 9

As I mentioned several times throughout the first chapters of this book, there are several HTML tags that are deprecated (in other words, no longer being developed) in version 4.0 and higher. Of particular note are those tags which involve general page layout and formatting—specifically, many of the tags I introduced in Chapters 2 and 4.

What does this deprecation mean? First, it does not mean you can no longer use the tags in question. Indeed, all of tags will still be read and function properly in today's browsers; however, it's a bit like driving a car that is no longer in production. Sure, the car still runs great and you can still get parts for it, but it might be more difficult to get the parts or deal with problems because the car is no longer in active production.

So it goes with many of these tags. They have been replaced by cascading style sheets (or CSS, for short). Why CSS? As I noted in Chapter 4, in an effort to bring more exact page layout control to HTML, different companies—especially Netscape Communications and Microsoft—decided to develop special proprietary tags for their browsers. Although many of these tags worked great and added some useful functionality, this was only the case if you used the appropriate browser. Clearly, this led to some serious design issues because Web developers had to code for two (or more) versions of their sites in order to best serve their content to all browser types.

CSS answers this (in theory) by trying to provide a common and advanced method of page element and page layout control. Moreover, it allows you to make global changes to your layout and formatting in one spot, as opposed to updating every HTML tag in your page. In short, there are many advantages. There are some disadvantages too, but it is clear that CSS is the future; thus I will explore it in detail in this chapter and Chapter 10, "Working with Cascading Style Sheets, Part 2."

NOTE

When I write that CSS answers these concerns "in theory," I mean that (as with all things Web) there is no common agreement on how CSS should be implemented. A universal formatting- and tag-definition list is highly desirable, of course, but it remains (like so many things in the IT arena) a kind of Web-based Tower of Babel, with different manufacturers developing different methods of communicating via their software.

 NOTE

As you will see, CSS is a complex topic. Not a difficult one, necessarily, but there are a lot of things to cover, as there is literally a new way of formatting your HTML in CSS for every old tag you learned about in previous chapters. That said, I've decided to present the material in two chapters to help clarify and "slow the pace" of the discussion, which should help you to get a better handle on the information being presented.

CSS Basics

You can think of CSS as a control template for your Web page because you define all the layout and formatting styles up front and then simply reference those definitions within your document.

There are basically two types of style sheets:

◆ **Internal Style Sheets.** These sheets are placed at the beginning of a single document (Web page). They are particularly useful if that single Web page has a lot of formatting in it, and if that formatting needs to differ from other pages in your site.

◆ **External Style Sheet.** If you have many pages within your Web site that will utilize common formatting, then external style sheets are the way to go. External style sheets are essentially independent documents that contain all the specific formatting decisions you want applied to multiple pages in your site. At the top of each page on your site, you simply reference this style sheet document, and the formatting commands contained therein are applied to the page.

NOTE

It is possible to have multiple style sheets referenced on a Web site. You might also have some pages with local style sheets all their own, as well as others that reference an external style sheet. Both types of pages can be contained within the same Web site.

Both types of style sheets work basically the same way. The difference is that one is referenced as a separate document and the other is contained within the Web page.

The best way to start working with style sheets is to, well, start working with them. Go ahead and do that now.

1. Within your Inetpub folder, create a new folder called Styles.

2. Open your text editor of choice, create a new page, and save it as StyleTest in your newly created Styles folder.

3. On the page, enter the following code as you see it here:

```
<html>
<head>
<title>Working with CSS</title>
<style>
h1          { font-family: Times New Roman; font-size: 24pt; text-decoration:
underline; font-weight: bold }
p           { font-family: Arial; font-size: 12pt; font-style: italic }
a:link      { color: #FF0000; font-style: italic; font-weight: bold }
</style>
</head>
<body>
<h1>Welcome to ABC Computers</h1>
<p>We offer the latest in computer technology, at prices you can afford. For a
current listing of all our products, click <a
href="http://www.somewhere.com">here.</a></p>
</body>
</html>
```

4. Save this page and load it in your Web browser. Your screen should look like Figure 9.1.

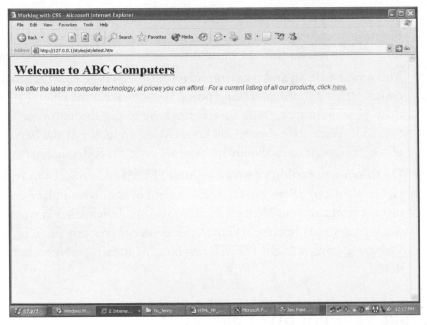

FIGURE 9.1 *By utilizing style sheets, you save yourself a tremendous amount of time in formatting your HTML.*

Style sheets are not difficult to learn; however, they do have their own unique syntax. Now I want to work through the preceding code listing to review exactly what is happening:

◆ The first thing you see is the use of the `<style>` tag. This and the corresponding closing `</style>` tag are placed within the `<head>` tags to begin the document.

◆ Next, the first style is defined—`h1` (for a first-level heading). Although I'll discuss the syntax for the style definitions a bit later, you can probably figure this out: Each attribute is listed (such as `font-family`), and then a value is assigned to it. A semicolon separates each attribute. Note that each style definition is placed between opening { and closing }.

◆ After all the styles are defined (in this case, `h1`, `p`, and `a:link`), the closing `</style>` tag is applied.

From this simple example, it's not hard to see how incredibly useful style sheets can be. Specifically, learning how to use them effectively can do the following:

◆ **Save you a tremendous amount of time.** Even though the previous example is relatively simple, imagine if you had multiple sections of text on that Web page. For each section, you would have to apply the formatting tags to each and every heading, paragraph, and hyperlink. With style sheets, you do this just once at the beginning of your document.

◆ **Make your editing and post-implementation change control much easier.** Related to the preceding point, if you make a mistake in your formatting without using style sheets, you have to dig through your HTML to find it. With style sheets, you know where to look—at the beginning of the document or in the linked external style sheet document.

◆ **Do things you couldn't do with regular HTML.** Compared to regular tags, style sheets allow you far more control over how you place and format elements on your Web pages. This reason alone makes it worth using style sheets because trying to get elements properly lined up on a Web page using straight HTML can be a maddening exercise in frustration.

Configuring External Style Sheets

As I mentioned at the beginning of the chapter, there are basically two types of style sheets—internal and external.

You've already seen an example of an internal style sheet in the first code listing in this chapter. Again, an internal style sheet is defined within the page itself; they are useful when you want to apply styles to a specific Web page.

However, often (indeed, the majority of times) you will want to give the pages on your site a uniform, clean look—that is, you will want the same style definitions to apply to more than one page on your site. In cases like this, it is best to use an external style sheet and save yourself lots of time. Create a style sheet with all the definitions and then simply link to it all the pages in which you want those styles to apply.

To demonstrate external style sheets, create one now.

1. Open your text editor, create a new blank document, and save it in your Styles folder as StylesDemo.css.

 CAUTION

Be sure to save your external style sheet documents with the .css extension!

2. In this new document, enter the following code just as you see it here:

```
h1          { font-family: Times New Roman; font-size: 24pt; text-decoration:
underline; font-weight: bold }
p           { font-family: Arial; font-size: 12pt; font-style: italic }
a:link      { color: #FF0000; font-style: italic; font-weight: bold }
```

 NOTE

If this code looks familiar, it's because you are taking the style information from the first code listing and saving it as its own document.

3. Save this StylesDemo.css page again in your Styles folder.

4. Open the StyleTest.htm page once again.

5. Delete all the style information you previously entered on that page, including the opening and closing ⟨style⟩ tags.

6. After the closing ⟨/title⟩ tag in the StyleTest.htm document, enter the following code as it appears here:

```
<LINK REL=stylesheet TYPE="text/css" HREF="StylesDemo.css">
```

7. Save the StyleTest.htm page once again, and then load it in your Web browser. Your screen should appear exactly as it did in Figure 9.1.

To confirm, your StylesTest.htm code should now look like the following code listing:

```
<html>
<head>
<title>Working with CSS</title>
<LINK REL=stylesheet TYPE="text/css" HREF="StylesDemo.css">
</head>
<body>
<h1>Welcome to ABC Computers</h1>
<p>We offer the latest in computer technology, at prices you can afford. For a current
listing of all our products, click <a href="somewhere.com">here.</a></p>
</body>
</html>
```

CAUTION

When you link to your style sheet, be sure to provide the correct file path to the desired style sheet. In the code snippet in Step 6, the HREF value was set to the name of the sheet (StylesDemo.css) because that document is saved in the same directory as the StylesTest.htm page. If this were not the case, you would have to provide the complete file path to the style sheet.

NOTE

If you link to an external style sheet and then apply an internal style, the internal style will overwrite the definitions in the external style sheet.

Working with Local Styles

In addition to internal and external styles, there is a third way of applying styles—locally. When you apply styles locally, you literally apply them within your document, prior to the section of text you want to have that style.

The following code listing illustrates the use of a local style.

```
<html>
<head>
<title>Working with CSS</title>
</head>
<body>
<h1>Welcome to ABC Computers</h1>
<p style="font-family: Arial; font-size: 12pt; font-style: italic">We offer the latest in
computer technology, at prices you can afford. For a current listing of all our products,
click <a href="somewhere.com">here.</a></p>
</body>
</html>
```

Figure 9.2 illustrates how this page would appear when loaded in a browser.

Notice the differences between Figures 9.1 and 9.2. The only stylistic change that has been applied outside of regular HTML formatting is to the paragraph text itself, which has a 12-point Arial font and is italicized. The special hyperlink formatting, as well as the additional formatting that was applied to the heading in

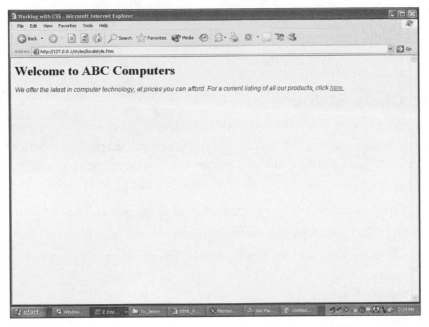

FIGURE 9.2 *Local styles only affect the specific section of text to which you have applied them.*

Figure 9.1, is not applied here. Again, local styles can be useful for on-the-spot changes, but you should use them judiciously. Too much individual local style application will defeat the global benefits of internal and external style sheets.

 NOTE

As I mentioned earlier, internal style sheets override external ones; however, local style applications trump both internal and external ones.

Defining and Creating Classes and Custom Tags

This chapter is really divided into two parts. The first part of the chapter was a general introduction to style sheets, including the differences between internal, external, and local applications. The second part of this chapter will deal with the level of customization you can achieve with these different types of applications, with particular emphasis on how to reference the styles within your document and how to divide your document into different sections to allow for more specific control over how your styles are defined.

Defining Class Styles

In your Web pages, you will need to differentiate sections with specific style formatting. Although you could use local styles (as described earlier), a better way to do this is to think of those different sections of your document as classes, and in turn create specific styles to suit those classes. Go ahead and try that out now.

1. Open your text editor and create a new page called ClassTest.htm.

2. Save this page within your Styles folder.

3. On the ClassTest.htm page, enter the following code as you see it here:

```
<html>
<head>
<title>Defining Style Classes</title>
<style>
h1          { font-family: Times New Roman; font-size: 24pt; font-weight: bold }
p           { font-family: Arial; font-size: 12pt; font-style: italic }
a:link      { color: #FF0000; font-style: italic; font-weight: bold }

h1.proinfo  {font-family: Arial; font-size: 48pt; font-style: bold }
</style>
</head>

<h1 class=proinfo>Product Catalog </h1>
<hr>
The above H1 heading uses the proinfo class.  Proinfo is a random name.
<hr>
<h1>Product Catalog</h1>
<hr>
The above H1 heading uses the non-class style for H1.  Note the different font
and font size.
<hr>
</body>
</html>
```

4. Save this page and load it in your Web browser. Your screen should look like Figure 9.3.

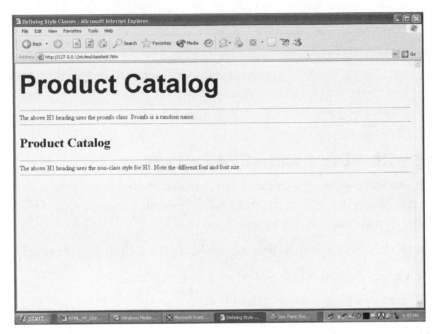

FIGURE 9.3 *Using class definitions can help you apply different formatting to specific sections of your text.*

Understanding Block-Level and Inline Elements

It is important to understand the difference between block-level and inline elements. Put simply, block-level elements begin a new line. The following are all examples of block-level elements:

◆ <p>

◆ <H2>

◆ <Table>

Block-level elements can contain other block-level elements as well as inline elements. Again, think of block-level elements as those which begin a new line in a document. For example, the <p> tag begins a new line in many an HTML document; however, you would not begin a new tag with the <b> tag. Indeed, a tag such as <b> is considered an inline element, which is used to format or enhance text.

Two other tags go hand-in-hand with block-level and inline elements:

◆ `<DIV>`. This tag is used with block-level elements. As you will see, `<DIV>` tags can be used to great effect to make your document appear to have different sections based on unique formatting.

◆ `<SPAN>`. This tag is used with inline elements. As with `<DIV>` tags, you can use `<SPAN>` tags to help provide individual formatting for letters, words, and so on. (Like the inline elements they support, `<SPAN>` tags will not begin a new section of your document.)

Working with <DIV> and <SPAN> tags

When you start working with these tags, you can really see the great functionality of style sheets in terms of the tremendous formatting options (and the ease of applying that formatting to your documents).

I want to start working with these tags now, via the following code example:

1. Open your text editor and create a new page called CustomTags.htm.

2. Save this page in your Styles folder.

3. On the CustomTags.htm page, enter the following code:

```
<html>
<head>
<title>Working with DIV and SPAN Tags</title>
</head>
<style>
DIV.Title {background: green; font-family: Times New Roman; font-size: 24pt;
font-weight: bold}
DIV.Preamble {background: yellow; font-family: Ariel; font-size: 12pt;}
SPAN.caps {font-size: 300%}
</style>
<body>
<DIV Class="Title">
The Constitution of the United States of America
</DIV>
<hr>
<DIV Class="Preamble">
<SPAN Class="Caps">W</SPAN>e the people of the United States, in order to form a
more perfect union, establish justice, insure domestic tranquility, provide for
```

the common defense, promote the general welfare, and secure the blessings of
liberty to ourselves and our posterity, do ordain and establish this Constitution
for the United States of America.
</DIV>
</body>
</html>

4. Save this page and load it into your Web browser. Your screen will
appear similar to Figure 9.4.

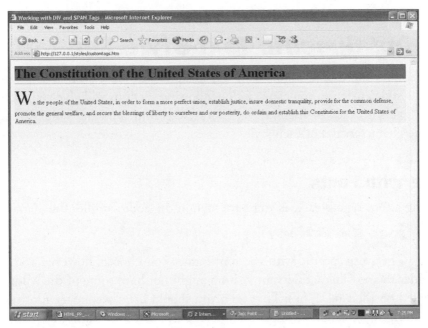

FIGURE 9.4 ⟨DIV⟩ and ⟨SPAN⟩ tags can bring a tremendous amount of formatting power to both
sections of your text, as well as to individual words or characters.

The definitions of the ⟨DIV⟩ and ⟨SPAN⟩ tags are very similar to the class definitions you learned about earlier in this chapter; as a result, they are similar in syntax to everything you work with in regard to style sheets. Specifically, the following rules apply:

◆ To name a specific ⟨DIV⟩ or ⟨SPAN⟩ tag, you first indicate the type of tag,
then a period, and then the name of the tag. As you can see in the preceding code listing, example names for a ⟨DIV⟩ or ⟨SPAN⟩ tag include
DIV.Preamble and SPAN.caps.

◆ After you name the tag in this manner, you apply the characteristics (between the { and } brackets), just as you learned to do with other aspects of style sheets.

◆ After you have defined the tags and set their characteristics, you reference them within your document just as you would any style. Note in the preceding code that for every opening `<DIV>` or `<SPAN>` tag, there is a corresponding closing `</DIV>` or `</SPAN>` tag to indicate when the specific formatting no longer applies.

Applying Specific Text-Style Formatting

Throughout the coding examples in this chapter, you have seen examples of the various style attributes you can set. The following sections will give you more specific details on each of these attributes (such as font type and bolding) and the unique characteristics of each style.

Working with Fonts

Setting a font type is easy, as you have seen in the code samples thus far.

```
{ font-family: "Times New Roman" }
```

You can get very specific with the font names you choose; however, you should consider the possibility that your visitors might not have some of the wilder fonts installed on their machines. That said, you should list a secondary font (perhaps something more common or generic) in case the first font cannot be displayed.

You can also set the font size.

```
{ font-family: "Times New Roman"; font-size: 24pt }
```

Note the following additional options with setting the font size:

◆ You can set an absolute font size by entering one of the following values: xx-small, x-small, small, medium, large, x-large, or xx-large.

◆ You can enter a relative font size by entering the value larger or smaller.

◆ You can enter an exact font size by setting a point value (such as 24pt) as I did in the example.

◆ You can enter a percentage value, which is relative to the parent size of the font (for example, 200%).

Setting Italics

To add italics as part of your style definition, use the following syntax:

```
{ font-family: "Times New Roman"; font-style: italic }
```

In this example, the font would be set to Times New Roman and it would be italicized.

Bolding Text

If you choose to bold your text with style sheets, there are some interesting additional formatting features you can utilize compared to traditional HTML. Consider the following code example:

```
{ font-family: "Times New Roman"; font-size: 12pt; font-weight: 800 }
```

Like the different options available for the font size, you have similar options for bolding text.

◆ You can use bold as the assigned value (for example, `font-weight: bold`) to traditionally bold the text.

◆ You can assign a value of `bolder` or `lighter`, which is relative to the current weight of the bolding.

◆ You can assign a number (as I've done in the example) between 100 and 900, where 700 is considered bold.

Adjusting Line Height

Line height is simply the amount of space between each line in a paragraph. You have three options for setting the `line-height` style attribute:

◆ Assign a number *n* that will be multiplied by the font size, which will in turn produce the desired line height.

◆ Enter a number *n* that will be a percentage of the font size.

◆ Enter the exact font size.

Consider the following examples:

```
{ font-family: "Times New Roman"; font-size: 12pt; font-weight: 800; line-height: 20pt }
{ font-family: "Times New Roman"; font-size: 12pt; font-weight: 800; line-height: 50% }
{ font-family: "Times New Roman"; font-size: 12pt; font-weight: 800; line-height: 5 }
```

Setting Text Color and Text Background

You can set text color in one of four ways:

- ◆ Assign a specific color name (such as red, green, or blue).
- ◆ Assign a hexadecimal equivalent of a color (for example, #FFFFFF).
- ◆ Assign the text color in the form rgb (x, y, z), where *x*, *y*, and *z* are integers between 0 and 255 that correlate to the amount of hue applied for each of the three values.
- ◆ Assign the text color in the form rgb (x%, y%, z%), where *x*, *y*, and *z* are the percentage values of red, green, and blue in the selected color.

Following are examples of how to apply text color:

```
{ font-family: "Times New Roman"; font-size: 12pt; font-weight: 800; font-color: red }
{ font-family: "Times New Roman"; font-size: 12pt; font-weight: 800; font-color: #ff00ff }
{ font-family: "Times New Roman"; font-size: 12pt; font-weight: 800; font-color: rgb (150,
78, 229) }
{ font-family: "Times New Roman"; font-size: 12pt; font-weight: 800; font-color: rgb(25%,
78%, 10%) }
```

You can use the background attribute to set the text background using the following methods:

```
{ font-family: "Times New Roman"; font-size: 12pt; font-weight: 800; background: yellow }
```

You can use a background image as your background, and you can specify whether your background should scroll with the rest of your document canvas. I will discuss these features in more detail in Chapter 10, and I will highlight them (along with other CSS features) in the project chapters in Part II.

Aligning Text

This basic attribute is easy to set. As you've seen in other chapters, there are four essential values you can assign—left, right, center, and justify. The syntax for this style attribute is

```
{ text-align: center; font-family: "Times New Roman"; font-size: 12pt; font-weight: 800 }
```

Underlining Text

There are three basic values you can assign in relation to underlining text.

- ◆ You can underline the text by assigning a value of underline.
- ◆ You can "overline" the text (that is, place a line above the text) by assigning a value of overline.
- ◆ You can strike through the text by assigning a value of line-through.

The following is an example of how to apply underlining as part of your style. Note the style name for this is text-decoration (which in this has a value set to underline, which produces the underline effect).

{ font-family: "Times New Roman"; font-size: 12pt; font-weight: 800; text-decoration: underline }

Changing the Text Case

One of the neater style attributes is the ability to globally assign a text case. There are three basic values you can assign to this style.

- ◆ Capitalize. This value puts the first letter of each word in uppercase.
- ◆ Uppercase. This value changes all the letters to uppercase.
- ◆ Lowercase. This value changes all the letters to lowercase.

Following is an example of how to apply this style attribute. Note the style name for this is text-transform.

{ font-family: "Times New Roman"; font-size: 12pt; font-weight: 800; text-transform: lowercase }

 NOTE

You can set other style attributes, including having your text blink, setting white space, and controlling spacing.

Summary

This chapter provided you with a general introduction to cascading style sheets, including a general definition of them and the great benefits to using them. You learned how to apply style sheets internally, externally, and locally. You also learned how to define custom tags and classes to gain more specific control over the formatting of your Web pages (and, via external style sheets, all the pages within your Web site). Finally, you were presented with several of the major style attributes you can assign, as well as the different values you can give them.

The next chapter will continue to explore style sheets, and you will learn how to work with the page layout attributes. The skills you learn in Chapter 10, combined with what you learned here, should give you all the tools you need to begin working with style sheets in your own projects. Again, you'll see style sheets in action in the projects of Part II, so you can get a real-world sense of how you can best utilize them.

Chapter 10

The last chapter provided you with an introduction to cascading style sheets and some of the general formatting options that are available with them. You also were introduced to the formatting possibilities with CSS in terms of the <DIV> and <SPAN> tags, which allow you far greater control over the look of your Web documents than regular HTML does.

This chapter will expand what you learned in Chapter 9 by taking a look at specific page layout options you can use with style sheets. If the last chapter gave you the pieces of the puzzle, then this chapter will allow you to start putting them together. More specifically, this chapter will show you how to use absolute positioning for elements on your Web page. That feature is really only available (with this level of control) via the use of style sheets.

Working with Absolute and Relative Positioning

Imagine you have an image you want to position in the upper-left corner of your Web page. You could use regular HTML to position the element close to where you want it by using the align attribute and getting creative with some of the basic tags. However, "close to where you want it" is often not good enough. Why can't you position the element in question exactly where you want it? This is when using style sheets for absolute positioning can be a very powerful tool to help you perfectly align your elements.

Consider the following code as an example of how you can do this:

```
<html>
<head>
<title>Working with Cascading Style Sheets</title>
</head>
<style>
IMG {position:absolute; left:50; top: 10}
</style>
```

```
<body>
<hr>
<align=center>Absolute Positioning of Elements</align>
<hr>
<IMG SRC="ComputerImage.gif">
</body>
</html>
```

Figure 10.1 illustrates how this will appear on your screen.

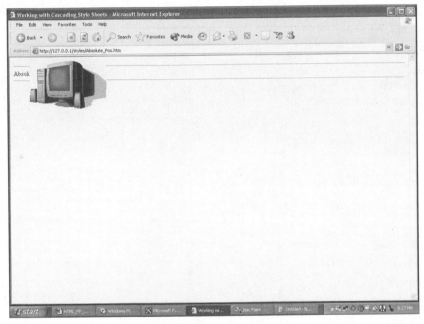

FIGURE 10.1 *Using absolute positioning, you can place an element at a specific location on your page. Note how it overlaps the other elements on your page.*

Note the following attributes of absolute positioning:

◆ You can apply four types of positioning—top, right, bottom, or left. Note that you can use more than one of these values (as illustrated in the preceding code sample) to define an exact position on the page.

◆ After each position attribute, you apply either an exact value (as illustrated in the preceding code sample) or a percentage of the parent element.

◆ You use a semicolon to separate each of the values.

NOTE

A *parent element* contains the element in question. For example, the `<body>` tag is the parent element of a `<p>` tag. Keep this in mind as you work with absolute positioning. If you assign a value that is a percentage of the parent element, it will affect the placement of the element relative to the parent element.

Relative positioning, by contrast, allows you to place an element without affecting the positions of the other elements on your page. Look at the following code listing to see an example of relative positioning:

```
<html>
<head>
<title>Working with Cascading Style Sheets</title>
</head>
<style>
IMG {position:relative; left:50; top: 10}
</style>
<body>
<hr>
<align=center>Relative Positioning of Elements</align>
<hr>
<IMG SRC="ComputerImage.gif">
</body>
</html>
```

Figure 10.2 illustrates relative positioning. Note the difference between it and Figure 10.1.

NOTE

Think of relative positioning as a way to keep the natural flow of your Web page intact with regard to each specific element. Put simply, relative positioning moves documents relative to themselves—other elements are not affected. In absolute positioning, you override this flow and force exact placement of an element at a precise location on the page, which can definitely affect the other elements on the page, depending on the location you specify. For example, if you use absolute positioning to place an element where another element already exists, the element that you placed will override the other one.

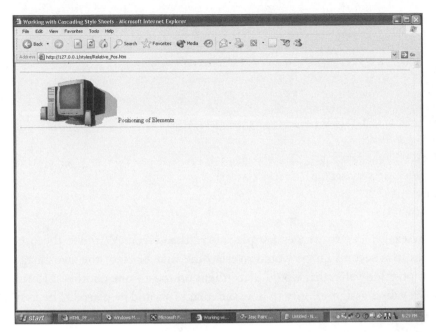

FIGURE 10.2 *Relative positioning moves elements relative to their natural positions on the Web page.*

Relative positioning is defined in the same manner as absolute positioning. (That is, the attributes are set in the same manner.) You can see this by comparing the two preceding code listings.

Preventing Image Overlap

As I mentioned in the discussion of absolute positioning, you can run into situations where your images overlap. (This can even occur in relative positioning, depending on how you place the elements.) Although in some cases you might want this to happen (such as for particular design effects), you can prevent it by using the z-index attribute.

```
<html>
<head>
<title>Working with Cascading Style Sheets</title>
</head>
```

```
<style>
IMG {position:absolute; left:50; top: 10}
IMG {position:absolute; left:50; top:10}
</style>
<body>
<hr>
<align=center>Relative Positioning of Elements</align>
<hr>
<IMG SRC="ComputerImage.gif" STYLE="z-index: 1">
<IMG SRC="ComputerImage2.gif" STYLE="z-index: 2">
</body>
</html>
```

In this example, two images are placed on the screen. Without the use of the z-index, the second image would overlap the first because the two images have a `left` position value that would place them on top of one another. However, the `z-index` values assign priority to how the images should be placed. The first image has a `z-index` value of 1, so it is positioned lower on the page and will thus appear behind the first image.

TIP

You can use positive or negative values for the z-index. For example, assigning one image a value of 1 and a second image a value of –1 would allow the image with the value of 1 to appear first. (The image with a value of –1 would appear behind the other image.)

Hiding and Displaying Elements

As you start to develop your Web pages with style sheets, you will quickly realize that style sheets can be wonderful strategy tools for how your content is presented. You can use the great functionality and level of layout control that is possible with style sheets to present your content based on certain parameters. Such parameters might include the following situations:

◆ You have an online store and you want to show specific product information only to those who have purchased from you in the past.

◆ You want to present information to users in a stepped order, so that specific information is displayed only after the user follows certain steps.

◆ Depending on the type of Web browser or other system specifications, you want to present information on your page in a different layout.

◆ You are integrating advanced scripting applications into your Web pages, and you want to use the power of style sheets to hide and display elements to enhance the presentation of your content.

 NOTE

Working with cascading style sheets in conjunction with a scripting language can bring unprecedented levels of control and design options to your Web pages. For more information on this integration, see *JavaScript Professional Projects* (Premier Press, 2003).

Hiding an element is quite easy. Take a look at the following code snippet:

```
<style>
IMG {display:none}
</style>
```

Displaying an element is equally easy. There are three distinct ways to display elements on your Web page:

```
<style>
IMG {display: block}
IMG {display: inline}
IMG {display: list-item}
</style>
```

Each of these methods has some interesting characteristics:

◆ If you use the block value, the element will be displayed as a block-level element and will start a new paragraph.

◆ If you use the inline value, the element will be displayed as an inline element. (In other words, it will not subsequently start a new paragraph.)

◆ Another neat feature is that if you assign the list-item value, the elements will be displayed just as if you had used the <li> tag that I discussed previously.

Specifying the Foreground Color and Backgrounds

Another general layout style that is easy to change is the foreground color. There are four ways to do this.

- ◆ You can assign an exact color name.
- ◆ You can provide the hexadecimal equivalent of the color in question.
- ◆ You can specify the amount of red, green, and blue that should be in the color. (You specify these amounts in numeric form, from 0 to 255 for each color.)
- ◆ You can specify a percentage of red, green, and blue that should be in the color.

In the following code, you can see how you could use each of these methods in a style sheet definition:

```
<style>
P:intro {color: red}
P:intro {color: #ff0000}
P:intro {color: rgb(125, 57, 229)}
P:intro {color: rgb(40%, 20%, 60%)}
</style>
```

Note that in each of the four examples, the foreground color change applies to the P/intro element so that wherever that style is called within the document, the foreground color will change to what was specified.

Changing the background is a bit different. The important thing to remember is that you are not changing the background of the entire Web page; rather, you are changing the background of a specific element. Once again, it should be easy to see that the level of control that style sheets give you is unprecedented when compared to traditional HTML tags.

You can set the background color for a specific element by using one of the following two methods.

- ◆ Set the background to a specific color or its hexadecimal equivalent.
- ◆ Use a background image. (Note that you can also specify whether you want the image to be tiled horizontally or vertically.)

TIP

You can also set the position of the background image using the x and y values. You can assign `top`, `center`, and `bottom` for the x value and `left`, `center`, and `right` for y. I will highlight this concept in the complete style sheet layout code example in the last section of this chapter.

Finally, you can determine whether the background should scroll with the canvas of the page or stay fixed. I will demonstrate this feature in the final code example in this chapter.

Specifying Text Wrap Options

There are two specific text wrap options available—`left` and `right`. Text wrapping is useful when, for example, you want the text to wrap around images placed on your page. As you will see in the code example at the end of this chapter, text wrapping is especially critical when you are working with images; it allows you to keep a natural, even appearance for your page layout.

You specify text wrapping in your images via the `float` attribute:

```
IMG {float: right}
```

Again, I'll demonstrate this attribute in the code example at the end of this chapter.

A Complete Style Sheet
Layout Example

Between Chapters 9 and 10, you've been presented with quite a bit of information about style sheets, in terms of general attributes (Chapter 9) and specific layout options (this chapter). This section will highlight many of the layout issues you have read about in this chapter.

NOTE

You will see style sheets used in more specific detail in the project chapters of Part II.

Follow along with this example by performing the following steps:

1. Open your text editor of choice.

2. Create a new page called StyleExample.htm and save it in the Styles folder you created in Chapter 9.

3. On the StyleExample.htm page, enter the following code as you see it here:

```
<html>
<head>
<title>Working with Style Sheets</title>
<LINK REL=stylesheet TYPE="text/css" HREF="StyleEx_Sheet.css">
</head>
<body>
<h1><img border="0" src="j0285750.gif" width="192" height="118"></h1>
<h1>Welcome to ABC Computers</h1>
<p>We offer the latest in computer technology, at prices you can afford.
For a current listing of all our products, click <a
href="somewhere.com">here.</a></p>
<hr>
<p>Remember, with ABC you get:</p>
<ul>
<li>Quality Products
<li>Unbeatable Prices
<li>Top-Notch Service
</ul>
<hr>
<h1>Why would you go anywhere else?!?
</body>
</html>
```

4. Save this page once again in your Styles folder.

5. Now it's time to create the actual style sheet upon which the references in the page you just created will call. For this example, you'll create an external style sheet. (Note the link in the preceding code listing to StyleEx_Sheet.css.) Create a new page in your text editor and save it as StyleEx_Sheet.css.

6. On the StyleEx_Sheet.css page, enter the following code as listed here:

```
h1 { font-family: Times New Roman; font-size: 24pt; text-decoration:underline;
font-weight: bold; padding: 20; margin: 20 }
p  { font-family: Arial; font-size: 12pt; font-style: italic; color: green }
```

```
a:link { color: #FF0000; font-style: italic; font-weight: bold }
IMG {position: absolute; left: 50; top: 80; border: thick groove red; float:
left}
BODY {background: yellow}
UL {list-style: lower-roman}
```

7. Save this page, and then load the StyleExample.htm page in your Web browser. Your screen should look like Figure 10.3.

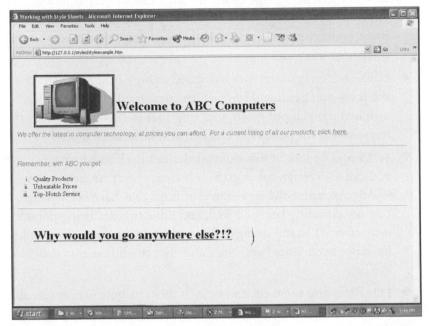

FIGURE 10.3 *Although it's not the most eloquent or well-designed Web page, it nevertheless illustrates several issues involved in layout with style sheets.*

I want to walk through both of these code listings to show you how style sheets are being applied, as well as their specific attributes and the values that have been assigned to them.

◆ First, the external style sheet (StyleEx_Sheet.css) is called from within the StyleExample.htm page. Remember that you can also apply style sheets locally or reference them internally.

◆ Next, the page is constructed with what would normally be regular (boring?) HTML tags. However, because several of these tags have been given special attributes in the style sheet, you can add a tremendous amount of additional formatting, as evidenced in Figure 10.3.

◆ The StyleExample.htm page is rather straightforward; however, the actual style sheet (StyleEx_Sheet.css) is where the action is. Several page elements are defined on this page.

   ◆ `H1`. The level-one heading is given several attributes. A specific font and font size are defined, underlining is applied, the font type is bolded, and padding is set, as well as a margin. The padding attribute is just extra space around an element. The number assigned to the attribute is a percentage of the parent element, just as in many other attributes. The margin attribute is simply the amount of transparent space between one element and the next (expressed as a percentage of the parent element).

   ◆ `P`. The paragraph element is assigned many of the same attributes as the level-one heading. However, the paragraph element also is assigned the color of green, meaning that in this case the text that resides with the paragraph element will be colored green.

   ◆ `a: Link`. The link in this element defines itself as being active. (Note you can also assign values to `a: visited`, `a: active`, and `a: hover`, which determine the appearance of links that have been visited, links that are currently being clicked, and links that are being pointed to, respectively.) In this example, the style is being defined for links that have not been visited yet. Note also that the link text is italicized and bolded.

   ◆ `IMG`. Referring to image, the style of this attribute is given an absolute position of 50, 80. The `border` attribute is just that—the style of border you want to apply around the image. (Options include `none`, `dotted`, `dashed`, `solid`, `double`, `ridge`, `groove`, `outset`, and `inset`.) Border width options include `thin`, `medium`, or `thick` (or an absolute value, such as `10px`). Finally, the `float` attribute has been given the value of `left`, which means that the text will wrap around the element (as you can see in Figure 10.3). You can set the `float` attribute to either `left` or `right`.

   ◆ `BODY`. In the `BODY` element in this example, you can see that the `background` attribute is set to `yellow`. Note that you can also assign the attribute of `fixed` or `scroll` (for example, `{background: yellow fixed}`), which determines whether the background should scroll with the canvas or stay fixed in one spot.

◆ **UL.** Finally, the `<UL>` tag is assigned a value of `lower-roman`. You can apply several different styles of formatting to your lists, including `circle`, `square`, `decimal`, `lower-alpha`, `upper-alpha`, `lower-roman`, and `upper-roman`. You can also assign a URL for an image to be used as your list marker, as shown in Figure 10.4.

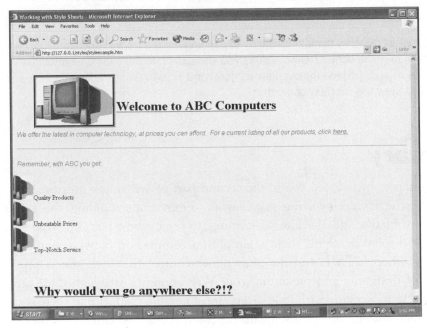

FIGURE 10.4 *An example of using images in the* UL *style definition.*

Think of this example as just a small sampling of the types of formatting you can apply. Clearly, with all the formatting options available to you with style sheets, your actual style sheet can be quite complex, regardless of whether it's internal or external. Remember to take advantage of what style sheets have to offer. Not only do they present you with more options; they also put all of your formatting in one place. This is critical because if you want to change how your level-one headings are formatted, for example, you simply change the formatting in your style sheet to apply the change globally to all Web pages that utilize that style sheet. When you think of even a medium-sized Web site, the tremendous functionality and timesaving features of using style sheets immediately become obvious. So take advantage of what style sheets have to offer!

TIP

You might find that when you are defining the attributes of a specific element, you make the element too small to contain all of the information. If this is the case, you will be presented with overflow content, and you will need to determine where that overflow content will go. To account for this, apply the overflow attribute. For example

```
{overflow: visible}
```

This makes overflow content visible by expanding the element in question so it can contain all of the content. Other values you can assign to the overflow attribute include hidden (to hide the overflow content) and scroll (which adds scroll bars so you can view the overflow content).

Summary

This chapter introduced you to the second part of working with cascading style sheets—the issues involving page layout. From understanding the difference between relative and absolute positioning, to seeing how you can wrap text and hide or display elements, there is simply no comparison between working with old-fashioned HTML and the tremendous control that style sheets provide in terms of designing and presenting your Web content. Although there are some drawbacks to working with style sheets (most notably the fact that there is still not a 100-percent agreed-upon standard for interpreting and displaying them across different browser types), it is still worth using them because they remove many of the HTML page-layout limitations. (From its beginning, HTML was not intended to allow for complex or specific placement of elements on a canvas.) Finally, as you gain more experience with style sheets and what they offer, you might want to learn more about integrating them with a scripting language (specifically JavaScript) to allow for new levels of design and content presentation.

TIP

If you are still unclear about some attributes of working with style sheets, don't be concerned. As with all Web design (and graphic design, for that matter), the more you work with style sheets, the more you will recognize the peculiarities of each style attribute, as well as how to best apply them. Moreover, you will see style sheets applied in a more real-world sense in the project chapters of Part II.

Chapter 11

Integrating Scripts and Other Advanced Functionality

You can do quite a bit of neat stuff with straight HTML to design and present your content. However, if you really want your pages to be dynamic (in the sense that you can gather, manipulate, store, and return information collected from visitors), you'll probably want to integrate some type of scripting language into your HTML.

This chapter will look at two such technologies, ASP (*Active Server Pages*) and JavaScript, both of which you can integrate easily with your HTML to produce some useful additional functionality. Specifically, this chapter will show you how to add several benefits that come with script integration.

◆ You'll learn how to actually process form data with ASP (specifically, through the use of Visual Basic Script, better known as VBScript) so when a user completes the form and clicks on the Submit button, you can grab that data and further manipulate it in your Web site.

◆ Similar to the preceding function, you'll learn how to pull data from a querystring so you can manipulate it within another Web page, just as if you had passed the information via a form.

◆ You'll learn how to call a JavaScript function that goes through each field in a form to make sure at least some type of information has been entered before the user submits it. (In other words, you'll learn how to call a form validation script to help ensure you are collecting accurate information.)

Although this chapter will only provide a cursory introduction to the power of ASP and JavaScript, when you finish reading it you should have a good understanding of how to integrate the functionality presented with your own HTML forms.

 NOTE

As I mentioned, this chapter is only the tip of the iceberg as far as integrating scripting with your HTML. For a far more detailed discussion of these scripting languages, check out *JavaScript Professional Projects* (Premier Press, 2003) and *ASP Programming for the Absolute Beginner* (Premier Press, 2002).

Gathering and Manipulating Form Content with VBScript

You learned how to work with HTML forms in Chapter 8. However, you might recall from that chapter that a critical piece of the form equation was missing. How do you process or work with the information you collect with forms?

Unfortunately, there is no very basic way to do this with plain HTML. However, the good news is that by understanding just a little scripting, you can really make your forms (and thus your Web pages) come alive by not only accepting form input, but actually doing something with it! This section will show you how to do just that using VBScript and ASP.

You can follow along with this and other sample scripts in the chapter, but first you need to perform the following steps:

1. Within the Inetpub folder on your computer, create a new folder and call it Scripting.

2. In your text editor, create a new page called ProductForm.htm and save it in your newly created Scripting folder.

CONFIGURING YOUR COMPUTER FOR "ADVANCED HTML"

As you've seen so far in this book, you can work with general HTML with very little "configuration" to your computer; that is, you can create Web pages in a simple text editor, save them to a regular folder, and pull them up for display in a Web browser. Moreover, by just creating relationships between pages, you can also see additional HTML functionality in action (hyperlinks, for example) with little to no extra configuration of your machine.

However, working with scripts is going to require a little more work. Specifically,

◆ ASP is short for active server pages, which means that the great functionality performed by this technology is performed primarily on the server. That being true, you need a server that can be "active" enough to work with this technology. The Microsoft Internet Information Server (IIS) is one such example (there are others, too—for example, Apache). If you are using Microsoft Windows XP Professional or Windows 2000 Professional, you can install IIS on your own computer (if it's not already installed); for more information, see http://support.microsoft.com/default.aspx?scid=kb;en-us;262632

◆ If you do choose to work with IIS (and for the sake of simplicity, I have assumed in many cases within this book that you are), you should be able to work with ASP (at least the functionality described in this chapter) with little to no configuration; moreover, your default Web site address (that is, the address of your root Web directory) will be the "http://127.0.0.1" that you have seen in many screen shots throughout this book. Also, the root directory of your Web server will be located at c:/Inetpub/wwwroot (within the wwwroot folder will be the folders that relate to your actual Web sites, just as you have been creating them at the start of many chapters in this book).

◆ JavaScript, on the other hand, is not (generally speaking) a server-based technology but a client-based technology: that is, it runs within the user's own Web browser on his computer. That said, you don't need to do any additional configuration to work with JavaScript (other than ensuring you have a Web browser capable of working with it). Note, however, that JavaScript can behave differently depending on the type of Web browser you are using, so again, testing of your pages that utilize JavaScript is a real requirement. For a far more extended discussion of JavaScript, see the other books that are referenced throughout this chapter.

◆ You should be aware that a full discussion of the configuration (and proper security) of IIS is well beyond the scope of this book. These are important topics and should not be ignored, so if you really start to work with advanced Web development like the topics that are introduced in this chapter, you should strongly consider learning more about server security and configuration.

◆ Finally, if you are using an HTML editing application (Microsoft FrontPage, for example), such a program may want to install "server extensions" in order to provide additional functionality. Such extensions work in conjunction with the Web server to ease the development time (and give you access to advanced design features that you wouldn't otherwise have access to). These extensions are discussed in more detail in both Chapter 12 and the third project of this book.

Ideally, you are in an environment where you are developing applications and there is someone else—such as your network administrator—who is responsible (and who has expertise in) configuring and maintaining Web servers. While this might seem like a simple answer that avoids an extended discussion of "how to configure a Web server," the bottom line is that configuring and maintaining a Web server is **serious** business. As this book was being written, the "blaster" worm made its joyous way through many an unprotected network. While this is perhaps an extreme example (and in this case, an attack that targeted regular workstations as much if not more than network servers), in today's networked world, you have to protect vulnerable machines. So, in a nutshell, if you have any questions about Web server administration ask an expert or, better yet, leave the administration and configuration issues to said expert.

Creating the HTML Form

The first thing you need to do is create the actual form that will be completed on the ProductForm.htm page you just created. Do that now by entering the following code exactly as you see it here in your ProductForm.htm page.

```
<html>
<head>
<title>ABC Company: Product Catalog Request</title>
</head>
<body>
<p align="center"><font size="7"><b>ABC Online Catalog</b></font></p>
<hr>
<p align="center"><font size="4">Product Information Request Form</font></p>
<form method="POST" action="FormProcess.asp">
Which product catalog are you interested in receiving:
  <select size="1" name="Catalog" tabindex="1">
  <option>Widgets</option>
  <option>Fidgets</option>
  <option>Gadgets</option>
  </select></p>
<table>
   <tr>
     <td width="24%">Your name:</td>
     <td width="76%"><input type="text" name="Name" size="20" tabindex="2"></td>
   </tr>
   <tr>
     <td width="24%">Your street address:</td>
     <td width="76%"><input type="text" name="Street" size="20" tabindex="3"></td>
   </tr>
   <tr>
     <td width="24%">Your City:</td>
     <td width="76%"><input type="text" name="City" size="20" tabindex="4"></td>
   </tr>
   <tr>
     <td width="24%">Your State</td>
     <td width="76%"><input type="text" name="State" size="20" tabindex="5"></td>
   </tr>
   <tr>
     <td width="24%">Your Zip:</td>
     <td width="76%"><input type="text" name="Zip" size="20" tabindex="6"></td>
   </tr>
```

```
        <tr>
          <td width="100%" colspan="2">Additional Comments:<p>
          <textarea rows="5" name="Comments" cols="30" tabindex="8"></textarea></td>
        </tr>
        <tr>
          <td width="100%" colspan="2">
          <p align="center">
          <input type="submit" value="Submit Your Request" name="Submit"></td>
        </tr>
      </table>
</form>
</body>
</html>
```

Save your ProductForm.htm page with the code you just entered. When you load this page into a Web browser, it should look like Figure 11.1.

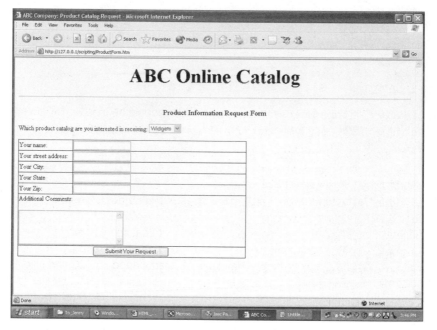

FIGURE 11.1 *A simple HTML form that gathers mailing information from potential customers.*

TIP

Notice that the use of a simple table on the ProductForm.htm page allows for neater formatting of your form elements. Please refer back to Chapter 6 for more information on table formatting, as well as Chapter 8 for a full description of these and other form elements.

Creating the Form Processing Page

Now that you have a form with which to gather information from potential customers, you need to create a form that will actually process the information.

As I briefly discussed in Chapter 8, there are many ways to process forms, but all involve some type of script. In the old days (pre-1996), this involved some fairly extensive knowledge of programming. However, when Microsoft introduced ASP technology and later integrated the ability to work with it directly in their HTML editing tool (FrontPage), more advanced Web design opportunities became possible even for non-programmers.

ACTIVE SERVER PAGES: THEN AND NOW

Before you go too much further into this chapter, you should be aware of some of the issues—both past and present—involved in working with ASP.

As I mentioned, when Microsoft first introduced the technology in 1996, it was revolutionary in the sense that it provided an easy way to add tremendous dynamic functionality to HTML. However, as with all things that are Microsoft-proprietary, working with the technology required that you also utilize other Microsoft products, most notably their IIS (*Internet Information Server*). Also, even though ASP was fairly easy to learn, it was not the most elegant technology because longer, more involved ASP pages would often result in *spaghetti code*—long, rambling lines of code that are difficult to follow and debug when the inevitable problems appear. Still, working with ASP allowed programmers to do all kinds of wonderfully advanced things in a fraction of the time it would have taken in other scripting languages. Before long, the .asp extension was showing up all over the Web.

However, with the introduction of the .NET platform in 2002, Microsoft radically changed the format and structure of ASP. Indeed ASP.NET (or ASP 4.0, as it is sometimes called) is really nothing like ASP 3.0, which is what you will use in this chapter. It uses a different programming language (C#) instead of VBScript. (You are using VBScript in the FormProcessing.asp page.) And unlike ASP 3.0, ASP.NET pages are compiled. Not surprisingly, the learning curve for ASP.NET is significant, and to really work with it you need to make a serious commitment to not only programming, but also the larger development platform (.NET) that supports ASP.NET. It is also worth noting that there is no "migration path" from an ASP 3.0 application to one written in .NET. Basically, if you want to move an ASP 3.0 application to the new technology, you're going to have to rewrite it from scratch.

Although the .NET platform is undoubtedly here to stay and is the supported platform for all of Microsoft's Web initiatives, you can still feel comfortable working with ASP 3.0. It is still supported within IIS and you can still work with it in FrontPage, as you will see in Chapter 12 and the project chapters of Part II. Moreover, if your scripting demands involve such requirements as form processing or inserting information into a backend database like Access or SQL Server, then ASP 3.0 can still suit your needs quite well.

The important point to take from this is that this chapter is a very brief introduction to scripting languages in general—not just VBScript and ASP, but also JavaScript. Also, when you begin to work with these scripting languages, you have to be aware of larger issues such as Web server configurations and so on. However, don't let these issues or the ever-evolving nature of Web development dissuade you from exploring and learning about scripting in more detail. I am confident that you will see, even from the simple examples in this chapter, that integrating scripting with your HTML opens all kinds of exciting doors in Web development and that it is something you will want to explore further. In the Part II projects (especially the third and fourth projects), you will see that real-world applications will require the type of functionality that basic HTML simply cannot provide, and thus knowing how to work with scripting languages will be to your advantage.

Of course, ASP is still a complicated technology—especially its latest iteration, also known as ASP.NET, which is part of the larger Microsoft .NET Web development platform. However, by understanding a few basic components of ASP, you can add some pretty advanced functionality to your Web pages, such as directly processing form input.

The following sections will walk you through how to build an ASP form-processing page so you can retrieve and manipulate the information entered on the ProductForm.htm page you created earlier in this chapter.

Go ahead and create the form-processing page right now.

TIP

Go back and look at the HTML you entered to create the ProductForm.htm page. If you look at the `action` attribute of the `<form>` tag, you will notice it is set to FormProcessing.asp. The form will be submitted to this page for processing, and it is this page you will create in this section.

1. In your text editor, create a new page called FormProcessing.asp. Be sure to save it with the .asp extension. (This is critical for the page to work, as you will see in a moment.)

2. Enter the following code exactly as it appears here:

```
<html>
<head>
<title>ABC Company: Product Catalog Request</title>
</head>
<body>
<p align="center"><font size="7"><b>ABC Online Catalog</b></font></p>
<hr>
<p align="left"><font size="4">Thanks for submitting your information! 
Your <font color="Red"><%=Request.Form("Catalog")%></font> catalog will be sent
to the following address:</font></p>
Name:<br>
<%=Request.Form("Name")%><p>
Address:<br>
<%=Request.Form("Street")%><br>
<%=Request.Form("City")%>, <%=Request.Form("State")%><br>
<%=Request.Form("Zip")%>
<hr>
<i>Your comments:</i><p>
<%=Request.Form("Comments")%>
</body>
</html>
```

3. Save the page, once again making sure you use the .asp file extension.

Figures 11.2 and 11.3 illustrate the two pages in action.

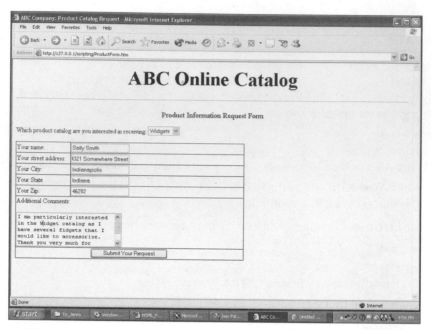

FIGURE 11.2 *The ProductForm.htm page, which is a typical HTML form.*

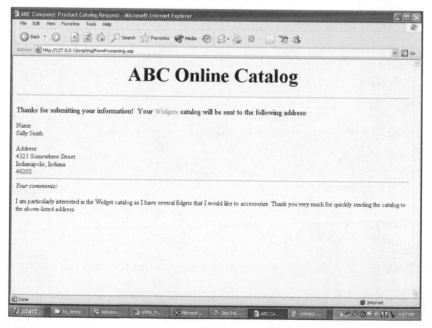

FIGURE 11.3 *The information that was entered on the request form is processed, formatted, and displayed here. Note how the requested product catalog is listed in a different font color to draw attention to it.*

The ASP Request Object

The FormProcessing.asp page can read and manipulate the information entered on the ProductForm.htm page via the ASP Request object.

The Request object is but one of several objects in ASP 3.0, but it is certainly one of the most useful and probably most-used objects. Moreover, the Request object has several collections available for your use. You can think of collections as special subsets of objects that expose unique information about an object for extended manipulation. In a large company, you can have a manufacturing component, a sales component, a human resources component, and so on. Relating this analogy to ASP, think of these company collections as exposing specific attributes of the company.

Certain collections are available for your use, depending on the ASP object with which you are working. For the discussion in this chapter, I want to focus on two specific collections within the Request object:

◆ **Form.** You've already started to work with this collection via the code listings in this chapter. Simply put, the Form collection takes all the values passed by an HTML form and submitted as part of the form request and makes them available for manipulation. The FormProcessing.asp page utilizes the Form collection.

◆ **QueryString.** Another oft-used collection within the Request object is the QueryString collection. Similar to the Form collection, the QueryString collection makes available to the Web server all values contained with the URL of the user's request. I'll discuss the QueryString collection in more detail a bit later in the chapter.

NOTE

There are additional collections available within the Request object, and obviously this and other ASP-related issues warrant a far more in-depth discussion than I have provided here. Please consult the books mentioned at the beginning of this chapter for a far more comprehensive discussion of ASP and other scripting languages and topics.

NOTE

ASP code is inserted into regular HTML using opening (<%=) and closing (%>) tags. When the page is loaded on the server, this indicates that anything enclosed within these tags needs to be processed on the server before it is displayed on the page.

So how does the FormProcess.asp page work? If you look at the code, it's pretty straightforward.

◆ First, the type of catalog selected from the drop-down form field on the ProductForm.htm page is displayed on screen. To draw attention to it, the font color is changed to red. This is done via the line `<%=Request.Form("Catalog")%>`, where `Catalog` is the name of the drop-down field.

◆ Next, each of the values passed for the specific form fields are displayed on the screen—`<%=Request.Form("Name")%>`, `<%=Request.Form("Street")%>`, and so on. Note how some general HTML formatting tags (`<br>`, `<p>`, and `<hr>`) are used to help display the information in a more attractive manner.

◆ Finally, the value of the `Comments` text-area field is displayed on the screen by the code `<%=Request.Form("Comments")%>`.

TIP

Remember that you can reference the form fields in your ASP script by simply referring to the name attribute given to the specific form field. In the example given here, the "Your Name" field was assigned the name of "Name"; this name attribute, then, is what is requested by the `Request.Form` object. The form example here is simple, in that the form field names are given the same "name" as they appear to the user (for example, the "Your Name" field is given the name of "Name," the "Your City" field is given the name of "City"). Note, though, you can assign any name to a form field; for example, you could have assigned a value of "City" to the "Your Name" field. Obviously, this would be a foolish (and confusing!) thing to do, so it's good practice to name your form fields something that is indicative of the values they will probably contain.

If the `Request` object form collection seems easy to use, it's because it is—there really isn't much to it. It is a simple way of processing information passed in a form and displaying it on the screen.

Working with the Request Object QueryString Collection

In addition to form fields, you can also read information from within the querystring itself. Imagine you have a Web page that, when loaded into a browser, has the following querystring:

`http://127.0.0.1/Scripting/FormProcessing.asp?Name=Smith&Catalog=Widgets`

Two variables are passed in this querystring:

◆ **Name.** This variable is assigned the value `Smith`.
◆ **Catalog.** This variable is assigned the value `Widgets`.

TIP

Note how the structures of querystrings are appended to the URL. After the file extension of the page being referenced (in the example here, "FormProcessing.asp"), there is a "?" to indicate querystring values will follow; then each individual value is amended and separated from the other by the "&" sign. Note that some browsers will put a limit on the number of values you can pass in a querystring.

CAUTION

You should also use caution in what values you pass in a querystring, as they are visible to the user. For example, a querystring of `http://www.bank.com?password=123ABC` is probably not a good idea, as the customer's password would be visible in plain view.

By utilizing the `QueryString` collection of the `Request` object, you could pull the values of these variables and display them on your Web page.

You do this exactly the same way you did for the `Response.Form` collection. Indeed, the only thing you have to do is replace `Response.Form` with `Response.QueryString`.

1. Create a new Web page called Query.asp and save it in your Scripting folder.

2. In this page, enter the following code as you see it here:

```
<html>
<head>
<title>ABC Company: Product Catalog Request</title>
</head>
<body>
<p align="center"><font size="7"><b>ABC Online Catalog</b></font></p>
<hr>
<p>
Name: <%=Request.Querystring("Name")%><br>
Catalog you wish to order: <%=Request.Querystring("Catalog")%>
</body>
</html>
```

3. Save the page in your Scripting folder.

4. Open your Web browser and type **http://127.0.0.1/scripting/query.asp? Name=Smith&Catalog=Widgets**. Be sure to type in the complete address.

When the page loads, your screen should look like Figure 11.4.

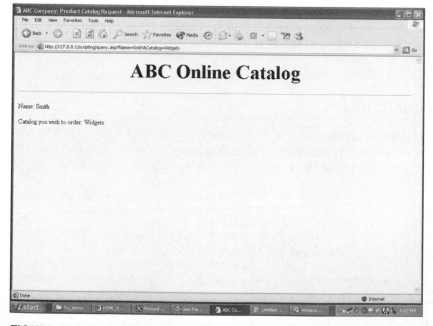

FIGURE 11.4 *You can pull information directly from the querystring of a page via the* Response.QueryString *collection.*

You should keep a few things in mind when you're working with `Response.QueryString` or deciding whether to use it or `Response.Form`.

◆ Using the `Form` collection is a more secure method of passing data. When data is passed in the querystring, as shown in Figure 11.4, it is obviously open to the public eye and therefore is not secure.

◆ Depending on the type of Web browser, there might be a limit on the maximum length of the querystring, as well as the manner in which the data can be passed within the querystring. (For example, the browser might not allow spaces or special characters to be included in the querystring.)

Integrating JavaScript with HTML

Originally developed by Netscape Communications and Sun Microsystems, JavaScript is a wonderful tool for enhancing your HTML and bringing new levels of functionality to your site. Creative uses for JavaScript with HTML are still being explored. Do a search on Yahoo! or another favorite search tool using the term "JavaScript," and you will see hundreds (if not thousands) of pages dedicated to the subject, many of which will include tutorials or free JavaScript code examples.

That said, I won't go too far into the use of JavaScript here because there are so many excellent tutorials on the Web, as well as an excellent book, *JavaScript Professional Projects* (Premier Press, 2003). However, because this chapter has dealt with additional ways to work with HTML forms, I want to include an example that illustrates how you can use JavaScript to help validate your form fields. In this case, the sample JavaScript code that follows ensures that at least some type of data has been entered into each form field in question.

Validating Forms with JavaScript

Take another look at your ProductForm.htm page. If this were a form on a live Web site, the information being gathered would be critical to the proper delivery of the catalog (with the possible exception of the comments field, which would probably be optional). That said, you would not want the form to be submitted with one of the fields left blank.

There are many ways to validate a form, but using JavaScript to do so is a great example of how useful it can be. For this example, you'll add some JavaScript to your ProductForm.htm page.

1. Open ProductForm.htm in your text editor.

2. Retype the code so it appears exactly like the following listing.

```html
<html>
<head>
<script>
<!--
function validateform()
{
if((document.orderform.Name.value=="")||
(document.orderform.Street.value=="")||
(document.orderform.City.value=="")||
(document.orderform.State.value=="")||
(document.orderform.Zip.value==""))
{
window.alert("In order to give you best service, please complete all fields.
Thank you!")
return false;
}
}
//-->
</script>
<title>ABC Company: Product Catalog Request</title>
</head>
<body>
<p align="center"><font size="7"><b>ABC Online Catalog</b></font></p>
<hr>
<font size="4">Product Information Request Form</font><p>
<form name="orderform" method="POST" action="formprocessing.asp" onSubmit="return
validateform( this.form)">
<p>
  Which product catalog are you interested in receiving:
  <select size="1" name="Catalog" tabindex="1">
  <option>Widgets</option>
  <option>Fidgets</option>
  <option>Gadgets</option>
  </select></p>
```

```
<table border="1" style="border-collapse: collapse" bordercolor="#111111"
width="58%">
  <tr>
    <td width="24%">Your name:</td>
    <td width="76%"><input type="text" name="Name" size="20" tabindex="2"></td>
  </tr>
  <tr>
    <td width="24%">Your street address:</td>
    <td width="76%"><input type="text" name="Street" size="20"
tabindex="3"></td>
  </tr>
  <tr>
    <td width="24%">Your City:</td>
    <td width="76%"><input type="text" name="City" size="20" tabindex="4"></td>
  </tr>
  <tr>
    <td width="24%">Your State</td>
    <td width="76%"><input type="text" name="State" size="20"
tabindex="5"></td>
  </tr>
  <tr>
    <td width="24%">Your Zip:</td>
    <td width="76%"><input type="text" name="Zip" size="20" tabindex="6"></td>
  </tr>
  <tr>
    <td width="100%" colspan="2">Additional Comments:<p>
    <textarea rows="5" name="Comments" cols="30" tabindex="8"></textarea></td>
  </tr>
  <tr>
    <td width="100%" colspan="2">
    <p align="center">
    <input type="submit" value="Submit Your Request" name="Submit"></td>
  </tr>
</table>
</form>
</body>
</html>
```

CAUTION

JavaScript is case sensitive and can be very picky. After you type in this code and test it successfully in a browser, go back and change the names of the form fields (within the form itself) so they begin with lowercase letters, but leave them referenced in the JavaScript function as beginning with uppercase letters. Your JavaScript won't function—I guarantee it!

3. Save the page again.

4. Load the page into a Web browser and try submitting the form with one of the form fields empty. Your screen will look like Figure 11.5.

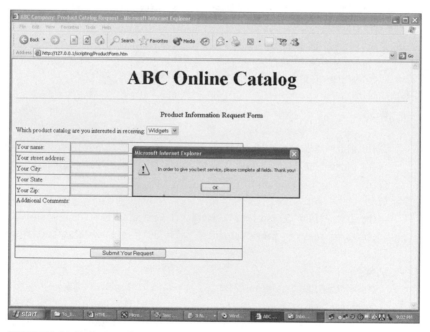

FIGURE 11.5 *Integrating JavaScript can be incredibly useful for ensuring the successful operation of your Web site.*

Although a detailed explanation of the JavaScript in this code example is beyond the scope of this book, there are a few things you should note about this code sample.

◆ First, the `validateform` function is declared.

◆ Next, each of the form fields (with the exception of the drop-down menu) is referenced within the function (for example, `document.order-form.Street.value`). The syntax of this statement is simply the Web page (`document`), the name of the form (`orderform`), the name of the form field (`Street`), and the value assigned to that field (`value`).

◆ The function looks at each of the assigned form fields. If nothing has been entered into the field (as noted by the `==""` code), the function displays the pop-up window alert:

```
window.alert("In order to give you best service, please complete all fields.
Thank you!")
```

◆ Finally, the function is called when the submit button on the form is clicked. This is done via the `onSubmit="return validateform( this.form)"` line of code within the `<form>` tag.

Another simple script, but one that should give you plenty of ideas (and hopefully interest) about the great power and functionality that is inherent within JavaScript.

Summary

The purpose of this chapter was to give you a brief overview of the extended functionality of integrating scripts with your HTML. First you saw two examples of ASP and the `Request` object. The first example utilized the `Form` collection, and the second utilized the `QueryString` collection. Both examples demonstrated how you can use ASP to process information that is passed via the form or a querystring. Next, you were shown a simple but quite functional example of JavaScript that you could use to validate a form to ensure that at least some amount of information is entered into each targeted form field. As I noted in that section, such a script could be quite useful (if not essential) for ensuring the accuracy of the information you gather from your HTML forms. Finally, I mentioned that although the scope of this book does not include detailed instructions on using scripting languages, there are many excellent references available to you (from Premier Press or the Web).

Chapter 12

**Working with an
HTML Editor**

U p to this point in the book, you have probably done all of your HTML coding by hand, using a simple text editor such as Notepad. While this is perfectly valid, you have probably found that this is a tedious process, and that several common HTML tasks (such as building and customizing tables) become quite repetitive and time consuming, to say the least. You might also find that a simple text editor allows you to take nothing for granted, so to speak, in your work with HTML. Unlike a word-processing program that automates some of your specific writing tasks (such as formatting a bulleted list), a simple text editor does nothing of the sort with your HTML coding.

Fortunately, there are several terrific HTML editor applications on the market that make these tedious, repetitive (did someone say boring?) HTML tasks yesterday's news and allow you to spend most of your time on the more interesting aspects of Web design. This chapter (along with the third project in Part II) will focus on one of those editors—Microsoft FrontPage XP. This application has been around for several years and has changed significantly, with each new version bringing more power and functionality (not to mention stability) to your Web-design tasks. Although it is by no means the only HTML editor out there, FrontPage is very easy to use, and if you have purchased the Microsoft Office application suite, you probably already have it installed on your computer.

The focus of this chapter is to give you an overview of the major features of FrontPage and to show you how you can enhance the skills you learned in the previous chapters (such as working with frames and manipulating images and graphics) by discovering the corresponding tools built into FrontPage.

 NOTE

To reiterate what I said in this chapter's introduction, the focus of this chapter is on introducing the major functionality and tools in FrontPage, and how they can facilitate and otherwise enhance the HTML skills you learned in Chapters 1 through 11. In the third project of Part II, you get a chance to put your knowledge of FrontPage to work by using the application to create a Web site. So use this chapter as an introduction to the powerful tools in FrontPage, and then use the third project to actually put those tools to use and build a full-featured Web site.

Creating a FrontPage Web

The best way to start your exploration of FrontPage is to open the application, see what is immediately presented, and then create a new Web.

1. If it is not already running, start FrontPage.

2. If you are working with FrontPage XP, your screen will look like Figure 12.1.

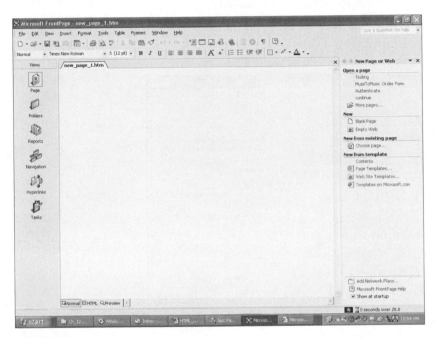

FIGURE 12.1 *The FrontPage XP work area.*

 NOTE

Earlier versions of FrontPage (especially FrontPage 2000) share much of the functionality and general look and feel of FrontPage XP. If you are using an older version, you probably will still be able to follow along and learn quite a bit from this chapter, as well as the third project in Part II.

If you've worked with other applications in the Office suite (such as Word or Excel), the general layout of FrontPage will look familiar. FrontPage includes the familiar menu options (File, Edit, and so on) and the Formatting toolbar (with bold, italics, and font options). Probably the biggest difference is the Views options listed along the left side of the screen (Page, Folders, Reports, and so on). Each icon in this list allows you to look in a different way at how files are stored in your Web site.

I'll talk more about these different views later in this chapter. For now, make sure you are in Page view (so your screen looks like Figure 12.1) because the first thing you need to do is create a Web site structure so you have something to work with.

3. Under the New heading on the far-right side of the screen, click on the Empty Web option. Your screen should look like Figure 12.2.

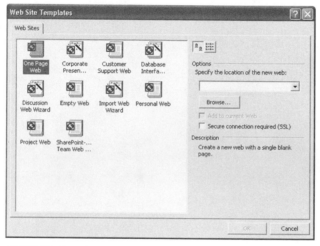

FIGURE 12.2 *FrontPage provides you with a number of templates you can use to design your Web site.*

TIP

The New heading may now show up every time. If it doesn't, you can choose File, New, Page or Web to get the Empty Web option.

4. For this first example you'll create a one-page Web, so select the One Page Web option, as shown in Figure 12.2.

5. Next you have to specify the location where you want your Web site to be created. Click on the Browse button and navigate to the c/Inetpub/wwwroot directory. Your screen should look like Figure 12.3.

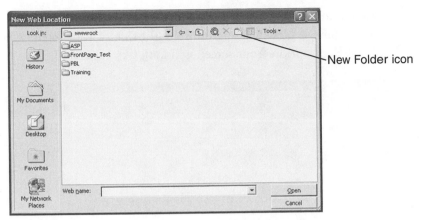

New Folder icon

FIGURE 12.3 *You will place your new Web site in the wwwroot directory of the Inetpub folder.*

6. Click on the New Folder icon and type **FrontPage_Test** in the dialog box that appears.

7. Back in the New Web Location dialog box, click on the Open button to return to the Web Site Templates window. Your screen should look like Figure 12.4.

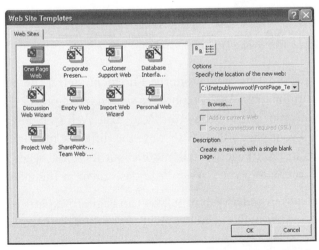

FIGURE 12.4 *Make sure the One Page Web option is selected once again.*

8. Click on OK. You will see a brief animation, showing you that FrontPage is creating your Web. After a few seconds you will return to Page view, but the primary work area will be grayed out. This indicates that your site has been created and that you need to create your first actual Web page.

9. From the File menu, select New, Page or Web. In the list of options that appears under the New heading on the right side of your screen, click on the Blank Page option. Your screen will look like Figure 12.5.

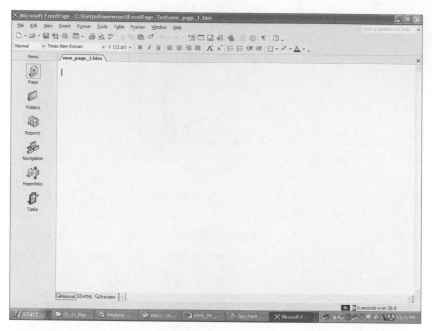

FIGURE 12.5 *You've created a Web site and opened a blank Web page on which to work.*

10. Go ahead and save the page now. From the File menu, select the Save As option to bring up the Save As dialog box, as shown in Figure 12.6. Make sure you are saving your page in the FrontPage_Test Web (the one you just created). Call your page FP_1. Also, note the different file types you can save pages as in FrontPage. I'll talk more about these file types later; for now, make sure the file type is Web Pages, as shown in Figure 12.6.

Now that you've created a Web and a Web page, you can begin to explore the tools and features in FrontPage that make it such a great tool for HTML coding and design.

Each of the following sections will take you through the FrontPage menus (File, Edit, View, Insert, and so on) so you will get a solid introduction to all the functionality contained in each menu. Once again, this chapter is an introduction to FrontPage. In the third project of Part II, you will put the application through its paces as you use it to develop an actual Web site for a small business.

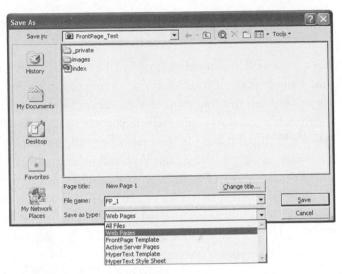

FIGURE 12.6 *Note the different file types with which you can work in FrontPage.*

The File Menu

Not surprisingly, the FrontPage File menu is similar to the File menu in many other Windows-based applications. However, there are some differences specific to FrontPage that I will discuss in this section. Figure 12.7 highlights the full File menu and the options it contains.

FIGURE 12.7 *The FrontPage File menu. Note the Publish Web and Preview in Browser options.*

Again, most of these options are standard Windows File menu fare. However, you should take notice of the following special FrontPage options:

◆ **Publish Web.** As you work in FrontPage, you will eventually come to a point when you want to publish your Web site so others can access it. Generally, you will publish to some remote Web server (remote in the sense that it is probably not the same machine you are using to create your pages). While Web publishing in general is beyond the scope of this chapter, it is safe to say the FrontPage Web publishing tool is automated (like many of the tasks in FrontPage). If you select this option, you will see a simple dialog box that asks you to enter the publish destination (see Figure 12.8). You'll learn more about Web publishing in the third project in Part II; for now, be sure to note where this functionality is located in the FrontPage menu system.

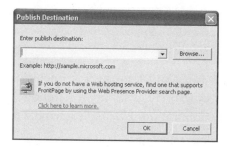

FIGURE 12.8 *Using FrontPage's Web publishing features, it's easy to take your work from development to production.*

◆ **Preview in Browser.** Although high-speed Web access is becoming more and more ubiquitous, the fact is that the majority of Web users are still connecting via a dial-up modem. When you're designing your Web pages, keep in mind that depending on the size of the page, it might take several seconds (or minutes) for it to load in the browser of a dial-up user. The Preview in Browser feature helps you consider these issues and see how your page will appear when it is published and live on the Web. When you select the Preview in Browser option, FrontPage asks you to set a few parameters so you can get the best idea of how your page will look, depending on how it is viewed. Figure 12.9 illustrates the options you can set to best determine the appearance of your page.

NOTE

Note that the list of Web browsers that appears is dependent on your own machine. FrontPage compiles and lists the browsers that are installed on your computer and displays them in this list.

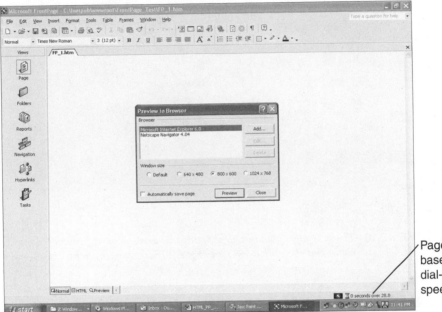

Page-load time based on a 28.8 dial-up modem speed

FIGURE 12.9 *You can set the browser type and the screen resolution to best determine how your Web pages will look under different configurations.*

When you click on the Preview button (refer to Figure 12.9), FrontPage will open a browser window (in the browser that you chose from the list) so you can get an idea of how the page will look when published. To get an idea of how long it will take for the page to load, look at the lower-right corner of your screen (see the callout in Figure 12.9). By using a lowest common denominator for connection speed (28.8 kbps), you can gauge how long it will take your pages to load in a visitor's browser.

Everything else in the File menu consists of standard Windows application options. Again, I'll return to the Publish Web and Preview in Browser options later in this chapter and in Part II.

The Edit Menu

The Edit menu in FrontPage is nearly identical to a typical Windows application. Although there are some features associated with document and project management related to the Tasks option (see Figure 12.10), most of these require special server configuration involving additional software. I will not discuss those features in this book.

FIGURE 12.10 *The Edit menu contains all the basic text-management features (such as Edit, Copy, and Paste) that you see in most Windows applications.*

The View Menu

The really great benefit to working with an HTML editor like FrontPage is that it allows you to quickly organize and view all the documents in your Web site. In addition to displaying a file directory with individual subfolders, FrontPage also allows you to view the hyperlink structure of your site. (By *hyperlink structure*, I mean a map of how all the pages within your site are connected via the individual hyperlinks they contain. FrontPage also has a Site Report view that allows you to see recent activity in your site (such as recently added files) as well as problems (such as broken hyperlinks or slow-loading pages). All of this functionality is contained in the View menu. I will preview the functionality in this section and discuss it in more detail in the third project of Part II.

As you can see in Figure 12.11, the View menu supports six major types of view options.

NOTE

Why am I only previewing the View menu options here? Most of the great functionality contained in this menu is best seen in a site that has at least a few active pages (including pages that link to one another) and a site navigation structure. This introductory chapter to FrontPage will not present you with an opportunity to build a full-featured site using the application; you'll get to that in the third project of Part II, when you'll use FrontPage to build the MuseToMusic Web site that I'll introduce in the first project.

FIGURE 12.11 *The View menu allows you to see your FrontPage Web content organized in a variety of ways.*

♦ **Page.** This is the basic view—the one that has been illustrated in the figures up to this point in the chapter. In Page view, you see the current page with which you are working.

♦ **Folders.** In Folders view, you see (not surprisingly) the folders within your Web site and the contents they contain. It is possible to combine the Folders and Page views at the same time; you'll see how later in this section.

♦ **Reports.** The options in the Reports submenu provide you with all kinds of useful information about the operation of your FrontPage Web, including valuable information about when pages were updated and how they are performing. There are several sub-report options available; you'll learn about those in the section titled "Reports View."

♦ **Navigation.** The best sites have an intuitive navigation structure that allows visitors to quickly find the content for which they are searching. FrontPage has a useful tool that allows you build a site's navigation structure from pre-defined templates. If you do so, you can then use the Navigation view to customize this feature even further.

◆ **Hyperlinks.** If the Internet is the information superhighway, then hyperlinks are the road signs that direct visitors to the information they are seeking. In a specific Web, you will undoubtedly have several hyperlinks to allow visitors to move between pages. (For example, you might have hyperlinks that lead from a catalog to a checkout page so visitors can make a purchase.) Like the Navigation view, the Hyperlinks view gives you a graphical representation of how all these links work in conjunction on your site, allowing you to easily and effectively manage them.

◆ **Tasks.** The final view option is the Tasks view. You can use FrontPage as a collaborative Web design tool so multiple Web developers can work simultaneously on the design of a site. Tasks are assigned via the Edit menu, and they show up in Tasks view. Although this can be a useful feature, this chapter (and book) will focus more on a single-developer role and will assume that you are the only person working in FrontPage to design a project.

Folders View

As your Web site grows, you will have several subfolders in your main site directory. For example, you might want to divide into different folders the major functionality of your site (such as the shopping cart, company biographical information, and hours of operation) and the pages that support that functionality. This allows you to keep your site neatly organized instead of having all of the files dumped into one folder.

1. Open the FrontPage_Test Web you created at the beginning of this chapter.

2. In the View menu, select Folders. Your screen will look like Figure 12.12.

Figure 12.12 really isn't that impressive because at this point you have one file and no subfolders in your FrontPage_Test Web. Still, note the information provided to you in this figure. The name, size, file type, and modification date are listed for each file.

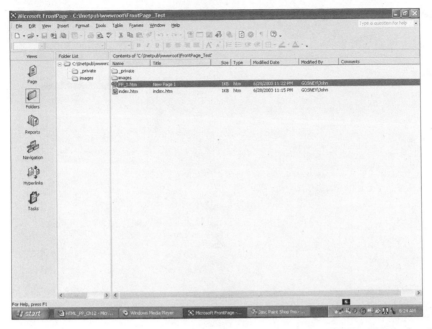

FIGURE 12.12 *Folders view allows you to see quickly the organizational hierarchy of your Web.*

You can also get and update information on a specific file by selecting the file and then right-clicking on it to view its properties.

1. Click on the file FP_1.htm, as shown in Figure 12.12. (This is the file you created at the beginning of this chapter.)
2. Now right-click on the file to bring up the menu shown in Figure 12.13. From this menu, select Properties.
3. The window that appears will give you specific information about the file in question (in this case, FP_1.htm). Click on the Summary tab, as shown in Figure 12.14.
4. Enter some text in the Comments space, as shown in Figure 12.14, and then click on Apply. The comments you added will be displayed in the Folders view screen, as shown in Figure 12.15.

TIP

Double-clicking on a selected file in Folders view will automatically take you to the Page view for that page.

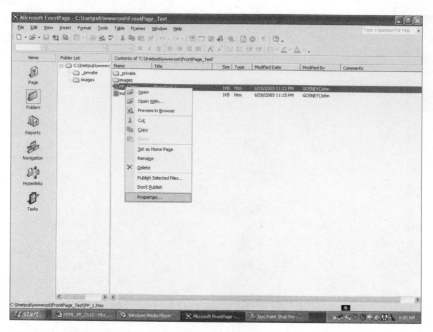

FIGURE 12.13 *These drop-down menus are available throughout FrontPage. They allow you quick access to a variety of features for the file or folder in question.*

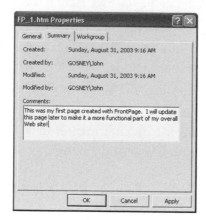

FIGURE 12.14 *You can enter detailed comments for a file on the Summary tab of the Properties dialog box.*

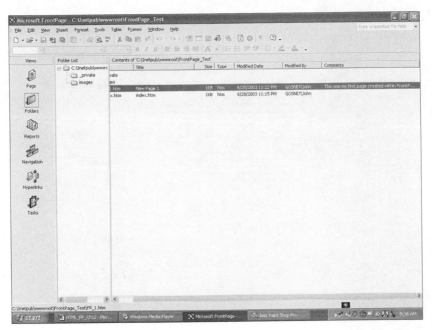

FIGURE 12.15 *Take advantage of the ability to enter comments to better organize your site and serve as a reminder of how a page functions, what issues exist with the page, and so on.*

Reports View

When you have your site up and running, you will find the Reports view to be an invaluable tool in administering your site and keeping everything running smoothly.

In the Reports view, there are five major types of reports you can utilize.

◆ **Site Summary.** This option gives a general overview or snapshot report of your Web. Figure 12.16 illustrates a Site Summary report. You can access those reports by clicking on their listing in this Site Summary report.

◆ **Files.** There are specific file reports you can view, as shown in Figure 12.17. Depending on the type of file report you select, FrontPage will display a file grid presenting you with options for how to get additional information about the file report with which you are working (see Figure 12.18).

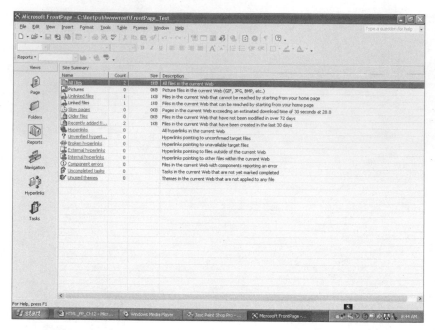

FIGURE 12.16 *Use the Site Summary report to get a quick overview of your entire site.*

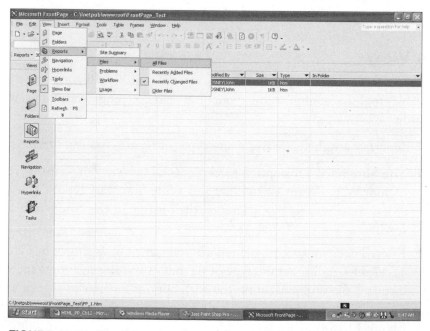

FIGURE 12.17 *The different types of file reports available in FrontPage.*

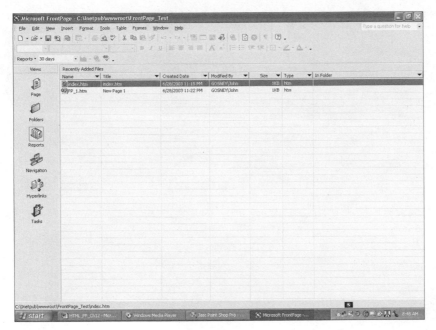

FIGURE 12.18 *The Recently Added Files report. You can click on the arrows in each column and sort by the specific options presented there (such as by file type or by folder).*

◆ **Problems.** The third type of report might be the most useful in practice. As you can see in Figure 12.19, you can view different types of site problems in this report.

Each of these four options displays a screen that provides specific information about the problem in question (see Figure 12.20).

NOTE

You'll really get a chance to see the great functionality of the Reports view in the third project of Part II, in which you will use FrontPage to build a Web site for a small business.

◆ **Workflow.** As I mentioned earlier, FrontPage allows you to work in collaboration with other developers and assign specific tasks that need to be accomplished to build a Web site. Although I will not discuss this functionality in this book, you should investigate the reporting options listed on the Workflow report if you are thinking of using FrontPage with other developers.

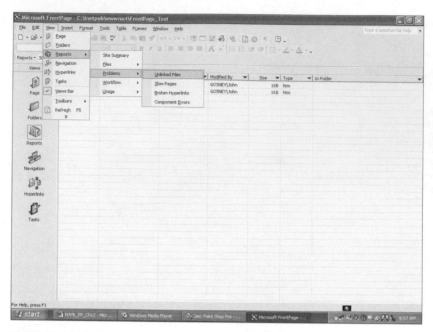

FIGURE 12.19 *You can use each of these specific problem reports to gain a better handle on the total operation and performance of your site.*

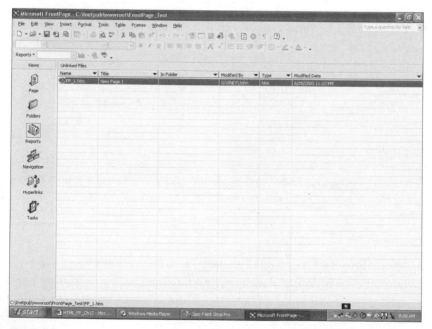

FIGURE 12.20 *The Unlinked Files report, showing that the file FP_1.htm does not have any links. This might not be a problem per se; nevertheless, the file is included in the report for quick viewing.*

◆ **Usage.** In addition to the Problems reports, the Usage reports will come in quite handy when you put your Web site into production and visitors begin to frequent it. Figure 12.21 illustrates the wide variety of reports you can obtain about how your site is utilized and how often it is visited.

 NOTE

Like the Problems reports, the Usage reports will be discussed in more detail in the third project of Part II. However, you should note that these two types of reports can provide you with critical business information in addition to providing you with vital technical information about how your site functions. For example, knowing that one section of your site is getting more visitors than another could lead you to further investigate why that is the case. Maybe it is because that section of the site is more visually appealing (or better designed!), or maybe it is because that section contains information that drives the capricious nature of the buying public for whatever reason. These are interesting questions that highlight the type of business intelligence that only technology can provide.

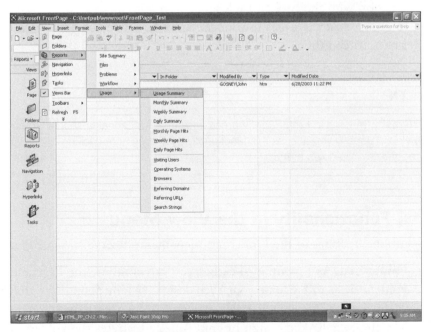

FIGURE 12.21 *Each of these reports can give you invaluable information about the activity of your Web and the information it contains.*

Navigation and Hyperlinks Views

As with all of the view options discussed in this chapter, the Navigation and Hyperlinks views really come into play and show their power in a full-featured site. Your very simple one-page FrontPage_Test Web site doesn't really offer much functionality at the moment, so the Navigation and Hyperlinks views don't come into play. However, I have provided a general description of each in the following list, and I will highlight both options further in the third project of Part II.

◆ **Navigation.** As I mentioned earlier, the best Web sites have an intuitive navigation structure that allows visitors to move back and forth between pages quickly and easily to find the information for which they are searching. FrontPage's Navigation feature builds this navigational structure for you. You can then use the Navigation view to manipulate and make changes to the resulting navigation structure.

◆ **Hyperlinks.** Similar in scope to the Navigation view, the Hyperlinks view gives you a graphical representation of how the pages in your site are linked via the hyperlinks included on each respective page. In conjunction with the Broken Link problem report, you can use this feature to ensure that the pages in your site are interconnected and functioning as you intend them.

TIP

Like so many features in FrontPage, there is additional functionality specific to each of these views. Usually you access this functionally by simply right-clicking to display a report-specific drop-down menu.

Additional Functionality in the View Menu

Two additional features of the FrontPage View menu deserve special attention.

◆ **Folder List.** As I mentioned earlier, you can combine the Page and Folders views to facilitate your Web design. (Many people like to have both views open to see how the page they are currently working on fits into the overall Web design.) Figure 12.22 illustrates the Folders and Page views together.

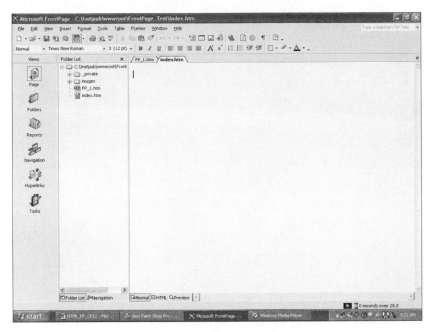

FIGURE 12.22 *You can work simultaneously in both Page and Folders views by selecting the Folder List option from the View menu.*

◆ **Toolbars.** As in most Windows applications, you can toggle on or off the toolbars you want to display on the screen. FrontPage has toolbars specific to Web design, such as DHTML Effects. Depending on the functionality you are using, you might want to display only related toolbars—in a case such as this, the toggle on/off functionality of the Toolbars option is useful. Figure 12.23 highlights the complete list of toolbars available in FrontPage XP.

The Insert Menu

There is a tremendous variety of functionality contained in the Insert menu. You will explore most of it in the FrontPage project of Part II; however, it is a good idea to get an overview of everything contained in this menu. Figure 12.24 highlights the functionality and how it is grouped.

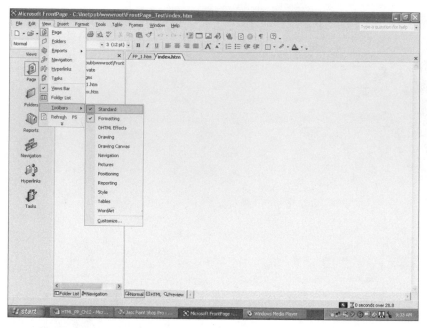

FIGURE 12.23 *You can toggle on or off specific toolbars. A checkmark next to each toolbar indicates that it is currently displayed.*

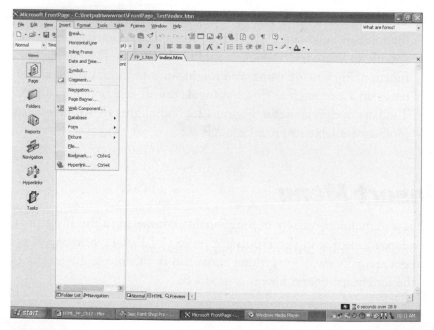

FIGURE 12.24 *The functionality contained in the Insert menu runs the gamut from basic HTML to some of the most advanced features of FrontPage and Web design.*

General HTML Options

This section will describe the options of the Insert menu up to and including the Comment option. Figure 12.25 shows the result of selecting each one of these options.

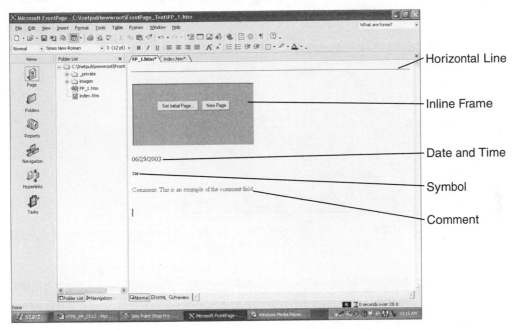

FIGURE 12.25 *The results of selecting the first five options from the Insert menu.*

Now take a look at each of these options in more detail.

◆ **Horizontal Line.** This option provides a good way to neatly divide content on your page. Because this basic HTML option is used so frequently, it's nice to have it as a quick option on the Insert menu.

◆ **Inline Frame.** This really neat feature of HTML allows you to place a frame inside a regular HTML page so you can provide more detailed information on a topic without using a traditional (and sometimes bulky) frameset. You'll learn more about this feature in the FrontPage project in Part II.

◆ **Date and Time.** This option allows you to insert two different options for date and time—the date and time the page was last edited or the date and time the page was last automatically updated. You are presented with these two options when you select Date and Time from the Insert menu.

◆ **Symbol.** When you select this option from the Insert menu, you are presented with a wide variety of special symbols that you can insert into your Web page (see Figure 12.26).

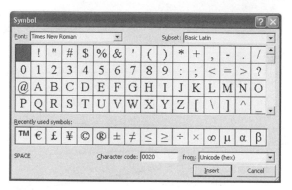

FIGURE 12.26 *You can easily insert a wide variety of special symbols into your Web page using the Symbol option from the Insert menu.*

◆ **Comment.** As you are designing your Web pages, you might want to insert a special comment so other developers can follow your train of thought. The Comment field allows you to do just that. (Note that these comments will not be displayed when you view the page in a browser.)

Advanced Functionality

The next set of options on the Insert menu (Navigation, Page Banner, Web Component, Database, and Form) present you with some of the more powerful benefits of working with FrontPage, as well as HTML and Web design in general. Although I'll discuss many of these features again in the FrontPage project of Part II, you should be familiar with what they are and how you can utilize them in your Web design.

◆ **Navigation.** This feature will allow you to automatically build a navigation hierarchy for your Web site. Then you can utilize the Navigation view (described in the previous section) to help you administer this functionality.

NOTE

While the automated navigation features of FrontPage can be useful, you might find that you want more specific control over the navigation scheme your site utilizes. For example, you might want to build your own menu system. (Many Web sites today use JavaScript-enabled menu systems to mimic the menu functionality present in most Windows applications.) I will discuss this design and process question in more detail in the FrontPage project in Part II.

◆ **Web Component.** Web components are special FrontPage features that allow you to automatically integrate functionality for which you would normally need to use advanced code (often with a scripting language). Figure 12.27 illustrates the different types of components that are available.

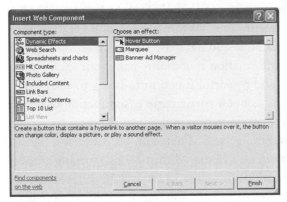

FIGURE 12.27 *Components can bring an exciting new functionality to your Web design.*

Some of the more popular components shown in the list in Figure 12.27 include the Dynamic Effects and Hit Counter options. You will learn more about these dynamic effects (or DHTML effects) in the discussion of the Format menu. You will also see these components utilized in the FrontPage project of Part II.

CAUTION

There are a few things you should be aware of with regard to using FrontPage Web components. Most important, for many of these components to work, the server that hosts your FrontPage Web must have the FrontPage extensions installed. Although many IPPs (*Internet Presence Providers*) provide these extensions, some do not. Keep that in mind before you depend too heavily on the functionality presented by these components.

The second issue is that these components add quite a bit of code to your HTML (more on this later) and are not easy to manually configure. Depending on your skill and interest, this might be a good or bad thing. You might not like the idea of having code that you have no direct control over inserted into your Web page. The bottom line is that you should use the FrontPage Web components cautiously—take advantage of their functionality when you can, but don't rely too heavily on them.

◆ **Database.** In the fourth project of Part II, "MS SQL Server 2000: Integrating a Database with Your Web Site," you will get a glimpse of how you can integrate a back-end database (in this case, Microsoft SQL Server 2000) and the information it contains with your Web pages. This is an incredibly useful and powerful function to bring to your Web design. Unfortunately, it is not a particularly easy function to use. It requires some extensive configuration and administration, as well as some advanced programming skills. That said, the Database option presents this functionality in an automated format. By working through the Database Results Wizard (see Figures 12.28 and 12.29), you can integrate a database into your Web page. The same cautions apply here as for the FrontPage components; however, the Database option is easy to use and allows you a modicum of control over how your data is presented. Figure 12.30 highlights the code that is automatically configured and inserted by FrontPage to deliver this functionality.

As shown in the text of Figure 12.29, you need to give the Web page that includes the database results region an .asp extension (short for *Active Server Pages*) for it to work properly. Also, the page will only function if it is first fetched (in other words, processed) from a Web server.

TIP

The Database Results Wizard and the functionality it presents are quite useful and worth discussing in more detail. However, this requires an explanation of some more advanced topics such as general database integration, the use of Active Server Pages, and SQL queries. I will explain these topics in more detail in the FrontPage project (Chapters 21 through 24) and the SQL Server project (Chapters 25 through 28).

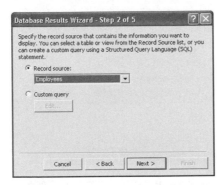

FIGURE 12.28 *In this example, I am connecting to the Northwind sample database that comes with Microsoft Access and SQL Server.*

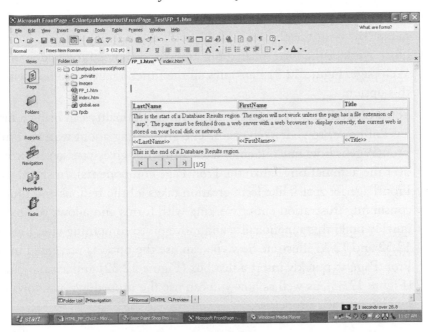

FIGURE 12.29 *The end result of the Database Results Wizard, highlighting a table that will pull information directly from the Northwind database into your Web page.*

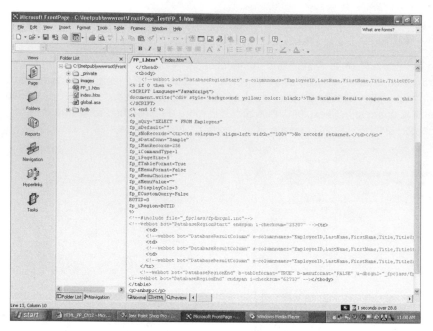

FIGURE 12.30 *An example of the auto-generated code that is included in your Web page for the Database Results Wizard to function.*

◆ **Form.** This is probably the most immediately useful option on the Insert menu. By using the choices available with this option, you can make quick work of the form-related functionality you need to include in your Web page. Figure 12.31 illustrates all the functionality included with this option.

You will recall from Chapter 8 that form functionality can bring a new level of power to your Web pages. The great thing about working with FrontPage is how much it automates forms but gives you specific control over the automation (unlike the FrontPage components). In short, using FrontPage for a task like form creation takes all the tedious and time-consuming frustration out of working with forms and allows you to quickly build this functionality and move on to something else. Figures 12.32 and 12.33 illustrate how you can use the options presented in FrontPage to quickly insert a text box (Figure 12.32) and a radio button (Figure 12.33), as well as how you can use the drop-down windows to quickly set their properties.

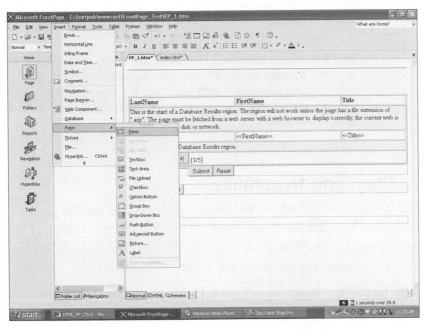

FIGURE 12.31 *Note all the specific fields (text box, radio button, and so on) you can quickly insert into your form.*

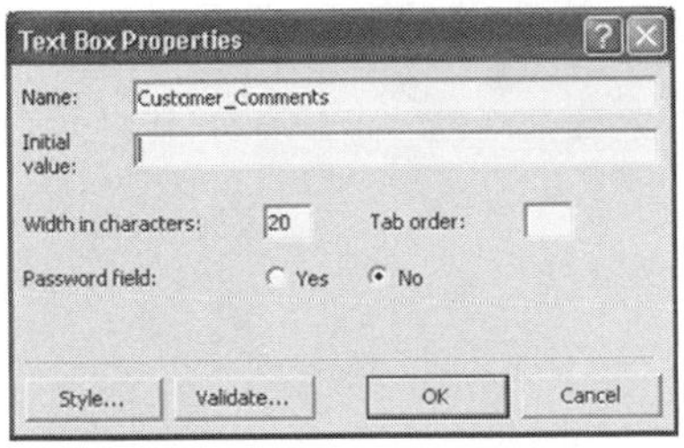

FIGURE 12.32 *You can set a default value and the size of the text box quickly.*

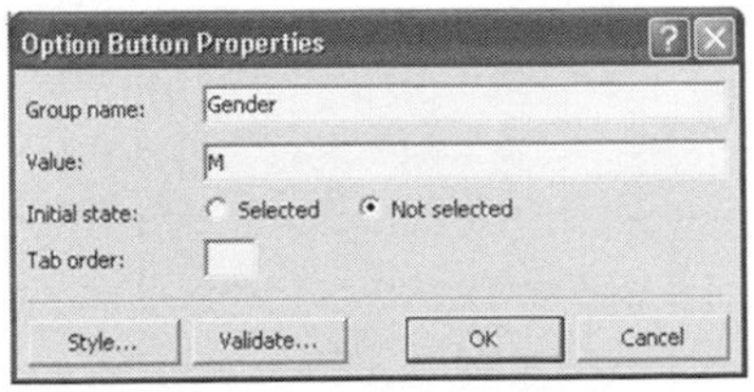

FIGURE 12.33 *Assign the radio button to a specific group and assign it a value.*

NOTE

You will see the form automation features of FrontPage illustrated extensively in the FrontPage project in Part II. However, you should note how you can facilitate the HTML you learned in Chapter 8 using the form functionality presented here. FrontPage presents you with an easy-to-use method for assigning specific parameters to your form elements. Take advantage of it!

Graphics, Files, and Hyperlinks

The final grouping of options on the Insert menu revolves around graphics, files, and hyperlinks. You can use these options to quickly insert additional files (such as sound, video, and graphics files; other documents; and hyperlinks) into your Web pages. These options are described in the following list.

◆ **Picture.** As you can see in Figure 12.34, you can insert all types of out-side documents using the Picture option. After you have inserted the files, you can further manipulate them using HTML, as you will see in the FrontPage project of Part II.

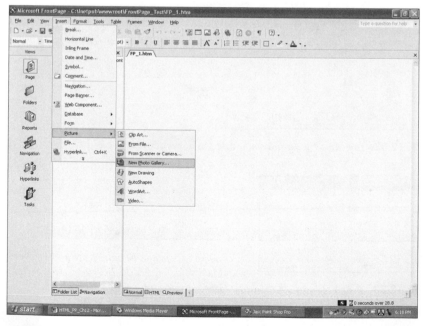

FIGURE 12.34 *You can insert a wide variety of multimedia into your Web pages using the Picture option.*

◆ **File.** This option brings up the familiar Windows Select File dialog box, which allows you to browse and insert a file into your Web page. Depending on the type of file you want to insert (such as a Microsoft Word document), FrontPage will convert the file so you can display it as a Web page.

◆ **Bookmark.** As you learned in Chapter 5, bookmarks are an easy, effective way to provide navigation within a single Web page. FrontPage makes it easy to insert bookmarks. First you define the bookmark (using the Hyperlink option—as shown in Figure 12.35), and then you select this option to actually pick your bookmark

◆ **Hyperlink.** No HTML editor would be complete if it didn't provide an easy way to insert a hyperlink. Figure 12.36 highlights the window that appears when you select this option, allowing you to easily set a hyperlink.

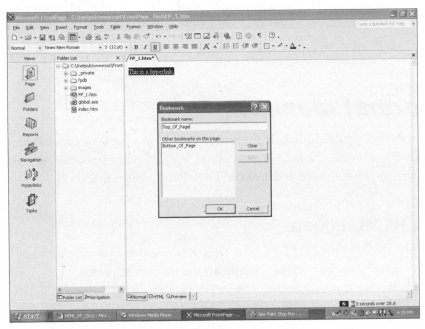

FIGURE 12.35 *Set your bookmarks in this window so you will be able to draw them directly from the list in the Hyperlink window by clicking on the Bookmark button (which will display a list of all the bookmarks you have defined).*

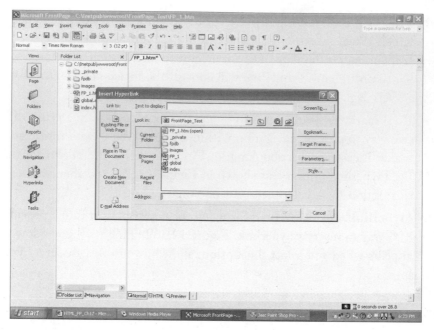

FIGURE 12.36 *Note the option to make your new hyperlink a bookmark or point to a target frame.*

The Format Menu

As in the Tools menu, much of the functionality presented in this menu is self-explanatory. However, I will discuss some Web-specific options here, and I'll (once again) present more detail in the FrontPage project in Part II.

Dynamic HTML Effects

Dynamic HTML (or DHTML for short) is a special subset of HTML that allows you to take far greater control over how text is presented in your Web pages, from exact placement to animation (such as text flying on and off the screen).

Although some DHTML effects are only supported in specific browsers, the functionality presented in FrontPage is generally fairly universal and can be applied across browsers.

NOTE

Unlike the FrontPage components, you can preview some of the DHTML effects directly in FrontPage. In other words, the effects don't require that you publish your pages to a server for them to be active.

Now take a look at an example of some DHTML.

1. Open your FP_1.htm page in your FrontPage_Test Web (if it's not still open).

2. Type the following text anywhere on your page: **This text will fly in from one side of the screen, and then exit to the other side.**

3. Highlight the text.

4. In the Format menu, select Dynamic HTML Effects. The DHTML toolbar will appear.

5. Select each option on the toolbar so your screen appears like Figure 12.37.

6. Close the DHTML toolbar by clicking on the Close button in the right-hand corner of the toolbar.

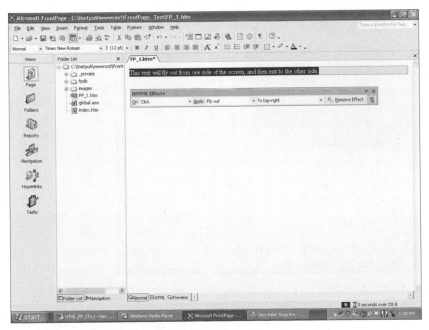

FIGURE 12.37 *Working with DHTML effects in FrontPage.*

7. At the bottom of the FrontPage window, click on the Preview tab. Your page will appear as it would in a browser.

8. Now click on the sentence you just typed and watch it fly off the page!

TIP

Admittedly, the DHTML effects made possible with FrontPage are fun to use, but remember to include them in moderation in your Web pages. Too much of anything—even neat DHTML effects—can distract from the message and content of your Web site.

Theme

FrontPage comes equipped with several predesigned templates or themes you can apply to your Web pages to give them a more visually attractive style. If you use these themes, you can carry them across your entire FrontPage Web to give it a uniform look. The following exercise will allow you to set a theme on the FP_1.htm page you have been working with in this chapter.

1. In the Format menu, select Theme. You will be presented with the Themes dialog box, as shown in Figure 12.38.

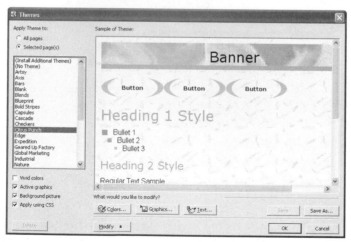

FIGURE 12.38 *Note the wide variety of themes that come prepackaged with FrontPage XP.*

2. Look through some of the themes until you find one that strikes you. For this example, I have used the Citrus Punch theme. You should notice a few things about the Themes window:

◆ You can apply the theme to the selected page (in this case, FP_1.htm) or all pages in your FrontPage Web.

◆ You can make your theme more visually dominant by toggling the Active Graphics and Background Picture options.

◆ You can utilize cascading style sheets (CSS) with the themes.

◆ You can further customize the colors, graphics, and text of the theme by clicking on the Modify button. (Doing so will display those three buttons as they are shown in Figure 12.38.)

3. After you have found a theme and set the options you desire for it (as discussed in the preceding bulleted list), click on OK. The theme will be applied to the FP_1.htm page.

 NOTE

When you use FrontPage to build the MuseToMusic Web site in Chapters 21 through 24, the Themes option (as well as the use of CSS) will be presented in more detail.

Page Transitions

The Page Transitions option is the last one I want to discuss in the Format menu. This option allows you to establish how a page will transition to another page when the user leaves it. Figure 12.39 highlights the Page Transitions dialog box and the configuration options it presents.

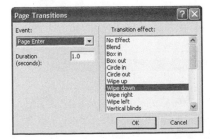

FIGURE 12.39 *You can set the duration of the transition effect and whether it will occur when you enter or exit the page or the entire site.*

If you've worked with Microsoft PowerPoint, you are familiar with slide transition effects. In essence, the Page Transition option works the same way; it allows you to specify how your Web pages will morph into other pages. When you build the Web site for the FrontPage project, you will see this option utilized.

The Tools Menu

I'm going to skip over the Tools menu for now because much of the functionality presented in it is beyond the scope of this chapter. (It includes working with the Visual Basic editor, setting macros, and integrating COM add-ins.) However, take a moment to notice that you will find the familiar Spelling and Thesaurus options in this menu. Also, note the Tools on the Web option, which will take you to a special Microsoft site for additional help with FrontPage, as shown in Figure 12.40.

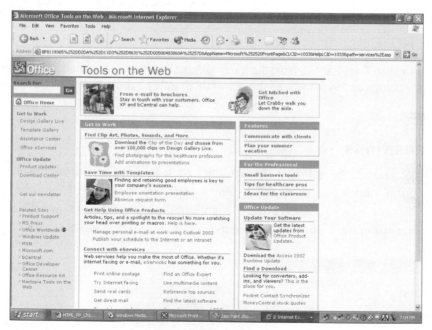

FIGURE 12.40 *Use the Tools on the Web option to gain access to up-to-the-minute online resources and other help for using FrontPage and applications in the MS Office suite.*

The Table Menu

Coding your tables using HTML can be tedious to say the least. As you learned in Chapter 6, there are many <TD> and <TR> tags in even the simplest tables. Multiply those tags by three or four for large, complex tables and add in the tags for special table formatting (such as cell width), and you're faced with some messy HTML.

If nothing else, using an HTML editor such as FrontPage is worthwhile for table creation and manipulation. Using the options in the Table menu, you can quickly build and format your tables and move on to more interesting aspects of your HTML.

Although most of the functionality within the Table menu is self-explanatory (especially if you are comfortable with the material presented in Chapter 6), you should work through the following exercise just to become familiar with the various windows and functionality presented in the Table menu options.

1. If it's not already open, go ahead and open your FrontPage_Test Web and then open the FP_1.htm page.

 NOTE

Don't worry if your FP_1.htm page looks different than what you'll see in the following figures. I encourage you to experiment with what you've learned in this chapter, so it's great if you've saved some of the work you've done in the previous sections, such as integrating DHTML effects and adding a template. The point of this chapter and the FP_1.htm page is to give you a scratchpad on which to learn about and experiment with the great functionality contained in FrontPage.

2. From the Table menu, select Insert, Table. The Insert Table window will appear. Set the parameters in this window to whatever values you want. The values illustrated in Figure 12.41 are just an example—you don't have to use them.

3. Click on OK. Your table will be inserted into your Web page, as shown in Figure 12.42.

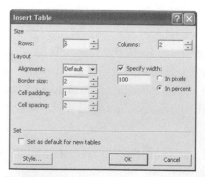

FIGURE 12.41 *Creating a table via the Table menu.*

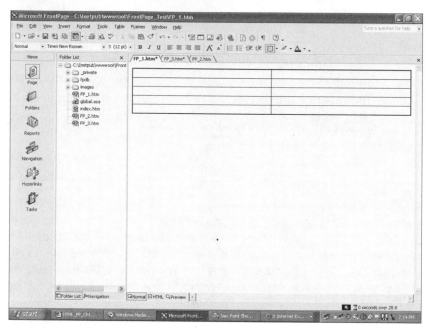

FIGURE 12.42 *You can create tables in seconds via the table creation options available in FrontPage.*

4. If you right-click within the table, a drop-down menu will display all kinds of additional table formatting options (see Figure 12.43). Note that many of these options are also presented in the Table menu once you have created a table.

That's all I'm going to say in this chapter about table creation in FrontPage. However, I suggest you experiment with the options presented in the Table menu to familiarize yourself with them and to further highlight what great timesaving features these options present to your Web design tasks.

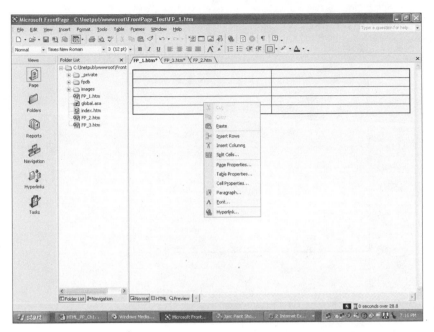

FIGURE 12.43 *Use these options to customize your table or make changes to it once it has been created.*

The Frames Menu

Just like when you're working with tables, the user-friendliness of FrontPage really shines when you work with frames. The frame design options presented in the application are incredibly easy to use and allow you to quickly customize various frame parameters.

The best way to illustrate this is to build some frame pages. I want to do that right now so you can learn how you can use FrontPage to enhance the frame skills you acquired in Chapter 7.

1. From the FrontPage File menu, select New, Page or Web.
2. Under the New from Template heading on the right side of the screen, click on Page Templates.
3. In the Page Templates dialog box, click on the Frames Pages tab, as shown in Figure 12.44. For this example, select the Contents option.
4. With the Contents option highlighted, click on OK. Your screen will look like Figure 12.45.

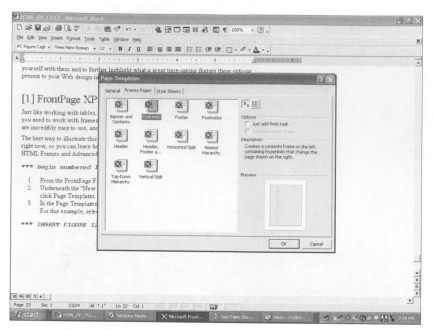

FIGURE 12.44 *For each option you select, you are given a description and preview of how that particular frame option will appear.*

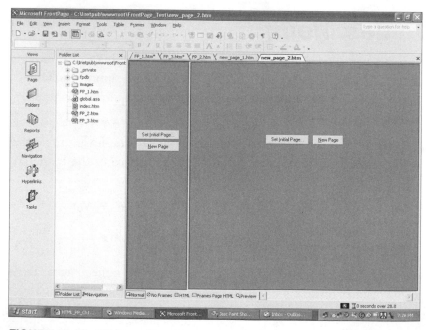

FIGURE 12.45 *When working with a frameset, you can either build pages from scratch (using the New Page option) or work from existing pages (using the Set Initial Page option).*

5. For this example, click on New Page for both the left and right frames. FrontPage will create blank pages.

6. Before you go any further, save these pages. In the File menu, select Save As to bring up the familiar Save As dialog box, which will include some additional functionality because you are working with a frameset (see Figure 12.46).

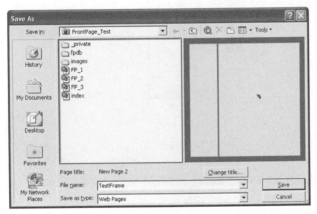

FIGURE 12.46 *Saving your frame pages in FrontPage.*

7. The first file name you need to provide is for the entire frameset. Name this TestFrame (as shown in Figure 12.46) and click on Save.

8. Next you will be asked to save the left frame page. (You can tell which frame you are saving because it will be highlighted in blue.) As shown in Figure 12.47, save this frame as TestFrame_Left.

9. Click on Save, and then repeat the process for the right frame. Save this frame as TestFrame_Right. You've now saved your entire frameset (TestFrame) and the two individual frames that comprise it (TestFrame_Left and TestFrame_Right).

10. At this point, you can apply all the skills you learned in Chapter 7 to the frames you just created. If you select Frame Properties from the Frames menu, you can set specific frame parameters, as illustrated in Figure 12.48.

11. Finally, notice the special tabs along the bottom of the FrontPage window: Normal, No Frames, HTML, Frames Page HTML, and Preview. Although some of these tabs (Normal, HTML, and Preview) are also present in Page view, the additional frame tabs allow you to view the

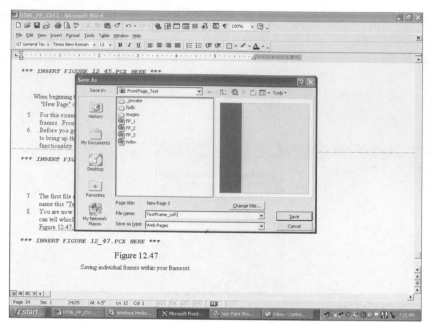

FIGURE 12.47 *Saving individual frames within your frameset.*

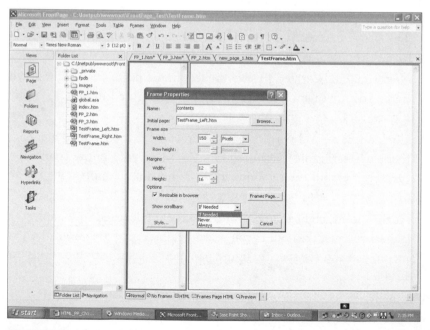

FIGURE 12.48 *In the Frame Properties dialog box, you can set when the scrollbars will be presented (if needed, never, or always).*

HTML code behind the frameset so you can customize it to your desire. Figure 12.49 shows the Frames Page HTML tab, where you can see how the entire TestFrame frameset is constructed and what pages (TestFrame_Left and TestFrame_Right) comprise it.

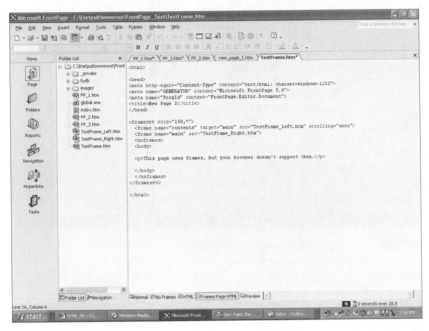

FIGURE 12.49 *You can quickly make changes to the frame structure via the Frames Page HTML tab.*

The Window and Help Menus

The Window and Help menus are standard for nearly all Windows applications. Use the Window menu to toggle between documents you have open at the same time.

The FrontPage XP Help menu is generally excellent; the included help files (as well as the available online help) can be extremely useful. Use the information contained in the help files to assist you in quickly locating answers. Figure 12.50 illustrates the friendly Office Assistant presenting possible answers to a question about using forms in a Web page. Note how the information returned is grouped into specific categories to aid in your search.

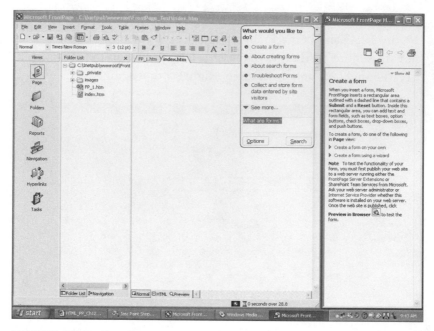

FIGURE 12.50 *FrontPage contains useful, detailed help files. Don't hesitate to take advantage of this information.*

Summary

This chapter has been a whirlwind introduction to FrontPage XP! Hopefully, you have gained some idea (and had your interest piqued) about how using an HTML editor such as FrontPage can really enhance the HTML coding skills you learned in Chapters 1 through 11. As I have stated repeatedly throughout this chapter, you will see FrontPage in action in the third project of Part II. Also, you will get a chance to see how the more basic HTML functionality is presented, as well as the advanced stuff (such as frames, DHTML, and the Database Results Wizard). Although you are free to use any development environment to code your HTML, I strongly encourage you to consider an editor like FrontPage if for no other reason than it can save you much time on the tedious and boring work and allow you to put more of your energy into the fun stuff!

PART II

Applied HTML: Coding Professional Web Sites

Now that you have an HTML skill set from which to work, you can apply those skills toward the creation of professional Web sites; however, there are other critical issues that you must consider if you want your Web sites to be really successful. Understanding and facilitating business processes and procedures (again, no matter what that business or process/procedure might be) is a central reason why technology—not just Web sites—has risen to such a prominent level in organizations of all types and purposes. As you will see in each of the first three projects, skillful recognition of this level of importance that technology plays in a business process/procedure can greatly benefit your Web design. From a small business to a nonprofit, as well as designing a site with an HTML editor, you will walk through the entire design process, from pre-implementation concerns to the final coding of the site, all along paying special attention to customer usability issues and other customer relationship management (CRM) concerns. In the fourth project, you will see how the integration of a database (in this case, Microsoft SQL Server 2000) can bring new levels of power and functionality to your Web design.

Project 1

The Small Business Web Site

Chapter 13

The first of the four projects you'll work with in this section of the book centers on the MuseToMusic CD Shop. MuseToMusic (or MTM for short) has been in operation for a little more than five years and has remained the only music store in a small college town. The owners of the store are both graduates of the local college and are very familiar with not only the town, but also the store's typical clientele. Even though the town is within driving distance of a medium-sized metropolitan area, MTM has managed to remain a successful business because of its reputation with the local community. This reputation has been strengthened by the store's desire to promote and encourage the local music scene by sponsoring many in-store concerts and aggressively promoting local bands by featuring their CDs with special pricing and large in-store displays.

Although e-commerce and the ability to sell items on the Web are of interest to the store, this is really a secondary level of importance in the design of the MTM Web site. The storeowners have come to you, as a well-respected Web developer, to build a site that will allow them to take their promotion of the local music community to the next level. They would like to develop into a central point of contact for the local bands by offering a place (the Web site) for anyone—regardless of their location—to find out about the music being performed and recorded in this small town.

 NOTE

As with all of the projects developed in this section of the book, the MuseToMusic store is a complete product of this author's imagination. The people, places, and events described in this project, as well as in all others in this book, are completely fictitious. Still, an effort has been made to keep the projects as realistic as possible and to present you with projects that include real-world problems you might be asked to help solve by developing a Web site.

MuseToMusic Project Outline

As I move through all of the projects discussed in Part II, each of the project chapters will follow a similar format. Specifically, each project will be broken into the following general chapters:

1. The first chapter of each project will, like this one, provide an introduction to the project, describe the events leading up to the design of the Web site, and provide background information on the fictitious company and their requirements for a Web site.

2. The second chapter will address the specific process issues of the Web site itself. Focusing on the overall business process requirements (such as navigation structure, major areas of content, and administrative issues), this chapter will essentially set the stage for the actual design and discussion of the Web project.

3. In the third chapter of each project, the focus will shift to specific design issues and how major functional components of a Web site will be targeted to address specific business concerns. Specifically, this chapter will discuss the various issues of customer relationship management (CRM), including defining customers, mapping business processes to the Web, allowing customers to customize their experiences on the site, keeping customers interested, and getting them to return.

4. Finally, in the fourth chapter of each project, the focus will shift to highlighting how you can actually use HTML (or the Web site itself) to meet each of the requirements discussed in the second and third chapters of each project. In these implementation chapters, you will see how HTML can provide the instruments to actually satisfy the business/process requirements set forth in the earlier chapters. Moreover, in this chapter you will see actual HTML examples of how this is done, as well as tips and hints for how to effectively implement similar solutions in your own projects.

 NOTE

The fourth project (devoted to SQL Server 2000) will differ in its approach, and not follow the format listed here.

THE FOCUS ON CRM AND CUSTOMER DEFINITION

Look at any technology magazine or industry trade rag, and you will be hard-pressed to find one that doesn't mention customer relationship management at least once in each issue or publication. Why all the interest? As the Web becomes more ubiquitous in our lives, it has become obvious that for a company or organization's Web site to be a truly successful component of its overall infrastructure, the Web site must be a viable and logical extension of the infrastructure. If the fall of the dot coms taught us anything, it was that a Web site cannot and should not be an end to itself. In other words, Web sites that are simply placed into existence so an organization can have a Web presence are usually failures. This is because such Web sites are like a human's appendix—they serve no purpose, and they only draw attention when something goes wrong! When your appendix gets inflamed, it is usually removed. If you carry that analogy over to a Web site, the result is the same. The Web site, after at best doing absolutely nothing or at worst wasting valuable company resources, is removed.

Enter CRM. Again, given the fact that the Web is here to stay, it makes sense to view a Web site as a component of a company's infrastructure. Rather than being an appendix that serves no useful purpose, the Web site should integrate with the organization's larger processes and be an essential component to the successful operation of those processes. CRM can be seen as a process in and of itself, but one that draws on all processes of an organization to be successful. A well-designed Web site can be an incredibly useful tool when it comes to CRM because it allows a company to communicate with its customers (and vice versa) in ways that were unthinkable in the days before the Web. From offering 24/7/365 information access to allowing customers to build a sense of identity and relationship with a company, Web sites can be the critical bridge over the otherwise huge chasm that separates a company (regardless of its size) from a personal relationship with its customers.

Finally, as you will see in each of these projects, the use of the word "customer" can take on various connotations depending on the type of organization under discussion. For example, for the elementary school Web site developed in the second project, the customers are teachers, students, and parents. However, regardless of the target audience, the CRM principles under discussion apply and can be used (as you will see) as a very effective method of larger Web site design.

MuseToMusic Process Issues

As I mentioned at the beginning of the chapter, the MTM storeowners have a real interest in promoting the local music scene and using their Web site as a tool to further highlight and draw attention to the great musicians within the community.

MUSETOMUSIC WEB SITE: PROJECT INTRODUCTION   Chapter 13   **275**

Each of the following sections describes the core process issues you need to address prior to writing the first line of HTML. This type of pre-implementation thinking is critical to ensure that the final product—the Web site—meets the desired requirements and fits into the larger infrastructure of the company/organization.

MuseToMusic Primary Goals

The MTM storeowners have several specific goals for the Web site. These issues will be discussed specifically and analyzed in Chapter 14, "MuseToMusic Web Site: Identifying Process Goals for the Commercial Site," but the following list provides an overview.

◆ First and foremost, the MTM Web site should be a mechanism for drawing attention to the local music scene. The storeowners have been long-time, aggressive proponents of local musicians, and they want to give a wider voice to the sounds being produced by these groups. Some initial ideas for presenting the local bands include placing short audio clips of their music on the site, providing group bios (including photographs), and allowing interested visitors to contact the bands (via the MTM site).

◆ In addition to its interest in promoting local bands, MTM has also built a reputation on being a great source for helping to locate rare or otherwise hard-to-find CDs. The store has had good luck utilizing a mail-order catalog, but this has become prohibitively expensive.

◆ Moreover, the Web site would allow a much greater number of potential customers to reach the store. To accomplish this goal, the MTM site should have a section devoted to this CD locator aspect of the business and allow interested customers to purchase these CDs via the site.

◆ The fourth major goal of the MTM site is really a combination of the first two. That is, the storeowners want the site to be a true music portal—a site music lovers can set as their home page, where they can find local and national music news, music updates, a place to purchase CDs, and, of course, a first look at new local bands.

NOTE

Web portals are also a very hot topic in today's Web/e-commerce industry. A Web portal is essentially a one-stop location for a variety of customer interests. You can think of Yahoo! and other similar sites as portals because they serve as gateways to a variety of information and other sites. Businesses and organizations are turning to portal design methodology to help generate customer interest and ideally to encourage customers to view the site as a launching pad for exploring interests related to those of the business/organization. In the case of the MTM Web site, it can be a portal to all things music, but it will act as a central location for accessing various areas of interest to music lovers, such as music updates, musician bios, information on new acts, and so on.

MuseToMusic Design Issues

The design issues for both the MuseToMusic Web site as well as the nonprofit site are all factors of CRM, and I will discuss them under that context in the specific design chapter for each project. You can think of those chapters and the issues they discuss as a procedural roadmap to the actual Web site that you will construct. Moreover, these issues will ensure that the final Web site is an integral component of the organization's function, and that it is not (as mentioned above) an otherwise useless "appendix" that serves no real purpose.

Defining the Audience

Audience definition is a major goal of any Web site, and the MTM site is no exception. Like the other projects discussed in this book, the MTM site will address different customers—casual music fans, dedicated music collectors, promoters, and other musicians. The site must clearly address each of these audience members individually, but at the same time be seen as a general music portal, serving the interests of all customers.

Defining Internal Business Processes

For any Web site to be successful, it must naturally integrate into the larger operational processes of the business/organization that it serves. In the case of MTM, there are specific business processes the storeowners want to facilitate via the use of the site.

◆ Ordering hard-to-find CDs

◆ Promoting the local music scene

◆ Advertising the store itself

◆ Tracking store inventory

The storeowners have been facilitating each of these processes using a pen and paper, but with differing results. As I mentioned, the promotion of the local music scene can be taken to a new level entirely by communicating via the Web. Moreover, ordering hard-to-find CDs can be increased exponentially by allowing customers from literally the entire world to order. But for each of these processes to be effectively mapped to the Web, the process must be clearly defined. The process design chapter for the MTM site (Chapter 15) will do just that.

Personalizing the Customer Experience

A central component of CRM is customizing the user experience or allowing visitors to personalize your site to suit their tastes. You can do this in a variety of ways, from allowing visitors to change the physical appearance of the site (allowing them to change the background and foreground colors, customize navigation menu preferences, and so on) to allowing customers to view a complete record of their visits (such as previous order history). By personalizing the site, customers will feel a sense of ownership. This can be invaluable if the site is to be a portal (like the MTM site wishes to be) because it encourages visitors to return often and perhaps make the site their home page—a place they visit every day when they first log on to the Web. Personalization and the methods used to accomplish it are a major (if not *the* major) issue of CRM. That said, this issue will take precedence in the design chapter of each project and will serve as a general framework for all CRM discussion.

The storeowners want to personalize the MTM site in a variety of ways.

◆ The site should allow audiophiles—especially those interested in the hard-to-find CD locator service that the store advertises as its strong point—the ability to join special mailing lists or otherwise be notified when a special selection becomes available.

◆ The site should allow frequent visitors the ability to add special links of interest so they can turn the site into their own personal music portal. For example, the site should have sections where visitors can add custom links to music-related Web sites, thus providing them a one-stop location for accessing all their interests.

◆ The site should allow all visitors the ability to view their music log. This might include all CDs they have ordered, a list of music-related sites they have visited, and so on. This component of CRM is critical because it ensures that customers have the ability to review all previous transactions (purchases or otherwise) on the site. Pre-, point-of-, and post-sale issues will all be addressed here. Note that customers don't have to buy something for this design issue to be important; as indicated earlier, customers should be able to view all of their prior transactions on the site, even if that includes simply reviewing the information or sections of the site they have previously accessed.

NOTE

In addition to the three major design issues described in the preceding sections, there are other CRM-related issues that you need to consider—for example, how the information and functionality presented on the site integrates with other technologies, such as the ability to download information from the site to a PDA via the use of an AvantGo channel. These and other related issues will be discussed in the design issues chapter for each project.

Implementing the MuseToMusic Web Site

The goal of each project is to see how these process and design requirements are actually facilitated via the use of HTML in a Web site. For the MTM Web site, this will involve a portal design, the use of multimedia technology (for example, placing short audio clips of local bands on the site), and various CRM issues, as described previously.

Chapter 16, "MuseToMusic Web Site: Building the Solution," will discuss all of these issues for the MTM site by highlighting actual HTML functionality as well as related Web technologies that will allow the process and design requirements to be fulfilled via the site.

It is now time to dig in to the specifics of the MTM site. The first step is to closely examine all of the process requirements, which will drive the overall functionality by defining two major components—clear definitions of the audience and the content that will be presented on the site.

 CAUTION

Regardless of the size of the Web site in question, you must not overlook the critical issues of change control and administration. Specifically, once the site is in operation, there must be a clearly defined and closely followed mechanism for making changes to the site, either in terms of content or operational functionality. Obviously, this involves clearly defining administrative issues so that those charged with maintaining the site understand the site in its own technical terms, as well as it how it integrates and facilitates larger company processes and procedures. I will discuss these change control issues throughout the project development and implementation.

Chapter 14

MuseToMusic Web Site: Identifying Process Goals for the Commercial Site

If there was one lesson to be learned from the dot com bust, it was that a Web site is not just a superficial, fancy add-on to an organization's business operations. Although it is possible for a Web site to serve an otherwise useless purpose, if you want to use it as a functional business tool, a Web site requires quite a bit of attention.

It's important to note, though, that "requires quite a bit of attention" does not imply that the site must be a major consumer of resources, be they manpower or time. However, if the site is to be effective, it must from the outset be considered a critical, functional component of your operation—not an appendage that gets no attention until it becomes infected and needs to be removed.

The MuseToMusic storeowners need and want their Web site to serve as a critical, viable business tool. Specifically, they want the site to facilitate the following process goals:

◆ The store has always supported the local music scene by allowing bands to use their location as a promotional venue for in-store performances, CD signings, and so on. That said, the storeowners would like to continue to facilitate this free promotion by giving local bands the opportunity to use Web space to advertise upcoming performances, provide band bios and short audio clips of their music, and so on.

◆ In addition to being a strong support of local acts, the store has also built a reputation as a great resource for locating hard-to-find music. The owners would like to take this service to the Web by allowing customers to search the store inventory for existing material, place special orders for hard-to-find CDs, and generally have access to a traditional online store. (In other words, they want to add an e-commerce component to their existing brick-and-mortar operation.)

◆ The final goal is somewhat nebulous but still a reflection of why the storeowners got into the business of selling music in the first place: They want the site to be an overarching resource for all things music. Are you looking for a biography on a particular performer? Are you interested in learning more about a particular genre of music, but you don't know where to start? Would you be willing to moderate an online discussion about a particular issue of interest in the world of popular music? In essence, the storeowners want to build off the inherent community aspect of the Web to enrich their customers' understanding, interest, and appreciation of music. They can accomplish this via the larger portal design concept, which I introduced in the last chapter and will discuss in more detail in the next chapter.

NOTE

You will notice that this chapter is shorter and might seem less involved than its counterpart in the Greenlawn School project (Chapter 18). There are two things to note about this. First, the non-profit sites at this level of design can be more complicated in their design structure because they must often serve a wider audience and address a greater number of issues internal to the organization in question. However, you should not infer that the process goals being facilitated via the MuseToMusic site are any less complicated or less important than the goals for the Greenlawn site. Still, the process goals of the MuseToMusic site might be more straightforward and business-typical, thus the shorter amount of space required to discuss them.

Process Goal: Promoting the Local Music Scene

When you first met with the storeowners to discuss building a Web site, it so happened that there was an in-store concert that afternoon for a local band. You knew this was going to be happening—the storeowners had asked you to come down and check it out prior to your meeting. As you enjoyed the sounds of the local band, you noticed a few important things about the overall scene in the store.

NOTE

As with the other projects, I'm asking you to role-play and pretend you are the Web developer working with the company and that you have met the people involved, attended design meetings, and so on.

1. Prior to the performance, you noticed many patrons asking about the band, either among themselves or to the storeowners. To help promote interest, the storeowners had a display of the band's CDs conspicuously placed at the store entrance, as well as at the counter.

2. As the band performed, customers walked around the store and browsed for music. You overheard at least three specific customers say something to the effect of, "Hey, I really like this music—they remind of [some other band]."

3. Finally, after the band finished performing, several customers waited for autographs and asked about future performances. The band had prepared paper flyers listing upcoming performances. You noticed, however, that only the name of the venue and the time was listed next to each date.

During your subsequent meeting with the storeowners, you elaborated on each of your observations with regard to how a well-designed Web site could build on each of these points (with specific reference to the goal of promoting the local music scene).

1. Obviously, there are few more effective ways to generate interest in a music CD than to perform that music live on stage. The storeowners did a good job of making sure the band's CDs were readily stocked and posted in plain view. However, you noted that the owners could enhance this in-store promotion of the band's recorded music by

   ◆ Placing a link on the Web site's home page to an in-store performances page listing upcoming events.

   ◆ Placing a link to the band's personal Web page on the store's page for the band's performance. Critically, the performance page should also include links to the online store so customers can purchase the band's CDs online.

   ◆ Placing links to similar bands that might also interest the customer. These links would be something along the lines of, "If you like [this band], you might also like…." The pages for the similar bands would then include the same sublinks as the page for the first band (such as links to the online store).

NOTE

The points listed here fall within the design principles of CRM with regard to an online store. You will be presented with more specific information on the CRM aspects of the MuseToMusic Web site in Chapter 15, "MuseToMusic Web Site: Addressing Customer Usability Issues."

2. The ability to cross-sell is highly desirable in any sales promotion, and the MuseToMusic Web site is no exception. As noted earlier, you indicated to the storeowners that they could capitalize on a local band's popularity by also displaying CDs by additional bands (both local and national acts). Moreover, they could carry this functionality over to the Web site, where they could cross-sell. Of course, direct links to the online store would be present on all pages that list information on any band.

3. Finally, you made sure to reiterate to the storeowners that they should take full advantage of how easy it is to disseminate large amounts of detailed information via the Web. For example, the band that was performing the day you went to the store had a simple flyer that only listed their upcoming performances with the venue, date, and time. This is a good start, but the same information could be presented on the Web along with directions to the venue, specific information about the venue (such as whether it is a 21-and-older club), and direct links to online ticket vendors.

Figure 14.1 highlights a news update about a local band, within the larger MuseToMusic site, illustrating how each of these points is being facilitated via the Web.

This particular process goal can be best summarized by this statement: You can make more people aware of more information by having a well-designed Web page than you can by using any other information-dissemination mechanism. In Chapter 15, you will learn about specific customer-usability issues with regard to how you present this kind of information on the MuseToMusic site. For now, however, be sure to note how you can enhance one business process goal—in this case, the promotion of local bands—to facilitate additional process goals (for example, providing links from a band's Web page to the online store, further enabling the e-commerce component of the site).

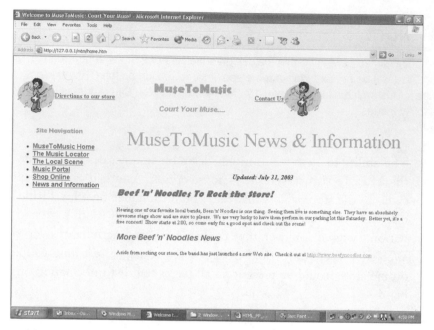

FIGURE 14.1 *Far more effective than a paper flyer, a well-designed Web page can give interested customers complete information on a band and provide tremendous cross-selling opportunities for the store.*

Process Goal: Facilitating the Music Locator Service via the Web

On the day you met with the storeowners during the in-store performance, you also had the opportunity to observe a customer who had come into the store wanting to find a special import-only CD by one of his favorite bands. Again, MuseToMusic has built a reputation in the local community by taking the time and having the resources available to find those hard-to-find CDs.

As you watched the exchange between the customer and one of the sales clerks, you noticed the following points:

◆ The first step in this particular business interaction was for the customer to complete a somewhat detailed product information form. On this (paper) form, the customer listed his name, address, and other pertinent contact information. Then he was asked to provide as much information as he could about the CD he was looking for, including the artist, the title, the label it was recorded on, and the year it was recorded.

◆ Next, the clerk took this information and perused an updated listing of music currently available on both domestic and international labels. (Such a listing, available in most music stores, is updated weekly by various cataloging organizations.) Given the size of these listings and the often limited information provided by the customer, these searches can take several minutes. Although customers are under no obligation to wait, they usually do because they want to know whether the CD they are interested in can be found.

◆ In this particular case, the CD was available. As luck would have it, the artist was one that the band performing in the store had listed as one of their major influences. (You found this out later when you talked to the drummer in the band.)

There are many things going on in this particular business interaction that could be enhanced via the Web. Once again, you noted these observations, and when you met with the storeowners, you gave the following suggestions with regard to the goal of enhancing their music locator service.

1. Why not automate this information-gathering process via a Web form (and thus Web-enable the entire music locator service)? Figure 14.2

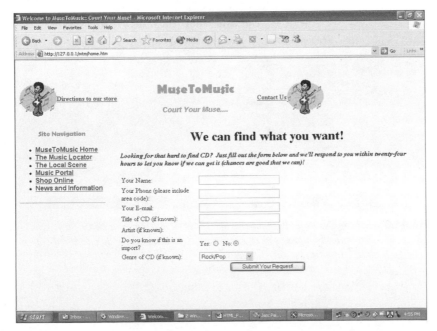

FIGURE 14.2 *Don't miss opportunities to use the Web to gather information via simple forms.*

highlights what this form might look like. (You will build this form in a later chapter of this project.) Customers can complete the form at their convenience at any time, day or night—truly one of the great benefits of any e-commerce shop.

2. Why not build a database of information collected from these forms to present additional products of interest to customers based on the types of music they search for? Again, this type of cross-selling can be greatly enhanced via the Web. You could, for example, present similar genres of music to customers based on the information they enter on the Web search form. Figure 14.3 highlights one of the menu options on the form. Assuming you capture this type of information, you could search the database that stores these records and provide the customer with similar music that matches this menu category.

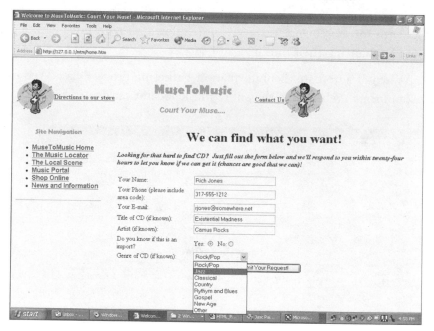

FIGURE 14.3 *Although you could ask for this specific information on a paper form, capturing it electronically allows you to categorize and subsequently do advanced searches to match specific customer interests.*

3. Related to the type of advanced searching mentioned a moment ago, once the form is submitted, you could immediately present links to other artists who customers might like based on the information they entered on the form. This also ties into the final benefit of facilitating this functionality via the Web—it is simply more efficient. The form can be submitted for immediate processing; the customer submits his order and moves on to other areas of the site.

Process Goal: Building a True Music Portal

This final process goal is really a culmination of all functions of the Web site, and it can be thought of as the ideology behind the total Web design.

Although you will see a more extended discussion of the customer-usability benefits of the portal design in the next chapter (as well as actually seeing it in action in Chapter 16, "MuseToMusic Web Site: Building the Solution"), it is important to note here the larger, tangible business process goals of utilizing a portal concept.

◆ Customers will be more inclined to see the MuseToMusic site as one that caters to their passion for music, not just with regard to purchasing music, but also with regard to online discussions forums and so on. The storeowners are adamant about keeping the local community informed about music (especially local bands), and they want the site to be an extension of this desire to deliver timely, accurate music information.

◆ The portal will allow customers to customize their online experience with MuseToMusic by having a site that is a reflection of their own personal interests. For example, customers will be able to have information that is based on their specific interests presented to them. Although some of this will come from their previous order history, they will also be able to choose to be notified when an artist they are interested in releases a new CD, for example.

◆ Finally, the portal allows the storeowners' many different business goals (such as promotion of local bands and provision of a music locator service and an online discussion forum for music lovers) to be presented in one place. Most important, the inherent ability of the Web to provide links to related items of interest will present customers with a much wider, comprehensive view of how their musical interests fit together. In turn, this will benefit the store by providing tremendous cross-selling opportunities. (For example, a customer might read about a local band and see links to related items on the same page. Each of these items would also include a direct link to the online store, as well as links to discussion forums and so on.) Figure 14.4 highlights a link to an external Web site; note, however, how the use of a frameset allows the visitor to view this information but still remain within the comfortable confines of the MuseToMusic Web site.

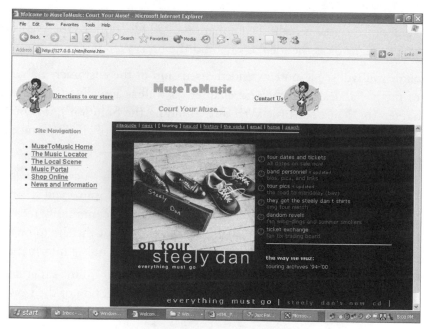

FIGURE 14.4 *Using the hyperlink capabilities of the Web, the MuseToMusic customers will never be more than one link away from a related item of interest—or more than one link away from the online store and an order form!*

NOTE

Note again that you will revisit the MuseToMusic Web (and this entire design process) in Chapters 21 through 24, when you build the site using FrontPage XP. You will still apply the portal concept, but you will see how you can further enhance it (and thus how you can enhance other site functionality) by using an HTML editor such as FrontPage XP.

Summary

This short chapter introduced you to the larger business goals of the MuseToMusic store and how the storeowners want to facilitate these goals via the Web site. As the site designer, you must be aware of these goals and be savvy enough to pick up on how technology (in this case, a Web site) can facilitate these business operations to further the successful business processes of the organization in question. In the case of the MuseToMusic store, the three specific goals of the company (promoting the local music scene, providing a locator service for hard-to-find music, and providing customers with a true music portal) can all be greatly enhanced by a well-designed Web site. The next chapter will look at specific customer-usability issues involving each of these goals, and how the Web facilitates them.

Chapter 15

As you learned in the previous chapter, the MuseToMusic storeowners have specific business goals they'd like to address with the store's Web site. Many of these revolve around the idea of a Web portal, so that the Web site will be seen not only as a reflection of the store itself, but as a current, dynamic, one-stop location for information on the local music scene.

Although a full discussion of Web portal design is beyond the scope of this book, there are nevertheless specific customer usability issues that should be addressed in relation to the MuseToMusic site, and thus other sites of this nature (portals) in general. This chapter will focus on these issues by specifically looking at

◆ **Providing optimal site navigation.** The best Web sites are those with conspicuous, intuitive navigation. The MuseToMusic Web site will need to address navigation issues by allowing direct access to information (both internal and external to the site) and making that information accessible at any time.

◆ **Personalizing the Web experience.** A central design concept of a Web portal is that it is user-centric. That is, in a portal, users are often allowed (indeed, required) to customize their experience so that the information presented to them is unique. To achieve this level of functionality, the portal component of the MuseToMusic site must address the entire customer experience, from allowing the development of a custom user profile to allowing the display (and related content manipulation based on that display) of previous order history.

◆ **Developing an online shopping cart.** As I discussed in the last chapter, the MuseToMusic site needs to have an online shopping cart or e-commerce component. The store has built a reputation as a solid resource for locating hard-to-find music, and the storeowners would like to extend this service via the Web site to reach a much larger audience. However, as you will see outlined in this chapter, a successful online shopping cart goes beyond the actual mechanism for placing an order. Rather, issues such as post-order customer support and larger, seamless integration of the cart with the entire site are requirements for this functionality.

Each of these points could be a book in itself! Still, the information presented in this chapter for each item should give you a good understanding of the underlying complexity of customer usability issues and ideally lead you to understand that the HTML you code for a site needs to consider these larger business-process issues—both in its actual functionality and in its design—for the resulting Web site to be the most representative, functional tool for the organization in question.

 NOTE

You might find it interesting to consider at this point how the use of an HTML editing tool such as FrontPage can further enhance or facilitate your meeting all these customer usability requirements. Chapters 21 through 24 will revisit the MuseToMusic site to discuss how it could be constructed using FrontPage. Furthermore, Chapter 23, "MuseToMusic Web Site with FrontPage XP: Addressing Customer Usability Issues," can be considered a mirror of this chapter because it covers the same issues. My intention in building the MuseToMusic site with and without the use of an HTML editor is to demonstrate how the design (including customer usability issues) and implementation would differ if you use the extra features that a tool such as FrontPage provides. So even if you are reading the chapters in this book sequentially, you might consider taking a look at Chapter 23 after you read this chapter to get an idea of how some of the issues presented here (as well as in Chapter 14) are handled differently when the advanced functionality and extra HTML toolsets of, for example, FrontPage are available to you.

Optimal Site Navigation

It's an obvious fact: When you really want to find something, you want to find it right now. Although you might be willing to put up with some amount of digging to get the information you need, you will quickly grow impatient if you are forced to slog through page after page of useless or unrelated information to find what you need.

Surprisingly, many Web designers have not learned this critical customer usability issue, and thus they give very little attention to the overall navigation schemes of their sites. Instead of having well-placed, conspicuous links to all the site content (either through a well-designed menu system or a clear image map placed on the site home page), many site designers make navigation a second thought and thus bury the most useful information deep within the Web site.

Obviously, this problem becomes paramount when your site is intended to help facilitate the sale or distribution of a product. Think about it—if your customers can't find the product they are looking for on your site (or if the order process is convoluted and non-intuitive, as you will see later in this chapter), they will quickly go somewhere else. One of the easiest things you can do to prevent this is to make sure your entire site has a clear navigation structure so all of your site content is clearly represented and can be accessed easily—not just from the home page, but also from each page on the site.

The following sections will look at some of the customer usability issues involved in site navigation, specifically as they relate to the MuseToMusic site.

CAUTION

It is critical that your site navigation extend beyond your home page. Too often a Web site will include only a comprehensive navigation tool on the home page. This means that as you move deeper into the site, you are forced to return to the home page to access other information on the site. You will explore this issue in more detail later in this chapter. Also, note the use of the navigation tool that is developed in Chapter 24 when the MuseToMusic site is constructed with FrontPage.

Readily Available Product Information

Successful navigation extends beyond just the e-commerce component of a site— that is, if you are thinking of a product as something to sell, as opposed to just information. However, in the case of the MuseToMusic site, the product indeed extends beyond the hard-to-find music that the store has built a reputation on providing. When considering the portal component of the site, the product really does include information because a visiting customer might be just as interested in knowing when a particular local band is next scheduled to perform as they are in purchasing a CD.

That said, easy accessibility to all the products made available by the Web site is an absolutely critical requirement. This does not have to be an overly complicated or extensive system. As shown in Figure 15.1, a simple table that shows on each page of the site and includes links to major products and functionality for the site will satisfy this requirement.

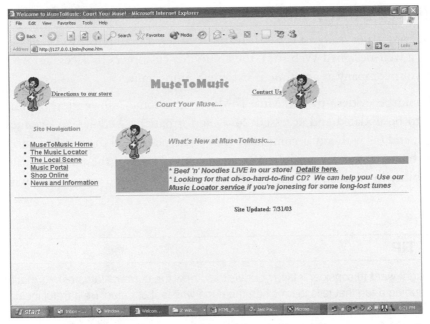

FIGURE 15.1 *A simple navigation structure still ensures constant accessibility to critical areas of your Web site.*

In addition to having the navigation bar present on each page, you also need to ensure that full information about your product (again, using a very general definition of the word *product)* is constantly available. Specifically, you should keep in mind the following points:

◆ A concise yet complete description of the product in question should be posted as conspicuously as the actual link to the product. Note in Figure 15.1 the description of the page (in this case, information on upcoming performances by local bands) that details what the page is, how often it is updated, how the information is gathered for posting, and so on.

◆ You should highlight how the product in question is related to other products or information on your page. As you can also see in Figure 15.1, the displayed page also provides direct links to other pages devoted to the band being discussed. This ability to provide quick links to related information is one of the most natural (and powerful) uses of hyperlinks and Web technology in general. Don't overlook it when you are constructing Web sites of any kind—not just those revolving around e-commerce.

Accessibility at Any Time

Although it is not really an HTML feature (rather, it is an effective by-product of having a well-designed Web site), the ability for customers to access information about your company at any time is extremely important.

As should be evident by the MuseToMusic site, some information on this site needs to be updated and accessed 24/7. Performance schedules and venues can change, and (as with any e-commerce site) some people do their online shopping at odd hours of the day or night. Keeping in mind both of these issues, real-time accessibility to products and information is critical when you are working with the Web.

 TIP

You might want to consider letting your visitors know the current status of information by including a tag that tells them when the page was last updated. Be careful including such information, though. If you choose to let visitors know when information is updated, be sure you update your update, so to speak. Visitors will quickly turn away from your site if they see a tag that shows the last update was several months (or years) ago.

Full Site Search

The ability to do a full site search is another important element of your overall site navigation. Although you might think you have designed the perfect site navigation bar and you have all your information accessible in an intuitive way, there will always be visitors to your site who come at your information from a different angle and thus manage to get outside of your navigation scheme. Put simply, they get lost within your site and subsequently can't find the information they need.

One way around this is to provide a full site-search tool on your Web site. Although you can't do this with straight HTML—you will need to employ some type of script or special Web tool—it is nevertheless something you need to consider. Many of these search tools are not difficult to install, and the benefits they bring far outweigh the effort involved in installing them.

NOTE

As you will see in Chapter 24, "MuseToMusic Web Site with FrontPage XP: Building the Solution," FrontPage includes a search tool that you can install automatically when you design your site (although it comes with certain limitations, as you will learn in that chapter). Moreover, some Web servers have indexing and search tools built into them or as plug-in components. (Microsoft IIS used in conjunction with Microsoft Index Server is one such example.) If you don't (or aren't able to) build a search tool into your actual HTML code, you should consider these other options. Also, depending on where you have your site hosted, your Internet presence provider might be able to provide indexing or search capabilities for your site.

Accessible Third-Party Information

For the MuseToMusic site, links to third-party information are very important. As you will read more about in the portal discussion in this chapter, the store-owners want their site to be seen as a one-stop resource for all the musical interests of their local community. Certainly a major component of this is providing Web space to local bands so they can advertise themselves and draw interest in their performances.

Figure 15.2 illustrates how you can use a frameset to open the outside information within the MuseToMusic site while still retaining the initial site navigation structure.

Providing links to outside Web sites in this fashion is becoming increasingly common. Larger Web initiatives in the business-to-business (B2B) realm increasingly focus on this information relationship by allowing related companies to interact with each other. This is a benefit to the companies because they are assured a greater overall audience. Moreover, it benefits customers because they can find everything they are looking for in one place. Obviously, you should use caution when linking to a competitor's site, for example. Generally, though, this strategy is successful and can add tremendous value to the usability factor of your site as viewed by your customers.

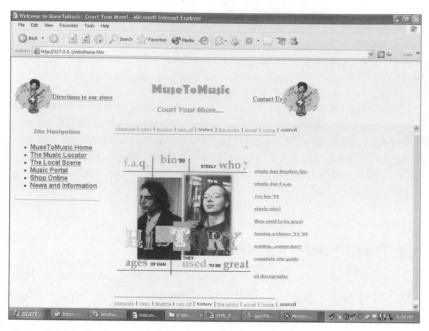

FIGURE 15.2 *Third-party links can open within a frameset, allowing visitors to remain within your site proper.*

Personalized Customer Experience: The Web Portal

As I mentioned numerous times in this chapter, the MuseToMusic Web site strives to be a true Web portal.

The definition of the term *portal* as provided at Webopedia.com (http://www.webopedia.com) is as follows:

> **Web portal:** Commonly referred to as simply a *portal*, a Web site or service that offers a broad array of resources and services, such as e-mail, forums, search engines and online shopping malls. The first Web portals were online services such as AOL that provided access to the Web, but by now most of the traditional search engines have transformed themselves into Web portals to attract and keep a larger audience.

Given this definition, how does this fit with the MuseToMusic site and the desire of the storeowners to have their Web site viewed as a portal? Consider the following:

◆ In terms of offering a broad array of resources and services, the storeowners want to provide an e-commerce tool for customers to purchase music over the Web, but they also want to provide space for local bands to generate interest in their music, to announce performance dates, and so on.

◆ Also, the storeowners want the site to be seen as a one-stop resource for current links to related Web sites, such as specific band Web sites, music magazines, and so on. Moreover, the storeowners would like to include space on the site for music discussion forums.

◆ The final part of the Webopedia definition is perhaps most relevant to the storeowners' overarching desire to have a Web site: They want to keep their current local community audience and attract a larger (regional? global?) audience. If the MuseToMusic site succeeds, it will be because the design allowed it to be a resource for all things music to a wide variety of people in different physical locations. The site needs to be empowered with an intuitive navigation tool. If the success of AOL can be attributed to anything, an argument could be made that it's due to the incredibly simple and intuitive design of the interface. Once AOL customers realized how easy it was to get an account and start utilizing the service, they were more inclined to continue their service and pay for the custom content AOL provides. It should be evident how important a good navigation scheme is for the success of any Web site.

Although there are many different elements to a Web portal (and each one warrants a much greater discussion than what is provided here), the following sections will highlight some of the important sub-components of the MuseToMusic portal and discuss why they are important to the overall success of the Web site.

Reviewing Previous Order History

This discussion could be included in the "Online Shopping Cart" section of this chapter. However, I wanted to include it in the portal discussion because it hits on one of the major aspects of a successful portal—the ability for customers to view and manipulate information that is specific to them.

Think about some of the better online retailers you have visited in the past. If they have a well-designed online shopping cart, you can review your previous order history. If the shopping cart is *very* well designed, your previous order information is used to customize how the site is presented to you. In other words, if you ordered Product A in the past, products associated with Product A will be displayed to you the next time you visit the site.

The MuseToMusic storeowners wanted to build this kind of personal touch into their online shopping cart. They have made it a long-standing practice to give friendly suggestions to patrons with regard to music they think the customer might like based on previous orders. Moreover, the store wants to build interest in the local music scene. Because the local bands cover a variety of different styles, as customers purchase a CD of a particular musical style (such as country, pop, or jazz), the site will display a link to a related local band. As a customer builds an order history, this information can be catalogued and used to personalize content for subsequent visits. Figure 15.3 highlights this type of personalized order history as facilitated on one of the best known commercial Web sites: Amazon.com.

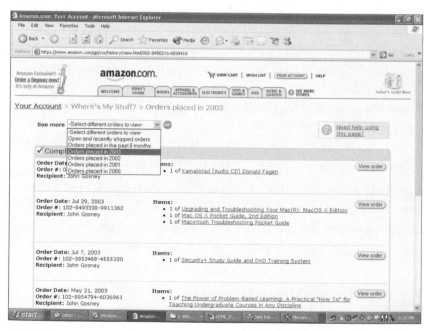

FIGURE 15.3 *The ability to view previous order history can be a key component in a personalized Web experience, as well as a successful marketing tool. Note the options to view order history, as shown in the drop-down menu.*

Customizable Profile and Interface

Related to the site's ability to display custom order information, an overall customized profile and interface are essential ingredients to a successful Web portal.

As you read in the previous section, allowing customers to view previous order history can lead to additional sales as well as a more personal feel to their experience at your Web site. However, this is really just the tip of the iceberg in terms of the benefits of allowing your site visitors to control how content is presented to them on your site.

While total customization is probably not realistic (or something you would desire), there are numerous benefits to why you should allow visitors to personalize your site.

◆ Visitors gain a sense of ownership of your site, and thus feel as if their experience (and critically, their time spent) on your site is by their choosing.

◆ As discussed earlier, personalization allows the development of a customer profile so you can target specific products and information based on visitors' previous Web visits.

◆ Allowing users to customize a page (or pages) on your site is critical to the portal concept because it encourages them to build a Web tool (the portal) that is functional and practical for their needs. This will potentially lead to a tool that is used on a daily basis.

◆ Generally related to all of the above, allowing personalization takes the guesswork out of your design. Not every user wants to have information displayed in the same fashion, and even the more mundane issues (such as screen background color) can be adjusted to suit specific tastes.

Finally, in conjunction with a well-designed online shopping cart, customers can build their own personal feedback sections where they can provide product reviews and link purchases to related products, for example. (I'll talk more about this in the following section.) As you can see nicely illustrated once again on Amazon.com, you know that customer feedback is an essential component of that site's overall design. Each product has an area for customer feedback, and customers build their own special lists of products they have found useful. Figure 15.4 highlights the Amazon.com site with regard to this functionality.

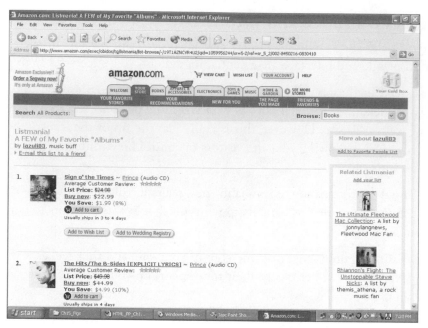

FIGURE 15.4 *An example of a user-created list of recommended products on the Amazon.com site.*

Online Support and Discussion Forums

Despite your efforts to build the most comprehensive, easy-to-use Web site, there is no substitute for "been there, done that" advice from one visitor to another. That is why online support and discussion forums are such invaluable tools for all areas of your site.

 CAUTION

It's a great idea to provide space for customer feedback, but you should closely monitor such forums to ensure that the online conversation remains on the subject at hand—and remains civil. Although some discussion forums are built for the sole purpose of allowing people to yell at each other, you don't want your professional, business-oriented site to fall into this category. Some heated discussion can be good, but only if it does not consist of purely derogatory remarks and is within the posted subject of the forum.

In addition to allowing your customers to post their comments and opinions, the online support function of a well-designed and moderated discussion forum is invaluable. For the MuseToMusic site, the discussion forums were designed to allow customers to talk about music—with regard to both the local music scene and commercially-produced music. Specifically, the storeowners want their discussion forums to fulfill these business requirements:

◆ First, the storeowners thought that an electronic forum could be a great way to allow more instantaneous feedback on a variety of issues in the local music community, especially as a mechanism for building interest in local bands. For example, the storeowners encourage fans to post feedback and reviews of local bands as soon as possible after a performance. This kind of feedback would not be possible without the Web.

◆ Another critical aspect of the MuseToMusic discussion forums is that they provide visitors a way of exchanging ideas on music in general. Not unlike the list-generating feature on Amazon.com (see Figure 15.4), the storeowners want users to be able to express their interests in music to each other. In conjunction with the general portal design concept, this encourages a wider discussion of products that are available and gives users a sense of ownership.

◆ Finally, the store is known as an excellent resource for locating hard-to-find CDs. The owners envision the discussion forums and online support made possible through them as a way for users to trade information on how to locate such hard-to-find music.

The Online Shopping Cart

The final major customer design issue to be addressed in the MuseToMusic site is the online shopping cart. The functionality of the shopping cart is fairly straightforward. However, the surrounding design issues (and how they are facilitated by HTML) are of particular importance for this book, and I will discuss them in detail in the following sections.

NOTE

It should be obvious that a functioning online shopping cart is beyond the capabilities of HTML and requires the integration of some advanced topics, including scripts and database access. Although the focus of this book is not specifically on such topics, you will nevertheless see how you can create a functioning cart when you construct the MuseToMusic Web site using Microsoft FrontPage (see Chapters 21 through 24). You will see an example of database integration (and the issues that surround it, including initial configuration and more advanced data access) facilitated via Microsoft SQL Server in Chapters 25 through 28.

Seamless Integration with Your Site

You definitely want to keep your shopping cart functionality within easy reach, but you don't want it to be so overbearing that it is a visual distraction to your customers. More important, however, is making the flow of your site naturally lead to your shopping cart. As your customers find an item of interest and follow a series of hyperlinks (such as links to related items or pages that give more information about the product), a list of items of interest that can naturally be posted to a shopping cart should be built.

TIP

Links to your online shopping cart should be conspicuous and omnipresent throughout your site. As with any marketing tool, you want this feature of your Web site to be easily recognized and—most critically—easily accessible.

Consider the following example of this process for the MuseToMusic site:

1. A customer searches for an item of interest on the main product page, and a list of items that match the search criteria is returned.

2. Based on the list of items returned, a list of possible related links appears in one frame of the larger frameset.

3. When the customer clicks on a product of interest, a complete description of the product is returned. Also, additional links are provided so the customer can add this item to his or her shopping cart, add the item to the cart and proceed immediately to checkout, or rate the product.

TIP

You will see how this integration concept can be facilitated via the use of an overall site design template when you build the MuseToMusic site in FrontPage (see Chapters 21 through 24).

4. A "rate this product" link provides a link back to the product information, as well as the same links to add the item to the shopping cart. Notice how this circular design always keeps customers within one click of a product order form, but at the same time allows them access to a variety of other pages within your site (in this case, a discussion forum).

Don't underestimate the power of this circular design; it allows you to provide full information access to your customers while keeping them just a click away from ordering. This approach is non-threatening and allows customers the ability to move freely within the site as they choose.

Full Product Descriptions and Direct Links to Products

Implied within the previous sections of this chapter is a simple rule: Don't be stingy with the amount of information you provide to your visitors. A well-informed user is a happy user who will be encouraged to explore deeper within your site and feel confident in his or her purchases. Indeed, if they know they can get all the necessary information on a product or issue, customers will be inclined to visit your site often and provide additional details on products (via an online discussion forum). As I have noted throughout this chapter, this type of direct user-to-user feedback is an invaluable information tool, both in furthering the power of your site as an e-commerce tool and in giving it more credence as a true information portal.

Also, as shown in the figures in the previous section, providing direct access to product information (via always-conspicuous product links) is critical. Customers should always be able to find complete product information easily, so be sure that information is never more than one or two (at most) clicks away.

Summary

This chapter's focus was two-fold. First, the intention was to generally describe customer usability issues. Second, the goal was to take those general principles and discuss them in the context of the MuseToMusic site. The chapter looked at three major customer usability issues—site navigation, portal design, and the online shopping cart. Although not all Web sites have these features, every Web site includes at least one of them (especially good navigation design). Each of these major areas contains specific subcategories you need to address if your HTML design is to be utilized in the most effective fashion possible. Finally, the chapter touched on how you can use a back-end database to facilitate many of these customer usability issues, especially an online shopping cart. Examples of how you can do this will be illustrated in later project chapters.

Chapter 16

In the previous three chapters you played the role of Web design consultant as you met with the MuseToMusic storeowners to determine their specific business process issues and goals they'd like to see facilitated by a working Web site. You have also worked with them to determine specific customer usability requirements so the Web site can deliver the same amount of excellent service that customers have come to expect from the store.

Now that you have all of this information, you are ready to code the actual Web site. To reiterate the primary goals of the site that you will need to factor into your design:

◆ The site will need to draw attention to the local music scene.

◆ The site will need to allow customers to request special order music. Again, the store has always been a great resource in this regard, and the owners want to expand this service via the Web.

◆ The site will need to act as a music portal by serving as a one-stop location for all kinds of music-related information.

To build this site, you will draw on nearly all the coding practices you learned in Part I of this book. In building the site, you will put into practice the following HTML coding skills:

◆ **Working with page layout.** Cascading style sheets (CSS) will give your overall site design a uniform, easy-to-administer look and feel.

◆ **Designing tables.** The MuseToMusic site presents lots of information to its customers. Use tables to help organize this information neatly.

◆ **Integrating frames.** A frameset design can help facilitate the portal concept by creating a structure that provides links to other Web sites but still keeps customers within the MuseToMusic site.

◆ **Working with forms.** From gathering customer information to presenting the music locator service, you should build and integrate forms directly into the site.

◆ **Integrating scripting languages.** Utilizing JavaScript with your forms will help you validate information entered by the customer.

◆ **Using advanced HTML design.** By designing a solid Web structure, you can plan for the integration of more advanced features (such as a database), which you will learn about in the third and fourth projects of this book.

Pre-Publishing Considerations for Your Web Site

At this point, there are a few things you should realize about publishing the Web site, which is the final step in the design process (and, in reality, the most important part).

◆ As a Web designer, you need to consider how and where you will publish and ultimately host the Web site. Are you going to do it yourself? If so, you must have the hardware infrastructure and expertise to host and maintain a Web site. Be forewarned: Web hosting is not an activity to be entered into lightly! Although you might have the technical expertise to bring a Web server online and provide a hosting service, do you have the wherewithal, patience, and perseverance to keep your servers patched against an ever-increasing range and severity of viruses and worms? Do you fully understand that your customers' Web sites are vital parts of their operations? (You have seen how this is possible in the previous three chapters of this project.) Unless you have a much larger business goal in mind than I think you do, you should let someone else handle the Web hosting for you. (I'm assuming you are interested in learning HTML in conjunction with some other technologies.) There are literally hundreds (if not thousands) of reputable Web hosting providers with very affordable prices, not to mention excellent support.

◆ Have you registered a domain name for your site? Many customers will want (and expect) to have their Web sites available at a specific address, such as www.musetomusic.com. Early in the process, you should confirm that the desired domain name is available. If it is not, you should suggest alternatives to your customers so this critical detail does not become a major stumbling block as you move toward the final steps of design and publishing.

◆ Does the server on which your site will be hosted support all of the functionality your site includes? As you will see in the third project, when you revisit the design of the MuseToMusic site using Microsoft FrontPage, much of the neat functionality possible with FrontPage is *only* possible if the server hosting the site has the FrontPage extensions installed. Although many Web hosting providers do support FrontPage extensions, many do not.

◆ Related to the previous point, if your site includes advanced functionality such as the integration of a database, does the Web hosting provider support this? Particularly with database integration, how does the provider allow you to administer the functionality?

◆ How does the hosting provider perform critical backup and security tasks? Will they charge you additional fees for backup service, and how often will they perform it? Also, what do they expect of you (or the customer) in terms of keeping your own site secure? Finally, if there is a problem with the site, how are you notified? These are all critical questions that you will need to address concerning the implementation and long-term administration of your site.

◆ What is the hosting provider's pricing structure? Will they charge you a set monthly fee or are there more long-term agreements possible, which might be cheaper than a month-to-month rate? If you add additional functionality in the future, will they charge you extra for it (probably), and if so, how will you and the customer handle this charge, assuming you are still involved in the ongoing maintenance and development of the site?

◆ Finally, with regard to nearly all of the previous points, how easy is it to access, administer, and make changes to your site once it is published? With Microsoft FrontPage, for example, many hosting providers will allow you to easily access the Web site on their server, so it's almost as if you are hosting the site on your own computer. However, other methods of administration may not be as easy; perhaps you cannot make changes to your site and then see those changes reflected instantaneously. This final issue can be a very critical point. Imagine you realize, after the site is published, that you have listed an incorrect phone number for your business. Clearly, this is something you would want to correct immediately, but what if changes to your site are only published to a live server twice a week? Although this is an unlikely scenario, it does happen, so be sure to consider this important issue as well.

Again, you should build the discussion of these issues into your overall project plan, and be sure you and your client are of the same understanding. Many clients will not realize there is an ongoing fee for Web hosting, or they might assume you will do it for them. Depending on the complexity of the site, hosting fees can be expensive, so don't get cornered into having to eat this expense simply because you did not communicate it to the customer in the early steps of the design process.

Developing the MuseToMusic Web Structure

I'm going to assume that you are developing your Web sites on a machine that is under your control and for which you have administrative rights. I will refer to this machine as the *development environment* (versus the *production server*, on which your site will be hosted when it is live).

The first thing you need to do is create a Web folder in which to store your pages.

 NOTE

Throughout this book, I have referred to the Inetpub folder as the place to create your Web sites. For Microsoft IIS, this is the default folder intended as a storage container for all the Web sites that are created on the computer. If you are using Windows XP Professional or Windows 2000, IIS is integrated into the OS: You simply add the IIS component via the Add/Remove Programs control panel. Figures 16.1 to 16.3 illustrate this process. In either case, you should be sure to create your individual Web folders within this folder, just as you have been doing throughout this book.

 TIP

If you are using an older version of Windows (especially Windows 98) or you don't want to install IIS, you can still create the Web site as it is described in this chapter. Follow along with the steps in this section and create the same folder, but just create it somewhere on your hard drive. The only difference will be how you load the site into your Web browser because you will use a different address to access the site and its pages. For example, instead of using the http://127.0.0.1 address you have seen throughout this book, you can just enter the exact file address in the address bar of your Web browser: such an address might be c:/Web_Folder/Muse_To_Music/Home.htm

FIGURE 16.1 *Click on the Add or Remove Programs icon within the Control Panel as a first step in loading IIS.*

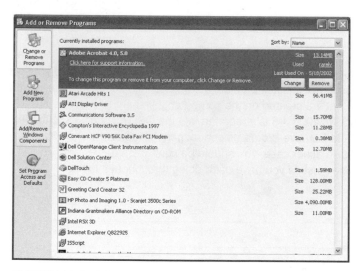

FIGURE 16.2 *Click on the Add/Remove Windows Components to access the component listing (IIS is included here).*

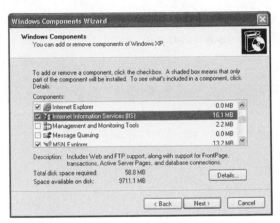

FIGURE 16.3 *Highlight the Internet Information Services (IIS) option, then click Next to begin the installation process.*

Okay, now you're ready to create the MuseToMusic Web folder.

1. Navigate to the Inetpub folder on your computer. The directory path to this folder is c:/Inetpub/wwwroot. You will create your individual Web site folders within the wwwroot subdirectory.

2. Within the wwwroot folder, create a new folder and call it MTM.

As you create the individual Web pages in this chapter, you will store them all in this MTM folder.

Creating the Frame Structure Layout

A frame layout is probably the best way to address all of the various functional requirements of the MuseToMusic site. A frame layout will help facilitate

◆ Easy site navigation

◆ Better organization of the site content

◆ Access to other Web sites, while keeping customers just a click away from all MuseToMusic services and functionality

 TIP

For more information on working with frames, refer to Chapter 7.

For the MuseToMusic site, you will utilize a Banner and Contents frame style. Figure 16.4 illustrates the basic structure of this layout, which you will code in this section.

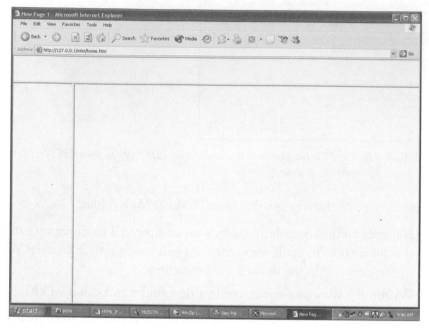

FIGURE 16.4 *The Banner and Contents frame structure.*

This frame structure is made up of four pages—the frame page itself (that is, the page which is actually referenced in the URL and which loads the other pages that constitute the frame structure) and three additional pages (the top frame, the left frame, and the right frame).

 NOTE

Chapters 21 through 24 will talk more about building the MuseToMusic site with FrontPage. If you have access to FrontPage and you want to use it as your editor of choice for this chapter, by all means do so. If you prefer another type of text editor (either another HTML editor or something as simple as Notepad), feel free to use it. If you have access to FrontPage and you are interested in using it, you might want to review Chapter 12, which focuses on FrontPage and provides a good general introduction to all of its features, many of which you can utilize in this chapter. The choice is up to you!

You should create the frame page first.

1. Open your text editor of choice.

2. Enter the following code exactly as you see it here.

```
<html>
<head>

<title>Welcome to MuseToMusic on the Web!</title>
</head>
<frameset rows="64,*">
  <frame name="banner" scrolling="no" noresize target="contents"
src="home_top.htm">
  <frameset cols="150,*">
    <frame name="contents" target="main" src="home_left.htm">
    <frame name="main" src="home_right.htm">
  </frameset>
  <noframes>
  <body>
<p>This page uses frames, but your browser doesn't support them.</p>
</body>
</noframes>
</frameset>
</html>
```

3. Save this page as home.htm in the MTM folder you created earlier.

Now it's time to create the three individual pages that will make up the site frame structure.

1. Open a new blank document in your editor.

2. Enter the following code as you see it here.

```
<html>
<head>
<title>Contents</title>
<base target="contents">
</head>
<body>
</body>
</html>
```

3. Save this page as home_top.htm in the MTM folder.

4. Open another new blank document in your editor.

5. Enter the following code as you see it here.

```
<html>
<head>
<title>Main</title>
<base target="main"
</head>
<body>
</body>
</html>
```

6. Save this page as home_left.htm in the MTM folder.

7. Open another new blank document in your editor.

8. Enter the following code as you see it here.

```
<html>
<head>
<title>Main Title</title>
</head>
<body>
</body>
</html>
```

9. Save this page as home_right.htm in the MTM folder.

10. Open your Web browser and load this page. (If you are working with the Inetpub folder, the address will be http://127.0.0.1/MTM/home.htm.) Your screen should appear exactly as in Figure 16.4.

Admittedly, this is a very basic structure; however, as you move through the design process, you will set specific frame attributes as you design and place additional content on the site.

Creating the Site Banner

The top frame will be used as the site banner and will include the store logo as well as contact information. The idea behind the site banner is that no matter what content is being viewed (content specific to MuseToMusic or information from outside sites), the customer will always know they are within the larger MuseToMusic site.

1. In your editor, open the home_top.htm page you created a moment ago.

2. On the banner, you want to include the site graphic and provide links to some general information about the store, such as contact information, hours of operation, and directions to the store. Figure 16.5 illustrates how this banner might appear.

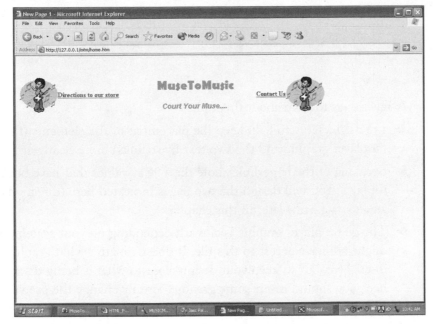

FIGURE 16.5 *An example of the banner frame as it might be designed for the MuseToMusic site.*

Enter the following code on the home_top.htm page, between the opening and closing <body> tags.

```
<p align="left"><p>
<table border="0" width="76%" style="border-collapse: collapse" cellpadding="0"
cellspacing="0">
  <tr>
    <td width="14%"><img border="0" src="j0382402[1].gif" width="94"
height="87"></td>
    <td width="27%">
    <p align="center"><font color="#FFFFFF"><b><a target="main"
href="directons.htm">
    Directions to our store</a></b></font></td>
    <td width="36%">
    <p align="center"><b><font face="Berlin Sans FB" size="6" color="#FF0000">
    MuseToMusic</font></b></p>
```

```
    <p align="center"><b><i><font face="Arial" size="4" color="#FF0000">Court
    Your Muse....</font></i></b></td>
    <td width="60%">
    <p align="center"><font color="#FFFFFF"><b><a target="main"
href="contact.htm">
    Contact Us</a></b></font></td>
    <td width="47%">
    <img border="0" src="j0382402[1].gif" width="94" height="87"></td>
  </tr>
</table>
```

A few things to note about this code:

◆ I've used a table to help keep the placement of the elements (the guitar player graphic and the two text hyperlinks) more neatly arranged.

◆ Speaking of the hyperlinks, note the a href values that have been set for both. You will design the two pages indicated here (directions.htm and contact.htm) later in this chapter.

◆ The guitar player graphic is clip art; depending on your system, you might not have access to this file. It doesn't matter what graphic you insert here, but to keep your design close to what is being discussed here, you should insert some graphic. Simply change the src value within the <img> tag to point to whatever file you use, and be sure you store the actual image source file in the MTM folder, along with the other pages you are creating for this site.

3. For the two hyperlinks ("Directions to our store" and "Contact Us"), you will want the pages to which these links point to open in the main content frame of the site, which is the right frame (home_right.htm). Note the inclusion of the a target attribute in the preceding code; this attribute specifies the frame to which the link will point, so be sure to include this important HTML as listed in the code.

4. Save this page as home_top.htm.

A GENERAL NOTE ON GRAPHIC DESIGN

I freely admit it: I'm not a graphic artist. In fact, you could say that I am graphically challenged. I have no problem with the underlying HTML code and I can integrate a Web site and database with the best of them, but ask me to design a cool-looking graphic or come up with a visually stunning design and I falter.

If you put yourself in this same category, you are not alone. There's a reason why graphic artists are paid well—they have the unique combination of natural talent and, quite often, several years of advanced training in the graphic design field. With the Web becoming ubiquitous in all of our lives, special training that focuses on designing just for the Web has started to develop. With an ever-widening set of tools for graphic design and Web manipulation (from image editors to advanced Web animation tools such as Macromedia Flash), the best graphic designers are helping to design Web sites that are both highly functional and visually stunning.

As you work through the projects in this book, you might find yourself wondering whether your site looks rather amateurish in design. But remember, the focus of this book is to teach you about HTML and to ensure that the functional requirements of the site are met. This should remain your first and foremost concern. Even though the Web is a visual medium, all of the visual pizzazz and whiz-bang animation won't mean much if the content is inaccessible or if the business requirements and process goals of the customers are not met.

However, when you revisit the MuseToMusic site using Microsoft FrontPage, you will see that there are tools you can use to help with the graphic design issues if you fall into the graphically-challenged category. As you will see in that project, you can use a site template design wizard to give your pages a standard look and feel. Not unlike the templates available in Microsoft PowerPoint, these tools can at least give your Web site some amount of design perspective, even if you struggle with drawing stick figures.

So keep in mind that the focus here is not on graphic design; rather, it is on ensuring that you understand how to code the underlying structure of a functional Web site. Still, clients in the real world will want their Web sites to look good and be functional information tools. That said, if you have the resources available to you, consider bringing a graphic artist into the project in the early stages of the design process. In addition to making the site look good, the best graphic designers can assist you with the functional information delivery requirements too. (If you've seen a well-designed Flash Web site, you know what I mean.)

Building the Site Navigation Scheme

If your Web site design is going to be truly successful, it must be easy to use as well as organized so all of the critical information and functionality can be accessed easily.

For the MuseToMusic site you are building in this chapter, there are six major functional components that will be presented in the site navigation. The navigation scheme will need to provide links to

- ◆ **The site home page.** You should always have a link that takes you back to the site home page: It serves as a good point of reference if the user simply wants to return to the initial point of entry into the site.

- ◆ **The music locator service.** As you know, a major business process requirement of the site is to facilitate MuseToMusic's reputation for being able to locate hard-to-find music. A primary link on the site navigation scheme will be to this service.

- ◆ **The local music scene.** The MuseToMusic owners are committed to promoting the local music scene, so it makes sense that a link directly within the site navigation should point to special pages devoted to announcing news and updates on local bands.

- ◆ **Outside Web pages that provide information on music.** If the site is to be a true music portal, then it must serve as a one-stop location for access to other sites. A link within the site navigation will take visitors to a page that lists such outside music sites, organized by category of music.

- ◆ **The online shopping cart.** The storeowners want customers to be able to find information on existing inventory via the Web and order music online. This is major functionality that deserves to be presented in the site navigation scheme.

- ◆ **General news and information about the store.** Store hours, history, special events, and so on all need to be readily accessible via the site navigation.

The left frame of the general frame structure will contain the site navigation. You will build and customize this in the following section.

Coding the Site Navigation Bar

This section will highlight specific hyperlink functionality, especially how it works within a frameset (in other words, clicking on a link and having the corresponding content load in a specific frame).

1. In your editor, open the home_left.htm page. You can think of this as your navigation frame.

2. For this example, you will use basic hyperlinks for your navigation. When a link is clicked, it will open content in the right frame of the frameset. In the home_left.htm page, enter the following code between the opening and closing <body> tags.

```
<p align="center"><b><font face="Berlin Sans FB" color="#FF0000">Site
Navigation</font></b></p>
<ul>
  <li>
  <p align="left"><b><font face="Arial" color="#0000FF">
  <a target="main" href="home_right.htm">MuseToMusic Home</a></font></b></li>
  <li>
  <p align="left"><b><font face="Arial" color="#0000FF">
  <a target="main" href="locator.htm">The Music Locator</a></font></b></li>
  <li>
  <p align="left"><b><font face="Arial" color="#0000FF">
  <a target="main" href="local.htm">The Local Scene</a></font></b></li>
  <li>
  <p align="left"><b><font face="Arial" color="#0000FF">
  <a target="main" href="portal_home.htm">Music Portal</a></font></b></li>
  <li>
  <p align="left"><b><font face="Arial" color="#0000FF">
  <a target="main" href="store_home.htm">Shop Online</a></font></b></li>
  <li>
  <p align="left"><b><font face="Arial" color="#0000FF">
  <a target="main" href="news.htm">News and Information</a></font></b></li>
</ul>
<hr>
```

3. Save the page again as home_left.htm.

4. Reload the frame page in your browser. Your screen should now look something like Figure 16.6.

Note that for each of the hyperlinks in the preceding code, the target frame is set to "main", which will allow the content to open in the right frame.

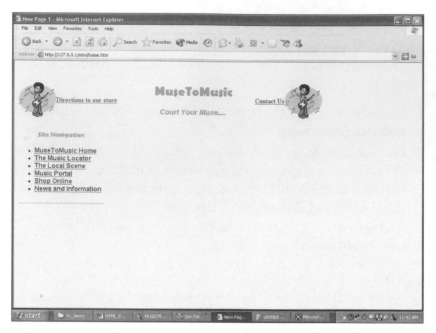

FIGURE 16.6 *The site starts to take shape with the addition of a navigation structure.*

Coding the home_right.htm Page

Let's see this in action now. Up to this point, you have included hyperlinks but you have not designed the corresponding pages yet. So far, you need to build the following pages to correspond to associated links:

- contact.htm
- directions.htm
- home_right.htm (the page that loads in the right frame when the site is initially loaded in a Web browser)
- locator.htm
- local.htm
- portal_home.htm
- store_home.htm
- news.htm

When the site initially is loaded into a Web browser, you don't want the right frame to be blank, as it currently appears in the figures provided so far in this chapter. You can create the home_right.htm page now.

1. You already created this page when you set up the initial frameset for the site, so open the home_right.htm page in your editor.

2. As you can see in Figure 16.7, I have included the same guitar player graphic, and I've done some formatting with font type and color. The code for this follows. You can use the same code (remembering to replace the graphic file with something specific to your system, as noted earlier) or design your own page using your HTML skills.

```
<table border="0" cellpadding="0" cellspacing="0" style="border-collapse:
collapse" bordercolor="#111111" width="100%">
  <tr>
    <td width="18%"><img border="0" src="j0382402[1].gif" width="94"
height="87"></td>
    <td width="82%"><b><i><font face="Arial" size="4" color="#FF0000">What's New
    at MuseToMusic....</font></i></b></td>
  </tr>
  <tr>
    <td width="18%" bgcolor="#FF0000" bordercolor="#FF0000"> </td>
    <td width="82%" bgcolor="#FF0000"> </td>
  </tr>
  <tr>
    <td width="18%" bgcolor="#FF0000"> </td>
    <td width="82%"><b><i><font face="Arial" size="4" color="#008000">* Beef 'n'
    Noodles LIVE in our store!  <a href="news.htm">Details
here.</a></font></i></b></td>
  </tr>
  <tr>
    <td width="18%" bgcolor="#FF0000"> </td>
    <td width="82%"><b><i><font face="Arial" size="4" color="#008000">* Looking
    for that oh-so-hard-to-find CD?  We can help you!  Use our<a
href="locator.htm">
    Music Locator service </a>if you're jonesing for some long-lost
tunes.</font></i></b></td>
  </tr>
</table>
<hr>
<p align="center"><b>Site Updated: 7/31/03</b></p>
```

3. Save this page and reload the site into your Web browser. It should appear similar to Figure 16.7.

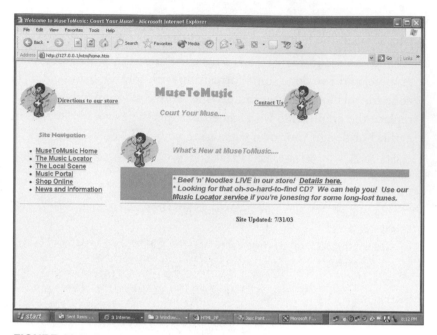

FIGURE 16.7 *Providing recent news and other updates when the site first loads is a good use of the right frame in this particular layout.*

Now if you click on the MuseToMusic link in the navigation frame, this page will always load. Also note that for this example, the home_right.htm page includes a "last updated" tag, as shown in Figure 16.7. It is important that you keep this type of information current. If a visitor loads the site and the last update was more than a year ago, it will not bring much credibility to your site or the information it contains.

Integrating Forms: The Music Locator Service

As you know from your meetings with the storeowners, they'd like to offer their music locator service via the Web. Ideally, they envision the process as follows:

1. The customers enter the site and click on the Shop Online link, where they can browse the store's online inventory.

2. In case they can't find what they are looking for, the online store pages contain links to the music locator service.

3. The music locator service is an online form that asks visitors to provide specific information about the CD for which they are searching. The form is completed, submitted, and sent to store administrators, who in turn contact the customer for more information and/or to give him or her the order status.

BRINGING E-COMMERCE FUNCTIONALITY TO YOUR WEB SITES

The online store that the MuseToMusic owners would like to see implemented requires some advanced coding and Web functionality. Moreover, there is a significant issue of accepting online payment. (This requires an external credit card verification service, such as CyberCash or PayPal.)

Still, you can bring e-commerce functionality to your site without worrying about these other issues if you keep your definition of e-commerce very basic. In this example, the storeowners' primary goal is to use their Web site simply as a means of addressing a wider audience. As you'll see in this section, they can achieve e-commerce in the sense that they are extending their selling opportunities via the Web. Even though the functionality is terribly automated, the fact that they are gathering information from a customer concerning a purchase item of interest (in this case, a hard-to-find CD) and then responding to that customer, either via e-mail or telephone, constitutes the extended marketing of their services via the Web and can ultimately result in a sale, even if the actual exchange of money is not facilitated via the Web.

In the third project of this book (Chapters 21 through 24), you will see how this definition of e-commerce can be widened by the use of FrontPage, and its Database Results Wizard, which allows easy integration of a database with a Web site. As you will see in that project, the database in question could be, for example, the current inventory of the MuseToMusic store. Customers could browse this inventory and have a link immediately available to an online order form in case they find an item they are interested in purchasing. Again, this is somewhat limited functionality with regard to a typical e-commerce site, but it nevertheless allows the storeowners to benefit from the extended selling opportunities that the Web presents.

So you should not immediately think your e-commerce options are limited simply because your site is basic in its coding. Rather, you need to think of the options presented to you via traditional HTML—"traditional" meaning HTML without any scripting languages or database integration included. You also need to consider how you might extend those options because your Web site allows you to reach a potentially huge audience (or at least a larger and more geographically diverse audience than those who would visit your brick-and-mortar establishment). It's all in how you define the situation and the level of creativity you possess in taking advantage of the opportunities a Web site presents.

Building the Music Locator Form

You learned all about form elements in Chapter 8, and now you will build on that knowledge to construct a functioning Web form. You will also utilize some simple JavaScript to help you validate the information entered into your form.

1. In your editor, create a new page and save it as locator.htm in your MTM folder.

 NOTE

You can call these pages anything you want; however, if you name them something other than what is listed here, be sure to go back to your navigator bar (the home_left.htm page) and change the name of the file to which each of the hyperlinks points.

2. Enter the following HTML in the locator.htm page.

```
<html>
<head>
<title>Music Locator Service Form</title>
</head>
<body>
<form>
<p align="center"><font size="6"><b>We can find what you want!</b></font></p>
<p align="left"><b><i>Looking for that hard to find CD?  Just fill out the
form below and we'll respond to you within twenty-four hours to let you know if
we
can get it (chances are good that we can)!</i></b></p>
<table border="0" width="100%" cellspacing="1">
  <tr>
    <td width="26%">Your Name:</td>
    <td width="74%"><input type="text" name="Name" size="30"></td>
  </tr>
  <tr>
    <td width="26%">Your Phone (please include area code):</td>
    <td width="74%"><input type="text" name="Phone" size="30"></td>
  </tr>
  <tr>
    <td width="26%">Your E-mail:</td>
    <td width="74%"><input type="text" name="Email" size="30"></td>
  </tr>
```

```
  <tr>
    <td width="26%">Title of CD (if known):</td>
    <td width="74%"><input type="text" name="Title" size="30"></td>
  </tr>
  <tr>
    <td width="26%">Artist (if known):</td>
    <td width="74%"><input type="text" name="Artist" size="30"></td>
  </tr>
  <tr>
    <td width="26%">Do you know if this is an import?</td>
    <td width="74%">Yes: <input type="radio" value="Yes" name="Import"> 
    No:<input type="radio" value="No" checked name="Import"></td>
  </tr>
  <tr>
    <td width="26%">Genre of CD (if known):</td>
    <td width="74%"><select size="1" name="Genre">
    <option>Rock/Pop</option>
    <option>Jazz</option>
    <option>Classical</option>
    <option>Country</option>
    <option>Rhythm and Blues</option>
    <option>Gospel</option>
    <option>New Age</option>
    <option>Other</option>
    </select></td>
  </tr>
  <tr>
    <td width="100%" colspan="2">
    <p align="center">
    <input type="submit" value="Submit Your Request!" name="B1"></td>
  </tr>
</table>
<p align="left">
</form>
</body>
</html>
```

3. Save this page again as locator.htm, and then reload the MuseToMusic site into your Web browser. When the site loads, click on the Music Locator link in the left-frame navigation bar. Your screen should look like Figure 16.8.

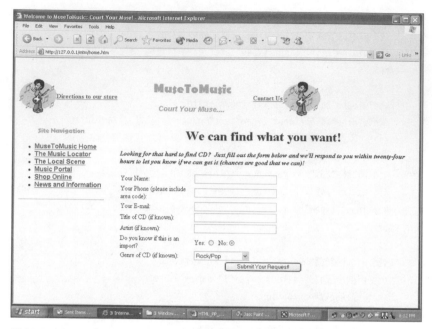

FIGURE 16.8 *The music locator form, which greatly extends the functionality of the store and brings an e-commerce viability to the entire site.*

Utilizing JavaScript to Validate the Music Locator Form

As you learned in Chapter 11, you can use a simple JavaScript function to validate the information entered into your form. Although the code listed for the previous form will work just fine, there is nothing in it that will prevent users from submitting blank fields (that is, not providing a telephone number, e-mail address, or another piece of critical information).

You can help safeguard against blank fields by integrating a JavaScript function into your HTML to ensure that something is entered for each form field. The following code is a revised locator.htm file that includes this function.

1. Open the locator.htm file in your editor.

2. Add the following code between the opening and closing `<head>` tags in the code you entered in the preceding section.

```
<script>
<!--
function validateform()
```

```
{
if((document.orderform.Name.value=="")||
(document.orderform.Phone.value=="")||
(document.orderform.Email.value==""))
{
window.alert("In order to give you the best service, please complete all fields.
Thank you!")
return false;
}
}
//-->
</script>
```

3. Also within the code you entered, replace this line of code

   ```
   <form>
   ```

   with this line of code:

   ```
   <form name="orderform" method="POST" action="formprocessing.asp" onSubmit="return
   validateform( this.form)">
   ```

4. Save your page again as locator.htm.

5. Load the MuseToMusic site into your browser once again, and click on the Music Locator link. The form will load, as per the previous example; however, try to click the submit button without entering anything into one of the first three form fields. You will receive an error message, as shown in Figure 16.9.

FIGURE 16.9 *You must enter some value for the first three fields on the form; otherwise, you will receive this friendly message.*

Your entire locator.htm code should now appear as follows:

```
<html>
<head>
<title>Music Locator Service Form</title>
<script>
```

```
<!--
function validateform()
{
if((document.orderform.Name.value=="")||
(document.orderform.Phone.value=="")||
(document.orderform.Email.value==""))
{
window.alert("In order to give you the best service, please complete all fields. Thank
you!")
return false;
}
}
//-->
</script>
</head>
<body>
<form name="orderform" method="POST" action="formprocessing.asp" onSubmit="return
validateform( this.form)">
<p align="center"><font size="6"><b>We can find what you want!</b></font></p>
<p align="left"><b><i>Looking for that hard to find CD?  Just fill out the
form below and we'll respond to you within twenty-four hours to let you know if we
can get it (chances are good that we can)!</i></b></p>
<table border="0" width="100%" cellspacing="1">
  <tr>
    <td width="26%">Your Name:</td>
    <td width="74%"><input type="text" name="Name" size="30"></td>
  </tr>
  <tr>
    <td width="26%">Your Phone (please include area code):</td>
    <td width="74%"><input type="text" name="Phone" size="30"></td>
  </tr>
  <tr>
    <td width="26%">Your E-mail:</td>
    <td width="74%"><input type="text" name="Email" size="30"></td>
  </tr>
  <tr>
    <td width="26%">Title of CD (if known):</td>
    <td width="74%"><input type="text" name="Title" size="30"></td>
  </tr>
```

```
<tr>
  <td width="26%">Artist (if known):</td>
  <td width="74%"><input type="text" name="Artist" size="30"></td>
</tr>
<tr>
  <td width="26%">Do you know if this is an import?</td>
  <td width="74%">Yes: <input type="radio" value="Yes" name="Import"> 
  No:<input type="radio" value="No" checked name="Import"></td>
</tr>
<tr>
  <td width="26%">Genre of CD (if known):</td>
  <td width="74%"><select size="1" name="Genre">
  <option>Rock/Pop</option>
  <option>Jazz</option>
  <option>Classical</option>
  <option>Country</option>
  <option>Rhythym and Blues</option>
  <option>Gospel</option>
  <option>New Age</option>
  <option>Other</option>
  </select></td>
</tr>
<tr>
  <td width="100%" colspan="2">
  <p align="center">
  <input type="submit" value="Submit Your Request!" name="B1"></td>
</tr>
</table>
<p align="left">
</form>
</body>
</html>
```

Some things to note about the JavaScript integration and the music locator form:

◆ JavaScript is case sensitive, so be sure to reference the form fields within the function (specifically, Name, Phone, and Email) exactly as you reference them in the form itself.

◆ You only validate the first three form fields because the rest of the fields either default to a value (the Genre and Import fields) and/or are optional (the Artist and Title fields).

◆ The HTML code that initiates the form now includes the appropriate JavaScript to initiate the function (onSubmit). This line also has an action attribute of "formprocessing.asp". If this site were being utilized on a Web server that facilitated Active Server Pages (the .asp extension listed here), the form would be sent to this page, and the results would be processed. Because you aren't processing this form in any way here, it doesn't really matter what value you assign to the action attribute.

 TIP

FrontPage has built-in support for Active Server Pages, as does Microsoft IIS. If you have access to either of these tools, you can learn about ASP and see an example of this in action in Chapter 11. Note that the phrase "built-in support" means that FrontPage contains certain tools that allow you to more efficiently code Web pages that utilize ASP; however, to actually view these pages in action, you will need to run them on a Web server (IIS, for example) that supports ASP.

Integrating Cascading Style Sheets for the Local Scene and News and Information Links

You will recall from Chapters 9 and 10 that utilizing CSS is a great way to make quick and easy work of your text formatting. As an example of CSS in action, you will learn how to integrate them to better present information for the Local Scene and News and Information links.

As a quick review, these two links are designed to present the following information:

◆ **Local Scene.** The page that corresponds to this link is designed to present information about local bands, including links (where applicable) to their own pages. This page will also include dates and venues where local bands will be performing (in other words, a schedule of performances).

◆ **News and Information.** This page will include information about the MuseToMusic store, as well as a listing of pertinent news flashes that affect the local music community.

This section will illustrate how to integrate CSS in the News and Information page. You can then use this knowledge as a guide to design your own Local Scene page.

 NOTE

Feel free to modify and experiment with the code listings you see throughout this chapter. They have been designed to show how you can facilitate the requirements set forth in the previous two chapters via HTML, but they are by no means the definitive answer to those requirements, so use them as a point of reference for your own design ideas.

Let's move to a CSS example.

1. In your editor, open a new page and save it in your MTM folder as news.htm.

2. This example will use an external style sheet, so create that file now. Open another page in your editor and save it in your MTM folder as NewsStyle.css.

3. On the NewsStyle.css page, enter the following code:

```
h1 { font-family: Berlin Sans FB; font-size: 18pt; color: #008000; font-style:
italic }
a:link { font-family: Arial (fantasy); color: #FF0000 }
h2 { font-family: Arial; font-size: 14pt; color: #008000; font-style: italic }
body { color: #000080; font-family: Times New Roman; font-size: 10pt }
```

As you can see here, four HTML tags have been configured with a specific style: h1, h2, the body text, and active hyperlinks (those links that are not currently being clicked or have yet to be visited).

4. Save the code you just entered on the NewsStyle.css page.

5. Open the news.htm page once again. On this page, enter the following code:

```
<html>
<head>
<title>News and Information</title>
<LINK REL=stylesheet TYPE="text/css" HREF="NewsStyle.css">
<body>
<p align="center"><font size="7" color="#FF0000">MuseToMusic News &amp;
Information</font></p>
```

```
<hr>
<p align="center"><font size="3" color="#000000"><b><i>Updated: July 31,
2003</i></b></font></p>
<h1 align="left">Beef 'n' Noodles To Rock the Store!</h1>
<p align="left">Hearing one of our favorite local bands, Beef 'n' Noodles is one
thing.  Seeing them live is something else.  They have an absolutely
awesome stage show and are sure to please.  We are very lucky to have them
perform in our parking lot this Saturday.  Better yet, it's a free
concert! 
Show starts at 2:00, so come early for a good spot and check out the scene!</p>
<h2 align="left">More Beef 'n' Noodles News</h2>
<p align="left">Aside from rocking our store, the band has just launched a new
Web site.  Check it out at <a href="http://www.beefynoodles.com">
http://www.beefynoodles.com</a></p>
</body>
</html>
```

6. Save the page.

7. Reload the MuseToMusic site in your Web browser and click on the News and Information link. Your screen should appear similar to Figure 16.10.

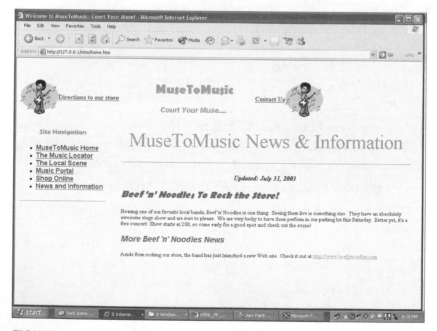

FIGURE 16.10 *Style sheets can help you maintain a consistent look and feel for all the MuseToMusic news and information.*

You might want to experiment on your own with the style attributes that have been defined for this page. Add more styles or change the style types that have been included here.

Implementing the Local Scene Link

Again, a major desire of the storeowners is to have the Web serve as an advertisement and promotional mechanism for the local music scene. The Local Scene link is intended to point to a page that will provide links to local bands' Web sites, as well as a listing of their schedules. Clearly, this page would include much textual formatting.

That said, such a page would be an ideal candidate for which to implement cascading style sheets. Not only would this give each band listed equal attention (because the formatting of each section on the page would be the same for each band), it also would make the page easy to update. Remember, a key benefit to CSS is that you set style definitions once so you don't have to go through every page and format individual sections of text. On pages with lots of text (or even a modicum of text), you should definitely take advantage of the power (and time-saving features) that CSS has to offer.

So experiment and create your own Local Scene page. To integrate it with the rest of the MuseToMusic site you've built in this chapter, be sure to save it as local.htm because that is the page you associated with the Local Scene link on the site navigation bar.

Other Site Functionality: The Online Store and Music Portal Links

The only two links on the navigation bar I haven't discussed are Shop Online and Music Portal. You were given extensive information about the portal concept in the previous chapters of this project. To reiterate, the idea is to make the MuseToMusic Web site a one-stop location so music lovers can type in one address (the address of the MuseToMusic site) and have access to a variety of music sites.

Again, you can design this page on your own based on the examples of the News and Information page and the site home page. As you experiment with the design, keep in mind the following points:

◆ The initial page (the page that contains all the links to the external sites) and the pages that are linked to it will all load in the right frame. Be sure to assign the appropriate target attribute in the hyperlinks (as you've seen done throughout this chapter). By having the pages in the right frame, you allow visitors to explore other sites on the Web but remain within the overall frame structure of the MuseToMusic site. Figure 16.11 illustrates this effect.

◆ Use CSS to help keep your formatting uniform and so that each page you are linking receives the same attention as the others (unless you want to give a page more emphasis).

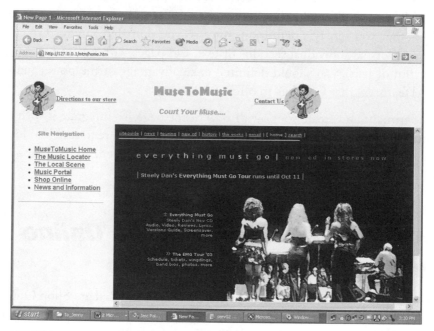

FIGURE 16.11 *An example of an external Web site (in this case, http://www.steelydan.com) displayed within the larger structure of the MuseToMusic site.*

The Online Store

Ideally, the storeowners would like customers to be able to browse store inventory online and then place (and pay for) orders online. This advanced functionality requires more than HTML can provide. However, as you will see in the third project of this book (in which you re-create the MuseToMusic site using FrontPage), you can bring a fair amount of this online store functionality to the site using the automated tools available in FrontPage.

Final Touches

At this point, I've addressed all the links in the navigation bar, and you have seen a variety of HTML tools utilized in the MuseToMusic site, from forms to CSS. However, some final touches are in order.

◆ Note that in all the figures for this chapter, the title bar at the top of the screen simply says New Page 1. This is because the frames page that loads for the site was not assigned a title. You can change that now!

1. Open the home.htm page you created at the beginning of this chapter.

2. Note that the title tag has the value New Page 1. Change this to "Welcome to MuseToMusic: Court Your Muse!"

3. Save the page and reload the site in your browser. Your screen should now look like Figure 16.12.

◆ Be sure to build pages for the two links in the banner frame (the "Directions to our store" and "Contact Us" links, currently pointing to directions.htm and contact.htm, respectively).

TIP

Don't overlook issues like the title bar! They are simple to fix, and if you don't address them, they can seriously detract from the professional look of your site.

◆ Finally, be sure to take care of obvious text editing issues such as checking for spelling errors. Additionally, make sure you have no broken links on your site.

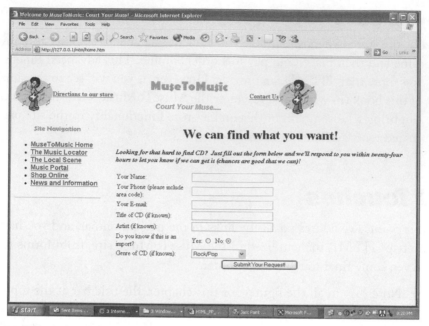

FIGURE 16.12 *Now your site has an official title!*

Summary

This chapter is the culmination of the design process that was outlined in the previous chapters of this project. You addressed all of the business process goals and customer usability issues that were outlined in Chapters 14 and 15 and you implemented several of the HTML coding skills that you learned in the first part of the book. Moreover, you were presented with tips and information on how to extend HTML functionality by thinking outside of the box in terms of how you define terms such as e-commerce. In the third project of this book, you will revisit the MuseToMusic site and rebuild it using FrontPage, in the process bringing more functionality to your site via the use of the special tools available in that application.

Project 2

**The Nonprofit
Web Site**

Chapter 17

For this project, you will be developing a Web site for the Greenlawn Secondary School. The school is privately funded, and thus is not part of a larger consolidated school district. That said, the school administrators want to push the envelope in terms of what they are doing with technology, and that includes developing an innovative Web site. In addition to somewhat standard fare, they also want the new Web site to allow online testing and present teachers, students, and faculty with customized schedules. For example, when students log on to the site, they should be presented with a customized schedule listing all of their homework assignments and other school-related responsibilities and commitments. Moreover, the school administrators want the site to include a Greenlawn Store where interested patrons can purchase school items such as T-shirts and hats.

 NOTE

Unlike the first two projects, this project will ask you to look at the concept of a "customer" a bit differently, in terms of both how you define the internal processes governing the function of the Web site and how you present information to the users (faculty, students, or teachers). However, you will see as you move through this project, the general principles of CRM are the same and can be neatly applied with regard to how you think about and implement HTML for this not-for-profit Web site.

Greenlawn School Project Outline

As with the other projects in this book, the Greenlawn School project is fictitious. However, you will see that the project brings many real-world issues and concerns to the topics of HTML and Web design. More challengingly, it also asks you to consider these design and CRM principles in a situation where the definition of the word "customer" is very different from how you understood it in the first two projects.

That said, the Greenlawn School project will be divided into the following four chapters:

◆ **Chapter 17** (this introductory chapter) will present you with the major process and design goals of the Web site, as communicated to you (the Web design consultant) by the school administrators. In this chapter, note the similarities between the CRM principles for the school's obvious not-for-profit functioning and those that were implemented via HTML in the first project.

◆ **Chapter 18** will look at the very detailed process issues for this site. In the next section of this chapter, "Greenlawn School Process Issues," you will be introduced to the major functional goals of the school Web site. These goals are quite varied and you will draw on many different aspects of HTML design to effectively implement them. Chapter 18 will describe these issues in specific detail, leading up to how they are actually implemented in Chapters 19 and 20.

◆ **Chapter 19** will discuss the design issues of the school's Web site. What is particularly interesting about the Greenlawn site with regard to HTML design issues is how you want to apply CRM and general business process design issues to the functioning of the school. You will learn (as described in this chapter) that the school has some disorganized internal processes and the school administrators are concerned that the development of the Web site will bring this to light. It is your job, then, to ensure that these processes are defined so you can map them over to the Web site for maximum functionality.

◆ **Chapter 20** will bring all of these design issues into perspective by highlighting various examples of actual HTML designs to satisfy both the process goals and the design requirements of the site. In this chapter you will see the Greenlawn project brought to life on the Web, as well as examples of other (real) schools and not-for-profit organizations that have utilized HTML to help meet their organizational goals.

Greenlawn School Process Issues

When the school administrators first contacted you (once again playing the role of Web design consultant) about this project, they had as many concerns about utilizing technology as they had project goals. Specifically, they were very concerned about how far they wanted to be on the bleeding edge of technology. Although other schools in the community (as well as surrounding communities) had experienced some success from having Web sites, those Web sites were purely window dressing for the schools in question. In other words, none of the Web sites played a critical role in the functioning of the school, and except for a few cases in which some general school information was listed, the sites offered no real informational (let alone educational) value to their visitors.

As a result of reviewing these sites prior to calling you, the Greenlawn administrators knew they wanted their Web site to be functionally critical to the larger operation of the school, as well as to the education of their students. Knowing that a firm understanding of technology is critical for success in today's world, the school administrators wanted to give their students a good start on this path to success by familiarizing them with how technology—in this case, a Web site—can be successfully integrated into their everyday lives.

But despite this optimistically ambitious goal, the school administrators also expressed serious concerns. Although they also expressed the usual questions about security and unauthorized access to potentially sensitive student grade information and other data, the real concern from the Greenlawn administrators was that the site would fall victim to some readily apparent disorganization within the school itself. In other words, the school administrators knew that some processes within the school (business, curriculum, and otherwise) were haphazard at best, and they feared that the development of a Web site would bring this disorganization painfully into the light.

However, you were able to assuage their fears by stating (truthfully) that this type of internal business process confusion is not uncommon and that very often the development of a Web site, while drawing attention to this confusion, can also be an opportunity to correct it. You were truthful with the administrators, and you told them that this would be hard work. But you also told them that a final Web site reflecting an organized school would be an excellent tool for furthering all the goals of the school—technology-related or otherwise.

Greenlawn School Primary Goals

A description of the technology goals of the Web site follows:

1. The first goal is the most important, but also the most general. To summarize, the school administrators want the Web site to be customized for each user. They want the site to be a school information delivery portal—a site that will present individual students, teachers, and parents with a customized listing of information. Students will see a listing of the day's homework assignments and a schedule of activities in which they are involved. Parents might see a listing of PTA meetings or a list of practices and games for the events in which their children are involved. Teachers would have access to an online course delivery system in which they can utilize a Web-based testing component to create tests and quizzes for students. Although each of these audience members will have a specific set of design issues related to them, the customized user information delivery concept will be common across the site, to all users.

TIP

The Greenlawn School (and their emphasis on different information delivery views for different users) is touching on a critical aspect of CRM and Web design. Indeed, for a site like this to function most efficiently and be seen as a true portal, it must be able to deliver information that is unique to the specific user. For example, a student would not (and should not) want to view information that is applicable only to teachers. However, despite this compartmentalization of users with regard to how information is presented, the site should still appear exciting and vibrant to whoever is using it.

2. Next, the school administrators want the site to be seen (and used) as a true portal. Although they are smart enough to know that the Greenlawn students think of other things besides school, the school administrators know that by making the site informative and easy to use, they can encourage students to check it daily (if not more often) and perhaps make it their home page within their Web browser software. This portal concept should also carry over to the other "customers" of the Web site, specifically the parents and teachers.

3. Another required major piece of functionality is the ability to do online testing. This could potentially be used for students who must be home-schooled for a period of time (such as students who get sick and are out

for a week or more). However, the administrators also want this functionality for in-class exercises so that students sitting at individual workstations can take tests in a multimedia format. For example, the Chemistry department wants to use animation and other multimedia aspects of the Web to present their students with illustrated tests for which they must perform lab studies on the computer and then answer questions based on the visual results of the chemical reactions (displayed via animation on the screen).

 TIP

Yet another component of CRM that relates to the school Web site can be found within this online testing component. If you make an analogy between being able to view your past test scores and being able to view past orders on your favorite e-commerce site, you can see what is implied here. If you utilize good design CRM principles when you construct the site, students should be able to view their past tests scores and see a customized grade book and other individualized information. Again, like an e-commerce store that allows ready access to personal order information, the Greenlawn School Web site should allow the same personalized access to its users.

4. Yet another functional goal of the school Web site is to provide an online store that will sell school-related items such as T-shirts and sweatshirts with the school logo, tickets to school events, and so on. Although in this regard the site will closely resemble an e-commerce site, the school does not want the online store to be the focus of their site, nor do they want it to be overly complicated. Still, there are basic CRM principles involved in even the most basic online store, such as the ability to quickly view items in your shopping basket, see your past orders, and easily change or update your current order.

5. The school administrators want the site to be a real source of information to the entire community. The school plays a vital role in the education of many of the community's young people, but it is also seen as a central, active element to the town as a whole because it reflects the same social framework (in its policies and procedures) as other local businesses and organizations. Ideally, the school administrators would like to see the Web site serve as a type of community bulletin board to encourage frequent visitors from the community at large—not just parents who have kids enrolled in the school.

6. Finally, the school administrators want a site that is easy to administer. While there will be a level of complexity to the site that will probably demand ongoing professional IT administration (for example, the database which would undoubtedly power the online testing component), the school administrators would still like a site that is "user-friendly" enough from the administration perspective so they can go in and make small-to-moderate content changes on their own; ideally, they would also like the online store to be easy enough to configure so they can update information (prices of items, current inventory, and so on) with minimal hassle.

It should be clear that although this is a school Web site, it is not uncomplicated. Rather, the Greenlawn Web project might prove to be the most complex and demanding project presented in this book, if for no other reason than it wants to specifically address so many different user groups (teachers, students, parents, community members, businesses, and so on).

Greenlawn School Design Issues

As mentioned earlier, the design issues of the Greenlawn Web site—that is, how the goals listed in the preceding section will actually be thought of in terms of practical implementation via a Web site—are interesting as processes, as well as in how they relate to CRM principles applied to the site.

Again, the word "customer" takes on a very different connotation if you think of the site's customers as students and the commodity being delivered as education. But as you will see in the next two chapters, this analogy works because the underlying design issues are the same if you want to build a Web site that is as user-friendly and accessible as possible.

That said, the Greenlawn site presents myriad design issues that you can address neatly and creatively using HTML. The following sections describe these design issues.

Defining the Audience

The audience definition for the Greenlawn Web site is critical, especially in relation to how the term "customer" is defined. In early meetings with the school

CRM in Education: What's the Real Worth?

As someone who works with technology in higher education, I have seen firsthand the benefits of applying CRM principles to the design and implementation of education-based Web sites. It never ceases to amaze me that a project (no matter how small) can be derailed by bad planning in an institution of such astounding creativity and energy. Moreover, when such projects have a technology/Web component (and frequently this is the case), the Web site is often viewed as the answer to the problems produced by bad organization or planning.

As you saw in the first project, Web sites can be (and should be, in order to be effective) essential components of an organization's larger operating infrastructure. But as you have seen, if a site is brought online as a quick fix or just as window dressing, it will quickly resemble the appendix analogy I brought up in the first project—it will serve no purpose and only draw attention to the problems when something goes wrong.

Obviously, this is not a situation you want to be in, especially if you are charged with developing the Web site (as I am, in my technology management role in higher education). The good news is that more and more CRM design principles are being utilized in education. Although when reading this chapter you might think that I'm making a very big stretch in conceptually trying to apply these principles to an educational Web site, in reality these principles are applied to educational Web sites all the time.

The concept of customer-focused Web sites is taking increasing precedence in education, not only as technology pervades education in greater detail, but also as students are seen as "customers." If technology within higher education is achieving any goal, it is getting educators to think about a student's school experience in holistic terms. Specifically, how does class A, taken during freshman year, relate to class B, taken during senior year? By utilizing technology (in other words, a student-centric, portal-based Web site), students can and should be able to view their entire educational experience, retrieve information about all of their classes, and so on.

In short, students can be seen as customers, and CRM principles dictate that their information should be presented to them in a format they can customize and manage to their liking. Moreover, this information should reflect well-organized business processes. For example, students should be able to access their grade information in a way that reflects the manner in which they took classes—that is, it should be organized by year, instructor, and so on.

When you read the following sections of this chapter and move into Chapters 19 and 20, think in terms of the student as a customer. This will bring new insight to how you think of the Greenlawn Web site, and in turn how you will view other not-for-profit Web sites that you might be asked to develop in your professional career.

administrators, it was very clear to you that they wanted the site to offer customized views of information depending on who was using the site. In streamlining these definitions, you were able to divide the audiences into four major groups:

◆ The students are the major audience group that you need to define and address. Keeping the level of personalization will be critical to this audience. With students' short attention spans and less-than-stellar organizational skills, content on a Web site must be presented in a manner that is as clear, concise, and personal as possible. (I use the term "personal" to describe information that is specific to the user—in this case, the student.)

◆ The second group to be addressed by the site is the Greenlawn teachers. Like the students, the teachers need to have information presented to them in a customized, personal format. But unlike the students, teachers need to have access to the full range of curriculum on the site. For example, Mr. Smith in the Chemistry department might be very interested in seeing what Mrs. Jones in the Physics department is doing to present her information. Given the larger goals of the Web site—to present students with a complete academic portfolio so they can see at a glance how their work in one class integrates with another—this type of cross-curriculum integration is essential for both teachers and students.

◆ The third major audience group is the parents. A sort of cross between the teachers and students, the parents need access to a wide range of information, but they also need to be able to strictly limit the amount and type of information they receive. For example, a parent might want to closely monitor a student's progress in a course in which he or she is having difficulty, but at the same time only receive sporadic updates from areas in which the student is excelling. Moreover, some parents might have a particular interest in one school activity and want only temporary updates (or no updates at all) for other functional aspects of the school. While the portal design of the Greenlawn Web site will encourage interest in all functional aspects of the school, the school administrators realize that parents will have specific areas of interest, just as their children do. That said, the Web site should be customizable to present information to parents in a limited or full-access mode.

As I mentioned earlier in this chapter, other audience groups are interested in the Greenlawn School, including local businesses and educators from surrounding communities. These audiences will have guest access (as a default) to the

Greenlawn site. Upon request, they will be able to receive special access to present information deemed appropriate by the school administrators and the PTA.

Defining Internal Business Processes

From your early meetings with the school administrators, you quickly realized that they had serious reservations about developing a Web site where internal business processes were perhaps not readily defined.

Some of the business processes for Greenlawn School are defined as follows:

◆ There is some debate within the school about how to best integrate the curriculum. This is not so much an issue of how, for example, the reading and language classes complement the science coursework, but rather how this integration is communicated to the students. One group of teachers thinks that students only need access to information about their coursework in the most basic terms (in other words, they feel that holistic communication of a student's academic progress over four years is not necessary). However, another group of teachers thinks that students should be made aware immediately that what they do in class A during their freshman year can directly affect how they perceive class B during their senior year. Clearly, this is a communication process issue that needs to be defined prior to working on the Web site because the outcome of the process debate will determine how the information is presented on the Web site.

◆ Related to the preceding point, the level of student access to information is under debate. Some of the faculty think that students' schedules should be presented on a need-to-know basis. (Their thinking is that if students can see months ahead in their schedules, they will improperly prioritize their workloads. The other side of this camp says that a well-informed student is a successful student, and that there is no reason why they should not be able to see their schedules for the entire year. Of course, this debate hints at a larger issue of faculty being prepared to present students with a year's curriculum schedule at one time, versus having to develop it on a month-by-month basis.

◆ Another critical business process issue is how much involvement the local community should be allowed. Greenlawn School is like other schools in that budgets are tight. Despite the fact that they are privately funded, Greenlawn School is in constant need of additional funds, and they would like to draw on a support community. Aside from a Web store, there has been much discussion lately about how to best "sell" the school to the local community without exploiting the students or any of the school's educational activities.

 CAUTION

It should be clear from reviewing these larger business processes (or lack thereof) that there is much to be resolved prior to the successful implementation of a Web site for the school. Educators are (good-naturedly) notorious for wanting things done at the last minute or moving ahead with something without considering the full ramifications of their decisions. In short, they aren't the greatest planners. Although this is often not their fault because they must work within shoestring budgets and other administrative constraints, you—as Web designer in this arena—must be able to hold a firm line with regard to the changes you allow in your project, and you must hold the administrators to a clear definition of what exactly they want to Web-enable. There is a good rule that says, "The process should drive the development of the system, and not the other way around." In short, if your Web site becomes the driving force in defining your business processes, you probably need to go back to the drawing board and more clearly and accurately define your business processes. This is not to say that a Web site can't be an instrument for change, but it should be clear from these process issues (especially the first two) that some internal processes need to be worked out first for the resulting Web site to most accurately facilitate the desired functionality.

Personalizing the Customer Experience

The Greenlawn School wants (needs) to put a real emphasis on customizing the user experience depending on who is logged on to the site.

Students will want and require a different content presentation than teachers, who in turn will want a different content presentation than parents. However, the common thread in all this is the administrators' stated desire to make the school Web site an information portal for these different groups (as well the community and other educators).

That said, the site should:

◆ **Allow for individual, customized information views depending on user type**. If students log on to the site, they should see content specific to their interests, such as homework schedules and listings of extracurricular events in which they're involved.

◆ **Allow for further customization of individual user information**.
Students involved with the school band, for example, might want to add
a listing of the football team's schedule to their information views.
Teachers in the English department, for example, might want to add
links specific to the History department to their information views. This
type of customized information delivery should be put into the hands of
the users as much as possible, so they can shape the Web site to their
liking and thus be more inclined to visit the site often.

Indeed, personalizing the customer experience is once again the primary driving
requirement of the Greenlawn Web site, and this goal will be the focus of much
of the discussion in the remaining chapters of this project.

Implementing the Greenlawn School Web Site

It should be clear from reading this chapter that just because the Web site is for a
school, it will not necessarily be simple to implement. Indeed, this site might be
the most difficult of all when you consider the high degree of customization that
is required for custom user views and how information will be presented.

Working through Chapters 18 and 19, you will be prepared to see the final Web
site implemented in Chapter 20 because you have the necessary technical HTML
skills (which you learned in Part I of this book), and you also have a critical understanding of the rather complex business processes that are lurking within the
Greenlawn site.

As you work through this project, keep in mind these design and process issues,
as well as how the principles of CRM are adjusted appropriately for this not-for-
profit site. Again, the Web functionality across all the projects in this book is basically the same; only the definition of the initial process goals and design requirements separates them. In the final implementation, you should be able to draw on
your HTML skills and organizational insight to deliver the best Web site possible. The Greenlawn School project will be no exception.

Chapter 18

**Greenlawn School
Web Site:
Identifying
Process Goals for
the Nonprofit Site**

As you learned in the previous chapter, the fictitious Greenlawn School Web project presents a special set of challenges, from the actual HTML behind the site to the challenging business processes the site hopes to facilitate. Moreover, compared to the commercial MuseToMusic project, the customer base for the Greenlawn site is varied and complex and asks you to consider new definitions of the term *customer*.

So before you start to code the school's Web site, you need to consider these issues and how they will affect the Web site. This chapter will provide specific detail on the five major goals of the school's Web site, as initially discussed in Chapter 17. The school administrators want to build a site that

◆ Facilitates direct communication among a diverse user base—specifically teachers, parents, and students.

◆ Allows for a personalized user experience by following the same Web portal concepts that drove the MuseToMusic site design.

◆ Allows for online testing and interactive content-driven online instruction.

◆ Provides space for an online store so different school groups can sell items of interest on the Web.

◆ Serves as a true information resource for the local community via the development of online discussion forums, bulletin boards, and so on.

This chapter will look at all these issues in specific detail. Chapter 19, "Greenlawn School Web Site: Addressing Customer Usability Issues," will look at the unique CRM issues for the school's Web site development. Finally, Chapter 20, "Greenlawn School Web Site: Building the Solution," will highlight the development and coding of the Web site.

 NOTE

If you've already worked through the MuseToMusic site (Chapters 13 through 16 and 21 through 24), you might find it interesting to consider the CRM issues discussed there and how they translate to a non-profit site such as the Greenlawn School. I will discuss these CRM-specific issues in more detail in Chapter 19, but I will lay the groundwork for how they will be implemented in the process goals covered in this chapter.

Greenlawn School: Identifying the Underlying Process Goals and Challenges

In the last chapter, I wrote that CRM methodologies are being applied via technology utilized in education. Specifically, I mentioned that a major benefit of using technology in education is that it allows (forces) educators to think of their curriculum in holistic terms—that is, how does Class A, taken during freshman year, relate to Class B, taken during senior year?

Although it might at first reading seem like an obvious issue to consider, the fact of the matter is that this holistic approach to curriculum development is something of a new idea. Too often in education (especially at the secondary and post-secondary levels), the curriculum is fractured into isolated components with no direct correlation to one another.

This is an interesting and complicated challenge when you look at these process issues from a technology perspective, specifically with regard to answering the following questions.

♦ How do you facilitate these educational processes via technology—specifically via a Web site?

♦ How do you apply portal design concepts and larger business intelligence methodologies (including CRM) so that you bridge the compartmentalized "silos" and thus make the entire educational process a holistic, integrated experience?

One of the hottest technology topics in secondary and post-secondary education is the CMS (*Course Management System*). Such applications seek to present teachers and students with a Web-based, portal-influenced design in which all aspects of the learning process—from posting of course syllabi to providing online testing—are presented in one shell. What is fascinating and incredibly challenging about implementing these applications is that they are often the impetus for serious review of the underlying educational processes that drive the development of the curriculum in the first place. As I have said many times in this book, the development of a system should be the end result of well-defined processes. If the opposite is true—that is, where the system drives the process—you are asking for trouble because the system will quickly spiral to account for everyone's requests and desires. (This is also known as *scope creep*.)

That said, when you first sat down with the Greenlawn administrators, you told them (being the excellent Web developer that you are) that much predesign work would be required if the Web site was going to be the most functional tool possible. The following sections of this chapter will look at these process issues and goals. Chapter 19 will build on those goals to look at specific implementation at the customer level. Collectively, these two chapters will represent the predesign work that will see its fruition in Chapter 20, with the actual construction of the school's site.

 NOTE

As with the MuseToMusic site, I'm asking you to slip into the role of Web design consultant and to read these project chapters as if they represent a project diary you might have kept while working with the organizations.

Process Goal: Facilitating Better Communication

The Greenlawn Web site will ultimately have to address three major types of users:

◆ Students

◆ Teachers

◆ Parents

Prior to considering a Web site, the school's mechanism of addressing these diverse groups was at best a mediocre success. In addition to the typical communication issues between parents and students, the school administrators recognized there were serious curriculum process gaps developing due to this lack of communication among the different user groups. For example, if a student was performing poorly in class, the teacher could contact the parent directly. However, to keep this level of communication going, it was necessary to initiate a complicated, paper-based tracking process. For example,

1. A student is identified as having difficulty in a particular class, so the teacher initiates a first contact with the parent (either via a letter or telephone call).

2. The parent requests a conference with the teacher.

3. The conference is held, and an action plan consisting of weekly progress reports between teacher and parent is initiated.

4. After the first two weeks of exchanging paper-based reports, a second conference is initiated.

5. For this example, assume that the student is still having problems in the class. A second conference is requested with the teacher, the student, the parent, and a development specialist within the school corporation.

6. More paper-based progress reports are exchanged.

7. The process repeats throughout the semester.

At first glance, this process might seem like an effective method of approaching the student's problems in class. But consider the following concerns:

◆ All of the parties involved must coordinate their schedules (never an easy task) to physically meet.

◆ The progress reports are static in that they are only as current as the last report that was sent.

◆ Although involved in this process with the others, each party is nevertheless isolated in their role. Other than the actual meetings, the three groups don't have much direct integrated communication.

◆ Most important, the student's difficulties in this particular class are isolated from his or her educational development in other courses, unless the time-consuming process of organizing multiple meetings with different teachers and administrators is undertaken.

Although some of the challenges of face-to-face meetings could be alleviated via e-mail, this still does not answer the challenges of addressing the problem in the context of the student's entire curriculum development. Although you will see how this issue is addressed to a greater extent by the portal design concept, the school administrators have realized that a major goal (indeed, the primary goal) of the site must be the facilitation of improved communication among parents, teachers, and students. In relation to the process outlined earlier for addressing a student's problems in a class, consider how that process could be facilitated via a well-designed, portal-based Web site.

1. Each student at the Greenlawn School has an electronic curriculum portfolio in which teachers post current grades and assignments, moderate online discussions, and so on. At a glance, students can see

assignments due for all their classes (via a curriculum-wide calendar). In turn, parents can log on to the site and get a snapshot of their children's progress as information is culled from each of the student's courses within the portfolio.

2. Since this is a communication tool viewed and owned by each party, each party has an opportunity to review the information at any time. (In other words, there is no need for physical meetings to take place.)

3. The holistic approach of such a communication tool means that reports on a student's progress are not limited to one course; rather, they can be seen in the context of the entire curriculum.

4. Finally, given the access to such integrated information, students, parents, and teachers can have a more comprehensive discussion about how to help the student address his or her academic challenge.

 NOTE

A sense of ownership is critical to the success of a Web tool such as the one described here. As you saw in the discussion of the MuseToMusic site, allowing customers to customize and personalize their Web experience provides them with a sense of ownership of the site and encourages them to return. They feel more in control of their experience on your site—not as if they are being force-fed information or the process they must use to access that information. The same applies to the communication goals of the Greenlawn Web site. Given that it is a well-acknowledged fact that the best facilitation of education occurs when there is active involvement from parents, teachers, and students, it makes sense that a Web tool that facilitates this involvement should allow each group the ability to personalize and own their role in this process.

Clearly the Greenlawn Web site has an opportunity to better facilitate this communication among its users, and this will remain a major design goal. Again, you will see the issues discussed here—sense of ownership, personalization, integration of information—discussed in regard to the portal design concepts that will also be applied to the Web site development.

Process Goal: Integrating Information Delivery

As I mentioned earlier, CMS is a major topic of interest in how technology is used in secondary and post-secondary education.

A course management system draws from several functional aspects of a Web portal in that it seeks to integrate isolated "silos" of information across the delivery of the curriculum. Additionally, as illustrated in the previous section, CMS seeks to facilitate better discussion among all users.

There are major commercial CMS applications available on the market today, such as Blackboard and WebCT. Moreover, there are efforts underway among higher education institutions to develop a collective process for the development of such CMS applications. (See http://web.mit.edu/oki for more information.) But the focus of this project (and this book) is to show you how you can facilitate the development of these tools on your own via HTML. As you saw in the MuseToMusic project, the benefits of a portal and the issues involved in its development can both be numerous.

In Chapter 15, which discussed specific CRM issues of the MuseToMusic Web site, there were three specific subsections on the benefits of a portal design for the MuseToMusic site:

◆ Access to previous order history

◆ Customizable profile and interface

◆ Online support and discussion forums

The following sections will look at each of these three issues in the context of the Greenlawn School, with the focus again being on how these issues can translate to a nonprofit site.

 NOTE

Regardless of whether you work in education, the Web design issues surrounding course management systems are fascinating. For a more extended discussion of these issues, check out the following links:

◆ http://www.educause.edu/ir/library/pdf/eqm0311.pdf

◆ http://www.cren.net/know/techtalk/events/cms.html

Accessing Previous Order History

If the analogy of a typical business is applied to the Greenlawn School, then some interesting comparisons emerge. One of the more intriguing issues, especially from a design perspective, is thinking about the students as customers of the school's Web site, and how they would like to review the products (which in this case translates to their specific grades and other aspects of their instruction).

In your initial meetings with the school administrators, it was made clear that the Web site needed to provide this comprehensive information access. As noted already in this chapter, the school administrators want to utilize the site to bring together various aspects of the school operation (curriculum or otherwise) and thus provide a more holistic view of the entire operation. The administrators believe that allowing students to see all of their current coursework, as well as how that current work fits in with previous work, is a central requirement for improving the overall delivery of the curriculum.

However, it is not just students who will benefit from this. You saw earlier a comparison of a student-teacher-parent discussion that was performed via traditional methods and then facilitated via a Web tool. If a parent, for example, could also access a student's work and compare past academic performance trends to current work, the parent would be better informed and ideally able to contribute more effectively to the solution for his or her child's specific academic problem.

Clearly the relationships between accessing this previous order history and how this goal was facilitated via the MuseToMusic site are readily apparent. Although the context is quite different, the underlying goal is the same—to give users a greater sense of empowerment in accessing information that is theirs to begin with and to facilitate stronger communication between users and your organization.

 NOTE

The Greenlawn School's efforts to construct a student portfolio via their Web portal is a concept that is gaining acceptance in all levels of education. As you will see in more detail in the next chapter, this type of tool provides an excellent method of managing and addressing the students' specific demands for how they want their product (their academic work) to be viewed and manipulated by themselves and other potential audiences (such as prospective employers who are looking for a more comprehensive view of a student's work).

Providing a Customizable Profile and Interface

Going hand in hand with the discussion in the previous section, all users of the Greenlawn Web site need the ability to customize the level of interaction they have with the site.

As you've already seen, students will want different views of information than their teachers and parents will. Moreover, local businesses will not (and should not) have access to a student's specific grades, but might want more general access to a student's e-portfolio.

There are many specific CRM-related issues with regard to how this information should be presented. These issues will in turn affect how you code the infrastructure of the site to best present audience-specific views. This will be discussed in more detail in the next chapter.

Providing Online Discussion and Support

If customers of the MuseToMusic site benefited from being able to talk to one another via online discussion forums, this functionality reaches new levels of effectiveness when used in an educational context. Students at all levels benefit from peer feedback, which can be an invaluable tool for providing a non-threatening (yet extremely constructive) environment for addressing specific questions and concerns.

The Greenlawn Web site will include several areas for online discussion. However, in addition to simply providing a forum for this interactivity, the online discussion forums will also seek to:

◆ Allow online moderation by teachers or other school administrators with regard to how to best facilitate the learning process.

◆ Provide students with the ability to personalize their discussion access (for example, so they can be prompted when a new message string develops that pertains to a question they have).

◆ Allow information that is generated in the discussion forums to be manipulated (cut and pasted) by students into other areas of their e-portfolios. For example, students might want to show how a particular discussion facilitated another student's learning, supported a project they were working on, and so on.

Clearly the focus in all of these subrequirements of the Web portal is on personalization and custom access to specific information. Once again, you should compare how these issues are addressed in the Greenlawn Web site versus their implementation in the MuseToMusic site. This will allow you to see how the general Web design principles are the same despite the different audiences involved.

Process Goal: Providing Online Testing

The ability to develop online testing is important to the Greenlawn administrators, but from a limited perspective. That is, they want to be sure that the internal process infrastructure is in place before online testing is fully integrated.

What does *internal infrastructure* refer to? You can think of the online testing issue as a key example of how Web sites (or any technology tools, for that matter) *must* be the result of a well-defined process and not force unstructured changes on a business process that may or may not be well defined in the first place.

When you met with the school administrators, you became aware of the specific issues and concerns surrounding online testing. Specifically,

◆ The school faculty and administrators (as well as parents) expressed concern that online testing cannot be accurately policed. That is, students—being creative as they often are—will devise ways to impersonate other students and cheat on the tests.

◆ There are questions about how online testing can be implemented into the curriculum. Specifically, when should online testing be utilized and to what degree should it substitute for regular testing procedures within the curriculum?

◆ How should the general online teaching environment be utilized best, especially in conjunction with traditional classroom lectures? Some teachers are quite technologically savvy and are working independently to devise multimedia presentations that can be accessed remotely by the students, for example. However, other teachers who are not as savvy or who see this type of instruction as secondary are raising concerns about the amount of time and resources that could be required by these types of technology initiatives.

These are good questions about how this component of the Greenlawn Web site should be addressed. As the Web developer, you need to recognize these issues and consider them when coding the site so that the site is an accurate representation of agreed-upon school polices and procedures. (This is not an easy task when the level of agreement is tenuous at best!)

READING BETWEEN THE LINES IN WEB DEVELOPMENT

The questions raised here about the online testing component of the Greenlawn Web site are very important and should not be ignored. As a Web developer, technology consultant, or anyone charged with developing and facilitating the implementation of a technology solution, you must constantly be aware of the underlying process issues that are at the center of any technology implementation. Remember that a Web site is ultimately just a tool. If the underlying process is corrupt or has serious problems, no Web site, no matter how well designed, will be able to solve them. In fact, the Web site will only exacerbate the problem because it will more than likely bring the problems in the underlying process to light.

As you work with customers and clients you can address these issues, but you might have to wear the psychologist hat as well as the Web developer hat. Organizations of all types often are looking for your services because they are seeking a panacea for their specific business process problems. They have heard and perhaps seen real cases of technology being the end-all, be-all solution, and they want to tap some of that magic to help address their own problems. Although technology can help to solve business problems, it cannot be overstated that the underlying processes that the technology is meant to facilitate must be well developed.

If you read between the lines in the bullet points regarding the online testing issue, you can see there is some real disagreement among the Greenlawn faculty and parents for how online testing should be implemented. Although it is not your job as a Web developer to tell the customer how to use the tool, it is your responsibility to build a tool that considers all of the functional requirements. That said, you should be aware of situations like this one because they are prime candidates for scope creep (that is, where the ultimate list of functional requirements grows and grows because the final list of requirements cannot be agreed upon). Don't be dissuaded from tackling projects like this; however, do stay aware and read between the lines about what your customers are saying in terms of what they want, the procedures they want to facilitate, and the possible contingencies you might have to consider, such as conflicting customer opinions about how the tool you are building can be utilized best.

Process Goal: Developing the Greenlawn Web Store

Compared to the requirements of the MuseToMusic online shopping cart, the Greenlawn online store is fairly straightforward. The store will seek to address different customers (just like the MuseToMusic site), but it obviously does not have the same aspirations as the MuseToMusic Web.

Still, you can apply the issues surrounding that site's online shopping cart to the Greenlawn site:

♦ **Conspicuous access.** Different organizations within the school (such as sports, academic clubs, and the school band) want to use the Web site for fundraising activities. The online store is the perfect place for this. By integrating a simple JavaScript (which you'll see in Chapter 20), you can rotate advertisements for each of these groups so they each get an equal amount of airtime on the site. When visitors click on the advertisement, they are taken to the page for the specific organization, where they can see a list of the products the organization has for sale.

♦ **Seamless integration.** Throughout the Web site, there should be links to the store, as well as a sense that the store is seamlessly integrated with the rest of the site content. Although not as overt as the MuseToMusic site, where band profiles link directly to order forms for their CDs, the Greenlawn Store can still be integrated with, for example, links to the stores on the individual Web pages for the different school organizations.

♦ **Full product descriptions.** Just because the store is on a school Web site, that doesn't mean the products in question should be glossed over quickly. Indeed, such products might need more description than those from a typical online store. Not only do you have to describe the product, but you probably want to describe why it is being sold and whom it will benefit. (Customers will want to know these details.)

 NOTE

Unlike much of the advanced functionality described for the Greenlawn site, it is possible to achieve a fairly complex online store with some simple JavaScript integration. See Chapter 11, "Integrating Scripts and Other Advanced Functionality," and the last chapter of this project (Chapter 20) for more information on this issue.

Process Goal: Providing a Community Bulletin Board

I want to close this chapter with a discussion of another important process goal of the Greenlawn site—for the site to serve as a community bulletin board. Similar to the general portal concept, the school administrators were quite adamant in their early meetings with you that they wanted the Web site to be a reflection of one of the major missions of the school—to serve as a community resource for information.

The good news is that this type of functionality isn't that difficult to build using some simple HTML. By using cascading style sheets (see Chapters 9 and 10 for more information on CSS), you can create, for example, a template for announcing different types of community events. CSS also makes these events easy to administer. Also, as mentioned in the previous section, you can integrate some simple JavaScript to make community and school announcements rotate and neatly integrate into the larger site design. (In other words, you can make them not overbearing to visitors.)

Again, you will learn more about the specific customer benefits of this functionality in the next chapter and you will see how it is implemented in Chapter 20. Stay tuned.

Summary

This chapter looked at the major process goals that the Greenlawn administrators, teachers, students, and parents want to see facilitated via the Web site. Even though the site is for a nonprofit organization, it still can follow the same conceptual design as that of a commercial site, such as the MuseToMusic site. Moreover, you can also apply terminology that is utilized for a commercial site—especially the term *customer* and the issues that surround it (CRM)—to a site like the Greenlawn Web to help facilitate user interaction. Finally, I mentioned extensively in this chapter that you must be sure to keep an eye out for scope creep, and that no matter how well a site is designed, the underlying business and organizational processes must be well designed too for the site to live up to its maximum potential.

Chapter 19

One of the more interesting things about Web development in today's environment is the emphasis and connotation placed on the word *customer*. As I discussed in the first two chapters of this project, the word customer takes on a special meaning when it is applied to a nonprofit site such as the Greenlawn School site. The customers (the students) are not shopping for products in the traditional sense, but they can still very much benefit from the design methodologies of customer relationship management applied to the site.

Why worry about CRM in the first place, let alone with a project like the Greenlawn School, where the definition of the word customer is really stretched, at least in the traditional sense? Well, there are many good reasons, not the least of which includes the following:

◆ Regardless of its focus, the best Web sites should give visitors a sense of ownership so they are more in control of the information that often belongs to them in the first place (such as order history). By applying this line of thought to the school Web site, the school administrators hope the students will take a greater sense of ownership of their academic progress (due to the ready availability of their grades and how their various courses fit together to form a larger curriculum) and thus strive to perform better.

◆ The process in which a student will move through the school site is similar to how a customer of an e-commerce site would look for, review, and order a specific product. For example, if the products in this analogy are the results of an online test, the student will need to be able to quickly navigate to the test (the product), have the questions and general format of the test (the product details) be neatly and clearly presented, be able to take the test (make a purchase), and then be able to review the results of the test (review their order history). All of this can be thought of as an extended process goal. These goals were described in the last chapter (and will be developed in Chapter 20), and this chapter focuses on the customer usability issues surrounding each step in this process.

◆ Finally, other aspects of the Greenlawn Web site (including its online store) can be easily paralleled in a real e-commerce site, thus basic CRM issues will apply to these functional components of the site as well.

I don't want to push the CRM analogy between e-commerce and a nonprofit site so much that I confuse you with regard to the actual Web design issues; however, keeping these issues in mind is critical to the overall planning process. As you learned when you met with the school administrators (in the previous two chapters of this project), there are some significant process issues in this project (for example, the differing views on online testing), as well as questions about how to best resolve them. This short chapter will give you an idea of how to consider these issues from what is perhaps the most important perspective—that of the customer or user of the site.

Accounting for Different User Viewpoints and a Sense of Ownership

Students are a fickle group, and having them as your primary customers will present a challenge to even the most talented Web designer. Indeed, the real obstacle in the Greenlawn project is trying to develop a Web site that is functional but also appeals to the habits and attitudes of the students. Although you would do this with any Web site, of course, it is of particular importance here.

However, students are not the only customers of the Greenlawn site. You must also consider the school faculty, as well as parents and the Greenlawn community in general. Each of the following sections will describe how you should consider addressing these ownership issues in your actual design.

 NOTE

Another challenge with this particular site is that although you need to address individual ownership requirements for each user, you must also integrate each of these different requirements into a collective whole. For example, you must include the student interaction with the Web site within the teacher interaction (in other words, the teachers will need to determine when online tests will be made available or how class-specific information will be presented to the students). Moreover, you will need to consider the teacher interaction with the parent view because parents will want to see their children's progress (the student view) as well as the manner in which the curriculum is being delivered (the teacher view). Put simply, there is a chain of interaction in terms of how much information is seen by each group, with the students at the bottom and the parents at the top. Of course, there might be information at each level of interaction that is private to just that level (for example, teachers might not want to expose every method or style of teaching they apply). Still, you need to consider these different interaction views when you design any Web site. This will be particularly important when you consider larger site navigation and how each type of user/customer moves through the site depending on their area of interest.

Figure 19.1 illustrates the site home page.

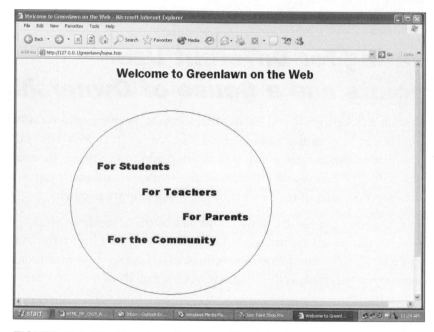

FIGURE 19.1 *The Greenlawn home page. The design is a simple image map, which you will construct in Chapter 20.*

Take a moment to consider the different user viewpoints in terms of this initial page, and how these views will need to be addressed by the individual user home pages (illustrated in the next set of figures):

◆ Students are entering the site, probably in a hurry, to try to find the specific information for which they are searching. Although they might be spending an extensive amount of time on the site, they are not going to meander from one section to another. They want quick access to particular sections, such as grades, discussion forums, and so on. That said, they want quick navigation to the point of interest.

◆ Teachers also want direct access, but they want to be presented with a more comprehensive view of all possible functionality on the site. In other words, they want to see how each section fits with another to account for all information requirements. As you will see in the design of the site, they will want the site design and links to be a representation of how the actual curriculum links together, so the site essentially becomes a conceptual map of their style of teaching.

◆ Parents likely will be attracted to information specific to their child. Although they might be interested in school activities (such as the school store—more on this later) or the community bulletin board, they will want direct access to information about their own child. However, as you will see later in this chapter and in the next chapter, the pages that subsequently load must give more specific, direct access to areas of interest specific to each user group.

◆ Finally, the community at large likely will want access to the school's community bulletin board feature or the Web store.

This is only the site home page, and already there are significant design issues that you need to consider. Again, these issues all have a customer usability component, depending on the information needs of the specific visitor. However, as Figure 19.1 shows, the design need not be overly complicated to include all these different usability issues; indeed, it can be radically simple as is illustrated here.

Figures 19.2 and 19.3, illustrate two specific audience/customer "sub-home" pages (the pages that load when one of the four specific links on the site home page is clicked). Considering the information presented earlier, note how the design of each of these pages is geared toward the specific audience and tries to be a functional representation of how the specific audience likely will access information on the site.

 NOTE

As with any site, much of the functionality presented here would be secure. For example, the user would be asked to provide a password or other identifier to access specific information. Although the complete design of such a site is beyond the scope and focus of this book, this type of secure access would obviously be required on the Greenlawn Web site.

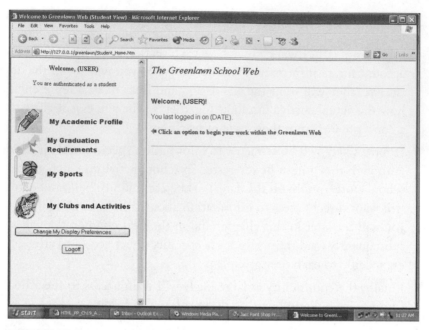

FIGURE 19.2 *The student home page.*

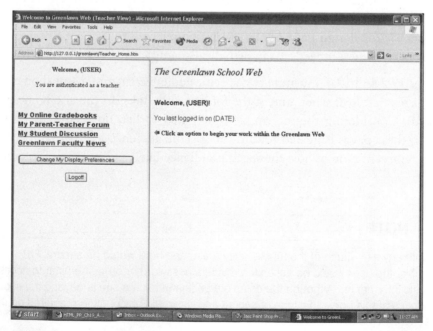

FIGURE 19.3 *The teacher home page. Again, a different design and placement of links tries to reflect the teacher's desire to have the site be a representation of his or her entire curriculum presentation, with links to gradebook, parent-teacher discussion forums, and so on.*

What is interesting about the actual HTML design of each of these customer views is the larger CRM requirements that you should consider—especially the issues that concern the order or process in which information is accessed, depending on the specific user. The next section will focus on these issues and how they differ from user to user.

The User-Specific Information Access Process

As I mentioned in the previous sections, how users move through the site will be unique based on their specific information requirements. For example, students will want access to different things than their parents, and in a different order.

If you apply e-commerce CRM design principles to account for the user-specific information access requirements, you can neatly account for some major design concerns. Recall from Chapter 18 some of the user-access questions and process goals that you uncovered in first meeting with the school administrators:

◆ How can the Web site facilitate a holistic view of the curriculum so students, teachers, and parents can share in all aspects of the educational process? And how can the site decrease the silo effect that each of these roles traditionally plays in education. (By silo effect, I'm referring to the communication between each group being isolated.)

◆ How can the Web site help address larger curriculum delivery concerns? Specifically, how can the use of online testing enhance the curriculum delivery?

◆ Related to each of these points, how can the Web site, using a portal design concept, deliver information to all audiences in a more integrated manner?

◆ Finally, how can the Web site deliver information to the community at large via the use of bulletin boards and an online store?

Certainly, the last point lends itself to the e-commerce aspects of CRM, as discussed in the MuseToMuse project. However, it is just as viable (and perhaps more interesting) to consider the first three bullets under the auspices of CRM, especially if the users are viewed as customers who are coming to the site in search of information that is viewed as a product.

Each of the following sections will examine major CRM aspects of this product access to better examine how the site design can account for each user's specific information access requirements.

Providing Access to Complete Product Information

Providing succinct yet comprehensive information is the goal of any Web site and is of particular concern to some of the specific user types of the Greenlawn site. As mentioned, students will want to quickly get to a particular area (more on this navigation aspect in a later section). However, once they are at the page they want to access, the product that is being "sold" there (in other words, online test information) needs to be comprehensive in its presentation.

Personalizing the Information Access Process

I have already mentioned that information on the Greenlawn site should be presented in a user-specific fashion. As the designer, you need to consider the various ways in which different user types access information.

However, there is another level of this user-specific access. Once the information is uniquely presented, it should be customized further to the individual user. Continuing the CRM e-commerce analogy, this would be considered personalizing the order process. You can carry this analogy through by thinking of the product not as an appliance, a CD, or a new pair of shoes, but instead as test grades or a progress report on a student's academic progress throughout the semester.

 NOTE

The issues discussed here go hand-in-hand with what was discussed in the section that began this chapter—"Accounting for Different User Viewpoints and a Sense of Ownership." In a nutshell, once you consider the different types of user access viewpoints (as described in that section), you then need to consider the specific, individual user ownership and customization of the information that is presented.

There are a few design issues you should consider to allow the highest degree of personalization within the site.

◆ **Allow access to previous order history.** For example, students should be able to access previous semester grades, and parents should be able to see previous academic progress reports from past years. This will give the users the feeling that their work is valued, and that you consider the ability to view it an important criterion for their continued use of the site.

◆ **Allow customization of data views.** Although this is beyond the scope of straight HTML, by integrating a database (or a little JavaScript) into your site, you can allow users to view information in a way that is specific to their tastes. This will also empower them with the much-discussed sense of ownership toward their own information, as well as the site in general.

◆ **Provide complete access to the product in which users are interested.** If a student is taking an online test, the information presented should be clear and easily accessible. The student shouldn't have to jump through HTML design hoops. Remember, even though a Web site is being used to facilitate the test, the Web site is not what is most important—the test is! The Web site is merely a tool used to facilitate a process.

TIP

The third bullet point here reflects perhaps the most basic point in HTML design (or any technology implementation): The Web site should be the end result of a well-defined process, and it should not be used initially to define the process. If the latter is the case, then you are headed down a slippery slope where technology is used to try to constantly patch problems that are the result of a poorly organized process infrastructure. Technology can lead you in the right direction, but it must always be placed atop a solid, well-defined process, regardless of the organization (e-commerce, nonprofit, and so on).

◆ **Don't lock how information is presented based on user profiles.** People change their opinions and preferences for how they want information to be presented. This is especially true when you use personal information to guide how information is presented. For example, a student initially might have requested that his or her current grades be displayed upon first logging in to the site. This is all fine and good, but this type of information access should be changeable at any time to reflect the user's personal preference.

Keeping Site Navigation Product-Oriented

This is perhaps the most critical issue in the larger e-commerce CRM analogy I am attempting to draw in this chapter. As I have mentioned repeatedly in the project chapters of this book, you should consider as a major design issue your overall site navigation. This becomes especially important—indeed, *critically* important—when you want to map what you feel to be information access preferences (based on user type) to your overall design scheme.

To illustrate this example, I want to once again compare the student and teacher home pages, as initially illustrated in Figure 19.2 and 19.3. Note the comparisons between the navigation features of the two pages, as described in Table 19.1.

Table 19.1 Comparison of Student and Teacher Home Page Navigation Schemes

Navigation Feature	Student Home Page	Teacher Home Page
Graphics	Multiple graphics used as hyperlinks to specific pages	One single image map used to reflect an integrated view of the curriculum the Web site hopes to facilitate.
Links to other sections of the Web site	Links to a wider variety of functions within the site, including the online store and discussion groups	Links tend to stay focused on the curriculum management aspect of the site and how it is facilitated. There is a single link back to the home page, where the user can access other functions of the site.
Links to personalized information	Links to student-specific grade and assessment information	Links to specific courses and online curriculum-development folders.

Now I want to compare and contrast each of these navigation features in more detail across both specific user types.

◆ **Graphics.** This is really a design issue in terms of trying to appeal to a specific user aesthetic. The more visually-direct graphics on the student page are intended to liven it up. In contrast, the single image map graphic on the teacher home page is intended to be a reflection of how the Web can be used as a tool to help effectively present an integrated approach to curriculum delivery (in other words, to allow teachers to see how each piece of the curriculum fits with the others to form a whole instructional methodology).

♦ **Links to other sections of the Web site.** Based on their interests, students probably will be inclined to want to visit different areas of the site. However, as I mentioned earlier, they want direct access to those sections, so note the unique graphical links used to represent each specific section of the site. The teacher home page is more limited in this regard because the design assumes that teachers will probably utilize the site primarily as a curriculum development tool; therefore, limiting the navigation links to just this area makes the page less confusing and (ideally) easier to navigate.

♦ **Links to personalized information.** This is an essential navigation tool for all user types; thus a similar approach is used on both teacher and student home pages.

 NOTE

In the next chapter, I will detail the underlying HTML used to facilitate the different types of navigation features highlighted here, including the development of an image map. However, refer back to Chapter 5 for a general primer on links and image maps.

Customer Usability Issues: The Greenlawn Web Store and Community Bulletin Board

The final two Greenlawn Web issues that I want to discuss with regard to the CRM analogy revolve around the online store and the community bulletin board sections of the site. Each of these site features has specific discussion points that can fit within the CRM analogy, so I want to discuss them individually in the following two sections.

CRM and the Community Bulletin Board

An interesting way to look at the bulletin board component of the Greenlawn Web site, especially with regard to the CRM analogy, is as a form of post-order support.

What do I mean by this? Imagine that you go to a commercial Web site to buy a product, such as an advanced piece of computer software or another technical purchase. Although you might be able to get the product to function properly, you realize that due to its complexity, there is a lot you could learn from the experience or help of others. This is where post-order support becomes invaluable.

You can carry the same idea over to the community bulletin board concept. In this case, if you think of the initial order as an investment or just general interest in the school or community, then the post-order support can be seen as a way of getting the most out of that interest. Consider the following:

- **Discussion forum.** You can use the bulletin board to help resolve various arguments or debates revolving around the school or the community in general.

- **Online support.** Members of the community can post a question or concern to the bulletin board and use it as method of gaining expert advice from other individuals or groups who are knowledgeable about the issue in question.

- **Customer retention.** Having a well-designed, well-moderated bulletin board is a great way to encourage interest in the site and should (ideally) encourage users of all types to continue to frequent the site.

CAUTION

You must use caution in allowing open postings to a Web site bulletin board or discussion board, lest an inflammatory topic be introduced. Things can get out of control, with users flaming one another (that is, slinging insults and other derogatory comments back and forth) or posting derogatory or inappropriate comments. (This is especially true in the case of a school Web site, where you would not want this type of discussion to occur.)

Basically, the bulletin board can serve a vital role in keeping users interested in your site. Moreover, with regard to the Greenlawn School, it can funnel attention to specific school events such as PTA meetings, sports, and band activities.

CRM and the Online Store

You can apply each of the points discussed in the earlier section, "User-Specific Information Access Process," directly to best practices for the design of the online store. Indeed, the points discussed in that section are really intended to serve as design principles for an e-commerce site, but I translated them for the CRM analogy I've been using throughout this chapter.

In the best e-commerce sites, there are basically three major design and process points you need to consider.

◆ **Pre-order customer support issues.** Issues here include inventory integration with the online store, real-time access to product information, and shipping and tracking of ordered products.

◆ **Point-of-order customer support issues.** Basically, this issue includes the points of discussion in the "User-Specific Information Access Process" section, including personalizing the order process, providing an intuitive navigation scheme, and so on.

◆ **Post-order customer support issues.** Major issues here include tracking orders and resolving problems. Also, many of the CRM issues discussed in the bulletin board section can be thought of as post-order customer support issues.

 NOTE

For a complete discussion of each of these CRM design and process issues, see *Customer Relationship Management Essentials* (Premier Press, 2000).

For a more complete discussion of an e-commerce site, please be sure to see the MuseToMuse project if you have not already done so.

Summary

This chapter looked at the specific customer-usability issues of the Greenlawn Web site by using a CRM analogy to consider the different issues based on specific users of the site. First, the chapter considered these different user viewpoints and how your HTML design should consider not only the user aesthetic, but also the different ways in which these users like to access information. Next, you looked in more detail at this process of information access based on the different user types by considering an analogy to a product-order process for a typical online store. Finally, the chapter considered two other major functional components of the site—the community bulletin board and the school's online store—to see what specific user-accessibility issues need to be considered in the design process for these areas of the site.

The next (and final) chapter of this project will consider the predesign issues discussed in this chapter and Chapter 18 in order to build the Greenlawn School Web site structure. The chapter will account for all the process goal requirements set forth in Chapter 18, as well as ensure that those goals are addressed in the most customer-friendly fashion, as discussed in this chapter.

Chapter 20

If after reading the opening chapters of this project, you feel that the Greenlawn Web site is a complicated challenge, then… congratulations! I say that because it means you have recognized the subtle complexities, in terms of design and audience requirements, that you will need to address if this Web site is going to be successful.

I also give you kudos if you recognize that to successfully answer all the challenges of this site, you will need to utilize additional Web design tools and methodologies (such as scripts and database integration) along with straight HTML. The focus of this book is not on these advanced technologies (although you will get a chance to learn about them in some detail in the third and fourth projects), you can still build the Greenlawn Web site so that it provides the framework for the total required functionality.

That framework (and how you might implement it in a real site) will be the focus of this chapter. Specifically, you will look at the following issues as you build the Web solution for the Greenlawn School:

◆ The Web site will need to serve a wide range of interests, including that of students, parents, teachers, and community members. That said, the sections in the site devoted to the interests of each of these user types need to vary in design. (This issue was discussed extensively in Chapter 19, in which I initially discussed customer usability issues.)

◆ The site will need to facilitate communication between these different user types. As an example of how you might facilitate such communication, you will return to the example given in Chapter 15, concerning how a parent and a teacher might use the Web site to facilitate a discussion about a student who is having trouble in a particular class.

 NOTE

This example was first discussed in Chapter 15. Given the complex process design considerations that you must address for the Greenlawn site, it might be a good idea to read Chapters 17 through 19 prior to beginning work on this chapter, if you haven't done so already.

◆ Finally, this chapter will examine the construction of the Greenlawn online store, as well as the community bulletin board, and how you can facilitate both requirements using HTML.

Again, this site presents significant challenges, not only to your technical skill, but also to your ability to manage a project, communicate with your customers, and help facilitate the integration of a technology resource (the Web site) with a complicated process (the functioning of the school). You've reviewed these issues in the previous chapters of this project; now you can see how you might construct the Web solution to address these issues.

Pre-Publishing Considerations for Your Web Site

At this point, you should realize a few things about publishing the Web site, which is the final step in the design process (and in reality, the most important step).

> **NOTE**
>
> This information was initially presented in Chapter 16; however, if you are not reading this book in sequential order (and that's certainly fine if you are not), you can now review this critical information here. Otherwise, feel free to skip over this section and start digging in to the actual design of the Greenlawn Web site.

◆ As a Web designer, you need to consider how and where you will publish and ultimately host the Web site. Are you going to do it yourself? If so, you must have the hardware infrastructure and expertise to host and maintain a Web site. Be forewarned: Web hosting is not an activity to be entered into lightly! Although you might have the technical expertise to bring a Web server online and provide a hosting service, do you have the wherewithal, patience, and perseverance to keep your servers patched against an ever-increasing range and severity of viruses and worms? Do you fully understand that your customers' Web sites are vital parts of their operations? (You have seen how this is possible in the previous three chapters of this project.) Unless you have a much larger business goal in mind than I think you do, you should let someone else handle the Web publishing for you. (I'm assuming you are interested in learning HTML in conjunction with some other technologies.) There are literally hundreds (if not thousands) of reputable Web hosting providers with very affordable prices, not to mention excellent support.

◆ Have you registered a domain name for your site? Many customers will want (and expect) to have their Web sites available at a specific address, such as www.musetomusic.com. Early in the process, you should confirm that the desired domain name is available. If it is not, you should suggest alternatives to your customers so this critical detail does not become a major stumbling block as you move toward the final steps of design and publishing.

◆ Does the server on which your site will be hosted support all of the functionality your site includes? As you will see in the third project, when you revisit the design of the MuseToMusic site using Microsoft FrontPage, much of the neat functionality possible with FrontPage is *only* possible if the server hosting the site has the FrontPage extensions installed. Although many Web hosting providers do support FrontPage extensions, many do not. Also, you should consider what kind of database support is available (be it the FrontPage Database Results Wizard that you'll see demonstrated in the next chapter, or a more robust implementation of SQL Server, which you'll see in the fourth project).

◆ Related to the previous point, if your site includes advanced functionality such as the integration of a database, does the Web hosting provider support this? Particularly with database integration, how does the provider allow you to administer the functionality?

◆ How does the hosting provider perform critical backup and security tasks? Will they charge you additional fees for backup service, and how often will they perform it? Also, what do they expect of you (or the customer) in terms of keeping your own site secure? Finally, if there is a problem with the site, how are you notified? These are all critical questions that you will need to address concerning the implementation and long-term administration of your site.

◆ What is the hosting provider's pricing structure? Will they charge you a set monthly fee or are there more long-term agreements possible, which might be cheaper than a month-to-month rate? If you add additional functionality in the future, will they charge you extra for it (probably), and if so, how will you and the customer handle this charge, assuming you are still involved in the ongoing maintenance and development of the site?

◆ Finally, with regard to nearly all of the previous points, how easy is it to access, administer, and make changes to your site once it is published? With Microsoft FrontPage, for example, many hosting providers will allow you to easily access the Web site on their server, so it's almost as if you are hosting the site on your own computer. However, other methods of administration may not be as easy; perhaps you cannot make changes to your site and then see those changes reflected instantaneously. This final issue can be a very critical point. Imagine that you realize, after the site is published, that you have listed an incorrect phone number for your business. Clearly, this is something you would want to correct immediately, but what if changes to your site are only published to a live server twice a week? Although this is an unlikely scenario, it does happen, so be sure to consider this important issue as well.

Again, you should build the discussion of these issues into your overall project plan, and be sure you and your client are of the same understanding. Many clients will not realize there is an ongoing fee for Web hosting, or they might assume you will do it for them (in addition to the ongoing domain registration fee). Depending on the complexity of the site hosting fees can be expensive, so don't get cornered into having to eat this expense simply because you did not communicate it to the customer in the early steps of the design process.

Developing the Greenlawn Web Structure

I'm going to assume that you are developing your Web sites on a machine that is under your control and for which you have administrative rights. I will refer to this machine as the *development environment* (versus the *production server*, on which your site will be hosted when it is live).

The first thing you need to do is create a Web folder in which to store your pages.

NOTE

Throughout this book, I have referred to the Inetpub folder as the place to create your Web. For Microsoft IIS, this is the default folder intended as a storage container for all the Web sites that are created on the computer. If you are using Windows XP Professional or Windows 2000, IIS is integrated into the OS: You simply add the IIS component via the Add/Remove Programs control panel. Figures 20.1 to 20.3 illustrate this process. In either case, you should be sure to create your individual Web folders within this folder, just as you have been doing throughout this book.

TIP

If you are using an older version of Windows (especially Windows 98) or you don't want to install IIS, you can still create the Web site as it is described in this chapter. Follow along with the steps in this section and create the same folder, but just create it somewhere on your hard drive. The only difference will be how you load the site into your Web browser because you will use a different address to access the site and its pages. For example, instead of using the http://127.0.0.1 address you have seen throughout this book, you can just enter the exact file address in the address bar of your Web browser: For example, such an address might be c:/Web_Folder/Muse_To_Music/Home.htm

FIGURE 20.1 *Click on the Add or Remove Programs icon within the Control Panel as a first step in loading IIS.*

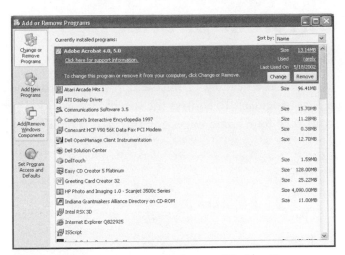

FIGURE 20.2 *Click on the Add/Remove Windows Components to access the component listing (IIS is included here).*

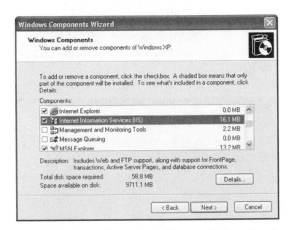

FIGURE 20.3 *Highlight the Internet Information Services (IIS) option, then click Next to begin the installation process.*

Okay, now you're ready to create the Greenlawn Web folder.

1. Navigate to the Inetpub folder on your computer. The directory path to this folder is c:/Inetpub/wwwroot. You will create your individual Web site folders within the wwwroot subdirectory.

2. Within the wwwroot folder, create a new folder and call it Greenlawn.

As you create the individual Web pages in this chapter, you will store them all in this Greenlawn folder.

Addressing Different Information Needs: The Site Home Pages

You might have noticed that the heading of this section refers to the site home *pages*—not just home *page* (singular). To address the specific information needs of each user, you will construct four home pages for this site. These home pages include

◆ A general home page

◆ A student home page

◆ A teacher home page

◆ A parent home page

On the general home page, there will also be a link for members of the community (refer to Figure 20.4). This will link to a section devoted to interests of the community at large. This page (which I will discuss later in this chapter) will include links to the online store and the bulletin board, as well as provide general information about the school (such as operating schedules, contact information, and so on).

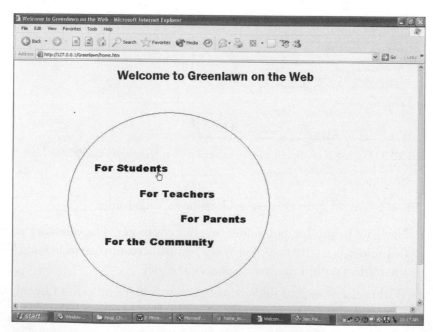

FIGURE 20.4 *The simple home page utilizes an image map: Here you are over an active hotspot, in this case the link to the student home page.*

The following sections will discuss the creation of each of these home pages, as well as issues (both HTML and process) you should keep in mind.

The General Site Home Page

The general site home page utilizes a simple design. (The individual user home pages will be more complex and will utilize a frame structure.) A single image map provides links to each specific user home page. You can start the construction of the Greenlawn Web by coding the page now.

1. In your text editor of choice, create a new page and save it as home.htm in your Greenlawn folder.

2. Enter the following code as you see it listed here:

```
<html>
<head>
<title>Welcome to Greenlawn on the Web</title>
</head>
<body>
<p align="center"><font face="Franklin Gothic Demi" size="6">Welcome to
Greenlawn on the Web</font></p>
<p align="center"><map name="FPMap0">
<area href="Student_Home.htm" shape="rect" coords="182, 175, 389, 214">
<area href="Teacher_Home.htm" shape="rect" coords="298, 242, 504, 277">
<area href="Parent_Home.htm" shape="rect" coords="399, 305, 585, 336">
<area href="Community_Home.htm" shape="rect" coords="213, 360, 505, 399">
</map>
<img border="0" src="home_image.JPG" usemap="#FPMap0" width="1018"
height="624"></p>
</body>
</html>
```

Some things to note about this code:

◆ You will need to insert your own image based on a file you create. The point of this example is to highlight the functionality of an image map so it really doesn't matter what image you use, but if you want to follow the text closely, you might want to create an image that is similar to the one shown in this example.

◆ The image map reference coordinates are based on the figure shown in Figure 20.1. Again, depending on the graphic you use, you will need to adjust these coordinates.

3. Save your page and load it into a Web browser. Although your figure might appear different, note how the sections of the image map are differentiated in Figures 20.4 and 20.5. (The hand icon indicates when you are over an active hotspot section, and the pointer icon indicates when you have moved off a hotspot.)

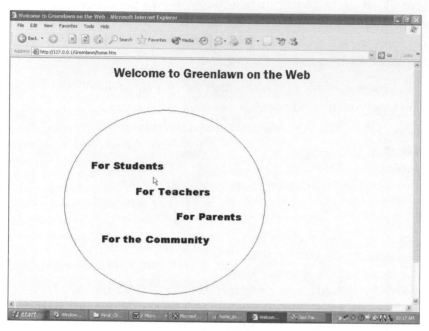

FIGURE 20.5 *Moving off a hotspot. The image map coordinates in the code define these individual sections of the image.*

 NOTE

As you move through this chapter, you might wonder about all the circles, squares, and triangles in the figures. Clearly, a Web site such as this (or any production Web site, for that matter) would benefit from the talents of a strong graphic artist. If, like me, you are not one of those people, you can use simple images as a way to storyboard your ideas. This allows you to focus on the underlying HTML code while developing the entire site functionality. Then, when you turn the project over to the graphic artist, he or she can see where you want to place specific images, as well as how such images facilitate your HTML. (An image map is a good example of this facilitation.)

TIP

Refer to Chapter 5 for a complete discussion of hyperlinks and image maps.

Following are some additional notes on the design of such a general home page.

◆ The simple facade of the page is purposely designed. If this were an actual site, users would be asked to enter a user name and password or some other type of identifying information when they click on one of the four major links. Why? Remember that throughout the first chapters of this project, I stressed that the school administrators want to utilize the Web to present a holistic view of the entire education process. (For example, students would be able to log on to the site and see grades for individual classes, as well as complete electronic portfolios of their entire academic career so they can see how all of their classes are interconnected.) Clearly, this often would be proprietary, confidential information that the student would not want viewed by others.

◆ The For the Community link is the exception to this rule because there is no need to password-protect it. Indeed, you want this link (and the information to which it points) to be very accessible.

◆ Finally, although the simplicity of the demonstration graphic is exaggerated, this site home page should be designed to be simple so it will load quickly. After all, what is the use of having an elaborate sign-in page when users are only accessing it as a launch pad for something else? In the real world, you'd probably want to have something slightly more visually appealing than this simple graphic, but probably not much more complicated.

CAUTION

You should most certainly keep page load time in mind when designing your sites. Although high-speed Internet access is becoming more commonplace, dial-up speeds (no more than 56 kb/sec) should remain the rule when you are determining how long it takes your pages to load.

A Note on Secure Login and the Greenlawn Web Site

As you read in this section, secure login would be a requirement in a real-world implementation of the Greenlawn Web site. It's important to note that such a secure login is critical not just for delivering confidential or proprietary information, but also for determining how information is presented.

Recall from Chapter 19 and the discussion of customer-usability issues that different users will want information presented to them in different ways. (Remember that we are using a very loose definition of the word *customer* for the discussion of the school's Web site.) By having a secure login, you can determine the type of user who is accessing your site. That way, you can present customized information immediately upon login, as well as while the customer moves throughout the site. Consider the following example.

1. A (student) user logs in to the site. He or she is immediately presented with a personal profile (including, for example, a current review of grades for all of his or her courses).

2. After viewing the grades, the student clicks over to the online store. Although the information presented could be the same as what is seen by an individual from the community at large, why not have the site design present student-specific information? Perhaps there is a current fund-raising activity specific to the student's class, and you could immediately present a related item for sale to the student.

3. Because you identified the user as a student, as he or she leaves the site, you are able to track which pages were visited and how long the student was on the site, as well as gather specific data on how the student interacted with the site. Such data can be very useful in assessing the value of the site; it can point the way to areas of the site (and areas of the curriculum the site is used to facilitate) that need to be improved or adjusted.

The point here is that you should think of a secure login as more than just a security measure. Although a secure login authenticates a user for presentation of confidential information, it also can identify the user as a particular type, which can be quite useful for a number of data-gathering, customer-usability, and site-design issues.

Although this type of functionality is beyond the scope of this book, you will get some idea of how you might facilitate it in the third and fourth projects of this book, in which you will integrate a database with your HTML. For an excellent discussion of how you might facilitate such secure login using JavaScript (and with another example based on a fictitious school), see *JavaScript Professional Projects* (Premier Press, 2003).

Building the Additional Home Pages

Once users log in to the site, they are taken (based on their specific user profiles, which are stored in a database with which the site interacts) to their specific home pages. Each page will utilize the same basic frame layout, so you can build them now. After you build the student home page, you can cut and paste the code (making some small modifications) to build the other two home pages.

1. First create the student home page. Open your editor of choice and create a page called student_home.htm. Save this page in the Greenlawn folder you created at the beginning of the chapter.

 NOTE

The pages you are creating in this section are named to correspond to the image map hyperlinks you created earlier in the chapter. Even if you are using different image files than what I am using here, you should name the pages the same as I have so you can follow along closely with the information presented.

2. This student_home.htm page will be the main frames page that loads the other pages that make up the entire student home page structure. On the student_home.htm page, enter the following code as you see it listed here:

```
<html>
<head>
<title>Welcome to the Greenlawn Web (Student View)</title>
</head>
<frameset cols="150,*">
  <frame name="contents" target="main" src="student_left.htm">
  <frame name="main" src="student_right.htm">
  <noframes>
  <body>
<p>This page uses frames, but your browser doesn't support them.</p>
</body>
</noframes>
</frameset>
</html>
```

3. Now it's time to create the two pages (student_left.htm and student_right.htm) that comprise this frameset. For now, just create and save two blank pages (being sure to place them in your Greenlawn Web

folder) and give them these two names. Use the following simple code for each page, but be sure to give each page a specific title (between the opening and closing `<title>` tags).

```
<html>
<head>
<title>INSERT YOUR TITLE HERE</title>
<body>
</body>
</html>
```

4. Load the student_home.htm frameset page into your Web browser. Your screen should look like Figure 20.6.

FIGURE 20.6 *Note the title bar that indicates this is a student view.*

You'll recall from the previous chapters of this project (specifically, Chapter 19) that changes in the home page design are necessary depending on the user being addressed. All of the individual user home pages should:

◆ **Allow access to previous order history.** Carrying the CRM analogy over to the Greenlawn Web, the pages should allow users to see previous information. For students, this might be a previous year's academic work;

for teachers, it might be grade books or course materials from previous semesters; for parents, it might be their child's progress over the years.

◆ **Allow customization of data views.** Not everyone likes to look at data in the same way. The home pages should allow the users to set preferences for how data is viewed. For example, a student might only want to see current semester grades and not be inundated with data from previous years' work.

◆ **Allow complete access to the product in which users are interested.** As was discussed in an earlier chapter, make sure your users don't have to jump through HTML design hoops to get to the information they need. This philosophy can and should carry over to the overall navigation structure of your site. Put simply, don't make it so difficult for users to find what they are looking for that they become frustrated in the process.

◆ **Allow for change.** The manner in which users access information can change on a whim, depending on their own preferences or their need to access some specific piece of data. Be sure your design allows these changes to occur. (Or make sure your site includes a mechanism for contacting the appropriate site administrators so that such changes can be put into effect quickly.)

Design Examples for Each Home Page

Each home page in the Greenlawn site will be designed to appeal to the specific interests and preferences of the user group. Figure 20.7 illustrates what a student home page might look like.

The HTML behind this page is fairly straightforward, especially if you've already worked through the MuseToMusic project (see Chapters 13 through 16).

1. In your editor application, open the student_left.htm page you created earlier in this chapter.

2. Enter the following code. Again, change the names of the files to correspond to the graphics you are using on your system.

```
<html>
<head>
<title>Student Navigation</title>
<base target="main">
</head>
```

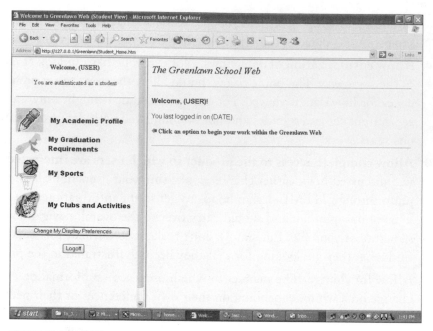

FIGURE 20.7 *The student home page. Note the extended use of graphics and a more active design than, for example, the teacher home page shown in Figure 20.8.*

```
<body>
<p align="center"><b>Welcome, (USER)</b></p>
<p align="center">You are authenticated as a student</p>
<hr>
<form>
<table border="0" cellpadding="0" cellspacing="0" style="border-collapse:
collapse" width="100%">
  <tr>
    <td width="28%"><a target="main" href="student_profile.htm">
    <img border="0" src="j0233363[1]1.gif" width="71" height="62"></a></td>
    <td width="72%"><font face="Arial Black"> My Academic
Profile</font></td>
  </tr>
  <tr>
    <td width="28%"><a target="main" href="student_graduation.htm">
    <img border="0" src="j0290508[1].gif" width="65" height="55"></a></td>
    <td width="72%"><font face="Arial Black">My Graduation
Requirements</font></td>
  </tr>
```

```
<tr>
  <td width="28%"><a target="main" href="student_sports.htm">
  <img border="0" src="j0305651[1].gif" width="58" height="89"></a></td>
  <td width="72%"><font face="Arial Black">My Sports</font></td>
</tr>
<tr>
  <td width="28%"><a target="main" href="student_clubs.htm">
  <img border="0" src="bd05105_[1].gif" width="66" height="69"></a></td>
  <td width="72%"><font face="Arial Black">My Clubs and Activities</font></td>
</tr>
<tr>
  <td width="28%"> </td>
  <td width="72%"> </td>
</tr>
<tr>
  <td width="100%" colspan="2"><a href="student_pref.htm">
  <input type="button" value="Change My Display Preferences"
name="B1"></a></td>
</tr>
<tr>
  <td width="100%" colspan="2"> </td>
</tr>
<tr>
  <td width="100%" colspan="2">
  <p align="center"><a href="signout.htm">
  <input type="submit" value="Logoff" name="B2"></a></td>
</tr>
</table>
</form>
</body>
</html>
```

3. Save the page. Depending on the graphics you are using, the general layout should appear similar to Figure 20.7.

TIP

Many of the graphics you see illustrated in this book are from the Microsoft ClipArt collection. Take advantage of the range and style of these graphics for inclusion in your own Web pages.

Note the following points concerning the HTML for this page:

◆ The target for all the hyperlinks is set to `"main"`. This will allow the associated linked pages to open in the right frame of the frameset.

◆ Although there are opening and closing `<form>` tags around the table, it is only to allow the graphics for the Change My Display Preferences and Logoff buttons to appear as Submit buttons. If you look at the code, they are actually just hyperlinks to two additional pages.

 NOTE

Note the identification markers on these home pages, including in the page title bars ("Welcome to Greenlawn Web (Teacher View)") and in the left frame of each page ("You are authenticated as a teacher"). On a live site with such authentication, these markers would be dynamic and would not be hard-coded into your HTML. However, for the sake of illustration, I have included them in the HTML for both the student and teacher home pages.

Comparing the Student Home Page to the Teacher Home Page

Okay, you have a design in place for the student home page. But as you'll recall, the other home pages will differ in their design because of the different user types the site intends to target.

Figure 20.8 illustrates the teacher home page. Note the more businesslike look and feel of the page and the difference in functionality (in terms of where the links point).

To continue following the site example in this chapter, build this page as well.

1. Open the teacher_left.htm page you created earlier in the chapter.

2. On this page, enter the following code:

```
<html>
<head>
<title>Teacher Navigation </title>
<base target="main">
</head>
<body>
<p align="center"><b>Welcome, (USER)</b></p>
```

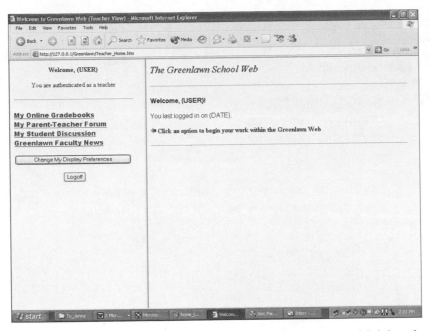

FIGURE 20.8 *The teacher home page has a decidedly different look and feel than the student home page.*

```
<p align="center">You are authenticated as a teacher</p>
<hr>
<form>
<table border="0" cellpadding="0" cellspacing="0" style="border-collapse:
collapse" bordercolor="#111111" width="100%">
  <tr>
    <td width="100%" colspan="2"><font face="Arial Black">
    <a target="main" href="teacher_gradebook.htm">My Online
Gradebooks</a></font></td>
  </tr>
  <tr>
    <td width="100%" colspan="2"><font face="Arial Black">
    <a target="main" href="teacher_feedback.htm ">My Parent-Teacher
Forum</a></font></td>
  </tr>
  <tr>
    <td width="100%" colspan="2"><font face="Arial Black">
    <a target="main" href="teacher_student_discussion.htm">My Student Discussion
</a></font></td>
  </tr>
```

```
  <tr>
    <td width="100%" colspan="2"><font face="Arial Black">
    <a target="main" href="faculty_news.htm">Greenlawn Faculty
News</a></font></td>
  </tr>
  <tr>
    <td width="28%"> </td>
    <td width="72%"> </td>
  </tr>
  <tr>
    <td width="100%" colspan="2"><a href="student_pref.htm">
    <input type="button" value="Change My Display Preferences"
name="B1"></a></td>
  </tr>
  <tr>
    <td width="100%" colspan="2"> </td>
  </tr>
  <tr>
    <td width="100%" colspan="2">
    <p align="center"><a href="signout.htm">
    <input type="submit" value="Logoff" name="B2"></a></td>
  </tr>
</table>
</form>
</body>
</html>
```

3. Open the student_right.htm page and resave it as teacher_right.htm.
   (Because this is just for illustration purposes, it's okay to use the same
   page.)

4. After you save your new teacher_left.htm and teacher_right.htm pages,
   reload the Greenlawn site into your browser. When you click on the For
   Teachers link on the home page, your screen should appear similar to
   Figure 20.8.

Keep in mind the following points when you are reviewing the teacher home page:

◆ The more businesslike design is a result of the predesign work you (as the
  Web consultant) did with the teachers to determine their preferences for
  how they want information presented. The overwhelming response was
  that the different links should be clearly marked and neatly organized.

◆ Speaking of those links, note the middle two—My Parent-Teacher Forum and My Student Discussion. As you know from the previous chapters in this project, a major focus of the Greenlawn Web is to help facilitate communication between all parties (student, teacher, and parent) in the educational process and to present a larger, holistic view of this process. A major component of the teacher section of the Web site is devoted to facilitating this communication, so it makes sense that the links to these pages should be clearly marked.

◆ As with the student page, teachers will want to have secure access to their online grade book and other confidential information. Such links might require further identification, such as asking teachers to re-authenticate themselves prior to being able to view the material.

A QUICK NOTE ON WEB SECURITY

Yet another topic worthy of an entire book-length discussion is Web security. However, the type of security I'm referencing here is not about viruses or worms; rather, it is about the types of security breaches that can occur when, for example, someone logs in to a secure site, steps out for some coffee (without logging back out), and leaves confidential information wide open for easy (unauthorized) access. That's why, as I mentioned here, you might ask teachers to authenticate themselves (enter their user names and passwords) once again when they click on the My Online Gradebooks link.

Ultimately, the most important thing is to train your users about the types of security breaches that can be prevented if they practice good common sense when accessing confidential information. In the case of the teacher home page and accessing the confidential grade information, teachers should understand that information viewable onscreen will be viewable to others on the same screen if they allow it. As part of your Web rollout and implementation planning (yet another topic worthy of a book), it would be a good idea to reiterate this issue of Web security, to instruct users to be protective of their personal information, and to log off the site if they must leave their computers unattended.

Designing the Parent Home Page

Although I will not discuss it specifically here, you might want to design the parent home page on your own. You can use the same frame layout as the teacher and student pages, or you can let your creativity take hold and implement something different.

Following are some things you might consider about the parent home page to achieve all of the design requirements set forth in the previous chapters of this project.

◆ The page should contain direct links for information on the child's progress. Again, during the authentication process, you will be able to determine which child belongs to the parent, and thus dynamically present the information.

◆ The page should contain direct links to teacher-parent discussion forums, a feature that I will discuss in the next section.

◆ The page should also provide links to other functional aspects of the school, including the school's bulletin board, news and updates about the PTA, and the online store.

Again, I'll leave the design of this page up to you; however, you should review the differences in the layout presentation between the teacher and student pages. Ideally, the parent home page (and the design scheme you use) would be somewhere between the teacher and student pages. That is, it should include some limited use of graphics, but also bring with it a more serious, direct presentation. Also, the functionality of the links should be very clear. There should be no uncertainty about where those links will take you—something that should be prevalent in all the user views.

The Web Site as a Communication Tool: Parent-Teacher Discussion Forums

You will recall that a major desired component of the Greenlawn Web site is a functionality that allows better direct communication between parents and teachers regarding student progress.

Having some well-designed forms can help you achieve this functional process goal of the site. This section will explore those forms and how to build them. Take another look at Figure 20.8, and the My Parent-Teacher Forum link. When teachers click on this link, they should be taken to a page that allows them to view information submitted by a parent and respond to it appropriately. Conversely, teachers should have a way to submit information to parents concerning a student's progress.

You can build such a form now.

1. Open your editor application, create a new page called teacher_feed-back.htm, and save it in your Greenlawn Web folder.

2. On this page, enter the following code:

```
<html>
<head>
<title>Teacher Feedback Form </title>
</head>
<body>
<p align="center"><b><font face="Arial Black" size="5">Parent-Teacher Feedback
Form</font></b></p>
<hr>
<p align="left"><font face="Arial">Use this form to send student progress
information to parents.  </font></p>
<form method="POST" action="Teacher_Response.asp">
<table border="0" cellpadding="0" cellspacing="0" style="border-collapse:
collapse" width="100%">
    <tr>
      <td width="14%">Parent e-mail:</td>
      <td width="86%"><input type="text" name="Email" size="30"></td>
    </tr>
    <tr>
      <td width="14%">Student's name:</td>
      <td width="86%"><input type="text" name="Student_Name" size="30"></td>
    </tr>
    <tr>
      <td width="14%">Name of class:</td>
      <td width="86%"><input type="text" name="Student_Class" size="30"></td>
    </tr>
    <tr>
      <td width="14%">Reason for this communication:</td>
      <td width="86%"><select size="1" name="Contact_Reason">
      <option value="New">New Feedback</option>
      <option value="Response">Response to Feedback</option>
      <option value="Update">Progress Update</option>
      <option value="Behavior">Behavior Concern</option>
      <option>Other</option>
      </select></td>
    </tr>
```

```
    <tr>
      <td width="14%">Comments:</td>
      <td width="86%"><textarea rows="4" name="Comments"
cols="50"></textarea></td>
    </tr>
    <tr>
      <td width="14%">Response required:</td>
      <td width="86%">Yes<input type="radio" value="Yes" name="Response"> No
      <input type="radio" name="Response" value="No"></td>
    </tr>
    <tr>
      <td width="14%">Conference:</td>
      <td width="86%">Yes<input type="radio" value="Yes" checked
name="Conference">
      No <input type="radio" name="Conference" value="No"></td>
    </tr>
  </table>
  <p align="center"><input type="submit" value="Submit this form" name="B1"></p>
</form>
</body>
</html>
```

3. Save this page and load the site into your browser. Assuming you have assigned the same file names and associated hyperlinks as I have presented in this chapter, your screen should look like Figure 20.9 when you click on the My Parent-Teacher Forum link on the teacher home page.

How might the larger functionality of this process be facilitated on the Greenlawn Web site? Consider the following options:

◆ Note the first field in the form—Parent e-mail. Although the form will not send all of the information to the parents (it will not send the teacher comments and so on), it will send them a prompt (with a link back to the Greenlawn Web site) indicating that a note has been sent to them by their child's teacher.

◆ When the parents click on the link, they will be taken back to the Greenlawn Web site. However, instead of just going to the site home page, the link will be within their section of the site. (They would still be required to log in.)

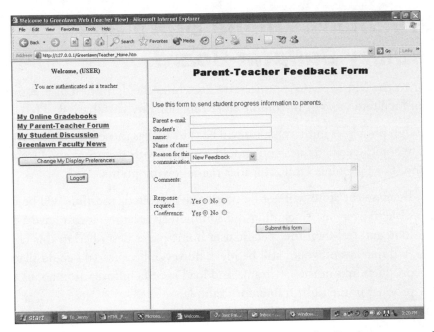

FIGURE 20.9 *Teachers can use this form to submit information directly to parents, who can in turn view this information in their section of the Greenlawn Web site.*

◆ After the parents are authenticated, they would be presented with their home page and a similar link called Parent-Teacher Forum (refer to Figure 20.8). When that link is clicked, the parents would be presented with a page similar to the form in Figure 20.9, but which includes the teacher's comments. Note that the comments would be within a form so the parents could respond. In turn, this would begin the construction of a message string so both parent and teacher could review previous comments as the conversation develops.

NOTE

Although this might seem like advanced Web design (and arguably, it is), you will see how you can facilitate this by using an HTML editor (in this case, FrontPage) in the third project of this book.

The Greenlawn Online Store and Community Bulletin Board

Similar to the MuseToMusic project, by stretching the definition of e-commerce you can facilitate some of the online store functionality with basic HTML.

The design principles in this chapter will be the same as those in Chapter 16. Still, there are some specific issues you should consider with regard to the Greenlawn Web site. For the online store, consider the following points.

◆ Because the store will not be password-protected, and thus will be accessible to everyone (including the community at large), it can have a looser look and feel than the specific user home pages described in this chapter. A frame layout would still be ideal, however, because you could place product links in the left frame and load specific information about that product in the right frame, for example.

◆ Unlike the MuseToMusic site, in which the focus on every page is to point customers toward the online order form, the Greenlawn online store does not follow this strategy. Indeed, the focus of the Greenlawn Web site is to provide a holistic view of the educational process; the online store is simply there to help with school fund-raising events and so on. Although there is nothing wrong with adding a link to the store on each of the individual home pages, it probably would not be warranted.

◆ In contrast to the preceding point, the store should function much like a typical online store in that it should present full product information and pricing. Although accepting payments over the Web probably is beyond the scope of a school Web site, you could still use a form to have an order confirmation e-mailed to a user, who could in turn bring that confirmation to the school as an order request. Or, a completed order form could act as an invoice when the products ordered are mailed out to the purchaser.

For the community bulletin board, consider the following points.

◆ The general design could be the same as the MuseToMusic News and Information page, on which you utilize CSS to keep a uniform format for all announcements.

◆ The announcements and news on this page would need to be closely monitored to ensure that messages were appropriate for display on a school's Web site (especially if individuals from the community at large were allowed to post messages).

◆ The announcements would need to be differentiated from confidential or private information that might be better placed in the secure site. As an obvious example, you wouldn't want parents and teachers communicating about a child's progress on this public forum. This issue once again recalls the larger process goals of the Web site (and some of the concerns) with regard to the information that is to be made available and the users who are allowed to see it.

WHAT ABOUT THE ONLINE TESTING REQUIREMENT?

A major functional requirement of the site is to allow for online testing. You will also recall that there is some significant concern and differing opinion among school administrators with regard to how online testing should be facilitated. All in all, this is a difficult issue that you, as the Web developer, need to keep in mind.

The successful integration of online testing will require the use of a database and advanced scripting within your site. Although you will acquire some of these development skills when you work through the third and fourth projects of this book, this truly is advanced functionality at a level that would require significant coding beyond what you can do with the HTML described in this book.

Still, you might consider how a scripting language (in this case, JavaScript) could help facilitate and lay the structural groundwork for such advanced functionality. Again, if this is an area of interest, consult *JavaScript Professional Projects* (Premier Press, 2003) to see how you can enhance such an online testing environment using JavaScript, as well as how you can address some of the design issues (for example, how information is displayed on the screen).

Summary

The Greenlawn Web site is a complicated project with requirements that far exceed the realm of traditional HTML. Still, this chapter revisited the design and process goal requirements set forth in Chapters 18 and 19 to look at how you could build the overall site structure (the individual home pages) and how you could use straight HTML (for example, forms) to facilitate communication and achieve the larger goal of the Web site, which is to enhance communication about the educational process. The chapter compared the Greenlawn site to the MuseToMusic project to show you how you could use comparable design concepts to achieve similar goals, albeit in a different environment. In this case, you can model the online store and the community bulletin board based on the functionality in the MuseToMusic project. Finally, although developing the complete Web site would present significant coding challenges, you can meet many of the requirements by using an HTML editor and database integration, two topics you will learn more about in the third and fourth projects.

Project 3

**MS FrontPage XP:
Building Web
Sites with an
HTML Editor**

Chapter 21

**MuseToMusic Web
Site with
FrontPage XP:
Project
Introduction**

We've discussed many issues with regard to the projects in this book. From early design issues to CRM principles to seeing how you can use HTML to facilitate real business requirements, we've covered a lot of ground. However, there is one major component of working with HTML that I haven't discussed —why (and how) you would want to use an HTML editor.

If you're a savvy reader—and undoubtedly you are—I'm sure you are considering (or perhaps already know about) using an HTML editor to make your Web development more practical, more efficient, and (never to be overlooked) just plain more fun.

Although there are several HTML editors on the market, Microsoft FrontPage continues to be an ideal tool for novice to advanced developers. Utilizing a familiar look and feel as other Microsoft Office applications (such as Word and Excel), FrontPage presents an inviting environment to get you working with HTML immediately. But don't let that easy-to-use interface fool you. FrontPage is a powerful development tool, and if you understand its functionality, you can do great things quickly with your HTML.

This project will show you how you can use FrontPage to develop a complete HTML solution. You will revisit the MuseToMusic project and see how, by utilizing FrontPage, you can build the same Web site for the company faster and with more functionality than if you just used a simple text editor like Notepad.

 TIP

It's perfectly okay to use Notepad or some other simple text editor; you shouldn't necessarily feel you are doing something wrong or missing out. Indeed in the early days, several HTML editors (especially FrontPage) were notorious for adding extra code or otherwise messing with the HTML that you often painstakingly coded by hand. Although the editor applications still try to exert their own will on your code from time to time, they (including FrontPage) have come a long way in being hands-off unless you specifically tell them to add their special coding to your Web pages. So view this project as an opportunity to see what's out there in terms of making your Web development life easier, but don't feel obligated to use an HTML editor if you don't want to!

Using FrontPage with the MuseToMusic Web Site (Project Outline)

For this project, the goal is to revisit the construction of the MuseToMusic site and, by working through the same chapter-by-chapter approach to building the actual Web site, to highlight how you can use an HTML editor to make your development easier and more productive.

I have divided this project into the following four chapters:

◆ **Chapter 21** (this introductory chapter) will highlight some of the major functionality of FrontPage XP, and how using it can significantly enhance the development of the MuseToMusic Web site from the first project (Chapters 13 through 16).

◆ **Chapter 22** will revisit the MuseToMusic process issues and discuss how you can use FrontPage to enhance those process goals in terms of the completed Web solution. In other words, you could bring certain HTML functionality to the MuseToMusic site if you use an HTML editor such as FrontPage. This chapter will discuss those issues.

◆ **Chapter 23** is a continuation of Chapter 22. It will highlight the MuseToMusic company, and how you can give their business process requirements new life via a Web solution. The chapter will also cover how FrontPage can make that process easier.

◆ **Chapter 24** the final chapter in the project, will be a step-by-step description of how to build the MuseToMusic site using FrontPage. As in the previous project chapters, this chapter will show you how you can make the site more powerful by working with FrontPage.

 TIP

This chapter will contain cross-references back to the initial MuseToMusic project, so you can compare and contrast the benefits (and possible drawbacks) of working with FrontPage versus working with a simple text editor like Notepad.

Using FrontPage with the MuseToMusic Web Site (Process and Primary Goals)

As you saw in the initial project, the MuseToMusic storeowners had three specific goals for their Web site.

◆ Drawing attention to the local music scene

◆ Expanding their mail-order service for locating hard-to-find music CDs

◆ Creating a music portal that frequent visitors can use as a central access point for all things music

How can you facilitate these ideas using FrontPage? Preview each one, and I'll show you how you can use FrontPage tools to help achieve each goal.

 NOTE

Again, I will discuss the functionality that is briefly described in the following sections in detail throughout the chapters of this project.

Working with Graphics and Multimedia

Achieving the first goal of the MuseToMusic Web site will require the use of some graphics and/or multimedia (sound and video). Local bands will want to provide their bios (including group photos) and perhaps short sound clips that interested visitors can download.

FrontPage makes this type of multimedia integration easy by allowing you to quickly insert graphics and audio/video files into your pages. Figure 21.1 shows such multimedia insert options on the main Insert menu.

In addition to directly inserting graphics and multimedia files into your Web pages, you can also utilize special formatting features to help you arrange your graphics. For example, Figure 21.2 highlights the use of the FrontPage Photo Gallery tool, which allows you to format and create links to specific pictures so you can create an attractive and functional display. The MuseToMusic site could use this functionality to help present an online band portfolio.

FIGURE 21.1 *FrontPage allows you to quickly insert graphics and multimedia files directly into your Web pages.*

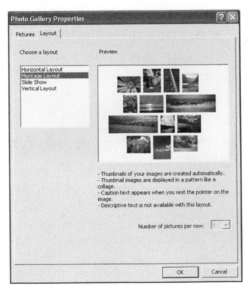

FIGURE 21.2 *A neatly arranged collage of photos that open large images when you click on them. When your mouse pointer hovers over each image, a caption appears, giving more information about the specific photo.*

Utilizing Special Text Formatting and Layout Options

One thing you will quickly learn about working with HTML (if you haven't learned it already) is that it can be quite tedious and repetitive to format text. For example, consider the use of tables. As you learned in Chapter 6, all those `<tr>` and `<td>` tags can be hard to keep straight!

An HTML editor such as FrontPage might be worth the purchase price if for no other reason than it makes designing and formatting tables a breeze. Figures 21.3 and 21.4 highlight the FrontPage Table tool. It should be obvious from these two figures that the frustration of working with tables becomes a thing of the past when you work with FrontPage.

You should also note that the tables created automatically (as well as all other functionality you create with the FrontPage tools and wizards) also automatically generate the underlying HTML. Figure 21.5 illustrates the HTML that FrontPage created for the table shown in Figure 21.3.

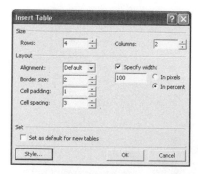

FIGURE 21.3 *FrontPage allows you to set the initial parameters for the table, including number of rows and columns, as well as cell and border width.*

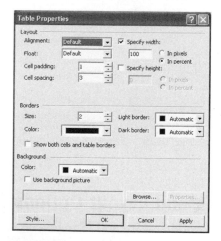

FIGURE 21.4 *Once the table is created, you can manipulate additional table properties.*

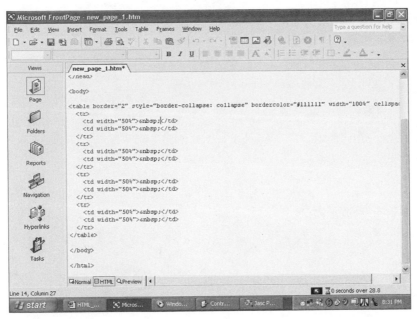

FIGURE 21.5 *Any material you create in the FrontPage WYSIWYG interface results in HTML being created automatically.*

WYSIWYG

WYSIWYG is an industry-standard acronym for *What You See Is What You Get*. It implies that what you see within the application is what you will see when the application document (such as a Web page or a report) is put into action.

As another example of the power of using a tool like FrontPage, you can also quickly insert some dynamic text-formatting effects. Figure 21.6 shows the dynamic HTML (DHTML) effects that will be applied to the highlighted text when the page is loaded in a Web browser.

 CAUTION

Although it is very easy to add in FrontPage, you should use the functionality illustrated in Figure 21.6 with caution. Not all Web browsers support this type of functionality. Moreover, this advanced functionality might not be present if the Web servers that host your FrontPage Web site don't have the FrontPage Extensions (a special set of code applications) loaded on them. I'll talk more about these issues (and how sometimes the functionality in FrontPage is too good to be true) throughout this project.

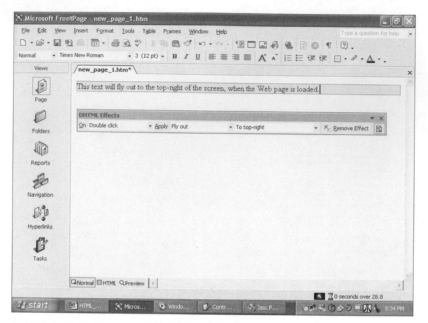

FIGURE 21.6 *You can easily add dynamic HTML effects, utilizing JavaScript and special FrontPage components, with just a few simple clicks. This will save you tremendous amounts of time in developing your own code.*

Finally, you can use additional layout options easily in FrontPage via the use of frames. Like you saw with the tables in Figures 21.3 and 21.4, you can easily set and customize frame parameters. Figures 21.7, 21.8, and 21.9 highlight how easy it is to create frames with FrontPage.

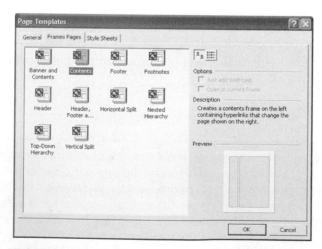

FIGURE 21.7 *The FrontPage Page Templates offer you a variety of frame design options.*

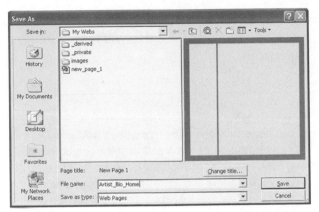

FIGURE 21.8 *When you save the frame layout, FrontPage asks you to save each frame individually. You can tell which frame you are saving by how the blue outline on the right side of the screen is highlighted; in this figure, you are first asked to save the entire frame shell (named Artist_Bio_Home in this example).*

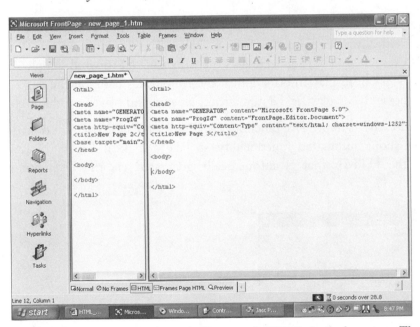

FIGURE 21.9 *FrontPage automatically creates the HTML for the frame page. The code is easily available for you to edit as required.*

Advanced Data Input and Manipulation Functions

One of the most exciting things you can do with a Web page is collect or manipulate information. Although most of this functionality requires advanced coding and integration of some type of database, FrontPage makes this easy. For example, you can use Microsoft Access, and FrontPage can automate the script and HTML so you can create a visitor feedback form that will input comments from Web site visitors into a database file.

 CAUTION

As I mentioned, FrontPage can powerfully automate this type of advanced functionality. Indeed, its ability to completely automate the creation of the link between a Web page and an underlying database is quite impressive. However, this type of automation is not without risks; most notably, it requires that the special components and code sets are installed on the Web server that is hosting your site. So before you depend too heavily on this advanced functionality to meet your project requirements, be sure you understand the Web server requirements for hosting a FrontPage-created site. You will learn more about this issue throughout the chapters of this project.

Figure 21.10 shows one of the steps of the Database Results Wizard, which is used to automatically pull information from a database and display it on your Web page. In this example, you are connecting to the Microsoft Northwind sample database so that you can display information in the Employees table on the page. Figure 21.11 shows the display field automatically created and placed on the Web page.

To be sure, this is impressive functionality. However, you've been cautioned in this chapter about automated functionality, so take a look at Figure 21.12, which shows the HTML that is automatically generated via the Database Results Wizard.

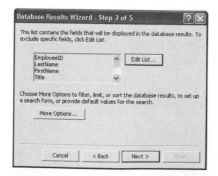

FIGURE 21.10 *Using the Database Results Wizard in FrontPage to automatically connect to a database.*

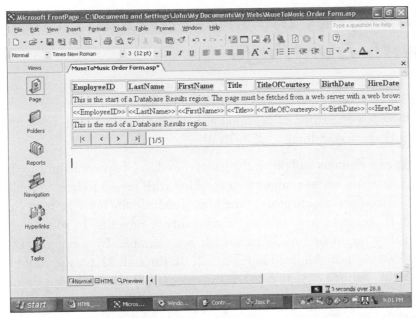

FIGURE 21.11 *Once the Database Results Wizard creates its display field (in table format), you can further define the table parameters of the display field.*

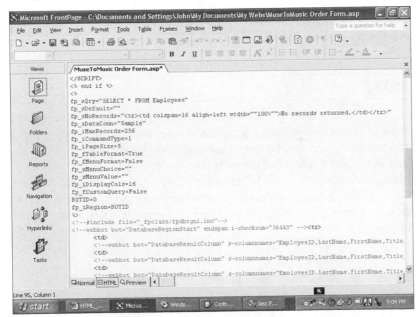

FIGURE 21.12 *If this doesn't look like straight HTML (or even regular ASP scripting, if you're familiar with that), it's because it isn't. Rather, this is special FrontPage coding that can only be run properly on a Web server that supports FrontPage Webs.*

Implementing the MuseToMusic Web Site with FrontPage

Now that you've been introduced to some of the functionality of FrontPage (including the potential drawbacks to that functionality), it is time to move on to a side-by-side comparison of developing the MuseToMusic Web site with a tool like FrontPage versus doing it all by hand.

The next two chapters will revisit the issues raised in Chapters 14 and 15, but will focus on how you might readjust your thinking with regard to how to achieve the specific process and design goals of the MuseToMusic site if you were to use a tool like FrontPage and the additional functionality it presents. In some cases, that functionality might be greatly enhanced. For example, by using the Database Results Wizard as highlighted in Figures 21.10 through 21.12, you could bring a new level of sophistication to how the site records, collects, and displays information, but at the same time you would have to consider the contingency if for whatever reason the Web server hosting the MuseToMusic site stopped supporting Webs developed with FrontPage.

As you move through the chapters in this project, keep this functionality and ease of use versus contingency planning issue in mind, especially when you look at Chapter 24 and building the MuseToMusic Web site completely with FrontPage.

 NOTE

Take this contingency planning issue with a grain of salt. Let's face it: If you work with technology, you must always have a good contingency plan because things are constantly changing, and those changes are often completely out of your control. Still, when working with a tool that presents many proprietary options (for example, the FrontPage components allow DHTML effects and database integration functionality), it is a good idea to plan ahead to see whether these tools—and the Web site you build with them—will be supported both from a technical (Web server) and an administrative side.

Chapter 22

**MuseToMusic Web
Site with
FrontPage XP:
Identifying
Process Goals**

As you saw when the initial business process requirements for the MuseTo-Music Web site were discussed in Chapter 14, there are several factors that the company owners wanted to consider in the development of their site. Specifically, those issues included

◆ Allowing the site to serve as a portal for not only the local music community, but also anyone (theoretically) who has access to the Web and can view the site content.

◆ Keeping the focus of the site content on the local music scene.

◆ Utilizing the site to extend the store's ability to fill special orders for hard-to-find items.

◆ Providing general information about the store (hours of operation, history, and so on).

◆ Ensuring that the site is easy to administer and integrate into the larger operations of the store.

Although all of these business requirements are important, the last point is especially critical. The storeowners, like so many small-business owners (or large-business owners, for that matter), have other things on their minds than worrying about whether their Web site is in operation. They are also working on a limited budget, and although they are very interested in having a functioning Web site and seeing the opportunities it might create for promoting their store, they can't afford to have someone update the content continuously. Put simply, they want to be their own Webmasters because they feel they are the experts in the operation of their store and the services they provide, and they want to extend that expertise to how they are represented on the Web.

For all of these reasons, it makes sense to give the MuseToMusic owners the ability to maintain and update their site content. That said, FrontPage XP is an excellent tool because it has a familiar interface (it shares the typical Microsoft Office menu system) and it is a great WYSIWYG editor. As you will see in this chapter, FrontPage opens up the possibility for extended functionality to meet all of these business process requirements, in addition to being easy for the storeowners to use.

This chapter will explore the benefits that using FrontPage can bring to the development, implementation, and long-term administration of the MuseToMusic Web site by looking at how you can use the special FrontPage features to address each of these issues.

 NOTE

When I talk about special FrontPage features, I mean the tools in the application (such as automated templates, the Database Results Wizard, site navigation tools, and publishing tools) that make development and administration of a Web site easier with FrontPage than with a simple text editor, such as Notepad.

Preparing to Design the MuseToMusic Web Site with FrontPage XP

Before you go any farther, you should take a few moments to prepare the MuseToMusic Web folder.

1. Navigate to the Inetpub folder on your computer.
2. In this folder, delete the existing MuseToMusic folder (if you created it when you read Chapters 13 through 16).
3. Re-create the folder, naming it MuseToMusic once again.
4. Open FrontPage.
5. From the File menu, select New, Page or Web.
6. In the list of options that appears on the right side of your screen, select Empty Web. The Web Site Templates dialog box will appear, as shown in Figure 22.1.
7. Click on the Browse button and navigate to the MuseToMusic folder you just created. Select it, as shown in Figure 22.2, and then click on OK.
8. After you've selected the MuseToMusic folder, click on Open. You will be returned to the Web Site Template dialog box, and the file path to your new Web site will be listed (c:\Inetpub\wwwroot\MuseToMusic).

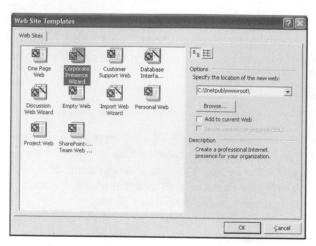

FIGURE 22.1 *The first step in creating a new Web with FrontPage.*

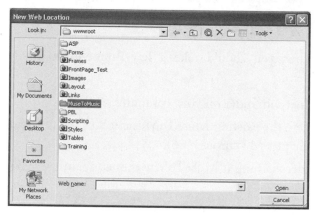

FIGURE 22.2 *The New Web Location dialog box. Select the MuseToMusic folder, in which you will create your new Web.*

9. Because this project is an illustration of how you can use FrontPage to create a Web, select the Corporate Presence Wizard option (as shown in Figure 22.1) and click on OK.

After a few seconds, you will be presented with the first window of the Corporate Presence Web Wizard, as shown in Figure 22.3. For now, leave this alone (that is, don't click the Next button—just leave it on screen); you will return to it a bit later in this chapter.

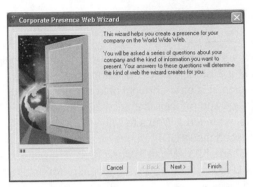

FIGURE 22.3 *You will utilize one of the Web design wizards (in this case, the Corporate Presence Wizard) to develop the MuseToMusic site with FrontPage XP.*

Meeting the Business Requirements: Developing the MuseToMusic Web Structure

One of the primary goals of the MuseToMusic owners is to build on their business' reputation as a strong proponent of the local music scene.

In your initial meetings with the owners, they had a fairly solid grasp that a simple Web site, while giving them a Web presence, would not fit all of the requirements they had in mind. In other words, they knew that a Web site with just one or two pages providing basic store information and a couple short profiles of local bands would not do much to promote local musicians or bring in additional business for the store.

However, the owners were not familiar with the concept of a Web portal. As a savvy Web developer, however, you immediately recognized that a well-designed portal would help deliver on all of the business process requirements and address specific customer issues critical to the site's success.

When you began to explain the benefits of a Web portal and how it would function, the storeowners greeted your ideas with skeptical eyes. Although they thought the idea sounded great, they were very concerned that a portal equaled complexity, and a complex Web site would lead to expenses (both financial and with relation to long-term administration) that they simply could not afford.

> **NOTE**
>
> The customer issues mentioned here are all part of the larger customer relationship management (CRM) features of the MuseToMusic Web site. Although CRM is not an issue related solely to Web design, it is often thought of in conjunction with e-commerce because the methodologies and principles that constitute strong CRM are the same ones that must be implemented in a Web site with a successful e-commerce component. I initially discussed these CRM issues for the MuseToMusic Web site in Chapter 15. However, in Chapter 23, "MuseToMusic Web Site with FrontPage XP: Addressing Customer Usability Issues," I will cover in more detail how you can further enhance and develop these issues using FrontPage.

Enter FrontPage. Given the application's many useful wizards and tools, you assured the storeowners that a portal could be constructed very quickly and that it would be easy for them to administer. The following sections will highlight how you can use FrontPage to enhance all aspects of the site (not just the portal concept), including

- **Web site planning.** Face it: If you are using a simple text editor, building even a modestly complex Web site is going to be an exercise in severe time consumption, as well as frustration. Although coding all of your HTML (and scripts) by hand might be a noble undertaking, it is probably not the best use of your time, and it will inevitably lead to errors. Knowing from the onset that you have a strong editing tool at your disposal will free you to consider the larger design and business issues that are so important to the most effective Web sites.

- **Web site development.** After you develop a strong plan, you can move on the actual development of the site. It's one thing to know about the advanced tools available within FrontPage (such as the Database Results Wizard); it is something else entirely to have a strong plan for how you can use these tools to meet your planning requirements. As you will see highlighted in this chapter (and in complete detail in Chapter 24, "MuseToMusic Web Site with FrontPage XP: Building the Solution," when you do the coding of the actual MuseToMusic site using FrontPage), you can use the development tools in FrontPage to help meet all of your planning requirements.

- **Web site administration.** As I mentioned previously, the MuseToMusic owners were skeptical about how much of an investment a Web portal would involve. This included not only the initial upfront development costs, but also long-term administration. Again, as you will see in this chapter and in Chapter 24, FrontPage has a strong user-friendly component, making the administration and maintenance of a Web site manageable even for those with limited Web design experience.

 TIP

As I have said many times throughout this book, planning is an essential component of a successful Web project. Think of this chapter (and the corresponding chapters in the other projects) as an exercise in planning. Not only are you thinking through the overall business requirements of your Web site, you are also considering the tools at your disposal (in this case, FrontPage) and—critically—how those tools can help facilitate meeting (and exceeding) these requirements.

Using FrontPage Site Templates to Build the MuseToMusic Web Structure

After you sold the storeowners on the concept of a portal, it was time to go back to your office and develop the plan for how the portal would be constructed within FrontPage.

If you are following along with FrontPage as you read this chapter, then you've already created the MuseToMusic Web folder and selected the FrontPage design scheme (Corporate Presence). Assuming you've done both of these things, you can move on and work through each step of the Corporate Presence Wizard.

1. If you are working in FrontPage as you read this chapter, the introduction step to the Corporate Presence Wizard should still be on your screen, as illustrated in Figure 22.3. Go ahead and click on Next.

 CAUTION

If you are using FrontPage 2000, you can still work with nearly all of the functionality presented in this and the other chapters of this specific project. However, using older versions of FrontPage (such as FrontPage 98) will result in significant discrepancies in the functionality presented, especially with advanced tools such as the Database Results Wizard.

2. The first step in the Wizard asks you to select the type of main/primary pages that will appear in your site. Click on all of the options, and then click on Next.

 TIP

Note the navigation buttons available in each step of the Wizard, allowing you to stop at any given point (Finish) or move forward or backward between the individual steps of the Wizard (Back and Next). Clicking on Cancel will stop the Wizard completely; it is not the same as clicking on Finish, which stops the Wizard at that particular point but creates all of the steps you've already completed.

3. The next step in the Wizard asks you to select specific sections of text that might appear on your home page. For now, select all of these as well, as shown in Figure 22.4.

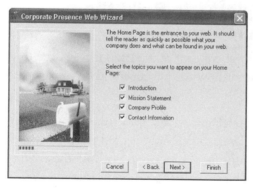

FIGURE 22.4 *You will adjust the content of your home page later; for now, select all of the options.*

4. Next, you are asked to select options that will appear on your What's New page. Think back to the Web portal concept and one of the primary requirements of the MuseToMusic site—to serve as a central location for information on the local music scene. Clearly, the What's New page will be visited often because you will include concert dates and other breaking announcements about the musicians and music events in the community. Again, select all of the options that appear here, as illustrated in Figure 22.5.

5. Click on Next. The next step of the Wizard asks you to select the number of individual products and services pages that should be created. As

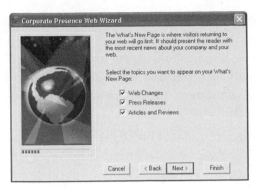

FIGURE 22.5 *Note how each of these options will fit in perfectly with the MuseToMusic site. For example, each band (as well as the store in general) will have press releases and articles or reviews.*

you'll see later, you will be integrating a database to pull information about your current inventory, so this step of the Wizard won't really apply. However, go ahead and change the default setting of three pages for products and services to one page for each so the Wizard will create these pages. (You can use them to build additional functionality, as you will see later.)

6. Again, click on Next. The next step in the Wizard asks you what type of content you want to present for each product and service. In this case, leave the default settings as they are (see Figure 22.6). As information about a particular CD is pulled from the database, for example, you can use the layout created by this step of the Wizard to display related content, such as price, cover image, and the request (purchase) form. Click on Next.

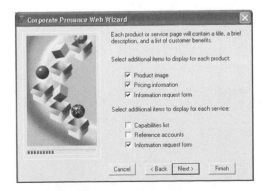

FIGURE 22.6 *Leave the default settings as they are shown here.*

7. The next step presents important information for your site. Given that you hope the MuseToMusic site becomes a vibrant communication tool for promoting all things music, you should expect lots of visitor feedback. This step in the Wizard addresses that very issue, so go ahead and click all of the options. You can remove them later if you find they don't fit into your overall design plan.

8. Collecting data (be it feedback or product orders) is obviously important. Although you'll be using a database to collect most of the information from site visitors, leave the default setting of Yes, Use Tab-Delimited Format selected in this step.

9. The next step asks you about your Table of Contents page. Leave the one default option (Use Bullets for Top-Level Pages) selected.

10. You're almost done! The next step in the Wizard asks you what information should appear at the top and bottom of each page. This header and footer information is very important for keeping an integrated look and feel for your entire site. To highlight all the functionality possible with this feature, select all the options in this step, as shown in Figure 22.7.

11. The next step asks whether you want the typical Under Construction graphic to appear for pages that might not be fully operational. Select this option and click on Next.

12. The following two steps of the Wizard ask you to provide contact information about the company. Enter whatever information you want, but use MuseToMusic for the name of the company.

13. After you complete these two steps, the next step of the Wizard asks whether you want to select a theme to apply to all the pages on your site.

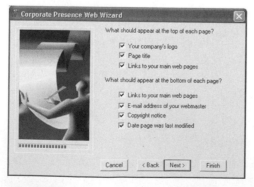

FIGURE 22.7 *It's important to have the same information appear at the top and bottom of each page. For now, check all of these options, as shown here.*

Click on the Choose Theme button to open the Choose Theme dialog box, as illustrated in Figure 22.8.

14. Note the four options below the list of theme choices—Vivid Colors, Active Graphics, Background Picture, and Apply Using CSS. After you select a theme, select all of these options, and then click on OK.

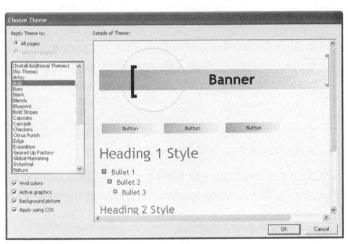

FIGURE 22.8 *Select a theme you find appealing. If you want to follow along closely, select the Axis theme, as shown here.*

 TIP

If you've used Microsoft PowerPoint, you may find that the FrontPage theme being discussed here is similar in look—as well as how you customize it—as a template that is used within PowerPoint to help you build a presentation. The similarities are certainly not coincidental: FrontPage and PowerPoint are both Microsoft products, but in addition to that obvious similarity, the methodologies that are utilized to build these themes are all constructed around the same general design principles. So, if you are comfortable using PowerPoint, you should feel extra assured that you will quickly recognize and become comfortable in working with the FrontPage themes, not just the one being illustrated here but all of them (as they all follow the same design process by asking you the same general questions).

 TIP

You don't have to apply a theme at this point in the Wizard, even though I have done so here. You can always go back and apply a theme later directly in FrontPage.

NOTE

FrontPage has some wonderful tools available for working with cascading style sheets, which you learned about in Chapters 9 and 10. Be certain to select the Apply Using CSS option, as shown in Figure 22.8.

15. After you click on OK in Figure 22.8, you will return to the "choose a theme" step. Click on Next, and you will be brought (finally!) to the step of the Corporate Presence Web Wizard. Click on Finish to have FrontPage create the site based on the information you provided in Steps 2 through 14.

After a few moments, FrontPage places you in Tasks view, where you will see a list of tasks to complete, as shown in Figure 22.9.

From a Web-development perspective, take a moment to reflect on the planning process that FrontPage has just facilitated for you. By working through a few short

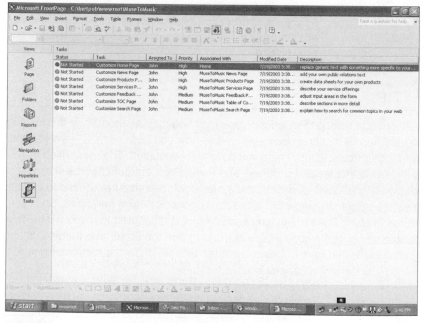

FIGURE 22.9 *Based on the default information you provided in the various steps of the Corporate Presence Web Wizard, you are now asked to go through and customize and provide specific information for each page.*

steps, you developed a well-structured shell for the entire MuseToMusic Web site. Granted, there is much work to be done, but the overall implementation plan—the focus of this chapter, which will govern the development of the site—is now in place.

Although you will customize the Web structure you just built in Chapter 24, there are a few things you should take the time to notice at this point. Specifically, these issues pertain to how the use of FrontPage (and specifically, the Corporate Presence Web Wizard) helps you to meet critical business process and Web design goals. Each of the following sections will briefly describe several of these issues.

Requirement Met: Portal Concept/Effective Design

Given that the local community has always viewed MuseToMusic as a cool store, the design of the Web site needed to reflect this emphasis on style.

Although some of the steps in the Corporate Presence Web Wizard might have seemed a bit, well, stodgy (not to mention the term *corporate presence*), the functionality represented in the design is nearly identical to what the MuseToMusic owners requested for their site.

Your screen should still look like Figure 22.9. If it doesn't, click on the Tasks icon in the left frame of the FrontPage window. Take a moment to get an idea of what the Corporate Presence Wizard and the theme you chose have done in terms of giving you a functional, attractive design from which to customize the pages of the MuseToMusic site.

From the list of tasks presented, right-click on the first task (which should concern the site home page). From the menu that appears, select Start Task. You will be taken to Page view for the page in question, which in this case is the site home page. Your screen should look like Figure 22.10.

A few things to note about this page:

◆ The overall portal requirement has been met via the design of the site home page. From the home page, there will be links to all facets of the store and the local music scene. (You'll see how this is developed in the next two chapters.) Through an easy-to-navigate design, visitors should find an inviting Web site full of pertinent information and links to related sites, both requirements for a successful portal.

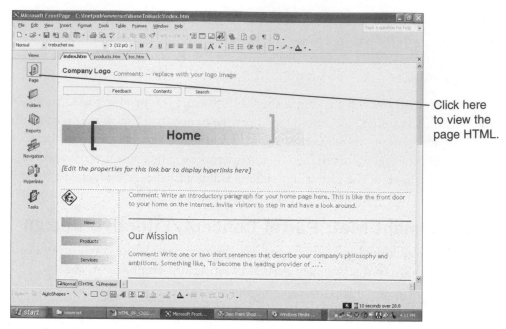

Click here
to view the
page HTML.

FIGURE 22.10 *The site home page. Note how the different content options you selected during the wizard creation process are reflected here.*

 NOTE

The portal concept is indeed critical. In the remaining chapters of this project, you will see how it is further developed in the design of the site, as well as how it addresses critical customer issues (CRM).

◆ As I mentioned, you should notice how the content options you selected in the various steps of the Corporate Presence Web Wizard are presented here. For example, placeholders for the MuseToMusic mission, company profile, and contact information are all presented here.

◆ The design theme you chose has been applied, and it is reflected in the navigation bar and the graphics and background presented on the page.

◆ FrontPage has inserted friendly reminders on the page (in other words, the purple comment text).

◆ Various hyperlinks have been inserted and are ready to be customized, including the e-mail addresses you provided in the related Wizard steps.

◆ Cascading style sheets have been applied to all of the pages on the site. If you click on the HTML tab at the bottom of the screen, you will see the style sheet references, as well as the underlying HTML (see Figure 22.11).

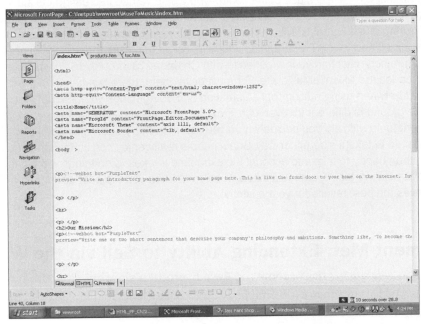

FIGURE 22.11 *FrontPage does its magic behind the scenes. Through external style sheets and other automated formatting, the actual HTML behind this page is fairly limited.*

You should note that although the HTML behind the site home page is not very complicated, the related FrontPage automation—that is, what FrontPage does to apply the themes and page layout styles—is extensive. However, you will need to perform significant HTML tweaking, so even though it might look like FrontPage has done all the work, there is still quite a bit for you to do.

As a final note on the home page, all the basic MuseToMusic store information (as well as more detailed information, such as the store's mission statement) has been included at the bottom of the home page. With some customization (which you will do in Chapter 24), you can add information such as hours of operation and directions to the store.

TO AUTOMATE OR NOT TO AUTOMATE: THAT IS THE QUESTION

The screen illustrated in Figure 22.11 is either the greatest thing in the world or something to completely despise, depending on your view of HTML editors. Although the Wizard you utilized to create the MuseToMusic site shell saved you a lot of time and helped you address the critical design and site functionality questions, there is no denying that it removed much of the control you would've had in creating the site. Even though there is much customizing to be done, as well as extensive tweaking and configuring of the actual HTML, there is no comparison between hand-coding all of this yourself and letting FrontPage do it for you. So as you work through the chapters in this project, reflect on your experience with Chapters 13 through 16, in which you hand-coded the MuseToMusic site. For most developers, there is a happy middle ground between using editing-tool automation and doing things yourself. But that middle ground is different for everyone. Experience in coding sites and working with different tools will help you decide where you stand on this issue. Again, don't feel compelled to take a side either way. Some people really enjoy coding by hand and are more than happy to take into account the extra time it takes to do things without the aid of an editing tool. You should follow whatever makes you the best developer and achieves the best results for your customers.

Requirement Met: Extending Ability to Sell via the Web

The term *e-commerce* has become somewhat verboten since the dot com bust. Yet there is no denying that e-commerce is here to stay, and that the use of the Web as an essential sales tool will only continue to grow.

When you were working on the "products and services" step of the Wizard, I mentioned that you would be integrating a database to help present the store inventory and gather customer feedback and other data. I will present this database functionality in more detail in the next two chapters, but you can see how the Wizard built pages that you can use to present store products and thus facilitate e-commerce.

Take a look at this page now. If you follow the Products link (by holding the down the Ctrl key and clicking on the Products link), FrontPage will take you to that specific page, as shown in Figure 22.12.

You will be utilizing another FrontPage tool—the Database Results Wizard—to dynamically pull product inventory from a back-end (Access) database and display it to your customers. This Wizard will also allow you to create a search form

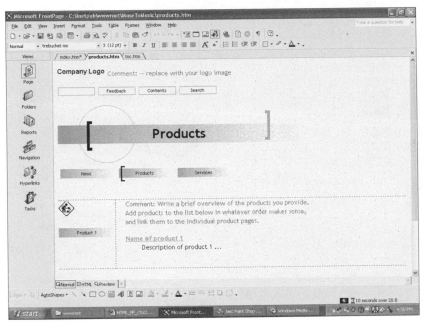

FIGURE 22.12 *The Products page, on which you will present items for sale (in other words, the current store inventory).*

so customers can quickly find items of interest based on title, artist, and other search criteria.

The important thing to notice here is how the Wizard generated a page for you to place product information. And, like all pages generated by the Wizard, the page prompts you with reminders about what to add to make it as effective as possible.

Requirement Met: Site Usability

Perhaps the greatest thing about working with a FrontPage site template such as the Corporate Presence Web Wizard is that it builds a site that is incredibly easy and intuitive to navigate.

Figure 22.13 illustrates the Navigation view in FrontPage, highlighting the overall site structure and how each page links to another.

You will revisit the navigation design and structure in the next two chapters. Take time now, however, to notice the functionality presented and how FrontPage

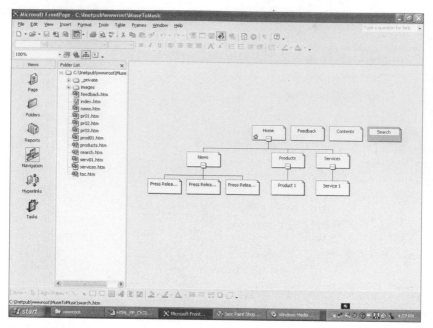

FIGURE 22.13 *You can easily customize and configure your entire site navigation structure.*

allows you to get a snapshot view of your entire site navigation structure. Also note that changes you make in Navigation view will be reflected on the pages themselves. For example, if you change the name of a page, it will be automatically changed on all the navigation buttons throughout the site.

Another user-friendly feature of the template is the inclusion of a search form, as shown in Figure 22.14.

There are other customer-specific features that involve an extended discussion of CRM principles. I will address these features in the next chapter.

Requirement Met: Ease of Administration

I will highlight this issue in Chapter 24, but it should already be obvious—especially if you look back at Figure 22.10—how useful FrontPage can be in coordinating the tasks associated with site development.

But what about once the site is built, when you want to turn the administration of the site over to the clients? Again, you'll learn more about this in Chapter 24,

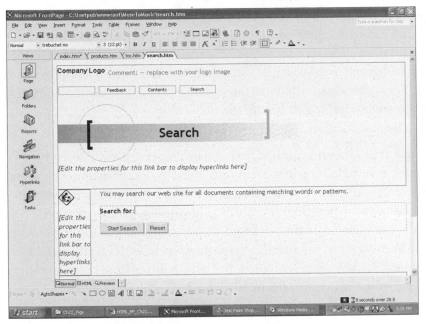

FIGURE 22.14 *A search tool is useful for allowing customers to quickly find the item for which they are searching.*

but you should note that FrontPage offers the following key benefits in long-term administration (as opposed to a site that was not developed with FrontPage):

◆ **An easy-to-use interface.** If you've used another Microsoft Office application (and who hasn't?), the general interface of FrontPage will be instantly familiar. Given that its overall text formatting is very similar to Word, even those users with very limited Web design experience will have no problem making basic to moderately complex content changes.

TIP

For a comprehensive review of essential FrontPage functionality, review Chapter 12.

◆ **Automated advanced programming requirements.** As you will see in the discussion and implementation of the Database Results Wizard, a process that would normally require some fairly extensive programming skills is reduced to a step-by-step wizard approach that results in pages that customers can later customize and update themselves.

◆ **A built-in, easy-to-use publishing tool.** FrontPage has a very user-friendly publishing feature that allows you to synchronize pages that have changed, so your Web site is always up to date. Moreover, the publishing tool is completely automated, so users don't need to worry about having to work with confusing command codes or file directories. Like nearly everything in FrontPage, publishing is achieved with point-and-click automation.

Of course, there are some drawbacks to using FrontPage. As I noted earlier, if you like to have complete control over your code, you might find the automation aspects of FrontPage irritating (even though FrontPage XP is better than previous versions about not changing your code without giving you explicit notice). Also, the use of some of the advanced automated functionality requires that the hosting Web server have FrontPage extensions installed. (I'll talk more about this in Chapter 24.) Still, even with these limitations, FrontPage is an excellent tool—and one that has many benefits to both the developer and the customer.

Summary

This chapter illustrated how you could build a Web site plan using FrontPage (and specifically a site template). For the MuseToMusic site, you worked through the Corporate Presence Web Wizard, creating all design aspects to meet the required functionality that was set forth by the storeowners. In working through the Wizard, you were introduced to some of the advanced functionally of FrontPage, including its ability to create a site navigation tool and apply an overall design scheme to your site. Finally, the chapter reviewed how you could meet the essential business requirements by using FrontPage. The following chapters will expand on these requirements by focusing on how FrontPage can help address specific CRM issues, as well as how you can use FrontPage to build the entire MuseToMusic site, including integrating a database.

Chapter 23

**MuseToMusic Web
Site with
FrontPage XP:
Addressing
Customer
Usability Issues**

The specific CRM components of the MuseToMusic Web site were discussed in detail in Chapter 15. This chapter will not repeat that information; however, it will look at how you can facilitate those same CRM requirements using FrontPage (and specifically, the special tools that FrontPage includes).

CRM-Specific Functionality in FrontPage

In this brief chapter, you will once again revisit the major CRM requirements, but you will also see how they are enhanced via the use of FrontPage. A list of these major CRM requirements follows.

 NOTE

Although it is not an absolute requirement to read these project chapters in sequential order, you might find it useful to read and work through Chapters 15 and 22, which lay specific groundwork for the discussion that is presented here, if you haven't done so already.

- ◆ **Intuitive site navigation.** As you saw in Chapter 22, when you used the Corporate Presence Web Wizard to re-create the MuseToMusic Web site in FrontPage, the Wizard automatically created a site-wide navigation scheme. Easy-to-use, intuitive site navigation is a critical component of CRM because customers must feel that they are in control of their experience when visiting your Web site. A well-developed site navigation structure tremendously aids in the achievement of this goal because any and all information the customer might request is quickly accessible. Related to this is the placement of a search form (which the Corporate Presence Web Wizard also created) on your site. I will discuss the functionality of this search form in this chapter as well.

◆ **Well-designed shopping cart.** In Chapter 22, I referenced the Front-Page Database Results Wizard several times as an easy way to integrate a database with your Web site. For real e-commerce ability on your site, you need a method of actively presenting product information—and, of course, capturing and processing product orders. Having a database to help facilitate this (so you can store and retrieve information) is critical. In the past, this has been a difficult task to accomplish for those without much programming experience; however, the Database Results Wizard makes this easy and can help you turn the MuseToMusic business requirement of using the Web to extend store sales into a reality when you combine it with other CRM features of the site.

◆ **Online forums and support.** Part of meeting all your customers' expectations is giving them a sense of ownership of your site. A great way to do this is to provide space for customer feedback and support forums, where visitors can post questions and respond to questions left by other visitors. As the site developer or the storeowner, you can use this same functionality to respond directly to customer questions about all facets of the site or company, from the status of online orders to general inquiries about the site or company.

◆ **Personalizing the Web experience.** Similar to the previous point, if your customers feel they are playing an active role in the operation of your Web site (or your company, for that matter), they will feel more inclined to return to it often. As I discussed in previous chapters concerning the MuseToMusic site, a key business requirement for the site is to have it be a portal to all things music—not just in the local community, but also for visitors' special interests (such as related music sites, music-related discussion forums, and so on). You can facilitate the portal concept and the online forums and support using the FrontPage Database Results Wizard because it provides you with a method of storing and retrieving (based on individual customer data queries) information specific to the customer. For example, you might request that customers log in to your Web site upon visiting certain pages. If this is the case, you could use the information they provide (such as user name) to search your database to see what products they have ordered or what discussion forums they have posted to, and then present only information related to them.

◆ **Enabling post-order support issues.** Related to the entire e-commerce perspective of CRM, after customers place an order on your site, you want to give them the ability to stay in touch by presenting options so they can track or ask you questions about their orders and (of course) reach you if there are problems with an order. Using special form-handling tools in FrontPage, as well as the Database Results Wizard, you can provide this interactive functionality so customers know you care even after the sale.

 NOTE

This chapter will explore in more conceptual detail many of the special FrontPage tools that were automatically integrated when you built the MuseToMusic site (in Chapter 22) using the Corporate Presence Web Wizard. The complete configuration of this site, including customization (via these tools and the actual HTML code) will be done in the final chapter of this project.

Building Intuitive Site Navigation

Think about it: If you had to monitor 20 different controls and adjust multiple settings while driving a car, it would be more like flying an airplane. Although there is something to be said for the joys of aviation, most of us prefer the simplicity of the modern automobile. You put the key in the ignition, maybe turn on the lights or windshield wipers, put the thing in drive, and go wherever you want. This analogy carries over to a Web site with a well-designed navigation structure. As visitors and customers move around the site, they want to be able to

◆ Know where they are at any given moment.

◆ Be able to go wherever they choose (in other words, find what they are looking for).

◆ Be able to return to where they previously were (after they have spent some time on the site).

The site navigation that was automatically created by the Corporate Presence Web Wizard helps the MuseToMusic site achieve many of these goals and allows for easy customization now or in the future. I want to move through the navigation features of the MuseToMusic site as they were constructed in the last chapter.

1. If you haven't done so already, open the MuseToMusic Web site in FrontPage.

2. Click on the Navigation view button. The navigation layout of the site will be presented, as shown in Figure 23.1.

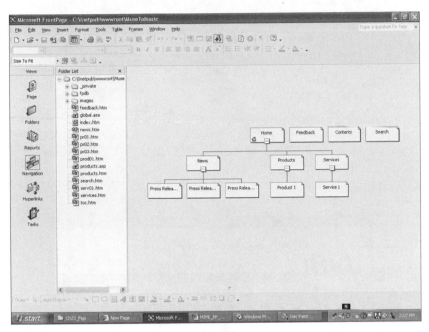

FIGURE 23.1 *The entire navigation structure of your site is easily configurable through the FrontPage Navigation view.*

3. Notice that the News page has three pages linked to it. Double-click on the News page. FrontPage will switch to Page view and display the News page (news.htm). Scroll down this page and you will see three links— Press Release 1, Press Release 2, and Press Release 3—as shown in Figure 23.2.

4. Now go back to Navigation view. From the File menu, select New, Page and select Blank Page from the list of options that appears on the right side of your screen. The blank page will be inserted in the Navigation view, as shown in Figure 23.3.

5. Click and hold on this new page and drag it so the connection line that appears links this page under the News page.

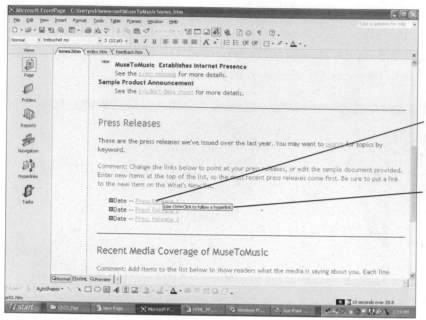

FrontPage allows you to view hyperlink functionality.

The page to which the specific hyperlink points

FIGURE 23.2 *The links for each page are also illustrated in Page view.*

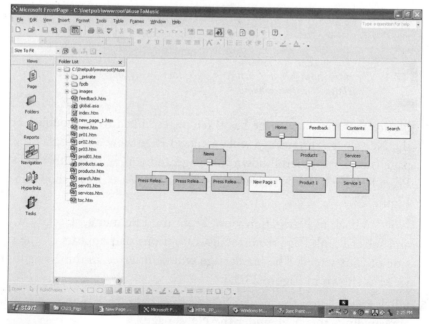

FIGURE 23.3 *You can easily add, delete, or customize pages in Navigation view.*

6. Now double-click once again on the News page. FrontPage will open Page view, and you will be able to see the link for the new page, as shown in Figure 23.4.

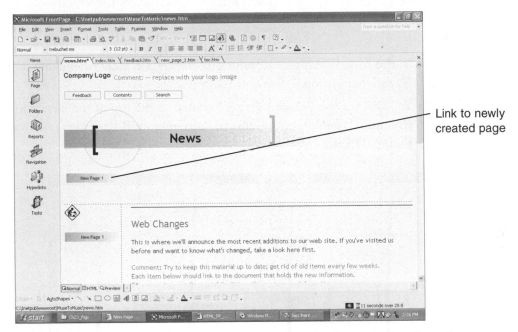

FIGURE 23.4 *The ease and power of the automated navigation features in FrontPage allow you a high level of customization and control in how customers will move about your site.*

You will customize the navigation features of the MuseToMusic site in the next chapter. Still, this brief overview of Navigation view and how the navigation features of the site were automatically inserted with the Corporate Presence Web Wizard are a clear indication of the powerful timesaving features of utilizing FrontPage, as well as the enhanced functionality possible. Although it is certainly possible to create your own navigation structure (indeed, some people prefer it), allowing FrontPage to build it for you gives you the assurance that changes you make will be reflected throughout the entire site. Not unlike the great functionality of style sheets, when you change something in a template-based Web site (using, for example, Navigation view), you are assured that all the associated changes are made as well. Nothing is more annoying or will turn a customer away from your site faster than a broken hyperlink. Utilizing the navigation features of FrontPage should help ensure that this doesn't happen.

Integrating a Search Form

Closely associated with a strong navigation structure is the ability for customers to search the site for a particular term of interest. Once again, the Wizard you utilized in Chapter 22 incorporated this search form functionality into the MuseToMusic site.

1. In the MuseToMusic site, return to Navigation view by clicking on the Navigation button.

2. You will see the Search page represented at the top of the navigation structure. Double-click on this page to open it in Page view, as shown in Figure 23.5.

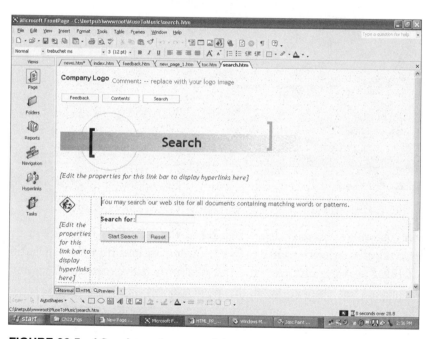

FIGURE 23.5 *A Search page is an essential component to ensure that customers find exactly what they want.*

A few things to note about this page:

◆ The Search page is an automated FrontPage component. It will only function if the server hosting your Web site allows for FrontPage extensions. (This is true of much of the functionality presented in this project.)

◆ As you will see a bit later in this chapter, the Search page will not search the Access database that you will also integrate with the MuseToMusic site. However, the Database Results Wizard has its own unique search form (and other navigation tools).

◆ The Search page is not a substitute for a well-designed general navigation structure. Rather than forcing your visitors to use a search form, why not make conspicuous links to major items readily apparent?

Enabling Dynamic Content with the Database Results Wizard

HTML is obviously an attractive tool for content presentation. Combined with cascading style sheets, scripting languages, and other tools that you are now familiar with from Part I of this book, you can bring a great degree of customization and power to your content presentation.

However, you will come to a point in working with Web sites where the content, no matter how convincingly designed, is *static*—in other words, it doesn't allow for any direct interaction with the visitor. Although it might be possible to have this content change or be altered to a limited degree through the use of JavaScript, you can't really ask customers to provide complex information and then return associated content based on the information they provide, for example.

Of course, if you integrate a data source with your Web site, the new functionality becomes very apparent. Specifically, your content becomes *dynamic* in that you can present it so it is specifically related to a product search request, for example.

Indeed, integrating a database can help you address many (if not all) of the CRM issues listed at the beginning of this chapter. Consider the following:

◆ If you store previous sales information about the customer in your database, the next time the individual visits your Web site you can present them with items similar to what they ordered on their last visit, thus increasing the chance they will find additional items of interest.

◆ Presenting a full-featured shopping cart on your site allows for real e-commerce because you can capture purchase information from customers and give them tracking information for when their orders should arrive.

Specifically, the customer places the order, and it is stored in your database. You pull this information from the database, process the order, and—as the product moves through the various stages of shipment—insert updates on this process back into the database. In turn, customers visit your site and retrieve this information by entering their e-mail addresses as their unique identifiers. This queries the database to return the shipment information you previously entered.

◆ Online discussion forums are more powerful with a database. Although there are several scripts that allow for Guestbook functionality, having a database behind this type of feature makes it searchable by the visitor. (Guestbook-type pages usually put the information entered into them in a text file, so the entire file must be read and displayed back to the interested user.)

◆ Generally, being able to store and retrieve information brings all kinds of wonderful content-presentation benefits to your Web site. You simply cannot bring the same amount of functionality to static content as you can to a dynamic, database-driven Web site.

TIP

As a developer, you can also use a database to make your coding more efficient. In conjunction with a scripting language (such as VBScript), for example, you could store layout information about your Web site in a database so a visitor could pick a desired layout. Rather than creating several individual pages to account for the various layout configurations of your site, you could store these options in a database. Then, by working with a script that is integrated with your HTML, you could dynamically build your page based on the customer's requests. In short, you would have one page template that gets specific layout values from the database, which in turn would be queried based on a specific request. For more information on this and other benefits of integrating a database with your Web site, see *ASP Programming for the Absolute Beginner* (Premier Press, 2002) or (for a .NET approach) *ASP.NET Professional Projects* (Premier Press, 2002).

So how do you accomplish this database integration with FrontPage? You do it using the Database Results Wizard. Best of all, you don't need any programming expertise to utilize this tool. (It is also easy enough for a non-developer to work with; thus there are added benefits for the long-term administration of a site that uses this feature.)

As usual, I want to work through how you might integrate the Database Results Wizard into the MuseToMusic site to facilitate all of the previously mentioned CRM goals. This exercise will get you familiar with the tool. In the next chapter, you will customize it as you build the final MuseToMusic site in FrontPage.

1. In the MuseToMusic Web in FrontPage, create a new page.

2. Call this page Database and immediately save it in the MuseToMusic Web. Be sure to save it with the .asp extension.

 NOTE

The Database Results Wizard is dependent on ASP functionality. In order to function, you must save the pages that utilize this functionality with the .asp extension.

3. After you have saved the page with the .asp extension, you can insert the Database Results Wizard. From the FrontPage Insert menu, select Database, Results. Your screen should now look like Figure 23.6.

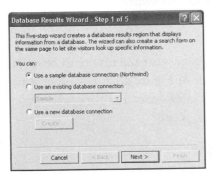

FIGURE 23.6 *Preparing to work with the Database Results Wizard.*

 NOTE

Remember that with scripting (and some other advanced functionality within FrontPage), you cannot see the script/functionality "in action" using FrontPage's Preview function: you must load these pages in a Web browser, and ensure that the Web server hosting them is able to facilitate (in this case) ASP.

NOTE

Until you save the page with the .asp extension, the Database Results option will not be accessible from the Insert menu.

4. Select the Use a Sample Database Connection (Northwind) option and click on Next. Northwind is the sample database that is loaded with many Microsoft applications. If for some reason you don't have it loaded on your system, you can still follow along with what is being presented here. In the next chapter, I'll ask you to create a simple database, at which time I'll provide you with more detailed information about the Database Results Wizard. (Again, the information presented here is intended to familiarize you with the tool and highlight what is possible for meeting customer usability requirements.)

5. You should now be on Step 2 of the Wizard. Leave the default selections as they are and click on Next.

6. In Step 3 of the Wizard, you must specify which fields in the database will be displayed on the Web page. Again, accept the default values and click on Next.

7. Step 4 of the Wizard asks you how you want the results to be displayed. Note the different options, as shown in Figure 23.7. For now, however, leave the default option of Table - One Record Per Row selected.

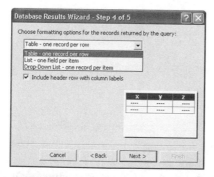

FIGURE 23.7 *You have different options available for how you want to format your database search results.*

8. For the final step (Step 5), accept the default values and click on Finish. Your screen should look like Figure 23.8.

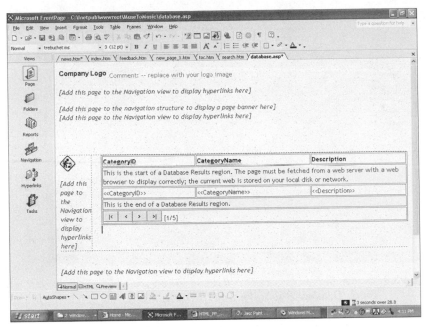

FIGURE 23.8 *The format of the Database Results Wizard, inserted directly into your page.*

9. Click on the HTML tab in Page view to see the underlying HTML that is inserted with the Database Results Wizard, as shown in Figure 23.9.

10. Save this page and load it into your Web browser. Your screen should appear similar to Figure 23.10.

Note that the Database Results Wizard also includes navigation buttons so you can move forward and backward in the returned dataset. Again, this is just a brief overview of the functionality that is possible with the Database Results Wizard. In the next chapter, you will configure this Wizard to access your own database, and you will include a database search form that customers of the MuseToMusic site could use to find a product. In other words, you'll create the first step for a well-designed e-commerce/online shopping cart.

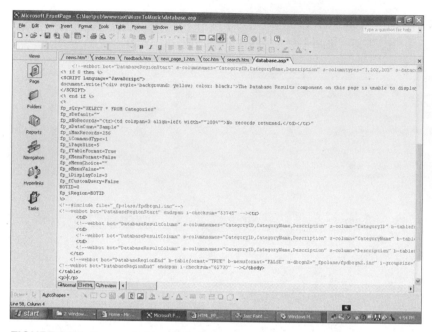

FIGURE 23.9 *In seconds, FrontPage inserts all the underlying code (HTML and script) required for the Database Results Wizard to function.*

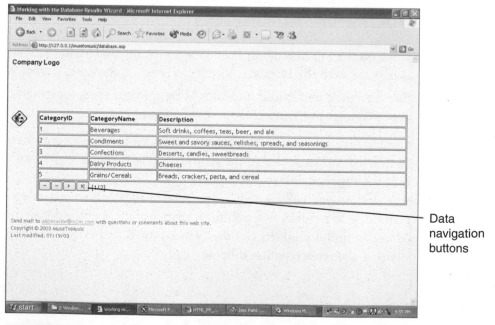

Data navigation buttons

FIGURE 23.10 *Integrating a database with your Web page opens up new avenues of content presentation and CRM benefits.*

> **NOTE**
>
> You may wonder, from Figure 23.10, why a music store has a database containing information about food and beverage items. If you caught this, congratulations on being a savvy reader! For this chapter, I am using the Northwind sample database that is included with both Microsoft Access and SQL Server (if you don't see this in your list of accessible databases within Access, check your original application CDs as it can be found there). The next chapter will work with a more appropriate database for a music store.

Other Customer Support Functionality in FrontPage

The navigation and database integration features previewed in this chapter address nearly all of the major CRM initiatives listed at the beginning of the chapter. In essence, the requirements for the MuseToMusic site are that it is well designed, with good navigation (FrontPage's Navigation feature); it allows for placement of online orders and facilitates online discussion groups (the Database Results Wizard); it has the ability personalize data presented to the customer; and it allows customers to retrieve information. (This last requirement is again met by the Database Results Wizard, as well as the search capabilities in that Wizard and the search form that was included in the Wizard you worked with in Chapter 22.) Also, as you will see in the next chapter, FrontPage is easy to use for even non-developers, so you—as the developer—can produce a site that your clients can take ownership of with limited ongoing support from you.

In the next chapter, you will configure all of these features so they are specific to the MuseToMusic site as it was constructed via the Corporate Presence Web Wizard you worked with in Chapter 22.

Summary

This chapter was intended to revisit the CRM issues for the MuseToMusic Web site, as initially presented in detail in Chapter 15. However, the focus of this chapter was to show you how you could enhance or facilitate those features using the FrontPage tools. You reviewed the automated navigation features in FrontPage and saw how changes made are updated throughout your site, thus decreasing the chance for errors. Also, you were introduced to the Database Results Wizard and how it can automate the integration of a database so you can further enhance your e-commerce, discussion and support forums, and other critical CRM components of your Web site. In the next chapter, you will configure the navigation and Database Results Wizard, and you will further customize the entire MuseToMusic site based on the Wizard you used to create it in the previous chapter.

Chapter 24

MuseToMusic Web Site with FrontPage XP: Building the Solution

If you're working through the chapters in this book sequentially, then you've already had quite a bit of exposure to the fictitious MuseToMusic company and the storeowners' desire to have a Web site to facilitate various business goals of the store. In the first project devoted to the company (Chapters 13 through 16), you read about the major business process goals that the owners would like to see enhanced by a well-designed Web site. Moreover, you were introduced to how that Web site could help the store address customer-usability issues with specific reference to CRM methodologies.

In the previous chapters in this project, you revisited these issues to learn how using an HTML editor such as FrontPage XP could further facilitate them. In Chapter 22, you saw how you could address the initial design and process goals using a FrontPage design template. Then in Chapter 23, you saw how you could use the special features and tools in FrontPage to further all of the requirements (design, business, or otherwise) from the first project. You can think of this final chapter in the MuseToMusic saga as a culmination of how to actually code the HTML to best accomplish all these goals. Specifically, this chapter will show you how the MuseToMusic Web site—constructed using FrontPage—can achieve the important design and process goals for the company by providing:

- A new forum for advertising and promoting the local music community.
- Links to external Web sites for local bands, as well as additional Web sites on music in general. This will further the Web portal design concept that has been stressed throughout the MuseToMusic discussion.
- Easy-to-use, intuitive site navigation.
- The ability to process form data.
- Integration of a backend database.
- An easy way for the storeowners to administer their site once you (as Web design consultant) are out of the picture.

Again, think of this chapter as a culmination of how to design a site using an HTML editor. There's a lot to cover in a relatively short space, so I want to get started now.

NOTE

This chapter assumes a few things. First and foremost, it assumes you are familiar with the basic and advanced tools of FrontPage. If this is not the case, you might want to go back and take a look at Chapter 12 (for that matter, all of the foundational HTML material presented in Chapters 1 through 12). Additionally, this chapter assumes you have worked through the material presented in Chapters 22 and 23. This chapter will continue to build on the basic site template you should have created when you worked through those chapters.

Establishing the MuseToMusic Site Template

In Chapter 22, you built the Web structure for the MuseToMusic site by utilizing the FrontPage Corporate Presence Wizard. This chapter will start from where you finished working through the Wizard, so if you haven't completed Chapter 22, you need to go back and do that now.

Assuming you are ready, I want to get started with some preliminary steps to confirm that your site structure is correct.

1. If it's not already open, go ahead and open FrontPage XP.

2. From the File menu, select Open. Navigate to the MuseToMusic Web you created (it should be stored in the Inetpub folder), and open the index.htm page. Your screen should now look like Figure 24.1.

3. Click on the Tasks icon to switch to Tasks view. Although you will complete more tasks than are listed here, this will give you an overview of some of the major content customization issues you need to address. Figure 24.2 illustrates what your screen should look like.

4. Click on the Page icon to return to Page view for the index.htm page. You will start your customization work there.

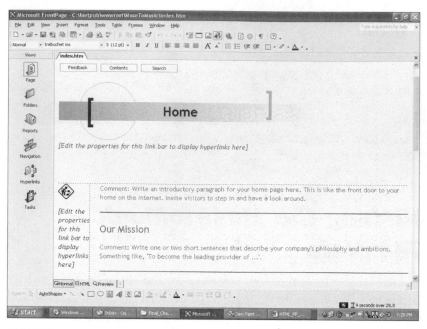

FIGURE 24.1 *For this chapter, you will build on the site structure you created with the FrontPage Corporate Presence Web Wizard.*

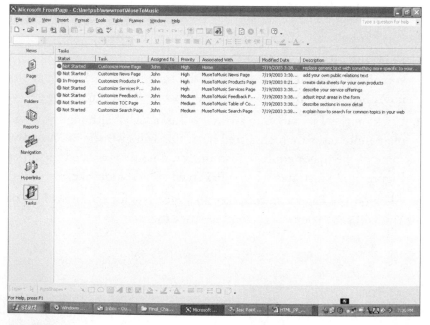

FIGURE 24.2 *It's fine if the status of some of your tasks is In Progress or Finished because you will be working through most of them again anyway.*

Modifying the Site Home Page

As it happens, the page you should now have open in FrontPage (index.htm) will be the site home page for the MuseToMusic Web.

To clarify both the FrontPage and HTML design issues on this page, I will present the different content customization issues for the home page in different sections. I want to start by describing how to change the page banner and customize the default text inserted by the Corporate Presence Web Wizard.

Customizing the Banner and Default Text

Obviously there is a lot of generic text on this and all the other pages of the site because they were created initially with the Corporate Presence Web Wizard. This section will focus on how to customize the banner and change some of the default text.

1. Right-click within the banner (the graphic that says "Home"). From the pop-up menu, select the Page Banner Properties option. The Page Banner Properties dialog box will appear, as shown in Figure 24.3. Enter **Welcome to MuseToMusic** in the Page Banner text box.

FIGURE 24.3 *This is only one example of how a site design template allows you to easily customize text and other elements in your site.*

 NOTE

You don't have to enter the customized text exactly as you see it in this chapter. The important thing is that you understand the HTML and FrontPage functionality being presented, so feel free to improvise and be creative!

2. Next, replace the default company logo. Scroll to the top of the index.htm page to the Company Logo text (it's actually a graphic). Click on it to select it, and then select Insert, Picture, From File or Insert,

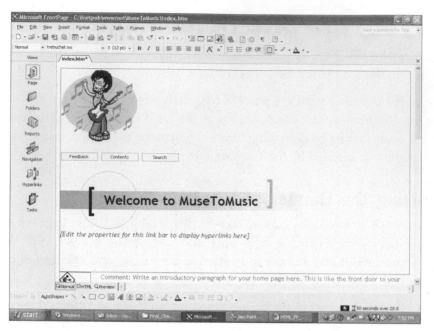

FIGURE 24.4 *Depending on the size of your image, you might want to resize it to make it appear more proportional to the rest of the elements on your page.*

Picture, From ClipArt. (If you have a picture you want to use as the company logo, you can select it using the From File option.) I'm going to use a ClipArt graphic, so if your logo is different than what appears in the figures from this point forward, it's no problem. Figure 24.4 illustrates the company logo I have chosen.

3. Finally, you should see three major text sections on this page—Our Mission, Company Profile, and Contact Information. There is default text under each of these headings (inserted by the Corporate Presence Web Wizard). Go ahead and change this text to something more descriptive of a music store. Feel free to use your imagination and insert whatever text you like in these sections. Note that the text under the Contact Information header was originally provided in a step of the Wizard. Figure 24.5 highlights the page as it appears with my new text.

4. Save your page.

Before you go any further, it's worth taking a look at how FrontPage does some customization of its own in terms of the HTML it automatically generates for this page and all others on the site. Click on the HTML tab at the bottom of the screen and take a look at what is presented, as shown in Figure 24.6.

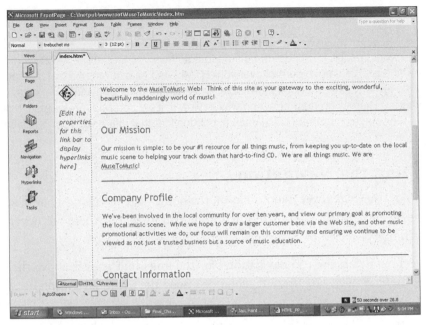

FIGURE 24.5 *As you enter text, be sure to delete the comment reminders that the Wizard inserted for you.*

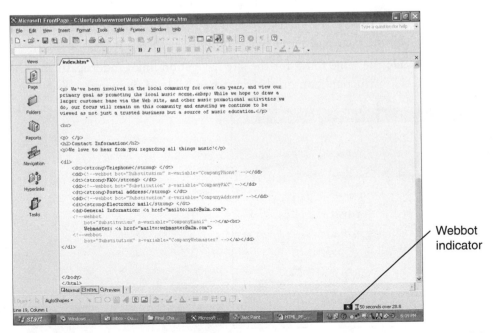

Webbot
indicator

FIGURE 24.6 *Notice the webbot indicator, which is the automated tool used by FrontPage to help build the site template, navigation, and so on.*

TIP

As you work through this chapter, be sure to note how you feel about having a tool like FrontPage exert so much control over your HTML. As I said in other chapters, some people view this as tremendous timesaver while others think of it as Web design anathema. There is no right or wrong way to view it; it's a personal preference. (I like using FrontPage and other HTML editors, but don't let that influence your decision!)

Customizing the Navigation

Right now there are three major links on the home page navigation bar: Feedback, Contents, and Search. These are OK for general links, but there are nevertheless some things you need to customize.

1. First delete the top navigation bar (the links that appear above the banner graphic). For this site, you don't need the extra navigation bar.

2. Underneath the banner graphic, right-click on the text that reads, "[Edit the properties for this link bar to display hyperlinks here]." From the drop-down menu that appears, select Link Bar Properties. The Link Bar Properties dialog box will open, as shown in Figure 24.7.

3. Select the Child Pages Under Home option, which should select the Home Page and Parent Page options, as shown in Figure 24.7.

4. Do the same thing for the site navigation link (underneath the Under Construction icon on the right-hand side of the page).

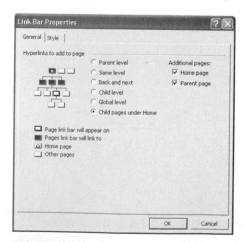

FIGURE 24.7 *You can easily configure navigation bar properties; the navigation features of the site were included when you worked through the Corporate Presence Web Wizard.*

5. Speaking of the Under Construction link, replace it with a graphic of your choice, as you did in the previous section. As you can see in Figure 24.8, I'm using the same guitar player graphic, but I've sized it down so it is proportional to the other elements on this page.

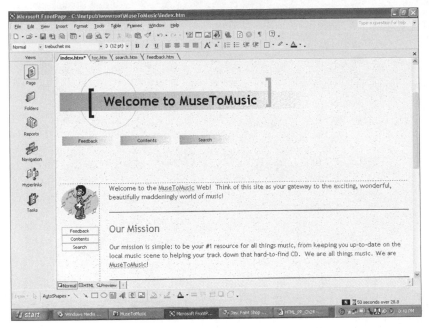

FIGURE 24.8 *Using the same graphic (albeit sized differently) gives your page a consistent look and feel.*

6. One last issue to address. Scroll to the bottom of the page, and you will see another text prompt to edit the link bar properties. Just as you did in Steps 2 and 3, set this so the text is replaced with the three major links. Note that the design of this navigation bar is different than the side and top navigation bars; this is the effect of the site template.

7. Save your page.

Before you move on to customize the site further, you can see the navigation bars in action. If you hold down the Ctrl key and right-click on one of the links, you will be taken to the corresponding (for now) default page that was initially created. Try it now.

1. Switch to Preview mode by clicking on the Preview tab at the bottom of the screen.

2. While holding down the Ctrl key, click on any one of the Feedback links on any of the three navigation bars.

3. The default Feedback.htm page will load, as shown in Figure 24.9.

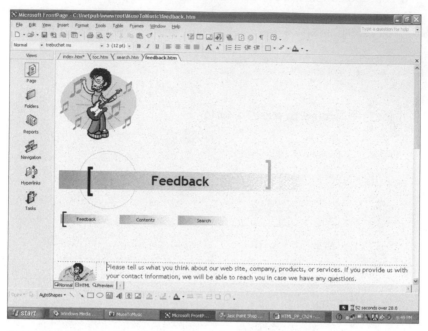

FIGURE 24.9 *Note how the link for the selected page is highlighted in the navigation bar. This is a neat way of letting the user know what page they are currently visiting.*

Allowing Customer Feedback

Allowing your customers to interact with your site via active forms is a critical functionality of any Web site. Fortunately, when you used the Corporate Presence Web Wizard to build the MuseToMusic site structure, FrontPage automatically included this functionality. This section will look at how to configure this functionality as it stands now, as well as how to further manipulate it with some simple scripting.

NOTE

Be sure to refer back to Chapter 8 for a full discussion of working with HTML forms. Also, see Chapter 11 for an example of how to process form data via the integration of a scripting language (VBScript).

1. Open the Feedback.htm page in FrontPage. Your screen should appear similar to Figure 24.10.

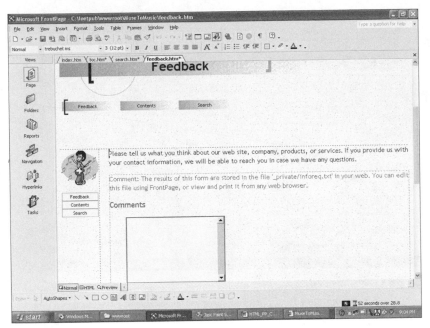

FIGURE 24.10 *If you saved the work you did in the previous section, notice how the graphic and changes to the navigation bars are copied down to this and other pages in your site. This is a major timesaving feature of working with a FrontPage design template.*

2. Before I go any further, I want you once again to click on the HTML tab to view what FrontPage is doing behind the scenes to your code. As shown in Figure 24.11, a webbot is being utilized to handle the processing of the feedback form you see on this page.

3. Switch back to Page view. Notice the comment (in purple text) that FrontPage inserted, telling you the location of the file that will store the form data that is inserted (for example, _private/inforeq.txt). You can see this file by going to Folders view, but don't worry about looking at it right now—it's empty anyway.

4. If you scroll further down the page, you can see the form in its entirety. If you click on the HTML tab, you can see the HTML code that builds this form and its elements, as shown in Figure 24.12. There should be no surprises here if you are familiar with the material presented in Chapter 8.

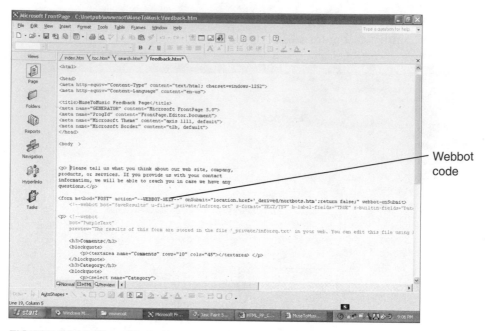

Webbot code

FIGURE 24.11 *You will also learn how to insert a simple form-processing script, in addition to working with the FrontPage webbot functionality.*

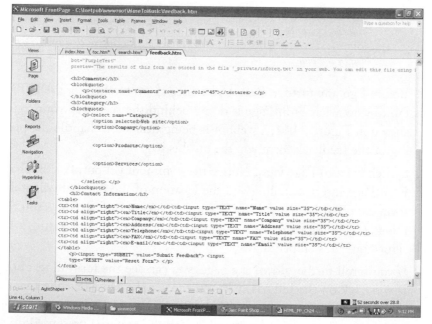

FIGURE 24.12 *A text area field, a selection box, several text boxes, and Submit and Reset buttons constitute this form.*

5. At this point, you really don't need to change any of these elements, although you certainly could if you wanted (by adding or deleting form elements, which you learned how to do in Chapter 8). However, go ahead and get an idea of how this will look in an actual Web browser by clicking on the Preview tab. Your screen will appear like Figure 24.13.

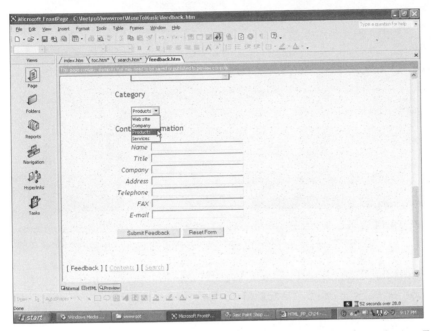

FIGURE 24.13 *This is basic HTML form functionality, but an important feature. Feedback forms are a great way to gather critical input from your customers on a variety of issues.*

You will see the form functionality presented in more detail in a later section of this chapter. For now, be sure you are familiar with the underlying HTML (as shown in Figure 24.12) that actually constitutes the feedback form.

Also, note how the form functionality (that you will see later in this chapter) will address the following specific goals in relation to the design and process goals listed at the beginning of this chapter.

Configuring Navigation Bars

One of the three major links on the site home page (index.htm) is Contents. If you were to click on this link now (or open the toc.htm file in the MuseToMusic Web), your screen would appear like Figure 24.14.

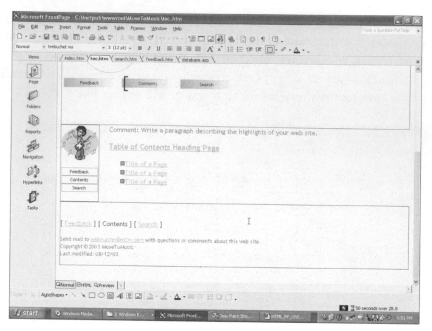

FIGURE 24.14 *The Contents page is literally a table of contents. It will serve as a launching point for more of the advanced functionality and information on the MuseToMusic site.*

Although the Corporate Presence Web Wizard helped you develop the overall look and feel of the site (via a template design approach), you can manually build some advanced functionality. Specifically, there are four important features (per your discussions with the MuseToMusic storeowners) that you need to build into the site:

♦ Another Web form so customers can place special orders for CDs.

♦ The ability to search for a CD and purchase it online. This will require the integration of a backend database that contains the inventory of the store so customers can search it and then place an order.

♦ A section of the site for local bands to advertise.

♦ A discussion forum so customers and visitors can comment on music (commercial CDs, local band performances, and so on).

From your discussion with the storeowners about the mandatory business and customer-usability requirements of the site (which you were introduced to in Chapters 14 and 15) as well as the list of functional requirements that began this chapter, you know that these issues must be addressed.

Although you could configure this Contents page, another option is to simply make this major functionality available on the site home page. To do this, you will configure the navigation bars on the site home page and change the names of the links.

1. Open the index.htm page in FrontPage.

2. Right-click on the top navigation bar. From the menu that appears, select the Link Bar Properties option. The Link Bar Properties dialog box will appear, as shown in Figure 24.15.

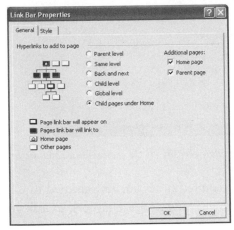

FIGURE 24.15   *You can easily configure the options for all navigation bars on all Web pages using the Link Bar Properties dialog box.*

3. Select the Child Pages Under Home option and be sure the two check boxes under Additional Pages are selected, as shown in Figure 24.15.

4. Click OK. Your screen should now look like Figure 24.16. Note the changes in the top navigation bar.

You should keep the side navigation bar the way it is to provide access to the functionality listed there (Feedback, Contents, and Search, although you will delete the link to the Contents page in just a few moments).

The remaining sections of this chapter will focus on the major links shown on this page, specifically:

◆ News   ◆ Feedback

◆ Products   ◆ Search

◆ Services

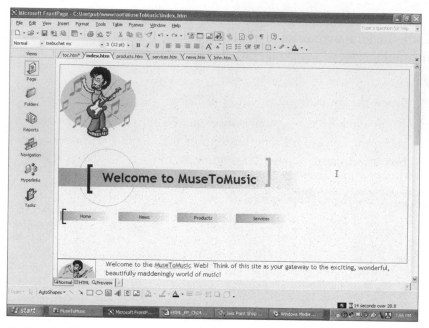

FIGURE 24.16 *This navigation bar will populate throughout the entire MuseToMusic site.*

I will explain and highlight all of the required functionality outlined in Chapters 22 and 23 (and reiterated again at the beginning of this chapter), so let's get to it!

The News Link

The News page is one of the most versatile on the site; it really highlights the power of using a design template like you did in Chapter 22 (the Corporate Presence Web Wizard).

This section will work through the following specific requirements, as outlined in the previous chapters and discussed in your meetings with the storeowners:

- ◆ A forum for promoting local bands
- ◆ A portal approach that allows customers a one-stop location for accessing all different kinds of music news
- ◆ An effective way to present announcements about the store

I want to work through the customization of this page in order to achieve all of the above goals.

1. Open the news.htm page in FrontPage. Your screen should look like Figure 24.17.

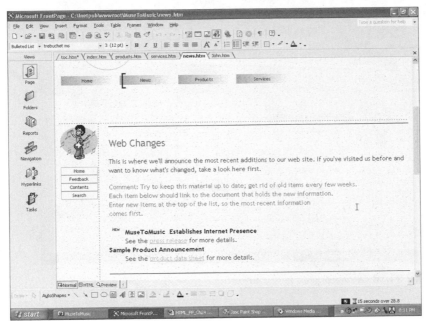

FIGURE 24.17 *The default text and links for the News page of the MuseToMusic site.*

2. Scroll up the page so the Web Changes section is visible. Note the comment text that has been inserted; this is good advice in terms of keeping your site content up to date. If you want, you can make up some imaginary updates for the MuseToMusic site and delete the comment text.

3. Next, notice the MuseToMusic Establishes Internet Presence heading. Also notice that the press release is a hyperlink that points to the file pr01.htm. You will recall from Chapter 22 that you created a number of default press release pages as you worked through the Corporate Presence Web Wizard. Follow this hyperlink. Your screen should now look like Figure 24.18.

   If you are so inclined, change the default text on this page to something MuseToMusic-specific, and then save the page. Note the navigation bar on the page, which includes an Up link. If you click on this, you will be returned to the main News page.

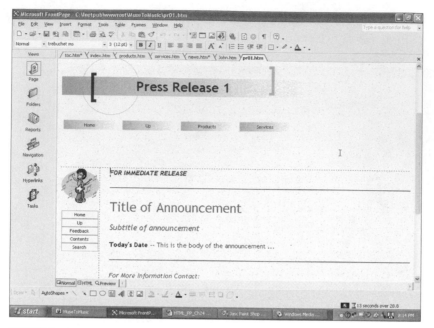

FIGURE 24.18 *A sample press release page.*

4. Before you leave this press release page, click on the Navigation button to switch to Navigation view. Your screen will look like Figure 24.19.

As you learned, you can add, remove, or change the names of the pages to which these links point. You do this by right-clicking on any one of the pages in Navigation view. Figure 24.20 shows the menu that appears when you right-click on a page and highlights all of the functionality mentioned here.

5. Return to the main News page (news.htm) and scroll down so your screen looks like Figure 24.21.

6. By changing some of the section headings and configuring the text, you can meet many of the promotional requirements originally presented by the storeowners. Specifically, the storeowners want the Web site to:

◆ Be a vehicle for the promotion of local bands

◆ Contain news updates about the store

◆ Serve as a portal for music news—not just news presented on the site, but on other music-related Web sites as well

7. Figure 24.22 highlights how the default layout and text of this page can meet all of these goals with some relatively simple modification.

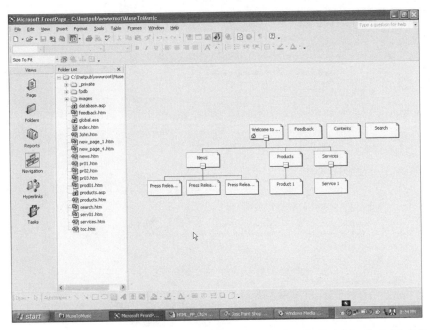

FIGURE 24.19 *Three default press-release pages have been included in the initial site design.*

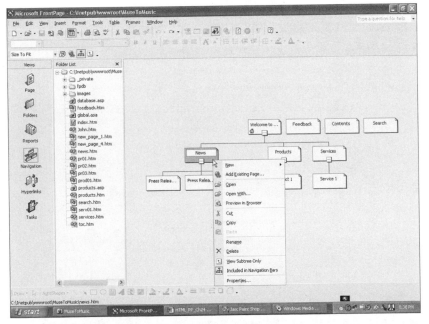

FIGURE 24.20 *You can address major site design tasks from within Navigation view.*

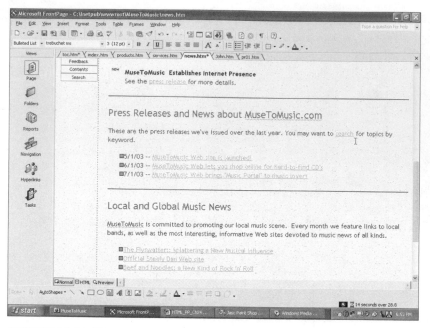

FIGURE 24.21 *You can change the Press Releases and News and Local and Global Music News headings to address some of the functional requirements originally listed by the storeowners.*

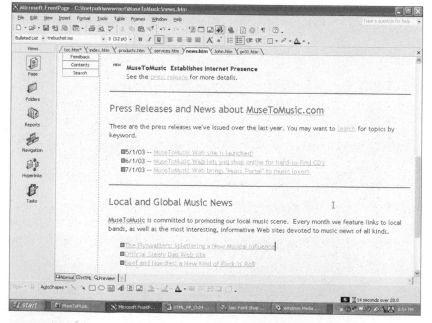

FIGURE 24.22 *By changing the default text and taking advantage of the pages and links placed by the site template, you can quickly achieve many functional process requirements.*

If this were a real site, you would want to update these sections of the News page with more detail, as well as provide (perhaps) more press releases and Local and Global Music News links. However, what you see in Figure 24.22 should give you some idea of what is possible with just the default text and links that were originally created by the Corporate Presence Web Wizard.

The Products Link

Again, one of the major business requirements of the Web site is to promote the store. That said, the storeowners would like to sell specialty items, such as hats and T-shirts, which promote the store. Additionally, the storeowners put together special CD compilations of local bands and sell them in the actual store. All of these items can be sold via the Web site, and the Products page is a good place to list them.

1. Open the products.htm page in FrontPage. Your screen should appear similar to Figure 24.23.

 NOTE

You might be thinking that the Corporate Presence Web Wizard used to create the site template for the MuseToMusic Web is too formal. After all, you probably wouldn't use the phrase, "Have a salesperson contact me" for information on a local band. Remember, the wording is not important; rather, the functionality that has been automatically created for you is the critical part. For example, if this product description page were for a local band's CD, you could change the three default check boxes on the form to read

◆ Add me to the band's mailing list
◆ Send me information on upcoming shows
◆ Send me information on other bands I might enjoy

The important point is that when you are using the FrontPage site templates, you should find one that you think matches the functional requirements you are looking for, and then use your creativity to modify the default text to fit your specific customer's needs and style.

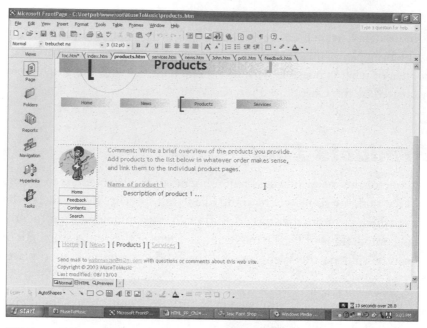

FIGURE 24.23 *The Products page will highlight special store-produced items.*

2. In Figure 24.24, you can see how I changed some of the default wording and created some hyperlinks. As with the default hyperlinks created on the News page, if you click on the first link (note how it points to prod01.htm), you will be taken to a default product description page, as shown in Figure 24.25.

3. Change some of the text and add some hyperlinks, as I have done in Figure 24.25, and then save the page.

The Services Link

The Service link is the final major link to discuss. This link will provide access to two of the major requirements of the site—the online store and the form for placing a special order request (in other words, the music-locator request form).

1. Open the Services page (services.htm) in FrontPage. Your screen should appear similar to Figure 24.26.

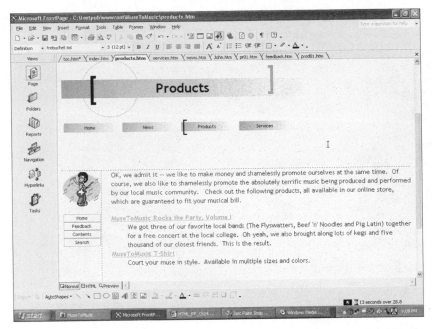

FIGURE 24.24 *Again, some simple configuration of the default text makes this a functional page in minutes.*

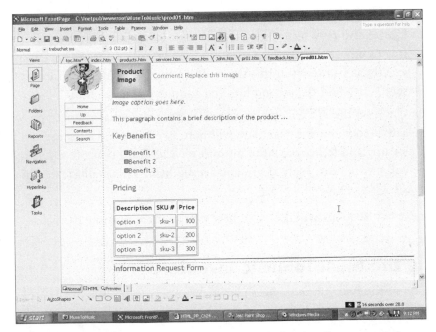

FIGURE 24.25 *The template product page. Note the functionality presented, from space for an image of the product to a product description to an information request form.*

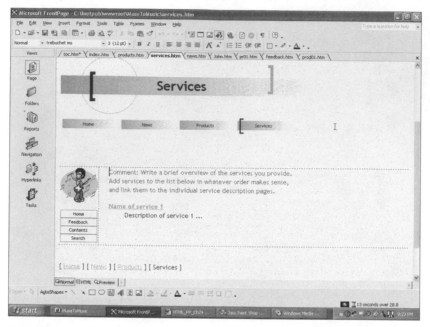

FIGURE 24.26 *The default Services page. Note the hyperlink to the serv01.htm, which was created when you worked through the Corporate Presence Web Wizard in Chapter 22.*

2. Create two new hyperlinks so your page looks like Figure 24.27. Feel free to adjust the wording to your own liking—it doesn't have to read exactly as you see it in this figure. Give the first link the address of serv01.asp and the second link the address of serv02.htm.

3. Click on the HTML tab in FrontPage to view what is going on with the actual code on this page. You will note two hyperlinks (to use the music locator and to browse store inventory). The links point to two pages you will create next—serv01.asp and serv02.htm. This is illustrated in Figure 24.28.

The next two sections will describe these two services in more detail.

Browsing the MuseToMusic Inventory

The first of the two online services allows customers to browse the MuseToMusic inventory and complete an online order form or arrange for in-store pickup.

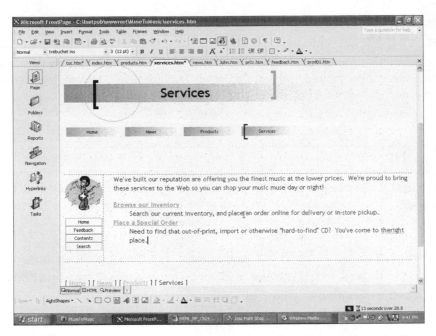

FIGURE 24.27 *The two major services are the ones that the storeowners initially requested be facilitated via the Web site.*

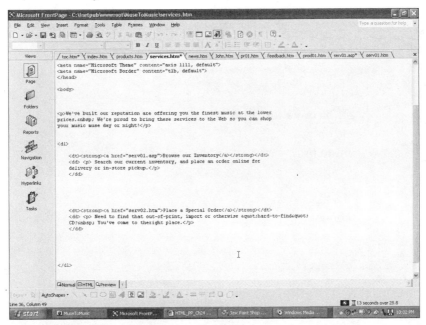

FIGURE 24.28 *The FrontPage site template is still taking care of much of the underlying HTML, but you can tweak some of the code. In this case, you are specifying the hyperlink properties and the pages to which the links are pointing.*

NOTE

This functionality makes extensive use of the FrontPage Database Results Wizard, which was originally introduced and discussed in Chapter 23. Therefore, I will assume that you are familiar with this tool and how to use it for basic configuration.

 TIP

This section also makes use of a Microsoft Access database. You can download this database from the Premier Press Web site (http://www.courseptr.com/downloads).

In working through this section, you will also see the benefits of integrating a database with your HTML pages, and the extended power and functionality it brings to the operation of your entire site.

1. Open the serv01.htm page in FrontPage. Delete the form at the bottom of the page and change the banner graphic heading so your screen appears similar to Figure 24.29.

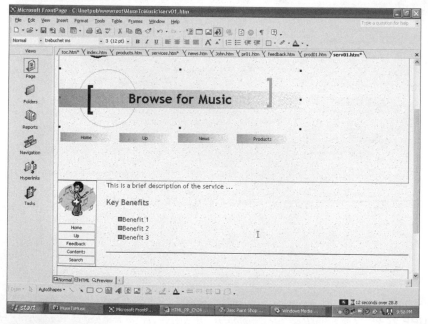

FIGURE 24.29 *Preparing the serv01.htm page for the insertion of the Database Results Wizard.*

2. Save this page now, but save it as serv01.asp. As you learned in Chapter 23, in order for the Database Results Wizard to work, it must be utilized in conjunction with an ASP Web page.

Configuring the MuseToMusic ODBC Connection

At this point, I am going to integrate the sample Access database that is available for download from the Premier Press Web site. If you don't have it or you want to use another database, you should still be able to follow along with the steps presented here.

1. Copy the CDShop.mdb database file into your MuseToMusic Web.

2. From the Windows Control Panel, click on Administrative Tools, and then click on Data Sources (ODBC).

3. In the ODBC Data Source Administrator window, click on the System DSN tab, and then click on the Add button.

4. In the Create New Data Source window, select the Microsoft Access Driver option, as shown in Figure 24.30.

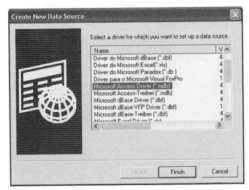

FIGURE 24.30 *Select the Microsoft Access Driver option because you are working with an Access database.*

5. Click on Finish. The ODBC Microsoft Access Setup window will appear. Complete the fields so that your screen looks like Figure 24.31. When you click on the Select button to select the database, you simply navigate to the MuseToMusic Web folder and select the CDShop.mdb file you just placed there.

6. Click on OK. Your database is now ready to be accessed through the Database Results Wizard.

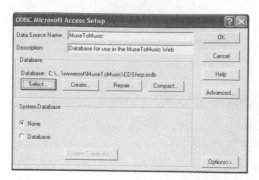

FIGURE 24.31 *Configuring the ODBC properties of the MuseToMusic System DSN.*

Integrating the MuseToMusic Database with the Database Results Wizard

Now that you have a proper ODBC configuration, you can use it in the serv01.asp page in conjunction with the Database Results Wizard.

1. On the serv01.asp page, click underneath the dividing line (see Figure 24.29). From the Insert menu, select Database, Results. The first step of the Database Results Wizard will appear.

2. Click on the Use a New Database creation option, and then click on Create. In the Web Settings dialog box that appears, click on Add. The New Database Connection dialog box will appear, as shown in Figure 24.32.

FIGURE 24.32 *Complete this window as illustrated here.*

3. Click on the Browse button. In the window that appears, you should see the MuseToMusic System DSN that you created in the previous section. Select it and click on OK. You will return to the New Database Connection dialog box. Click on OK. You will return to the Web Settings dialog box. Highlight the MuseToMusic listing and click on the

Verify button. The question mark next to the MuseToMusic listing will change to a checkmark. When this happens, click on the Apply button, then click on OK.

4. You are now back at Step 1 of the Wizard. Click on the second option (Use an Existing Database Connection), select the MuseToMusic option from the drop-down list, and then click on Next. Step 2 of the Wizard will appear, as shown in Figure 24.33.

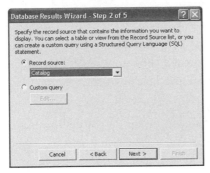

FIGURE 24.33 *Select the Catalog option for the record source.*

5. After you confirm your screen looks like Figure 24.33, click on Next to continue to Step 3 of the Wizard.

6. Click on the More Options button, and then click on the Criteria button to bring up the Criteria window. Click on the Add button to bring up the Add Criteria dialog box, as shown in Figure 24.34.

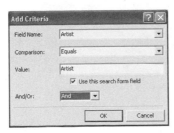

FIGURE 24.34 *Use the criteria functionality to build a search form so customers can search by specific field options (such as artist or title) within the database.*

7. Add the artist so your Criteria dialog box looks like Figure 24.35.

8. Click on OK, and then OK again to return to Step 3 of the Wizard. Click on Next.

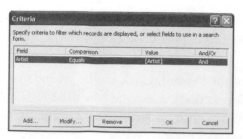

FIGURE 24.35 *When your page is loaded in a Web browser, customers will be able to search the database using the Artist field.*

9. You will proceed to Step 4. Note that this step allows you to configure how your database results will be returned. For now, accept the default values, but notice that you can change the layout of the results if you want.

10. Click on Next to proceed to the final step of the Wizard. Be sure the Add Search Form option is checked.

11. Click on Finish. The Database Results region will be inserted into your serv01.asp page, as shown in Figure 24.36.

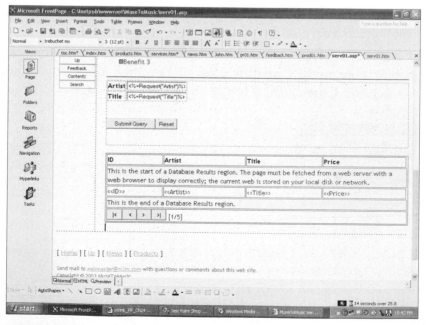

FIGURE 24.36 *The Database Results region is where the information pulled from the database will be displayed.*

As you might guess, FrontPage is adding quite a bit of custom code to the HTML to get the Database Results Wizard to function. Take a quick look at the HTML for the serv01.asp page now, as shown in Figure 24.37.

Save the page once again and load it into your Web browser. In Figure 24.38, the page is loaded, and the customer has entered a search criteria of Steely Dan. Figure 24.39 illustrates the number of hits, which corresponds to the number of matches in the database for the search term Steely Dan in the Artist field.

 NOTE

As you saw in the steps describing the Database Results Wizard, there are quite a few options you can set for the search form and the format in which data is returned. Because the Database Results Wizard is using (to some degree) VBScript in conjunction with ASP technology, you can modify your search results so that, for example, you could have the ID of the returned record (see Figure 24.39) be a hyperlink to an order form. For a more complete description of using the Database Results Wizard in this fashion (and with specific regard to a small business Web site), see *Web Enable Your Small Business In a Weekend* (Premier Press, 2000).

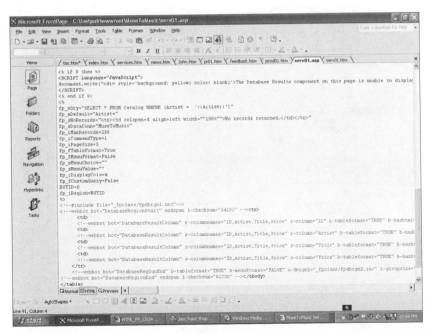

FIGURE 24.37 *FrontPage automatically adds to and adjusts the underlying HTML to account for this advanced functionality.*

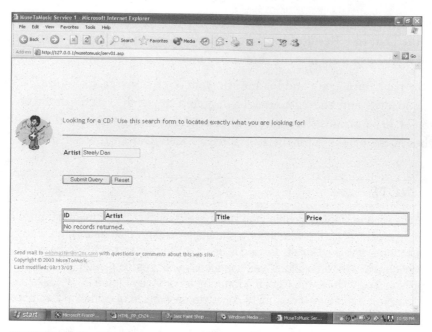

FIGURE 24.38 *Entering search criteria for the Artist field.*

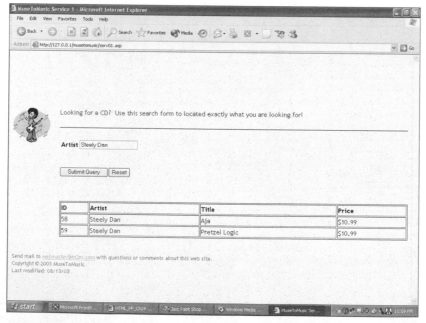

FIGURE 24.39 *The matching records for the Artist field are returned.*

Confirming Business Process Goals and Requirements

So how does the use of the Database Results Wizard meet the stated business process goals and requirements of the MuseToMusic storeowners?

Two specific business process goals and requirements can be facilitated via this functionality:

◆ Although it is not a specifically stated goal of the Web, the ability to link a database with a Web form allows the storeowners to present current inventory to their customers, as well as update this inventory via a Web interface. A possible second phase of your design project could be to design a MuseToMusic intranet, which is essentially a portal open only to authorized employees of the company. This could allow the employees to administer various store operations via the Web.

◆ An often-discussed requirement is that of an online store. Clearly, the ability to allow customers to browse current inventory points to the next step, which would be providing a Web form on which customers could order a product. In the next section, you will see an example of a combination of this functionality and the automated form processing that FrontPage allows.

 TIP

As you learned in Chapter 11, it is possible to utilize scripting languages (such as VBScript and JavaScript) with your HTML. The Database Results Wizard utilizes ASP to work in conjunction with the Web server and the ODBC connectivity to allow the database to be integrated directly with the Web page. With just a modicum of programming (in ASP, for example), you can bring even more advanced functionality to this type of integration. For more on this topic with regard to a small business, see *Web Enable Your Small Business In a Weekend,* as well as *ASP Programming for the Absolute Beginner* (Premier Press, 2002).

Creating the Music Locator Special Order Form

The other special service that is facilitated via the MuseToMusic Web is the music locator service, which allows customers to request special CD orders. The storeowners have prided themselves on being able to find such music, and they want to be sure this service is advertised via the Web.

This example will highlight the form processing capabilities of FrontPage.

1. Return to the services.htm page in FrontPage. Depending on how you configured the second hyperlink, your page should look something like Figure 24.40.

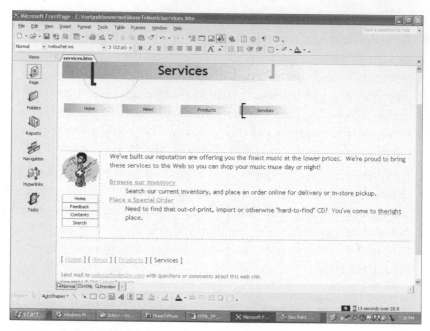

FIGURE 24.40 *You will configure the music locator form on the second service page.*

2. You will need to create the serv02.htm page. (If you have been following along in this chapter, serv02.htm is the name of the file to which you assigned the second hyperlink.) From the File menu, select New Page or Web. From the list of options that appears on the right side of your screen, select Blank Page. You will be presented with a blank Web page that nevertheless conforms to the overall site template, as shown in Figure 24.41.

3. You will create your form in the section to the right of the guitar player graphic. Switch to HTML view in FrontPage and enter the following code as you see it listed here:

```
<form>
<p align='center'><font size='6'><b>We can find what you want!</b></font></p>
<p align='left'><b><i>Looking for that hard to find CD? Just fill out the
form below and we'll respond to you within twenty-four hours to let you know if
we can get it (chances are good that we can)!</i></b></p>
```

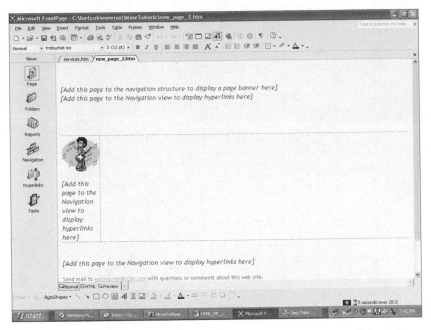

FIGURE 24.41 *Every new page you add to the site includes the overall site design.*

```
<table border='0' width='100%' cellspacing='1'>
  <tr>
    <td width='26%'>Your Name:</td>
    <td width='74%'><input type='text' name='Name' size='30'></td>
  </tr>
  <tr>
    <td width='26%'>Your Phone (please include area code):</td>
    <td width='74%'><input type='text' name='Phone' size='30'></td>
  </tr>
  <tr>
    <td width='26%'>Your E-mail:</td>
    <td width='74%'><input type='text' name='Email' size='30'></td>
  </tr>
  <tr>
    <td width='26%'>Title of CD (if known):</td>
    <td width='74%'><input type='text' name='Title' size='30'></td>
  </tr>
  <tr>
    <td width='26%'>Artist (if known):</td>
    <td width='74%'><input type='text' name='Artist' size='30'></td>
  </tr>
```

```
<tr>
   <td width='26%'>Do you know if this is an import?</td>
   <td width='74%'>Yes: <input type='radio' value='Yes' name='Import'> 
   No:<input type='radio' value='No' checked name='Import'></td>
</tr>
<tr>
   <td width='26%'>Genre of CD (if known):</td>
   <td width='74%'><select size='1' name='Genre'>
   <option>Rock/Pop</option>
   <option>Jazz</option>
   <option>Classical</option>
   <option>Country</option>
   <option>Rhythm and Blues</option>
   <option>Gospel</option>
   <option>New Age</option>
   <option>Other</option>
   </select></td>
</tr>
<tr>
   <td width='100%' colspan='2'>
   <p align='center'>
   <input type='submit' value='Submit Your Request!' name='B1'></td>
</tr>
</table>
<p align='left'>
</form>
```

4. Now switch back to Normal view. Your screen should look something like Figure 24.42.

5. Right-click somewhere inside the form and select Form Properties from the drop-down menu that appears. In the Where to Store Results section, select the first option (File Name) and browse to the _private folder in your MuseToMusic Web. You should see a text file called inforeq.txt. Select it so that your Form Properties dialog box looks like Figure 24.43.

6. Click on the Options button, shown in Figure 24.43, and you will see the Saving Results dialog box. Take some time to browse through each of the four tabs (File Results, E-Mail Results, and so on) to see the different options available to you in terms of additional data you can record and how you might send the form results to a specific e-mail.

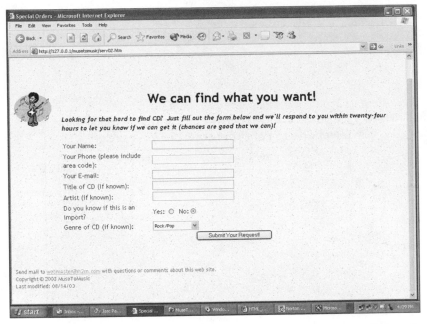

FIGURE 24.42 *The music locator form is created; now you just have to tell FrontPage how to process it.*

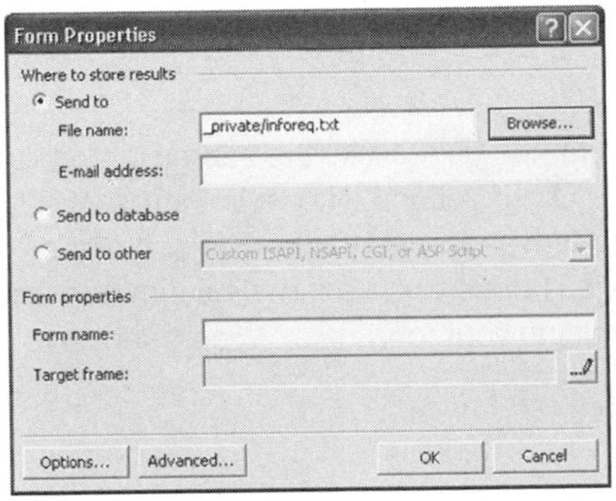

FIGURE 24.43 *FrontPage allows you to send form results to a variety of places, but for this example you will just send the form to a text file.*

7. Save the page, and then open the MuseToMusic Web in a Web browser and navigate through the site to this page. Complete the form and click the Submit button. You will see a confirmation screen that your form results have been submitted, as shown in Figure 24.44.

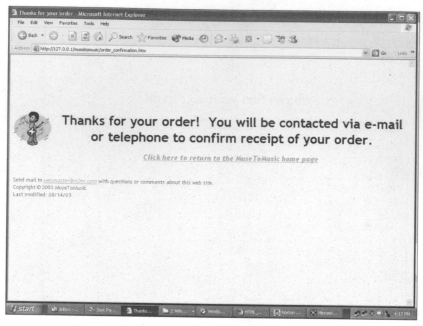

FIGURE 24.44 *Providing an order confirmation page gives your customers the peace of mind that their order has been successfully received by you.*

 TIP

You can load any form confirmation page after the user clicks the submit button. Under the Confirmation Page tab (visible once you click "Options" shown in Figure 24.43), you can enter the URL of any page you want to load when the form is submitted. Often designers will load custom confirmation pages when a form is submitted, saying something to the effect of "Thanks for submitting your form data. A representative will contact you shortly."

Reviewing Design and Business Process Goals Facilitated via FrontPage

Clearly, a tremendous number of functionality and customization options are available to you when you design a Web with one of the FrontPage site design templates and wizards. Moreover, the general features of FrontPage—from navigation structure to the Database Results Wizard—are worthy of an extended discussion. I encourage you to experiment with the tools described in this chapter and review the previous chapters (especially Chapters 22 and 23) to see how you can facilitate specific business process goals with FrontPage.

I want to review the specific goals of the MuseToMusic storeowners and how FrontPage can facilitate those goals, as you've seen in this chapter.

◆ **A new forum for advertising and promoting local bands.** The News page and the default text inserted by the Corporate Presence Web Wizard presented you with some predefined links and general formatting so you could, for example, provide updates on the MuseToMusic store, links to local bands' Web sites, and press releases on in-store concerts.

◆ **Links to external Web sites for local bands and other music sites (portal concept).** You can customize the News page to allow links to other sites. Using the default text and structure presented by the Corporate Presence Web Wizard, you can easily customize the content to make the MuseToMusic site a real music-information portal that addresses a wide variety of musical interests.

◆ **Intuitive site navigation structure.** As I discussed extensively, you can easily configure the navigation features that are automatically inserted by the site template. Using the Navigation view in FrontPage, it is easy to configure the navigation bars so they apply to all pages (in other words, so you can make a change in one place and have it applied to each page in the site).

◆ **Ability to process form data.** You worked with this when you designed the Music Locator form, as well as the Feedback form. Utilizing the FrontPage Server Extensions, you can easily integrate this type of advanced Web functionality without doing any programming.

◆ **Integration of a backend database.** Another benefit of working with FrontPage is the Database Results Wizard. Using this feature, you brought the MuseToMusic inventory online and allowed customers to browse for a CD of their choice. As I mentioned, there is a clear link between this functionality and an online order form. Putting those two components together essentially gives you the structure of an e-commerce site, which was also a major requirement of the storeowners.

◆ **Easy Web site administration by the storeowners.** Last but not least, this is an important issue for ongoing administration and functionality of the site. FrontPage is easy enough for anyone to use, so once you (as the Web developer) establish the site and the more advanced functionality (such as the navigation scheme, the form processing, the Database Results Wizard), you could feel comfortable allowing the customer to configure and make changes to the site. If you use a site template as you did in this chapter, then making changes is even easier. For example, if the storeowners wanted to add a new page (perhaps a press release), they could simply add it in Navigation view. The page would be added with the related navigation bars and site template design applied.

 TIP

You should compare the process of creating the MuseToMusic Web in FrontPage (and the additional functionality that is possible) with how you hand-coded the site in the first MuseToMusic project (Chapters 13 through 16). Which do you prefer? What was easier? Perhaps a combination of hand-coding and using an HTML editor to handle some of the more tedious or mundane tasks of Web development is to your liking. This is a personal choice, and there is no right or wrong answer. Bottom line, though: Don't ignore the great timesaving features of an HTML editor, such as FrontPage.

Summary

This chapter examined how to use Microsoft FrontPage XP to build the MuseToMusic site. By focusing on many of the advanced tools in FrontPage—especially the Corporate Presence Web Wizard, form-processing tools, the Database Results Wizard, and general FrontPage functionality (such as navigation features)—you were exposed to the power and timesaving attributes of using an HTML editor versus trying to code everything by hand. As a culmination of Chapters 22 and 23, this chapter took the approach of highlighting how the business process goals and requirements (including customer usability and CRM issues) could be facilitated via FrontPage. Although there are drawbacks to using an HTML editor (not the least of which is how such an editor will manipulate the underlying HTML code or in some cases make it inaccessible), the power and functionality is undeniable, and you should strongly consider using an HTML editor in any type of Web design work.

Project 4

MS SQL Server 2000: Integrating a Database with Your Web Site

Chapter 25

**Integrating HTML
with Microsoft
SQL Server 2000**

You've worked through three extensive HTML projects, as well as getting a strong hands-on introduction to Microsoft FrontPage XP. Hopefully by this point in the book, you have mastered the HTML essentials and seen (in the previous projects) how you can utilize solid Web design to help facilitate a variety of business processes, regardless of the type of business (small company, not-for-profit, and so on).

However, if you are now reading this chapter, you are looking for the next step in your HTML/Web design learning experience. As I've hinted throughout this book, you can really take your Web design to the next level by integrating a database. By doing so, you can make your Web pages dynamic in the sense that you can interact more directly with your visitors by not only capturing information they provide (such as shipping address and customer feedback), but you can also present customized information to your visitors based on their preferences. For example, perhaps the first time they visit your site they complete a customer survey form. Then the next time they visit, you query this information in your database and present only the information, products, and services in which they are interested.

So think of this final project as bonus material, but bonus material of real sustenance. As you will see, setting up and actually integrating a SQL database into your Web site isn't too difficult.

Welcome to SQL Server 2000

Perhaps the best place to start is with the actual installation of SQL Server 2000. But before you launch into that, you should be aware of the different flavors of SQL Server 2000.

◆ **Enterprise Edition.** This is the 100 percent full-blown version of SQL Server, and it comes equipped with every aspect of functionality and usability. This version easily handles complex tools for managing data across multiple server and network environments. The Big Daddy version of the application, it is perhaps not the best place to start if you are a relatively inexperienced database developer. However, if you own this version, consider yourself lucky. You have everything you will ever possibly want or need in a database solution.

◆ **Developer Edition.** The Developer Edition is significantly less expensive than the Enterprise Edition (relatively speaking, depending on where you purchase it and under what legal circumstances you make your purchase). It contains all the functionality. However, this reduction in cost comes at a price (no pun intended). The Developer Edition is not designed to run on a production server; rather, it is designed for use on a desktop in a development environment, free of network and server issues.

◆ **Standard Edition.** The Standard Edition is the poor man's SQL Server (with regard to cost), but don't let this fool you. If budgets are tight, the Standard Edition will do just fine, although you will lose a bit of the advanced functionality you find in the Enterprise and Developer Editions.

◆ **Personal Edition.** The Personal Edition is nearly identical to the Standard Edition, but it runs on Windows 2000 Professional, Windows NT Workstation, and Windows 98. This is a good edition if you are limited in your choice of operating systems.

◆ **CE Edition.** This very limited version of SQL Server is kind of nifty because it is designed to run on a handheld computer. The one tremendous benefit of this version is that it offers nearly full compatibility with its big brother versions, so if you are on the go, you can sync up your data on the CE version with a larger, more robust version back at the home office.

◆ **Desktop Edition.** This version of the application is designed purely to serve an application; it offers no real data management or administration features. If your client is a very small company or one with a tight budget (or both), you could conceivably develop your solution on one of the more robust versions, and the client could purchase the Desktop Edition just to serve up the functionality.

Although some would disagree, I have chosen to utilize the Standard Edition of SQL Server 2000 for this book because it provides a nice middle ground (especially with regard to price) with hardly any loss in performance or functionality at the level of experience and interest I assume you have. If you have the Personal, CE, or Desktop Edition, I highly recommend you acquire one of the other versions, though, because your ability to follow and understand the examples in this book will be severely limited without one of the more robust versions.

Installing SQL Server 2000

Now that you have a general understanding of the different variations of SQL Server 2000, it's time to install. Again, for this example, I am installing the Standard Edition.

1. Insert the SQL Server installation CD into your CD-ROM drive. After a few moments, the autorun installation welcome screen will appear (see Figure 25.1).

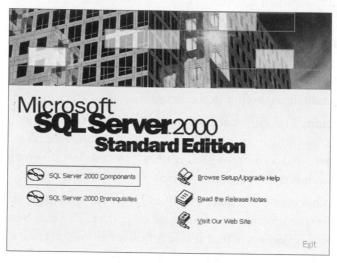

FIGURE 25.1 *To begin the installation process, click on the SQL Server 2000 Components option.*

2. Click on SQL Server 2000 Components. From the list of options that appears, click on (for now) the Install Database Server option (see Figure 25.2).
3. The installation wizard will begin. Click on Next.
4. The next screen asks you to enter the name of the computer on which you want to install an instance of SQL Server 2000. Select the Local Computer option, as shown in Figure 25.3.

FIGURE 25.2 *Depending on the version of SQL Server 2000 you are installing, your list of options might differ from what appears here.*

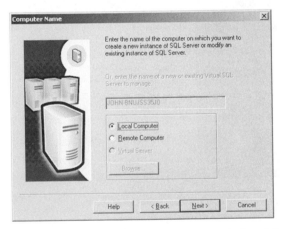

FIGURE 25.3 *For this installation, select the Local Computer option.*

5. Click on Next. In the dialog box that appears, select Create a New Instance of SQL Server, as shown in Figure 25.4.

6. The next two dialog boxes ask you to enter your name and company (if applicable) and accept the standard Microsoft licensing agreement. You are then presented with the screen shown in Figure 25.5, which asks you to pick the type of installation. For this installation, chose Server and Client Tools.

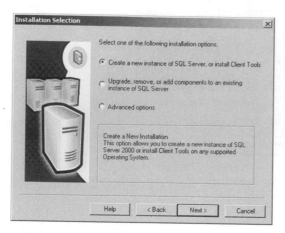

FIGURE 25.4 *Note that you can update, add, or remove components at a later time if you want to modify your installation.*

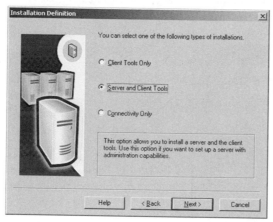

FIGURE 25.5 *Be sure to select both server and client tools for this installation.*

7. The next screen asks you to provide an instance name. Provide a descriptive title, as I've done in Figure 25.6, then click on Next.

8. As with most standard software installations, SQL Server 2000 now prompts you for the type of custom installation you prefer. Leave the default setting as Typical, but note the space requirements and the other installation options (see Figure 25.7).

9. You are next asked to provide information on the service accounts used to access SQL Server. For this dialog box, leave the default setting as Domain User Account, but go ahead and enter some type of password that satisfies the usual requirements—easy for you to remember, hard for

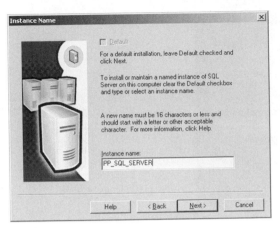

FIGURE 25.6 *Providing an instance name allows you to give your installation a more recogniz-able (and potentially useful) title.*

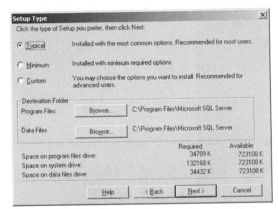

FIGURE 25.7 *Note that depending on the type of installation you choose, the disk space require-ments can vary significantly.*

others to guess (see Figure 25.8). Don't leave the password blank because that will make you an easy target for unauthorized access.

10. Just a few steps left! Figure 25.9 shows the dialog box that asks you to select the authentication mode. Select Mixed Mode and be sure to enter a password for the sa (system administrator).

11. Click on Next. The installation wizard will tell you it has enough information to proceed with the installation. Click on Next. After a few moments, you will see a confirmation screen telling you that the setup is complete. Click on Finish and reboot your server. (You might be asked to do this, but if not, you should go ahead and reboot anyway.)

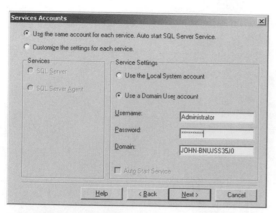

FIGURE 25.8 *Be sure to enter a password in the space provided.*

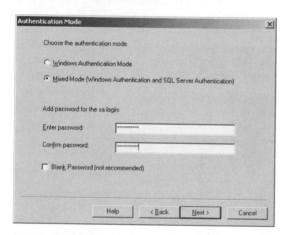

FIGURE 25.9 *Again, be sure to enter a password for the sa login.*

Understanding Security: Working with Windows Services

SQL Server 2000 runs as a Windows service, which in a nutshell means that if there is any problem with SQL Server, Windows can take care of it without a great deal of human intervention.

You can set specific SQL Server configuration options by navigating through the Services option, under Administrative Tools. (Note that this only works on

Windows NT, 2000, and XP because services don't exist on Windows 9x operating systems.) This Services option is in the Administrative Tools Control Panel applet.

Now take a look at configuring SQL Server service properties. This will help you gain a further understanding of how SQL Server operates within the Windows operating system, and it will lead into a more complete discussion of the security options that are available for your use.

1. In the Start menu, select Settings, Control Panel.

2. Double-click on the Administrative Tools icon, and then double-click on the Services icon (see Figure 25.10).

3. In the screen that opens, scroll down and select MSSQLSERVER, as shown in Figure 25.11.

4. Once you've selected MSSQLSERVER, right-click and select Properties from the drop-down menu that appears. The MSSQLSERVER Properties dialog box will appear, as shown in Figure 25.12.

5. Click on the Log On tab (refer to Figure 25.12).

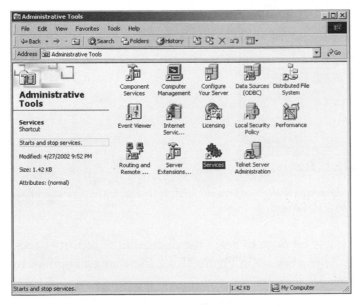

FIGURE 25.10 *Double-click on the Services icon in the Administrative Tools folder.*

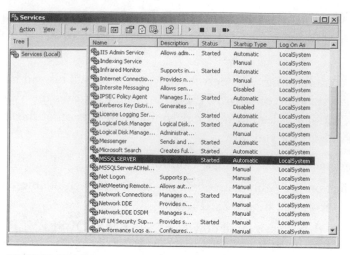

FIGURE 25.11 *Note the various services available for your review and customization.*

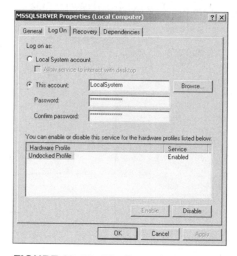

FIGURE 25.12 *The Properties dialog box provides access to several key configuration issues related to the SQL Server service options.*

The Log On tab is a good place to begin the discussion of security issues within SQL Server 2000. As you can see in Figure 25.12, there are two options to log on to SQL Server.

◆ **Local System account.** This simple account was designed to allow you to log on solely to a local account/local installation of SQL Server. Using this account, there is no way that you could log in to a remote server. In a way, this is a neat method of ensuring the instance of SQL Server with which you are working (in other words, you must be working on a local system account).

◆ **Domain account.** When you log on to SQL Server utilizing a domain account, the service will verify with the Windows security model to ensure that the user name and password you entered are indeed valid. Note that if you are on a network instead of a local machine, your user name will have a prefix of DOMAIN\USERNAME. In order for you to log on to the service in this fashion, the Window security model will verify that the domain account information you've provided matches a valid user name and password in the Windows Domain Controller.

 TIP

Regardless of whether your SQL Server installation is on a remote server or a local machine, it's probably a good idea to use the domain account setting. That way, the Windows security model (and your user name and password) can help secure the account. Of course, if you are working on a local machine, this might not be as big of an issue, but it is still probably a good idea. Also, in a network environment you might have to ask your system administrator to give you full administrative rights to SQL Server. (The user name should be able to alter the registry, so in essence you need to be made an administrator of your own machine.)

 TIP

It is not recommended to use your own domain account as a service account. If you must use a domain account, then create one that has the sole purpose of a SQL service account. Also, if you use your own account and you change the password of your account, you must then go back into the Services control panel and change it—it will not automatically change.

I'll talk more about security and account issues a bit later in the chapter. For now, take a moment to review the Recovery tab in the MSSQLSERVER Properties dialog box.

Determining SQL Service Recovery Actions

As I said earlier, running SQL Server as a service means that Windows can take care of the maintenance when something goes wrong (for the most part). However, it is up to you to determine what action should be taken. The Recovery tab on the MSSQLSERVER dialog box allows you to set these options.

1. Navigate to the MSSQLSERVER dialog box, as described in the preceding section, and click on the Recovery tab (see Figure 25.13).

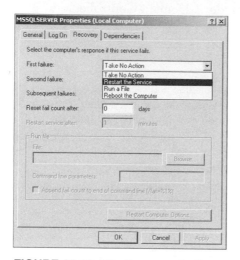

FIGURE 25.13 *The Recovery tab allows you to determine which actions Windows will take if the SQL service fails.*

2. Generally speaking, you might want to set these actions in the order of severity. As you can see in Figure 25.13, you can take four actions:

   ◆ Take No Action   ◆ Run a File

   ◆ Restart the Service   ◆ Reboot the Computer

   You might want to set the action for the first failure to either Take No Action (thus requiring human intervention to get the service running again) or Restart the Service. For the second failure, you might want to run a file for further diagnostics. Finally, for the third failure, you might want to reboot the computer. This is an extreme (but usually effective) action, especially in a production, multi-user environment.

> **TIP**
>
> You can also run a file as an alerter service. For example, you could send a warning e-mail or broadcast a message to the system administrator's desktop.

All of this material directly relates, in one way or another, to specific user account security, including the Windows authentication mode you chose when you installed SQL Server. That said, let me move to a more formal discussion of issues surrounding your choice of authentication mode and give you an opportunity to practice your administration in this area.

Working with Windows Authentication Mode

When you log in to Windows, SQL Server uses what is called a *trusted connection*. Basically, this means that SQL Server trusts that the user name and password you provided are in fact valid.

The best way to understand this is to actually administer the user name and password functionality, so let's do that now.

1. Be sure you are logged in to your machine with administrative privileges.
2. From the Start menu, select Control Panel, Administrative Tools and select the Computer Management icon (see Figure 25.14).
3. Double-click on the Computer Management icon to bring up the Computer Management snap-in tool. Expand the Local Users and Groups node so it appears as shown in Figure 25.15.
4. Right-click on the Users folder and select New User from the drop-down menu that appears.
5. The New User dialog box will appear, at which point you (as the administrator) can assign the user name and initial password (see Figure 25.16).

    Note the options regarding the user's password and account. Generally, once you set the user's initial password, you should select the User Must Change Password at Next Logon option. However, you have other options available to you, including the option to disable the specific user account.

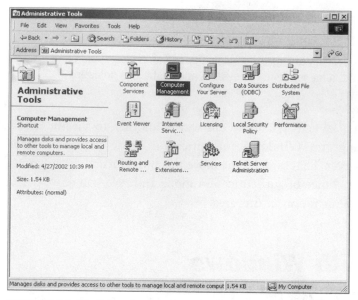

FIGURE 25.14 *Select the Computer Management icon to begin your Windows Authentication Mode work.*

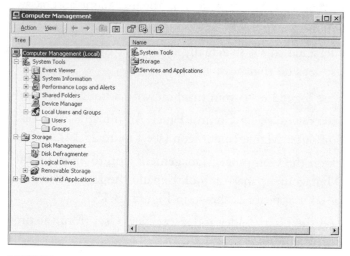

FIGURE 25.15 *Expand the Local Users and Groups node within the Computer Management snap-in tool.*

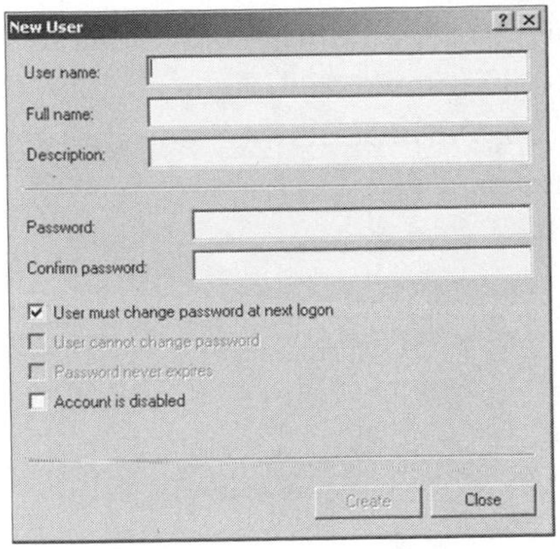

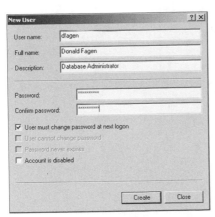

FIGURE 25.16 *The New User dialog box prompts you for specific account information about the new user.*

TIP

When setting up a service account, don't check "User must change password at next logon." The reason for this is that in the Services control panel, this is hard-coded in.

6. After you complete all the fields and click on the Create button, the user is added to the list of users, as shown in Figure 25.17.

FIGURE 25.17 *Take care when creating new user accounts and assigning the levels of administrative authority.*

7. For this new user (dfagen), assume that you want to make him an administrator. In the Computer Management tool, right-click on the user name and select Properties from the drop-down menu that appears. You should see something like Figure 25.18.

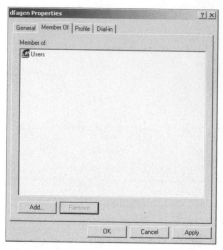

FIGURE 25.18 *You can set specific administrative privileges for individual users.*

8. Click on the Member Of tab, as shown in Figure 25.18, and then click on Add. Your screen should now look like Figure 25.19.

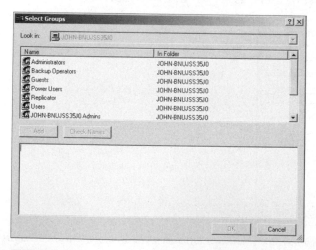

FIGURE 25.19 *You can add users to specific groups via the Add to Group functionality.*

9. In this example, you are making dfagen an administrator. Therefore, select the Administrators option (as shown in Figure 25.19), and then click on Add. The Administrators group will be added to this user name.

10. Click on OK. You will be returned to the Member Of tab of the Properties dialog box, where you should see Administrators added as a group to the dfagen account (see Figure 25.20).

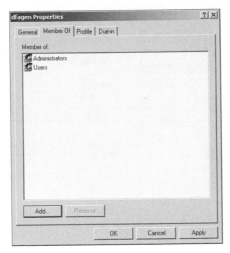

FIGURE 25.20 *dfagen now is a member of the Administrators group.*

11. Click on the Apply button, and then click on OK to close the Properties dialog box.

12. To test dfagen's administrative access, completely log out of your machine and then log in using the dfagen user name and password you just set. You should be able to log in using the user name and password that you just created.

13. Once you've verified that you can log in using this account, log out and then log in again using the administrator account.

The Enterprise Manager

Although the preceding example was a good introduction to the basic administrative tasks surrounding general Windows authentication, it really didn't provide you with an understanding of how to set specific access rights to SQL Server itself. In this section, you'll learn to do that by taking a look at SQL Server's central management tool—the Enterprise Manager.

1. Confirm that you are logged in to the machine as an administrator.

2. Navigate to the Enterprise Manager by selecting Start, Programs, Microsoft SQL Server, Enterprise Manager, as shown in Figure 25.21.

FIGURE 25.21 *Navigating to the SQL Server Enterprise Manager.*

3. When the Enterprise Manager opens, open the various nodes until your screen looks like Figure 25.22.

4. Take some time now to expand the various nodes so you have an idea of what each one contains.

5. Also, within the Enterprise Manager, note the menus (Action, View, Tools) that provide access to other SQL Server functionality. For example, select the Databases node and then take a look at the Tools menu, as shown in Figure 25.23.

For now, just be comfortable with how to access it and the general look and feel of how these tools and functionality are presented (via the menus, toolbar, and so on).

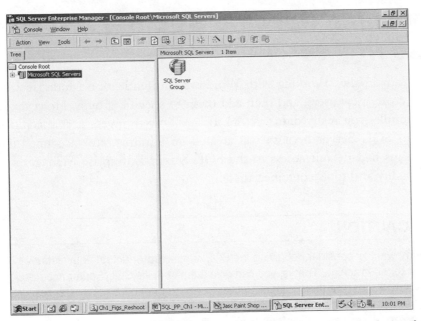

FIGURE 25.22 *The Enterprise Manager provides an easy-to-use navigation method for accessing all facets of your SQL Server installation.*

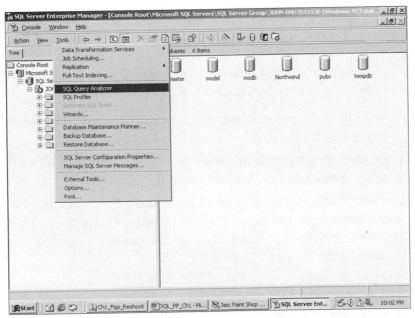

FIGURE 25.23 *The Tools menu provides access to extensive SQL Server functionality, including the Query Analyzer that will be discussed in Chapter 27.*

Establishing Specific SQL Server Access Rights

As you saw in the "Working with Windows Authentication Mode" section, it's easy to create new users, and then add them to specific groups. However, in the first example, you really didn't get an idea of how to give a user specific access rights to SQL Server because you created an administrator account (dfagen), which thus had default access to the SQL Server Enterprise Manager and the functionality and tools contained therein.

 CAUTION

You may want to consider not giving the SQL administrator actual administrative access to the machine: That is, you can give them specific SQL Server access rights but still not give them administrative access to the entire server ("server" in this case being the physical machine that the SQL Server 2000 application runs on). Depending on your security infrastructure, this is something you might wish to consider; conversely, you may find that you have SQL Server administrative rights, but your network administrator (if you are not that person!) has not given you full access rights to the larger server itself.

That said, in this example you will create another user account and then give the user specific access rights to SQL Server in terms of general access and the types of functionality (such as table creation and data manipulation) he or she is granted.

1. As you did in the previous section, create a new user account, as illustrated in Figure 25.24.

2. Since you want to keep this account as a regular user, do nothing else to it within the Computer Management tool.

3. Log out of your machine, and then log in using the rplant account. Immediately upon logging in, you will be asked to change the password (per the specifications you set when the account was created, as shown in Figure 25.24).

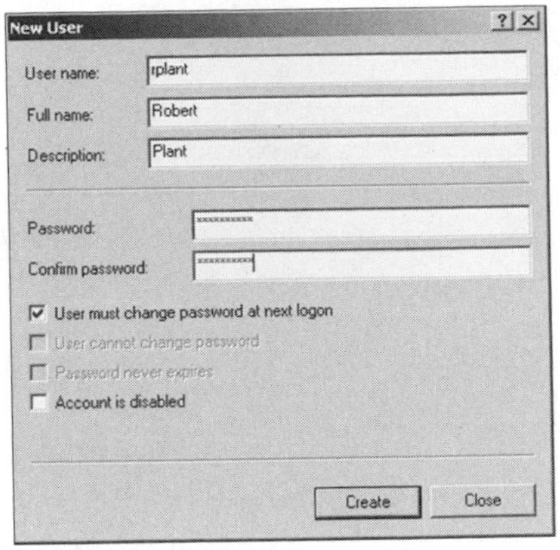

FIGURE 25.24 *Create the fictitious rplant account as shown here, setting the password to what-ever value you choose.*

4. Now when you try to navigate down into the SQL Server Enterprise Manager, you will be presented with this text:

```
- - - - - - - - - - - - - - - - - - - - - - - - - -

SQL Server Enterprise Manager
- - - - - - - - - - - - - - - - - - - - - - - - - -

A connection could not be established to JOHN-BNUJSS35J0.

Reason: Login failed for user 'JOHN-BNUJSS35J0\rplant'..

Please verify SQL Server is running and check your SQL Server registration
properties (by right-clicking on the JOHN-BNUJSS35J0 node) and try again.
```

5. For the user rplant to have access to the SQL Server Enterprise Manger, it is up to you (as the administrator) to assign this user-specific privilege. To do so, log out of the rplant account and log back in using your administrator account. Once you are logged in, open the Enterprise Manager and expand the Security node so that your screen looks like Figure 25.25.

6. Right-click on the Logins option (see Figure 25.25) and select New Login from the drop-down menu that appears. The SQL Server Login Properties - New Login dialog box will appear, as shown in Figure 25.26. Click on the button to the right of the Name text field to bring up a list of all user and group accounts.

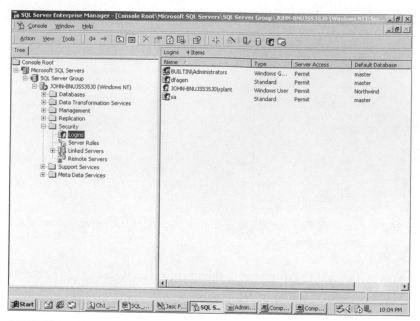

FIGURE 25.25 *You can assign specific user access to SQL Server via the Security node within the Enterprise Manager.*

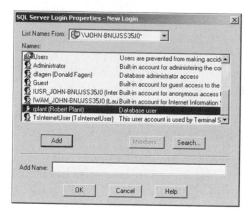

FIGURE 25.26 *You can set specific access rights to non-administrative users via this dialog box.*

7. Scroll down the list until you find the rplant (Robert Plant) account. Highlight it and click on Add. You screen should appear as in Figure 25.27.

8. Click on OK to return to the New Login dialog box. Note that you can either set Windows Authentication or specific SQL Server Authentication. For now, leave this set to Windows Authentication.

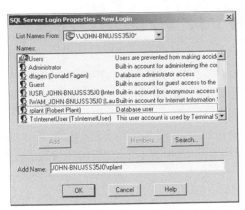

FIGURE 25.27 *To grant a user access rights to the SQL Server, first choose the user name from a list of all applicable users and groups.*

9. For this example, you want to give rplant access to only the Northwind sample database. The first step is to click on the Database Access tab, so that your screen appears similar to Figure 25.28.

10. Click on OK. The access and permissions settings you chose will be applied.

11. To test the permissions you've just set, log off the server and log in using the rplant account. You should be able to access the Enterprise Manager and the specified database.

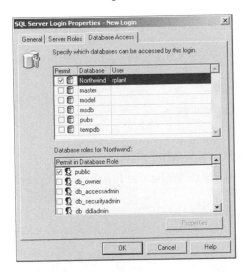

FIGURE 25.28 *You can assign specific access to databases and control the level of access and functionality permitted for various components (such as tables) within the selected database.*

Configuring SQL Server Properties

You can configure and specify several unique properties of SQL Server from within the Enterprise Manager. Primarily, you set these configuration options via the SQL Server Properties dialog box, which just happens to be the focus of this section.

1. In the Enterprise Manager, right-click on the actual SQL Server name node and select Properties from the drop-down menu that appears, as shown in Figure 25.29.

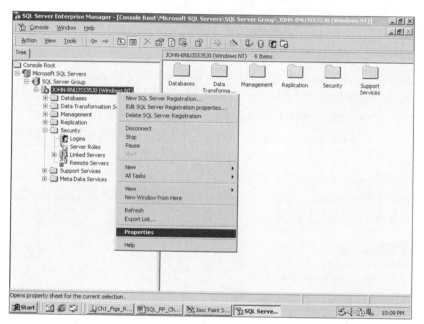

FIGURE 25.29 *Select Properties from the drop-down menu.*

2. The SQL Server Properties dialog box will appear (see Figure 25.30). The following short sections briefly describe the functionality present on each tab.

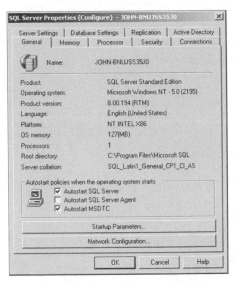

FIGURE 25.30 *Each of the tabs allows you access to specific functionalities.*

The General Tab

This tab allows you to quickly view general information about the particular SQL Server instance that you've selected. Note the check boxes for the Autostart options (see Figure 25.31).

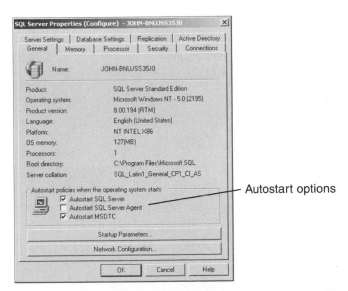

FIGURE 25.31 *The General tab gives you a quick overview of fundamental SQL Server configuration information.*

The Memory Tab

This is an important tab because it enables you to set SQL Server to configure memory dynamically or allow you to manually set it (see Figure 25.32).

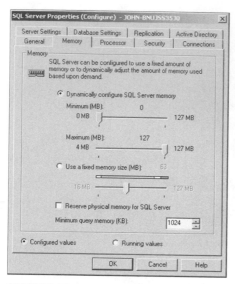

FIGURE 25.32 *Generally, you should be able to allow SQL Server and Windows to dynamically allocate memory.*

The Processor Tab

Depending on whether the machine on which you are running SQL Server has multiple processors, you can fine tune performance in this regard by adjusting the processor control and the number of processors to use for parallel execution of queries (see Figure 25.33).

The Security and Connections Tabs

Conceptually related, these two tabs control the authentication scheme used in accessing SQL Server. Moreover, the Connections tab allows you to specify the default connection options, as well as whether another SQL Server can remotely connect to this SQL Server (see Figure 25.34).

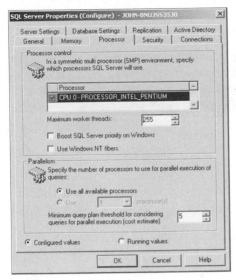

FIGURE 25.33 *A multiple processor environment that is properly configured can greatly enhance your SQL Server performance.*

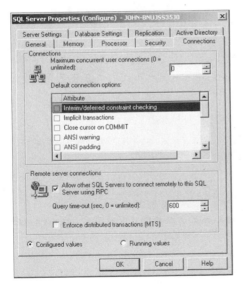

FIGURE 25.34 *On the Connections tab, you can enforce distributed actions.*

NOTE

As you start out with SQL Server, you can safely leave all of the default settings for each of the Server Properties tabs. Note, however, that specifically adjusting some of these settings (such as those on the Memory tab) can significantly enhance and improve performance and help you avoid system errors and crashes.

The Server Settings Tab

The Server Settings tab provides some general settings that you should understand and know how to access so you can change them, if necessary (see Figure 25.35).

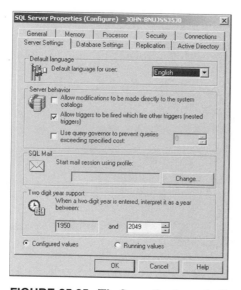

FIGURE 25.35 *The Server Settings tab allows you to specify how two-digit dates are read by the system, thus avoiding another Y2K-type conundrum!*

Within this tab, you also have the option to modify general server behavior. For example, the query governor can prevent queries from executing if they exceed certain memory or processor requirements. This tab also contains the seldom-used default language choice. (Seldom used if your language preference is English; otherwise, this might be the first thing you look for within the Server Properties!)

The Active Directory Tab

Active Directory and the Active Directory Service (ADS) is the all-encompassing container for a network's users and computers. It was officially introduced with the Windows 2000 operating system.

If you have a need and the required network administration knowledge, you can add your SQL Server to your particular ADS via this tab (see Figure 25.36).

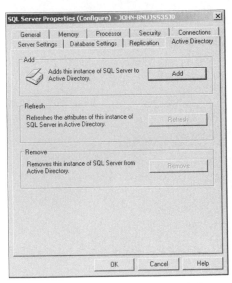

FIGURE 25.36 *Utilize this tab to bring your SQL Server to the ADS party.*

I won't say too much about the functionality of this tab, other than to suggest you consult your Windows system administrator for more information about how (and why) you would need to add SQL Server to your appropriate ADS.

Summary

This chapter presented you with a wealth of general administrative information, and it walked you through the steps to install SQL Server 2000. You also were presented with a short description of the different flavors of SQL Server 2000, so you can make a decision about which version will work best for you. In addition to installation, you were presented with security and user administration issues so you can immediately begin protecting your databases from unauthorized use. Finally, the bulk of the chapter introduced you to the SQL Server Enterprise Manager. Think of the Enterprise Manager as your command console, allowing you easy access to utilize and administer all the great functionality and power built into SQL Server 2000!

Chapter 26

**Creating a SQL
Server 2000
Database**

If you are familiar with database terminology (perhaps you've worked with Microsoft Access or some other desktop database application), then you will be pleasantly surprised by how straightforward the database creation process is within SQL Server. But even if you are relatively new to database design, terminology, and methodology, you will be surprised at how intuitive and powerful the SQL Server database creation tools are. This chapter will show you all of these tools by illustrating the creation of a sample database that you could use in conjunction with the MuseToMusic project.

Overview of SQL Server Databases

When you installed SQL Server, you also installed several databases by default. Although some of them are more important than others, they all serve some function and can assist you as you move through your own projects. Some of them—and this is critical—absolutely should not be altered; otherwise, you run the risk of doing serious damage to your SQL Server installation and the data stored within your individual databases! That said, the following sections will take you through each of these installed databases so you will know what each one does (and so you will know which ones not to mess with).

1. If it's not already running, start the SQL Server Enterprise Manager.

2. Expand the Databases node so that your screen looks like Figure 26.1.

3. Although you'll learn about the individual database components a bit later in this chapter, go ahead and expand one of the individual database nodes so you can see how the components are presented, as shown in Figure 26.2.

 NOTE

Don't see the MusicCatalog database in your list? Don't worry—it's the database you'll create in this chapter.

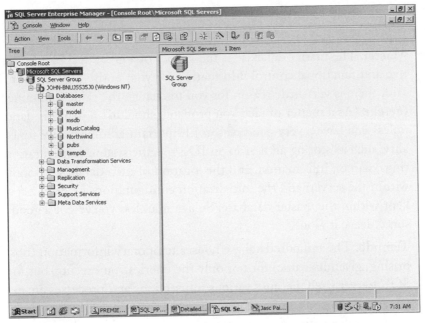

FIGURE 26.1 *Expand the Databases node so your screen looks like this.*

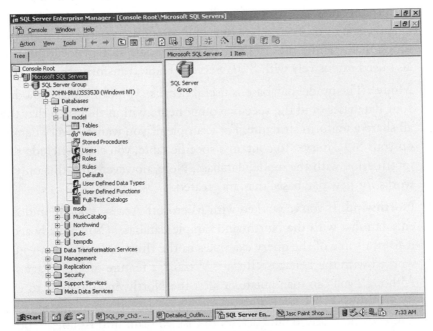

FIGURE 26.2 *Each database is composed of several components.*

Now that you have the default databases accessible and on your screen, take a closer look at each one.

- ◆ **Master.** The master database is the keeper of a great deal of administrative and functional control information for your entire SQL Server. That said, there is very little reason for you to change the values contained therein. (As a matter of fact, you probably shouldn't touch this database unless you have a very good reason.) Important administrative functionality, such as storing all user login IDs; specific system configuration settings; names, information, and the location of each database contained within the server; and the initialization configurations of SQL Server, is kept within the master database. So again, unless you've got a good reason... leave it alone.

- ◆ **Tempdb.** The tempdb database houses temporary information (not surprising, given its name) for not only the queries you execute, but for SQL Server itself, because various transactions and processes are executed within the application. You can use the tempdb database to temporarily store information for your procedures. This is fine as long as you remember that as soon as the database refreshes itself, the data stored within tempdb will be lost. I'll talk more about tempdb later in this chapter and in other chapters. For now, though, recognize its general functionality and usefulness as a temporary data storage location. It is also used extensively with SQL Server's Data Transformation Services.

- ◆ **Model.** The model database is useful because you can indeed "model" your databases (and the specific components within them) so that they all share a uniform structure. For example, if you wanted every database on your SQL Server to contain a specific table, you could include this information with the model database. Note, however, that this only works for new databases that are created.

- ◆ **Northwind.** If you've worked with Microsoft Access, you are undoubtedly familiar with the Northwind sample database. (You already accessed it to run some of the query examples in the third project, when you worked with the Database Results Wizard, a feature of FrontPage.) Although you can manipulate or alter the Northwind database to your heart's content, it's probably a good idea to leave it alone so you have a reference database to fall back on in case you run into trouble in other areas of SQL Server, or you need to test a query or procedure on a predefined set of data (the information contained with the Northwind database) as opposed to your actual live data.

- ◆ **Pubs.** Another sample database, the pubs database is based on a fictitious publishing company. Like the Northwind sample database, you can alter this any way you want, but it might be useful to leave it fairly unchanged so you can use it as a data reference.

- ◆ **Msdb.** Like the master database, you probably should not alter the msdb database. Used to control the functioning of various processes within SQL Server, any change in this database could have adverse results on other critical function areas of your server.

Understanding Specific Database Components

All databases, including those that you create with SQL Server, are made up of specific components. Some of these (such as tables and indexes) will be discussed in the chapters of this project; however, for this chapter you should at least have a cursory understanding of what each component is and how it functions in relation to the other database components.

Tables

Perhaps the quintessential database components, tables are the information repositories where all of your data is stored. All databases should have at least one table, and each table will consist of columns and rows, which are defined in the following sections.

Columns

Columns contain specific information that, when taken collectively, comprise a complete table. Each column has specific attributes assigned to it. For example, take a look at Figure 26.3, which illustrates the specific attributes of a column.

Rows

Once you have established a set of columns, each combination of columns represents one row of information in your database. The number of rows that can exist

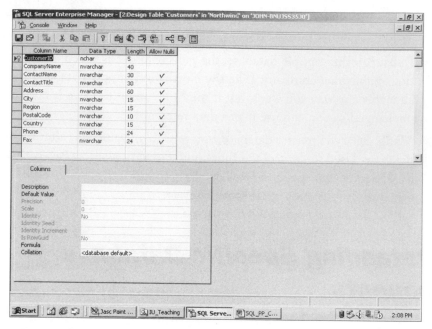

FIGURE 26.3 *Each column within a table has its own unique properties and specifications.*

within your individual tables is limited only by the amount of disk space at your disposal. Figure 26.4 illustrates several rows of information within the sample Northwind database.

Stored Procedures

As you move through your SQL Server development, you will quickly come to the realization that you must repeat some data manipulation tasks on a regular (daily? weekly?) basis. These tasks are good candidates for automation. Stored procedures are just the ticket for such tasks because they allow specific data manipulation functions and processes to be run automatically.

Indexes

Indexes allow you to determine how your information is stored, sorted, and (as a combination of these two attributes) ultimately manipulated. A well-defined index will allow your procedures and processes to run much faster and more efficiently, thus greatly increasing the speed at which critical data result sets are returned to you and your users.

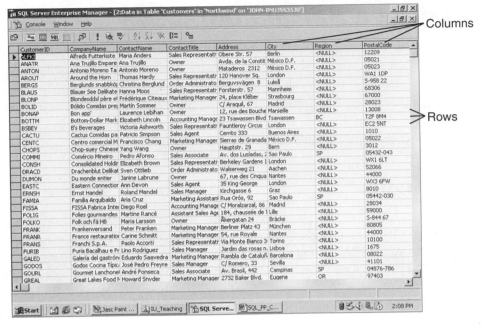

FIGURE 26.4 *The number of rows in your database is limited only by your available disk space!*

Views

Views allow you to create specific windows to your data. Not real tables in and of themselves, views are a specific amalgamation of information that consists of attributes and configurations that you specify. You can use views to streamline how data is presented, and they are also a somewhat effective data security measure because they allow users to view only specific pieces of information stored in the database.

Transaction Logs

Although perhaps not as essential as the components discussed in the preceding sections, transaction logs are still a critical component of any database. In essence, transaction logs give you the ability to track the successful (or unsuccessful) execution of various processes and procedures. Transaction logs can become quite lengthy and therefore take up a fair amount of disk space, and they can also be a bit confusing, at least initially. Note that transaction logs also allow you to restore your database to a certain point in time, if a problem occurs.

Creating a Sample Database

Now that you understand the essential database components, you can move on to actually creating your own database. For this project, you will create the Music-Catalog database, which you could utilize to enhance the MuseToMusic project. Although you will be working through the SQL database essentials in Chapters 25-27 of this project, you will see a more fully realized example in Chapter 28, "Web-Enabling Your SQL Server 2000 Database."

 NOTE

Despite my advice about keeping them in their original state, the Northwind and pubs sample databases are included as part of your SQL Server installation for a reason—to allow you a reference and a place to test your work. That said, you can always reinstall them at a later time if they become disjointed or otherwise changed from their original conditions.

Ready to begin? Okay then, let's get started. I'll show you different ways to create the MusicCatalog database. Depending on your experience and preference, you can ultimately determine which way works best for you. However, the end result will be the same—you'll have a new database with which to work.

Creating the MusicCatalog Database Using the Enterprise Manager

The first method of creating the MusicCatalog database will utilize the Enterprise Manager.

1. If it isn't already running, start the SQL Server Enterprise Manager via the Windows Start menu.

2. Expand the Databases node so it appears as in Figure 26.5.

3. Right-click on the Databases folder and select New Database from the drop-down menu that appears, as shown in Figure 26.6.

4. If all goes well, you should be presented with the Database Properties dialog box. Enter MusicCatalog in the Name field, but don't click on OK just yet.

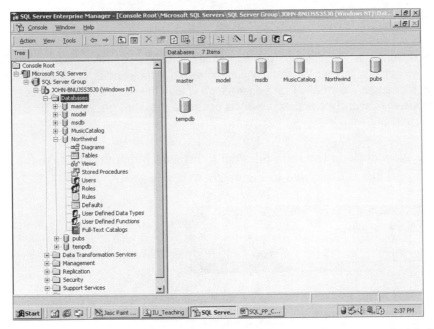

FIGURE 26.5 *Make sure the Databases node is highlighted before you proceed with the database creation process.*

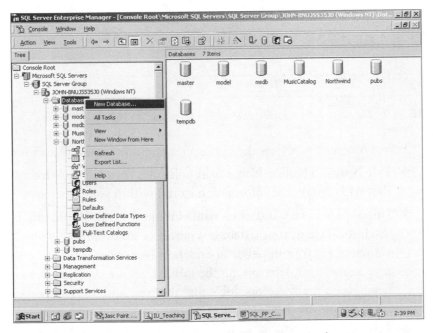

FIGURE 26.6 *Select New Database to begin the database creation process.*

TIP

As you work with and reference your individual databases, you will be asked on a consistent basis to enter the name of your database in the queries, processes, and procedures you create. That said, it's a good idea to keep the names of your databases as short (yet as descriptive) as possible.

5. Now click on the Data Files tab to inspect some important configuration options, as illustrated in Figure 26.7.

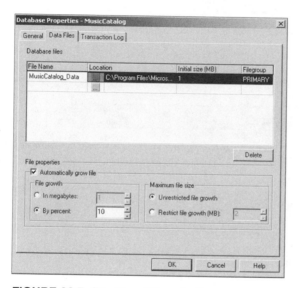

FIGURE 26.7 *The Data Files tab allows you to set critical database size specifications.*

Take a moment to review the options that appear on the Data Files tab:

◆ **File Name.** The File Name field holds the name of the physical file that will contain the information stored within your database.

◆ **Initial Size (MB).** Just as its name implies, this field asks you to set the initial size of your database. Generally, 20 to 26 MB should be sufficient for your initial databases; however, there is no real tried and true formula for determining the initial size of a database because it depends on many factors, including the type and initial amount of information the database will store.

◆ **Filegroup.** For now, leave this set to PRIMARY. In SQL Server, you can designate secondary data files as well, which allow you greater flexibility and control over how your database information is stored. In addition to the actual data, the PRIMARY filegroup also stores database system information (such as the tables) so it can increase or decrease in size based on the database system information.

◆ **Delete.** Use this button to remove any entry in the database files list.

Before you move on, take a look at the options presented in the File Properties section of the Database Properties dialog box (as shown in Figure 26.7).

◆ **Automatically Grow File.** You should always leave this critical little check box checked (for now). This allows your database PRIMARY file to grow as needed. Recall that I said your PRIMARY file can grow in size (and can in fact grow very large) based on just system information. If you uncheck the Automatically Grow File check box, your database can exceed the Initial Size specification very quickly.

◆ **File Growth.** With the Automatically Grow File check box selected, SQL Server will grow your database for you. However, you need to tell it how to grow the database—either in megabytes or by a percentage. Obviously, selecting the In Megabytes option will give you more accurate control over the incremental growth of your database. (Two megabytes is more precise than, say, 15 percent.)

◆ **Maximum File Size.** You can use this option to put a cap on how large your database can grow. You should use caution in setting the maximum file size (unless you or someone else keeps a very close eye on the database), as once the file size limit is reached, no other information will be written to the database!

6. Leave the default options selected in the Data Files tab (as shown in Figure 26.7). Now click on the Transaction Log tab, so that your screen looks like Figure 26.8. As with the Maximum File Size attribute, use caution in setting this unless, again, you or another administrator are going to keep very careful watch over the size of the database.

7. Notice any similarities between Figures 26.7 and 26.8? Although the functionality is different in the Data Files and Transaction Log tabs, the size of the database essentially controls both. Like the Data Files tab, the Transaction Log tab allows you to set specific growth parameters for the location, size, and degree to which the transaction log for the database is generated and allowed to grow. For now, leave all the default options as shown in Figure 26.8.

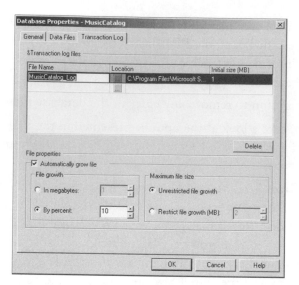

FIGURE 26.8 *The Transaction Log tab appears similar to the Data Files tab.*

8. Ready to create the MusicCatalog database? At this point, click on OK (regardless of the tab of the Database Properties dialog box you have selected). After a few moments, your MusicCatalog database will be created.

9. To verify that everything went as planned, return to the Enterprise Manager. You should see MusicCatalog listed within the Databases node, as shown in Figure 26.9.

Viewing the Database in the Enterprise Manager

Now that you've created the database, you can view it in the Enterprise Manager. As you saw in Figure 26.9, the MusicCatalog database is now part of your database listing, as shown under the Databases node. For a created and functional database, the Enterprise Manager presents different information options regarding the database. This section will highlight some of those options.

1. Under the Databases node, right-click on the MusicCatalog database you just created and select Properties from the drop-down menu that appears.

2. The Properties dialog box will appear. As shown in Figure 26.10, the General tab presents you with much of the general database parameter information (such as maximum size and creation date) that you established when you created the database in the preceding section.

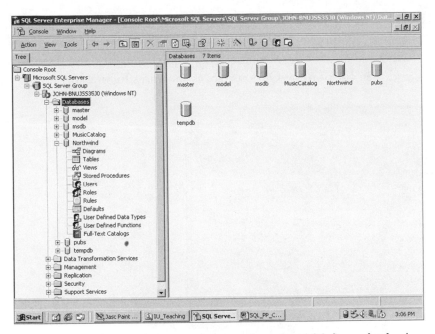

FIGURE 26.9 *Congratulations; you just created your first SQL Server database!*

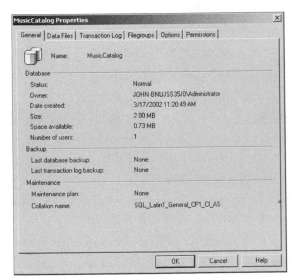

FIGURE 26.10 *The information here should look familiar because you specified it when you created the database.*

3. The General, Data Files, Transaction Log, and Filegroups tabs are fairly self-explanatory and similar (if not identical) to the options you saw when you created the database. Take a quick look at these if you want, and then click on the Options tab, as shown in Figure 26.11.

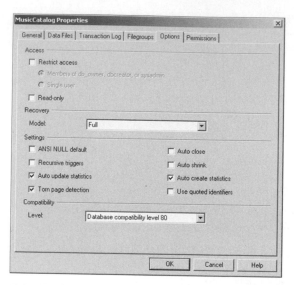

FIGURE 26.11 *The Options tab presents important configuration choices, especially with regard to database access.*

4. You should note the following important options presented on this tab:

◆ **Restrict Access.** Use this option to restrict access to members of the db_owner group, the dbcreator, or sysadmin. You can also restrict access to a single user. This is also good for troubleshooting purposes, as you can lock everyone without changing any permissions (which can be tedious and time-consuming to reset).

◆ **Read-Only.** As the name applies, no modification of any kind is allowed to the database when this option is selected.

◆ **Recovery.** This is an administrative function within SQL Server.

◆ **Settings.** I'll discuss these a bit later in this chapter.

◆ **Compatibility.** This is an important consideration given that you might have to integrate databases and information created under older versions of SQL Server. You can leave this set to the default.

5. Finally, click on the Permissions tab (see Figure 26.12). Right now, the only user access that is set is for the sa, or system administrator. You can tell this is the system administrator access because it is the only one listed and no options are selected.

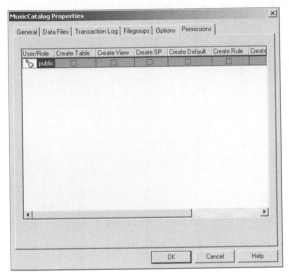

FIGURE 26.12 *Note that sa access is implied, thus Public is the only group that appears here.*

Deleting a Database in the Enterprise Manager

Okay, even though I just had you create the MusicCatalog database, I'm going to ask you to delete it. (I would hope this doesn't cause you too much stress; you've just seen how easy it is to create a database with SQL Server 2000.) Ready? Then let's delete a database!

1. In the Databases node in the Enterprise Manager, right-click on the MusicCatalog database and select the Delete option from the drop-down menu that appears (see Figure 26.13).

2. You will prompted to ensure that you really want to delete the database, as shown in Figure 26.14. Note the option here to also delete the backup and restore the history of the database. If you uncheck this option, you can review some information about the database at a later date.

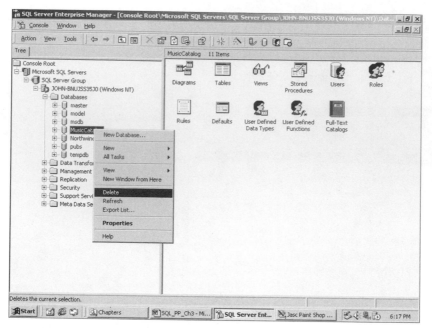

FIGURE 26.13 *Preparing to delete a database in the Enterprise Manager.*

FIGURE 26.14 *Before you are allowed to delete a database, you must confirm your action one last time.*

3. Click on Yes, making sure that the Delete Backup and Restore History option remains checked. (There's no need to keep any record of the database activity at this point.) Assuming the database is not active (open), no one else is connected to it, and you actually have the proper authority level to delete the database, it will be deleted. If not, you will be presented with a typical error message, indicating the reason why your delete request was not possible.

 CAUTION

Obviously, use caution when deleting a database. Once it's gone, it's (usually) gone, unless you've stored a backup somewhere else.

Creating a Database Using a Wizard

Now that you've created and deleted the MusicCatalog sample database, I'm going to ask you to create it one more time (well, maybe a few times) using other methods. One of those methods is by using a wizard.

1. To access the wizards, select Tools, Wizards in the Enterprise Manager or click on the Wizard button on the Enterprise Manager toolbar (see Figure 26.15). The Select Wizard dialog box will appear, as shown in Figure 26.16.

FIGURE 26.15 *Click on the Wizard button to bring up the Select Wizard dialog box.*

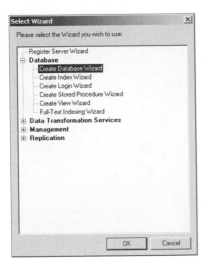

FIGURE 26.16 *Expand the Database node and select the Create Database Wizard option.*

2. Once you've selected the Create Database Wizard option, click on OK. You will be presented with the opening screen of the Create Database Wizard, as illustrated in Figure 26.17.

3. Click on Next. In the Database Name field, once again enter **MusicCatalog** (see Figure 26.18). Leave the Database File Location and Transaction Log File Location fields set to their default values.

4. Click on Next. In the next step, you are asked to set the initial size of the database. For now, leave it set to the default of 1 MB.

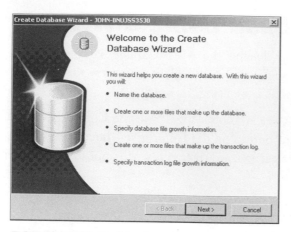

FIGURE 26.17 *Review the tasks you will accomplish with the Create Database Wizard.*

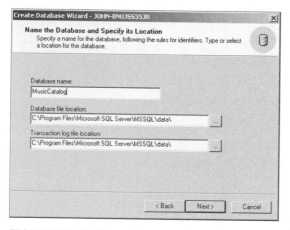

FIGURE 26.18 *Enter the name of the database (in this case, MusicCatalog) in the first step of the wizard.*

5. Click on Next. This step in the wizard should appear similar to what you saw in the Database Properties dialog box when you created a database using the Enterprise Manager.

6. Once again, click on Next. The next two steps in the wizard pertain to configuring the transaction log. They are very similar (with regard to the options they ask you to set) to the database file growth. Leave the default settings as they appear, and click on Next until you reach the final step of the wizard, shown in Figure 26.19.

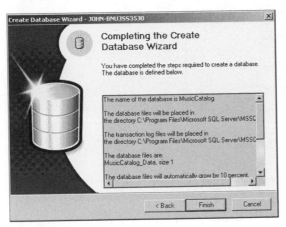

FIGURE 26.19 *The final step in the Create Database Wizard asks you to confirm and complete the creation process.*

7. Click on Finish. After a few moments, the database will be created and you will be presented with confirmation via the Create Database Wizard (see Figure 26.20).

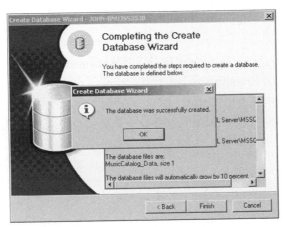

FIGURE 26.20 *The database creation process is complete once again!*

Think the Create Database Wizard is finished with you? Not quite! Once you click on OK, you are presented with another option that you didn't see when you created a database using the Enterprise Manager (see Figure 26.21).

For now, click on No. Also, go ahead and delete the database so you can re-create it using the Query Analyzer, as described in the next section.

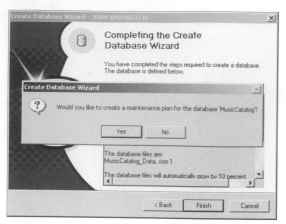

FIGURE 26.21 *The Create Database Wizard also inquires whether you would like to create a database maintenance plan.*

Creating a Database Using the Query Analyzer

There is one final method of creating a database that I'd like to show you, and that is via the Query Analyzer.

1. Open the Query Analyzer by selecting Tools, SQL Query Analyzer in the Enterprise Manager. Remember that you can also access the Query Analyzer via the Start menu.

2. Enter the following T-SQL script in the Query Pane of the Query Analyzer.

```
CREATE DATABASE MusicCatalog
ON (NAME='MusicCatalog_Data',
    FILENAME='C:\Program Files\Microsoft SQL Server\
    MSSQL\data\MusicCatalog_data.mdf',
    SIZE=1, FILEGROWTH=10%)
LOG ON (NAME='MusicCatalog_Log',
    FILENAME='C:\Program Files\Microsoft SQL Server\
    MSSQL\data\MusicCatalog_Log.ldf',
    SIZE=1, FILEGROWTH=10%)
COLLATE SQL_Latin1_General_CP1_CI_AS
GO
```

When you are finished entering the code, your screen should look like Figure 26.22.

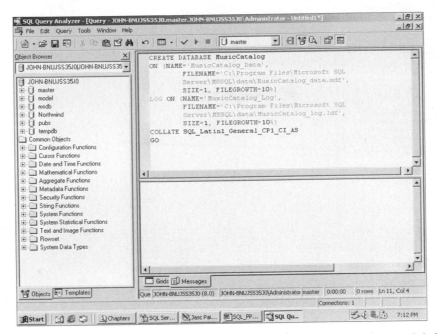

FIGURE 26.22 *The finished T-SQL script, ready to execute and create (once again) the MusicCatalog database.*

3. Execute your code by pressing F5, Ctrl+E, or the Execute Query button on the Query Analyzer Toolbar (see Figure 26.23).

FIGURE 26.23 *Click this icon to execute your query.*

4. You can confirm the creation of the MusicCatalog database (even though you know it is confirmed by the text you see in the Results Pane of the Query Analyzer after you execute the query) by refreshing the Object Browser. To do so, select Tools, Object Browser, Refresh (see Figure 26.24).

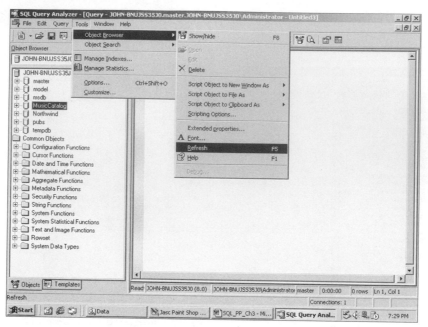

FIGURE 26.24 *Refresh the Query Analyzer Object Browser to view your newly created MusicCatalog database.*

Creating a Database Using Query Analyzer Templates

The Query Analyzer contains many useful templates that can greatly assist you in entering your T-SQL script (thus reducing the chances of coding errors and typos, and freeing you from having to remember the syntax for so many procedures and processes).

As you might expect, there is a template for creating a database. Once again, delete the MusicCatalog database so you can re-create it using a template.

1. Delete the MusicCatalog database that you just created.

2. In the Query Analyzer Object Browser, click on the Templates tab.

3. Expand the Create Database node.

4. Select the Create Database Specifying Collation template option. When you double-click on this option, the template code is placed in the Query Pane, as shown in Figure 26.25.

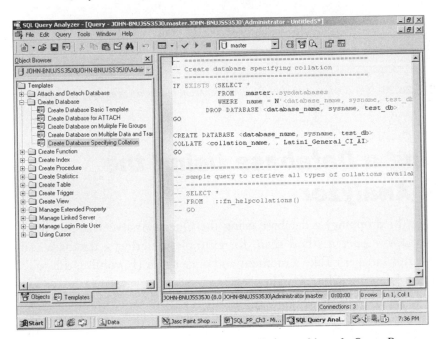

FIGURE 26.25 *The template code is automatically inserted into the Query Pane.*

5. You can make the template even easier to work with by replacing the various parameters. Do that now by selecting Edit, Replace Template Parameters from the Query Analyzer menu.

6. Change the default values in the dialog box that appears so that your screen looks like Figure 26.26.

7. Click on the Replace All button. The values you replaced will be inserted directly into the Query Pane.

8. Execute the query. Once again, the MusicCatalog database will be created.

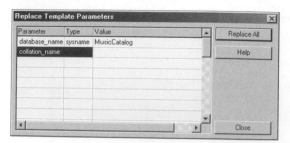

FIGURE 26.26 *The Replace Template Parameters option makes it even easier to work with a template's predefined code.*

Deleting a Database Using the Query Analyzer

Deleting (or dropping) a database using the Query Analyzer is quite easy. (It is also perhaps a safer method than, for example, deleting a database using the Enterprise Manager.) Take a moment and once again (I promise, this will be the last time) delete the MusicCatalog database.

1. If it's closed, open the Query Analyzer.

2. Make sure that the database you want to remove (in this case, Music-Catalog) is *not* selected in the database combo box. This is important: If MusicCatalog is showing in the database combo box, then the connection is still active and SQL Server will not allow it to be deleted (see Figure 26.27).

3. Enter the following code into the Query Pane:

```
DROP DATABASE MusicCatalog
GO
```

4. Execute the query. The MusicCatalog database will be deleted once again.

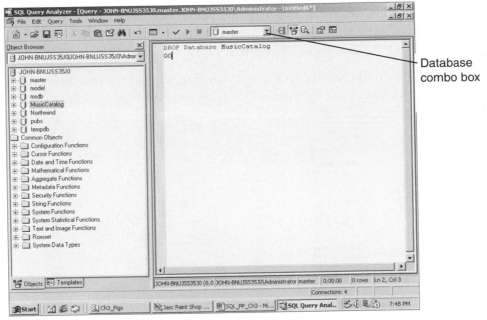

FIGURE 26.27 *Make sure the database you want to delete is not shown in the database combo box.*

Creating the Final Instance of the MusicCatalog Database

Take some time now and create the MusicCatalog database using one of the methods I've described in this chapter. You will be using the MusicCatalog database as your reference for the other chapters in this project.

Creating a Table in the Enterprise Manager

Befitting good data and information organization (which is the whole point of working with a database in the first place, right?), tables allow a high degree of internal organization and specificity so you can set parameters governing how each piece of data is initially entered into the table and later manipulated.

Creating tables within SQL Server is actually quite easy from a very general viewpoint. (The complexities of good design—and having the foresight to consider the ultimate use and required functionality of your database—is something else entirely. Although these intricacies are more complicated, you can certainly get control of them with some practice.) That said, let's jump right in and create a table using the Enterprise Manager.

1. With the Enterprise Manager running, expand the tree under the MusicCatalog database that you created (see Figure 26.28).

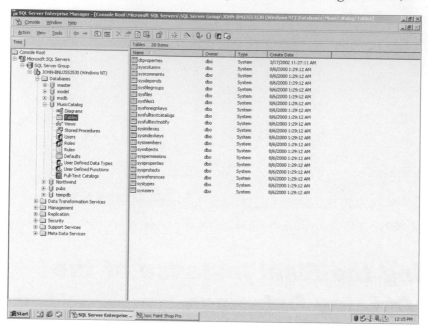

FIGURE 26.28 *The tree expanded under the MusicCatalog database, visible in the Enterprise Manager.*

2. Next, right-click on Tables. In the drop-down menu that appears, select New Table. The Table Designer window will appear, as shown in Figure 26.29.

 NOTE

If you've used Microsoft Access before, be sure to note the similarities between the Access Table Designer and the one you see illustrated in Figure 26.29. Take that similarity for what it's worth; if you feel comfortable with Access, then by all means build from that confidence when working with SQL Server. Obviously, SQL Server is a far more robust product and there are differences between the Table Designers and related tools in the two products, despite the superficial similarities. Still, you can feel comfortable assuming that some basic functionality will be the same in Access and SQL Server.

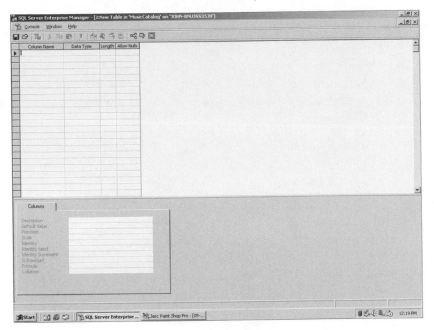

FIGURE 26.29 *Preparing to create a table using the Table Designer.*

3. All we have done so far is create the shell of the MusicCatalog database; we have yet to add any tables. The MusicCatalog database will have just two tables for now. (Remember, this is a simple database designed to get you comfortable with some basic SQL Server tools.)

◆ **Catalog.** This table will store information about the inventory of the actual music catalog.

◆ **Customers.** This table will store basic contact information about customers who have previously purchased items from the catalog.

With the Table Designer open, complete each of the fields (Column Name, Data Type, Length, and so on—refer to Figure 26.29), as shown in Figure 26.30. Press the Tab key to move between each field.

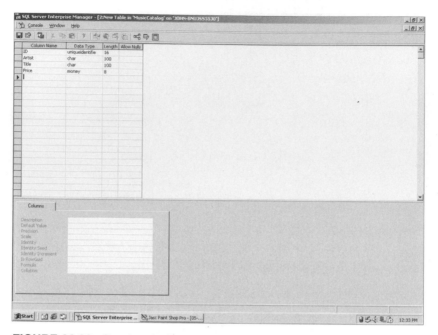

FIGURE 26.30 *Creating the first column within a table and setting data attributes specific to that column.*

What does all this information mean? Let's go through what you just entered to ensure that you understand each data attribute you've just set.

◆ **Column Name.** The Column Name attribute is just that—the name you will use to refer to this specific piece of data. In the Catalog table you are creating, there are four columns (ID, Artist, Title, and Price). It is a good design practice to name columns so they are indicative of the information that will be stored in the associated fields. (In other words, the Artist field you created will store the name of the artist of whose work is carried in the Music catalog.)

◆ **Data Type.** Probably the single most important (and sometimes the most confusing) design parameter of your table, the data type specifies the type of data that can be entered into the specific field. You can think of data types as the format in which data is stored (numerical, text, date/time, and so on). As you entered the information, you probably noticed several available choices in the drop-down menu that appears when you click in the Data Type column. Determining which data type to use can have a profound impact on the usability and functionality of your database and the information it contains. I want to reiterate that point here.

◆ **Length.** The length field corresponds to the size of each piece of information that can be entered in the field. For example, both the Artist and Title fields have lengths set to 100 characters. This simply means that if the character length of the field were to reach 105 (for example), only the first 100 characters would be captured.

◆ **Allow Nulls.** You probably noticed that as you tabbed to this field for each entry, the default value was checked (which allows for null values in the specified field). Generally, it is not a good design practice to allow for null values because this essentially allows a field to be passed (either accidentally or on purpose) without any information being recorded. Even if you want to allow some fields to not require information (such as a fax number field on a customer response form), it's better to record a value such as N/A or No Value Entered than to leave the field blank.

4. Now that you have the table parameters entered, it's time to save the database. Begin the process by closing the Table Designer window. You will be presented with the dialog box shown in Figure 26.31.

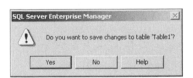

FIGURE 26.31 *SQL Server reminds you to either save or discard the changes you've made to each table.*

5. Click on Yes to access the Choose Name dialog box, as shown in Figure 26.32. In the field provided, enter **Catalog** (because you created the Catalog table of the MusicCatalog database).

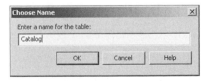

FIGURE 26.32 *Enter **Catalog** to properly name the table you've created.*

6. Once you click on OK in Figure 26.32, the table will be saved and you will return to the console root of the Enterprise Manager.

WHO OWNS THE TABLE VERSUS WHO OWNS THE DATABASE

Take a close look at your newly created table and the details that are displayed regarding the creation of your Catalog table, specifically the Owner column. More than likely (definitely, if you have administrator rights to the SQL Server on which you are working), the owner of this particular table is marked as dbo (which is short for database owner). However, you should note that dbo indicates not just the database owner but also anyone who has administrative rights to the SQL Server database. For example, if the user jgosney has administrative rights to this particular SQL Server database, any table he creates will show dbo in the Owner column of the Details Pane. But if the user dfagen only has the ability to create tables (and is not, therefore, an administrator of the SQL Server database), then the Owner field will display dfagen (as opposed to dbo). Also note that it is a good idea to change the database owner to sa for all databases that are created. If not—and the creating user was deleted from the SQL Server—some child objects may become orphaned.

Creating a Table Using the Query Analyzer

The Table Designer in the Enterprise Manager is a simple, straightforward way to create tables within your SQL Server databases. However, you can also create tables directly from SQL text itself, using the Query Analyzer.

In the preceding section, you created the Catalog table using the Enterprise Manager. In this section, you'll create the other table in your MusicCatalog database—the Customers table—using the Query Analyzer.

1. Start the Query Analyzer. Remember, you can access this feature by selecting SQL Query Analyzer from the Tools menu of the Enterprise Manager, as shown in Figure 26.33.

2. Once the Query Analyzer is running, make sure it is pointing to the correct database (in this case, MusicCatalog), as shown in Figure 26.34.

3. In the Query Pane, enter the exact statement shown in Figure 26.35.

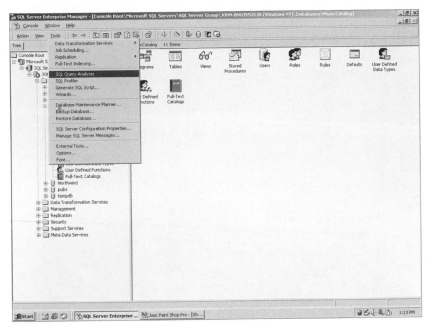

FIGURE 26.33 *Starting the Query Analyzer.*

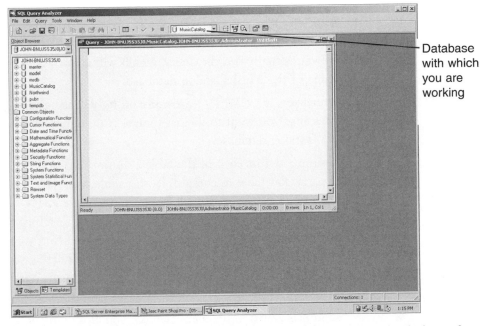

Database
with which
you are
working

FIGURE 26.34 *Whenever you work with the Query Analyzer, be sure you are pointing to the correct database!*

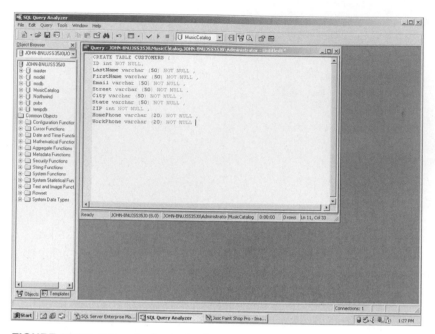

FIGURE 26.35 *Using the Query Analyzer to create the Customers table of the MusicCatalog database.*

So what does all the text you just entered relate to? I want to quickly break down the code so you have a basic understanding of what's happening before you actually run the query, which will in turn create the Customers table of the MusicCatalog database.

◆ First, you utilize the CREATE TABLE command (which is basic SQL, by the way) because you want to do just that—create a new table within your MusicCatalog database.

◆ Next you simply define each of the table columns and fields that you want this particular table to contain. In this table, you have ten fields (ID, LastName, FirstName, Email, Street, City, State, ZIP, HomePhone, and WorkPhone). Note that along with each of the field names, you also identify the data type to be used (int, varchar, and so on), as well as the length allowed for each field. (For example, the HomePhone and WorkPhone fields have maximum lengths set to 20.)

◆ Finally (and this is just basic query syntax), you close out the query with a closing) tag.

4. Once you are satisfied that your Query Pane looks like Figure 26.35, execute the query by clicking on the Execute button on the Query Analyzer toolbar. Assuming no error message appears, your screen should look like Figure 26.36. (Error messages usually indicate you've made some sort of typing error.)

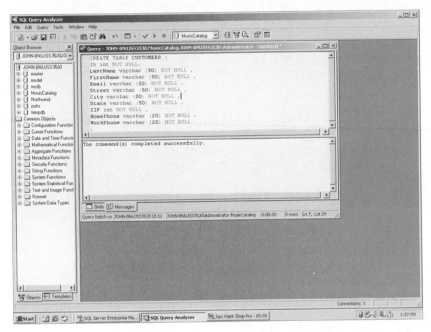

FIGURE 26.36 *When a query is successfully executed, you will see a confirmation message in the Results Pane of the Query Analyzer.*

Moving from the Query Analyzer to the Enterprise Manager

Once you execute a command in the Query Analyzer (especially in this case, because you have created a new table in your database), you might want to go back into the Enterprise Manager to verify your work and perhaps use the tools to further manipulate the actions you undertook in the Query Analyzer.

Because you are just beginning to work with both the Query Analyzer and the Enterprise Manager to create tables, take a moment to switch over to the Enterprise Manager to examine your handiwork in using the Query Analyzer and the CREATE TABLE command.

1. Close the Query Analyzer and took a look at the Details Pane. It should appear as in Figure 26.37, with the Customers table you just created added to the expanded Tables tree of the MusicCatalog database.

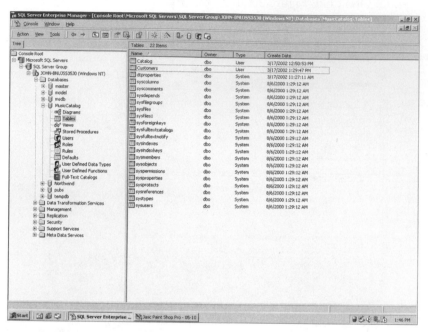

FIGURE 26.37 *The Customers table is now part of your MusicCatalog database.*

> **TIP**
>
> If you switch back to the Enterprise Manager (especially if it was still open when you worked in the Query Analyzer to create the Customers table) and you don't see the Customers table in the expanded Table tree, right-click in the Details Pane and select Refresh from the list of options. Once the screen is refreshed, you should see the Customers table.

2. Take a look at the attributes of the Customers table by double-clicking on its name. You should see all the attributes (field names, data types, and length) exactly as you specified them in the Query Analyzer (see Figure 26.38).

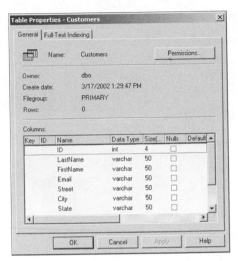

FIGURE 26.38 *Verifying the Query Analyzer by examining the properties of the Customers table. Note that the Nulls attribute for each field has been disabled.*

Creating a Table Using a Template

So far you've learned how to create a table in the Enterprise Manager and the Query Analyzer. Now I want you to take a quick look at yet another way to create a table—by using a template.

Imagine that in your MusicCatalog table, you want to create a third table that stores information on specific purchases made by individual customers. To create this table (call it Purchases), you utilize the Template functionality, which is actually part of the Query Analyzer.

1. Open the Query Analyzer as you did in the preceding section.

2. In the bottom-left corner of the Object Browser, click on the Templates tab, and then expand the Create Table tree.

3. In the Object Browser Pane, double-click on the Create Table Basic Template option. As soon as you perform this action, the Query Pane will be populated automatically with some code, as shown in Figure 26.39.

4. If you don't already know it (or you haven't already guessed), a template is a convenient way of automatically generating some standard code. From your work with the Query Analyzer in an earlier section, you probably recognize some of the placeholders (or, to use the correct terminology, *parameters*) in the T-SQL code, such as `table_name`, `column_1`, and

FIGURE 26.39 *T-SQL code is automatically generated when you click on the Create Table Basic Template option.*

column_2. These parameters are placeholders for which you need to enter details specific to the table you are creating.

5. You could simply type these parameters in the Query Pane; however, you can have them presented in dialog-box format to make them easier to fill in. Do this now by selecting Edit, Replace Template Parameters, as shown in Figure 26.40.

FIGURE 26.40 *Replacing the template parameters makes it much easier to enter the specific information for the table you are creating.*

6. After you select this option, you should be presented with a screen similar to Figure 26.41. Again, by presenting the parameters in this format, it is easier for you to enter the values specific to the table you are creating.

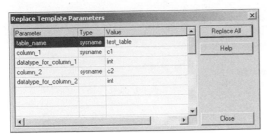

FIGURE 26.41 *Enter the specific information for your table after you have replaced the template parameters.*

7. Enter the values for each parameter, as shown in Figure 26.42. When you are finished, click on the Replace All button.

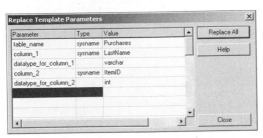

FIGURE 26.42 *Utilizing the Replace Parameters feature makes it easy to quickly complete the template.*

8. When you click on the Replace All button, you will be returned to the Query Analyzer proper. Note that in the Query Pane, the values you provided have been entered into their placeholder sections of the template.

9. The only thing left to do is execute the query and thus generate your table. Do that now by clicking on the Execute Query button on the Query Analyzer toolbar.

10. You should see in the Results Pane of the Query Analyzer that your command was successfully completed. As you did when you created a table using the Query Analyzer, switch over to the Enterprise Manager to view your new table. (Remember that you might have to refresh the Enterprise Manager Details Pane to view your new table.)

11. Double-click on the Purchases table in the Details Pane of the Enterprise Manager to view the specifications of your new table. It should appear like Figure 26.43.

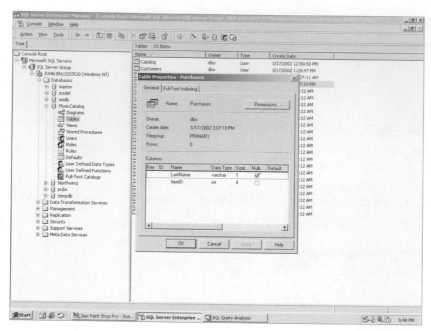

FIGURE 26.43 *You have created another table, this time with the help of a template.*

 NOTE

Don't worry if some of the attributes of the Purchases table are inconsistent with the two other tables you've created (such as the allowance of a null value for the LastName field). You won't really use this table in the continued discussions of essential SQL Server 2000 functionality; rather, it was intended simply to illustrate the template function.

Introducing the Index

Now that you've learned various methods of creating tables within SQL Server, it's time to turn your attention to a closely related and important topic—creating indexes.

What is an index? Put simply, indexes allow you to cross-reference information both within individual tables and across tables. Using your MusicCatalog database as an example, imagine that you want to perform a query to determine how many Beatles CDs were purchased by residents of Indiana, Ohio, and Illinois during the months of May, June, and July, 2001. With properly-indexed tables, such cross-reference queries are possible and really bring to the forefront the incredibly power and versatility of a well-designed database.

Fortunately, SQL Server allows you to work with different kinds of indexes within your tables, and each has its own specific attributes (although all of them share a certain commonality). Within SQL Server, there are two basic types of indexes:

◆ **Clustered.** In a clustered index, the physical order of the data is defined. For example, in the Catalog table of your MusicCatalog database, the ID field might be a good candidate for a clustered index because it meets the one major requirement: It is a column that will not be updated. (Once a new record is created, the ID field is assigned as a unique identifier. Although I'll talk more about unique identifiers later in this chapter, suffice it to say at this point that once a value is entered into the ID field, it is rarely changed or updated at a later date.)

◆ **Non-clustered.** A non-clustered index only points to the data. This can increase performance speed because your SQL Server can use multiple, parallel purposes to query and return data.

Defining the Primary Key

If you've worked with Access, you probably know the importance of the primary key. If you haven't, then take heed of this crucial element of table design. A primary key in your table serves critical purposes, including the following:

◆ First, a primary key ensures that a single row of data will be returned from a query. Put simply, if you query a database for a specific record and you have a primary key set, only the resulting data for that *specific* record will be returned. For example, imagine that you are querying the Catalog table in your MusicCatalog database to return the artist and pricing information for the CD *Countdown to Ecstasy*. If the ID field (for example) is set to the primary key, then the resulting query will return the artist (Steely Dan) and the price for this exact CD ($11.99). Without a primary key, you might get the incorrect artist and/or price returned if there were other CDs by Steely Dan stored within the Catalog table, even though you entered an exact search criteria (in this case, the CD title).

◆ A primary key also allows you to link data from one table to another. For now, suffice it to say that the linking of data across tables is critical so that advanced queries (not unlike the one just mentioned) can be performed.

There are other important terms and considerations when dealing with indexes. For now, though, take a look at actually creating an index. As with creating tables, there are a variety of methods (and resulting considerations) to do so.

Creating an Index Using the Table Designer

You'll create your first index using the Table Designer on the Catalog table of your MusicCatalog database.

1. From the Enterprise Manager, select the Catalog table. Right-click to display the menu and select Design Table. The Table Designer will appear.

2. Right-click within the table and select Properties. The Properties dialog box will be displayed.

3. Click on the Indexes/Keys tab. You will immediately notice that nothing is selected and that there are very few options open to manipulate (this will all change in a moment, however). To begin, click on the New button, which will automatically populate many of the fields for you, as shown in Figure 26.44.

4. Complete the Indexes/Keys tab of the Properties dialog box so that it appears as in Figure 26.45.

   Note the changes I've made in this dialog box:

   ◆ First, I changed the Index name to IX_Catalog_ID. The breakdown of this naming convention can be described as the Index Identifier code (IX) plus the table name (Catalog) plus the name of the table column I want to use as the index (ID). Although you can name your index whatever you like, this is a good naming convention to follow.

   ◆ Next, I ensured that the column name selected was in fact the column I want to use as the Index. (By default, SQL Server will select the first column that appears in the table to use as the index.)

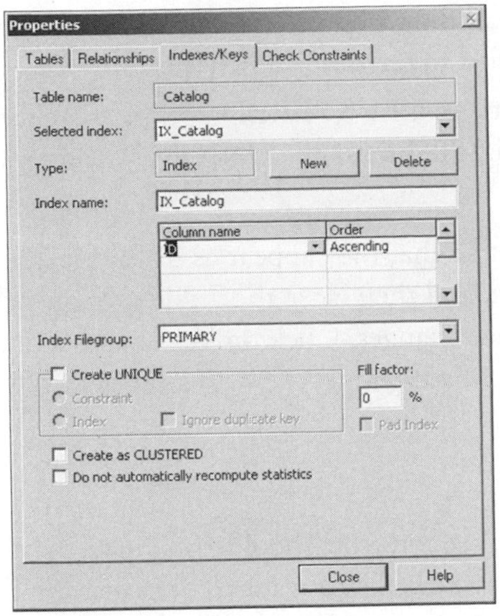

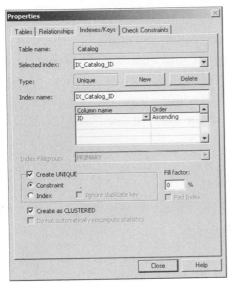

FIGURE 26.44 *Preparing to set the Properties of a specific index.*

FIGURE 26.45 *Completing the Index specifications for the Catalog table of the MusicCatalog database.*

◆ Also, I set the order to Ascending (the default value). Having the sort order match what is specified in queries can help performance.

◆ Finally, I selected the Create as CLUSTERED option and checked the Create UNIQUE field. (I'll discuss the UNIQUE qualifier a bit later in this chapter.)

5. Once you've made the changes so that they appear as in Figure 26.45, close the Properties dialog box, and then close the Table Designer. You will be asked if you want to save changes. Click on Yes to preserve the index information you just specified.

Setting the Primary Key

From the discussion in the preceding section, you should recognize the importance of properly establishing a primary key. Now I want to demonstrate how to set the primary key on the Catalog table, for which you just set the index values and parameters.

1. As you did earlier, open the Catalog table in the Table Designer mode. Select the ID column (by clicking within any of the fields in that row), and then right-click on it. From the menu that appears, select the Set Primary Key option, as shown in Figure 26.46.

2. After you have done that, you will notice a little key icon to the left of the ID field, which indicates that the field has been established as the primary key.

That's about it for setting a primary key; it is a very straightforward function. Now take a look at creating indexes using other methods available in SQL Server.

Creating an Index Using a Wizard

Imagine that your MusicCatalog database is in production. However, given the fluctuating costs of business (not to mention the fluctuating egos in the music business), the proprietor of the store needs a way to quickly locate specific CD titles and change their attributes (most notably their prices). So you want to create an index that allows the proprietor to quickly search for a specific title by just that—it's title.

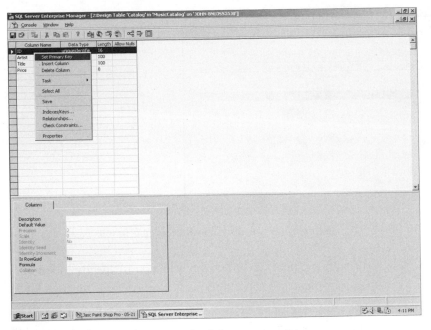

FIGURE 26.46 *Setting a primary key is just a mouse click away.*

You can do this in a variety of ways, but in this example I want to create an index using a wizard.

1. In the Enterprise Manager, select Wizards from the Tools menu. In the dialog box that appears, double-click on the Create Index Wizard option, which is found in the Database tree.

2. Click on Next in the opening dialog box. You will then be asked to select a database and an object name (in this case, table) with which you want the wizard to work. Make sure you select the MusicCatalog database and the Catalog table.

3. The next dialog box allows you to view previously created indexes. (This is a nice feature because it prevents you—potentially—from creating the same index multiple times.) Click on Next.

4. Next you will be asked to select the columns to include in the index. As I mentioned at the beginning of this section, you want to be able to quickly search for a specific CD by title. So on this screen, check the Include In field for the Title column, as shown in Figure 26.47.

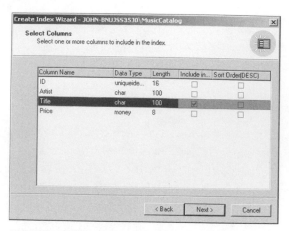

FIGURE 26.47 *Determining which columns you want to include in your index.*

5. Click through the next screen, which asks you to specify index options. (For this example, leave these options at their default settings.)

6. Finally, you are asked to give this particular index a name. Since you can use it to search for a specific CD by title, call it IX_Catalog_TitleSearch, as shown in Figure 26.48.

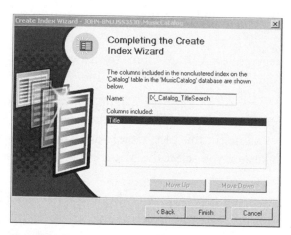

FIGURE 26.48 *The final step in using the wizard is to give your newly created index a meaningful name.*

7. Click on Finish, and you will be presented with a message indicating that your index was successfully completed.

Creating an Index Using Tasks

So far, you've seen how to create indexes in two different ways. Now take a look at yet another method—using Tasks. In reality, this method will have the same result (index creation), but along the way you might notice that this method has useful features not present in the other methods.

In the previous example, you created an index that allowed you to search using the title of a particular CD. For this example, expand your indexing capabilities and build an index that allows you to search using both the CD title and price. That way, the proprietor of the store will be able to search for CDs for a given artist at a given price.

1. From the Enterprise Manager Details Pane, select the Catalog table. Right-click on it and select All Tasks, Manage Indexes from the menu that appears.

2. The first thing you will notice is the existence of the two indexes you created in the previous sections. Some neat features to notice at this point (and a good reason to consider using Tasks to create your indexes) are the ability to quickly see and edit all existing indexes (by clicking on the Edit button) and the ability to quickly delete an existing index (by, you guessed it, clicking on the Delete button).

3. Rather than manipulate an existing index, you want to create a new one. Click on the New button. Select the Title and Price fields, and name this index IX_Catalog_TitleandPrice.

4. Before you click on OK in this dialog box, notice the Edit SQL button. Although I won't discuss it in great detail in this section, if you click on this button, the actual T-SQL code that is generated for this index will become available for your manual manipulation. This is another neat and handy feature that is readily accessible when you use the Tasks method to create an index.

5. Click on OK, and you will be returned to the opening screen, where you should now see three indexes (including the one you just created). That's all there is to it!

Other Methods of Creating Indexes

In addition to the methods you've already seen illustrated, there are still other ways to create indexes.

◆ **Creating an index using the Query Analyzer.** Similar to what you saw when you created a table in this fashion, you can use the Query Analyzer to create an index directly with SQL syntax, instead of the more graphical (dare I say user-friendly?) methods that I have described thus far.

◆ **Creating an index using a template.** Similar to creating a table using a template, you can also create an index via a template. And just as with a table, you can select Replace Template Parameters (from the Edit menu of the Query Analyzer) to more readily see the parameters that require specific input from you, the developer.

Depending on your preference, you can use any of these methods—the Enterprise Manager, a wizard, Tasks, the Query Analzyer, or a template—to create an index. However, because the Query Analyzer and Template methods are so conceptually similar to creating tables using these methods, I won't go into specific detail. (However, feel free to experiment with these two methods as your interest and inclination guide you.)

Other Index Considerations

Before I end this chapter, I want to take a look at some other important considerations and terminology when working with indexes.

Understanding Uniqueness

If an index is set to unique, it means that all data inserted into the table must be of unique quality. Put simply, a unique index will not allow duplicate records to be created. If such an attempt is made, an error will be generated. Generally, it is a good idea to identify all of your indexes as unique (which you've done in this chapter). This will greatly improve the consistently and validity of the data contained in your tables.

Avoiding a Bad Index

Fortunately, it's not that difficult to avoid creating a bad index. Like so many things in programming and development, a little common sense can go a long way.

When creating indexes, consider first and foremost what you want to get out of the index. In other words, what data do you want to have returned? As with so many aspects of database design, even a little bit of foresight and planning will save you much time and frustration further down the road. When considering your desired results, think about the columns you are selecting. Do they contain the data you want to query? If the column doesn't contain any type of data you are searching for, then leave it out of your index to speed up processing time. Also, think about the selectivity and uniqueness of the data you are querying, so that the data you are indexing is unique enough to return specific results.

Finally, consider the actual number of records in your database. If you have a small amount of records, you probably don't need to create an index when a quick visual inspection of the data (via the Enterprise Manager, for example) would produce the same results just as quickly.

Summary

This chapter presented you with a wealth of information on perhaps the central exercise in database creation—creating and manipulating tables and indexes. You learned what a table is and how it is defined in SQL Server. Next, you learned how to create a table utilizing various methods, and you took a look at how to manually manipulate the SQL code to create tables by hand, allowing you a much greater degree of control over how the tables function. Next, you learned about indexes and how to create them, including methods that are similar to creating and manipulating tables. You also were introduced to some fundamental index terminology, and you learned ways to avoid creating poor indexes.

You were also presented with a significant amount of information about how to create, delete, and configure databases via the Enterprise Manager, the Database Creation Wizard, and the Query Analyzer. For each method, you saw the similarities and differences in how a database is created, and you were exposed to the amount of time required to create a database using each method.

Chapter 27

Querying and Manipulating Data in SQL Server 2000

Y ou've got a database, and you've got data stored within the database. Somewhere within that data, you know there is one piece of information that can move you ahead of your competition or provide your customer with a more personal experience on your Web site. How do you retrieve this elusive piece of data? As you saw in Chapter 25, you can use the Enterprise Manager to dig down through the general navigation structure of your database to find the information you need. However, this can be time consuming and ultimately unnecessary because of the power the Query Analyzer brings to your SQL Server 2000 environment.

If you have worked with Microsoft Access or another database application, you might have experience with SQL. You will be happy to find that the basic syntax of T-SQL (short for *Transact-SQL*, or the specific variation of SQL that SQL Server 2000 utilizes) is really not that different from what you are accustomed to. The big difference—and the real focus of this chapter—is the tools that SQL Server presents to make working with these statements more flexible and powerful than any other database application you have worked with in the past.

 NOTE

It is critical that you understand the tools and concepts presented in this chapter so when you Web-enable your database (as you will do in the next chapter), you have a firm grasp of the underlying structure and methodology that is used in this process.

Opening the Query Analyzer

The first thing to do is start the Query Analyzer. If SQL Server is not running, start it now and access the Enterprise Manager. Your screen should look like Figure 27.1.

Now you are ready to open the Query Analyzer. From the Tools menu, select SQL Query Analyzer, as shown in Figure 27.2.

The Query Analyzer will open and be ready for you to use.

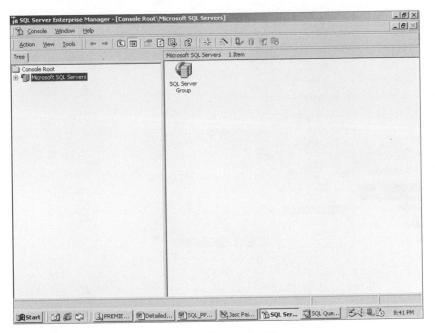

FIGURE 27.1 *The SQL Server 2000 Enterprise Manager.*

FIGURE 27.2 *Accessing the Query Analyzer in the Enterprise Manager.*

In addition to opening the Query Analyzer via the Enterprise Manager, you can also open it via the Windows Start button. Figure 27.3 highlights the path to open the Query Analyzer.

While in the previous section you probably saw the Query Analyzer open directly, using this method you are presented with the Connect to SQL Server dialog box shown in Figure 27.4.

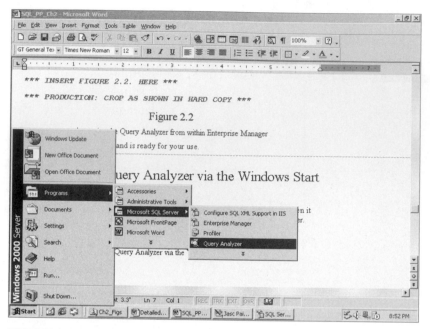

FIGURE 27.3 *Opening the Query Analyzer via the Windows Start button.*

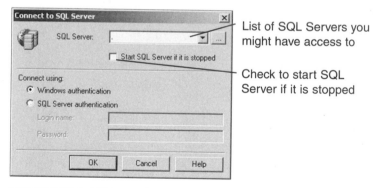

FIGURE 27.4 *When opening the Query Analyzer via the Start button, you are first asked to connect to the appropriate SQL Server.*

In Figure 27.4, there are two options to connect to SQL Server. Each has its own attributes:

◆ **Windows Authentication.** This is the preferred choice because you will be logging into SQL Server using your identified Windows information, thus ensuring that you are logging into SQL Server as yourself, with the proper security and other credentials.

◆ **SQL Server Authentication.** This is essentially the catch-all method of logging in to SQL Server. Although the sa user name can be assigned *a* password, the emphasis is really on the word "a." In other words, one user name and one password will prevent the proper tracking of who is doing what within the various databases. Put simply, this method of authentication doesn't allow you to go back later and determine precisely who did what because everyone will be identified as "sa."

 TIP

It is possible to create other SQL logins, so that everyone would appear as sa. SQL authentication can be used in a non-Windows domain where Windows credentials are not available; however, administration is much easier with Windows authentication because you only have to create one login account.

Now that you understand how to open and authenticate the Query Analyzer, it is time to take a closer look at the various elements of this powerful tool.

Query Analyzer Components

When you first open the Query Analyzer, it is divided into two major areas—the Object Browser and the Query Pane, as shown in Figure 27.5.

Take some time now to familiarize yourself with the navigational structure as it is presented in the Object Browser.

1. First take a look at the System Objects listing, as shown in Figure 27.6. System objects can also be identified as the specific database components because you can find each system object (system tables, views, and so on) within each SQL Server database. For now, click on the plus sign next to the sample Northwind database and expand the User Tables node, as shown in Figure 27.6.

2. To see a further node breakdown, click on the plus sign next to the dbo.Categories object, underneath the User Tables folder.

3. A new listing of objects will appear (Columns, Indexes, Constraints, and so on). Click on the plus sign next to the Columns object to see a listing of the columns that comprise the Categories table, as show in Figure 27.7.

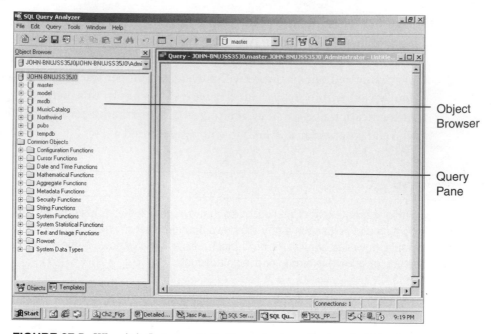

FIGURE 27.5 *When it is first opened, the Query Analyzer displays the Object Browser and Query Pane.*

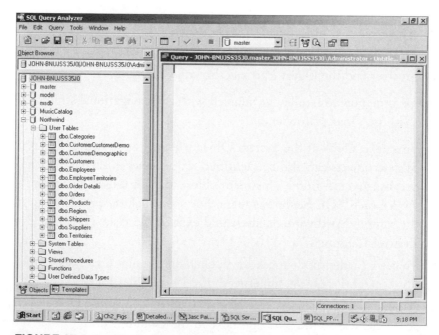

FIGURE 27.6 *In this case, expanding the various nodes will display the system objects they contain.*

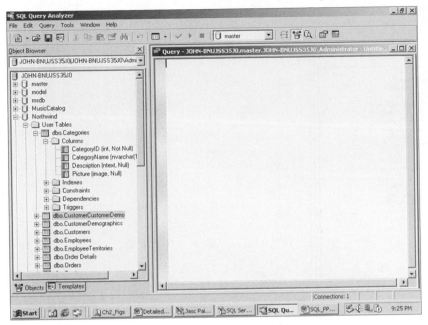

FIGURE 27.7 *You can see the individual column names, as well as information about the columns' specific properties.*

 NOTE

The dbo. nomenclature that appears in Figures 27.6 and 27.7 is short for *database object*.

The Common Objects

You should also take note of the Common Objects node in Figure 27.5 (Configuration Functions, Cursor Functions, and so on). These objects are not specific to individual databases; rather, they are common to all databases. As you work with the Query Analyzer, you will use the objects as a convenient reference in order to return the type of information you are seeking as you manipulate your data.

For now, take a moment to browse through the various common object listings by clicking on the plus button next to each one and examining the functions that are contained therein (see Figure 27.8).

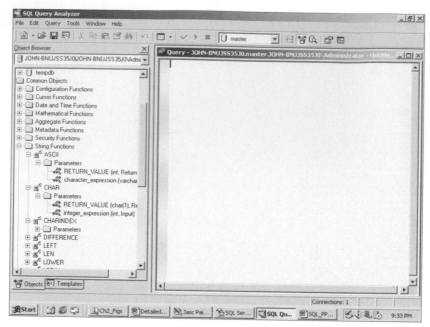

FIGURE 27.8 *The String Functions node, expanded. Note that a parameter listing is given for each function shown, so you can quickly identify each piece of the specific component.*

 TIP

The type of information and functionality presented in Figure 27.8 is a big reason why SQL Server continues to enjoy such phenomenal success. Compared to other database applications, the GUI (*Graphical User Interface*) of SQL Server is so easy to manipulate—yet so powerful—that you can quickly build and access powerful data solutions. The Query Analyzer is a prime example of this power.

That said, as you begin using SQL Server in your own applications, don't be afraid to experiment and dig in to all the functionality that is presented. Part of the real benefit (and fun) of using an application like this is that there is always something new to learn. Moreover, the help and general information available in SQL Server make your work that much easier.

The Templates

Templates are a wonderfully powerful and convenient way of accessing the data you seek. The templates in the Query Analyzer do most of the hard work for you—they complete the major framework and simply ask you to fill in the blanks.

To illustrate this, take a moment to explore the Create Database template option.

1. Click on the Templates node as shown in Figure 27.9. Once you do, a listing of the installed templates will appear in the Object Browser window.

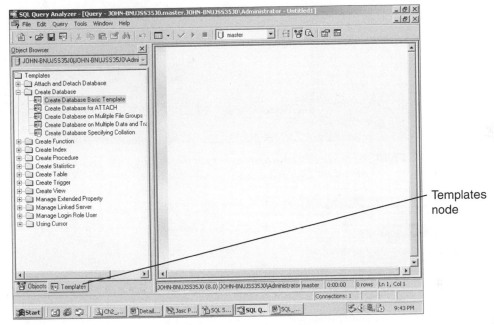

FIGURE 27.9 *Clicking on the Templates node displays the installed templates available.*

2. Now expand the Create Database node so your screen looks like Figure 27.9. Double-click on the Create Database Basic Template option. Your screen should look like Figure 27.10.

3. The parts of the code that are shaded in colors other than black are placeholders within the template, or areas where you need to provide information. Although you can type over these areas of text as they appear in the main pane of the Query Analyzer, you can also (in yet another great example of the first-rate SQL Server GUI interface) have these placeholders presented in a neatly formatted table. To see this, select Edit, Replace Template Parameters (see Figure 27.11).

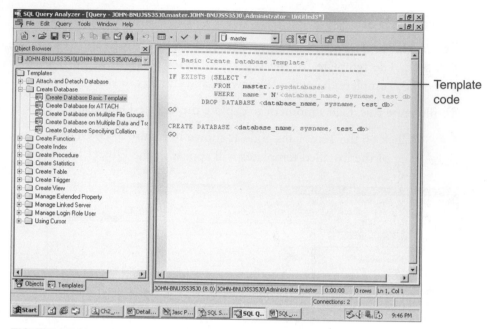

FIGURE 27.10 *When you click on a template option, the resulting code will appear in the main pane of the Query Analyzer.*

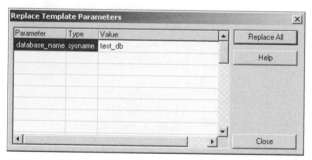

FIGURE 27.11 *When you replace template parameters, the parameter, type, and value are all neatly presented in a table for easier manipulation.*

Again, you'll look at the Replace Template Parameters function in far greater detail a bit later. For now, just take a moment to open some of the other templates shown here.

Examining the Query/Results Pane

The Query Pane basically consists of the entire right side of the Query Analyzer. When you execute a query, the results of that query are displayed in the Results Pane, shown in Figure 27.12.

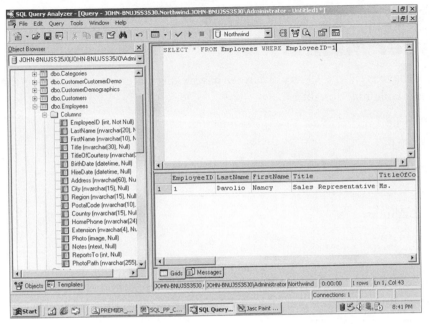

FIGURE 27.12 *The Results Pane shows the results of your query.*

In Figure 27.12, the executed query

```
SELECT * FROM Employees WHERE EmployeeID=1
```

returns the information shown in the Results Pane. (In this case, within the Employees table, Nancy Davolio has an EmployeeID equal to 1.)

 NOTE

The Results Pane only appears as a result of a query being executed. So if you don't see it on your screen right now, don't worry! It's there; it's just waiting for you to execute a query.

If you're familiar with Microsoft Access and the query tools available in that application, then you are going to be very happy with the tools at your disposal in SQL Server.

Investigating the Query Analyzer Menus

As you have seen, the Query Analyzer has six distinct menus containing the various available functionalities.

◆ File

◆ Edit

◆ Query

◆ Tools

◆ Window

◆ Help

Some of the options available in each menu are self-explanatory, but others will require a bit more discussion. That said, the next few sections will be devoted to an explanation of each menu and the exciting features of the Query Analyzer you can expect to find in each.

The File Menu

The File menu in the Query Analyzer isn't that much different from what you find in other Windows applications. For example, in MS Word you use the File menu for basic document navigation (such as opening, closing, and saving files). This is also the case with the File menu in the Query Analyzer, except that instead of documents, you are opening, closing, and otherwise manipulating connections to your SQL Server and printing, saving, or otherwise manipulating the queries you create.

Take a moment to go through each of the options in the File menu to make sure you understand the functionality of each one.

◆ **Connect, Disconnect, and Disconnect All.** These three options allow you to—surprise—connect to and disconnect from a specific SQL Server. When you access the Query Analyzer via the Enterprise Manager, you are presented with the Connect to SQL Server dialog box shown in Figure 27.13 when you select the Connect option.

When you choose the Disconnect or Disconnect All options, you are presented with a dialog box asking you whether you want to save your

FIGURE 27.13 *When you select File, Connect, you are asked which SQL Server you want to connect to.*

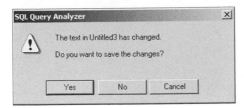

FIGURE 27.14 *Before you disconnect, you are prompted to save your changes.*

changes (see Figure 27.14). Again, this functionality is very similar to any Windows application. When you close a particular file, the application prompts you to first save your changes.

◆ **New.** When you select the New option from the File menu, you are presented with a list of predefined query templates (the same list you saw when you clicked on the Templates node, shown in Figure 27.9). Selecting the New option is just a different way of accessing these query templates (see Figure 27.15).

Once you navigate to a specific query template and select it, the resulting template code will appear in the Query Pane. You can then work with the code by utilizing the options discussed earlier, in the section titled "The Templates."

◆ **Save, Save As, and Save All Queries.** Just as their names imply, these options allow you to save the queries you created. As you might guess, saving long or complicated queries is analogous to saving long Word documents—you want to save them so you don't have to re-enter them later!

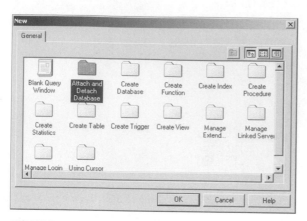

FIGURE 27.15 *Chose a query template by selecting the File, New option.*

◆ **Print.** As in other applications, selecting the Print option here allows you to print a hard copy of your query. Note that the Print option only works with a single Query Pane, and you cannot print a results set if it's displayed as a grid. (You also cannot print multiple Query Panes.)

The Edit Menu

Much like the File menu, the Edit menu contains basic operations that you will find in most Windows applications. Still, take a few minutes to go through the options listed to make sure you are familiar with them.

◆ **Undo, Cut, Copy, Paste, and Select All.** These are basic text manipulation functions that you will find in any application. They generally function the same within the Query Analyzer.

◆ **Clear Window.** This option clears the Query Pane. Note, however, that it does not clear the Results Pane.

◆ **Find, Repeat Last Find, and Replace.** Again, as with most applications, this is basic text manipulation that allows you to quickly locate and replace specific sections of text or a query, as required.

◆ **Go To Line.** This function allows you to quickly jump to a line in your query. This is useful when you are dealing with long queries.

◆ **Bookmarks.** This is yet another useful tool for quickly finding specific sections in your text. By inserting bookmarks, you can annotate specific sections within your query, which will help you locate and troubleshoot specific sections of the query.

- **Insert Template and Replace Template Parameters.** This is the same functionality described earlier in this chapter, in the section "The Templates."
- **Advanced.** The options presented here allow you to specifically format how your queries are presented in the Query Pane. Note the options to increase and decrease indents, as well as to comment out specific sections of your query.

NOTE

If you think I went through the functionality of the Edit menu very quickly, there is a reason! As I noted in my description of nearly every item, the functionality presented in this menu is conceptually very similar to most Windows applications.

The Query Menu

The Query menu is the central menu in the Query Analyzer; thus it contains most of the specific functionality options.

- **Change Database.** This allows you to quickly jump to a different database contained within your instance of SQL Server (see Figure 27.16).
- **Parse and Execute.** These basic query options actually execute (or run) your query to produce results. Note the shortcuts for these two options—you will use them often (especially the F5 option to execute a query).

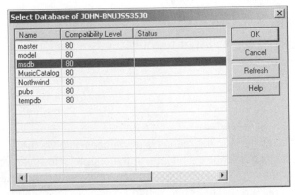

FIGURE 27.16 *You can quickly move between databases using the Change Database option.*

◆ **Display Estimated Execution Plan.** This option allows you to view specific performance details with regard to the query (or queries) you are executing. To demonstrate the level of detail available with this option, take a moment to enter a basic query so you can see how this option works with your queries.

1. If you are not connected to SQL Server via the Query Analyzer, do so now by selecting File, Connect.

2. For this example, work with the Northwind sample database. From the Query menu, select Change Database and select the Northwind database, as shown in Figure 27.17.

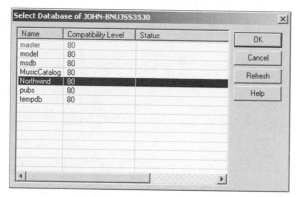

FIGURE 27.17 *Select the Northwind sample database for this example.*

3. In the Query Pane, enter the following query:

```
SELECT * FROM Employees WHERE EmployeeID=1
```

4. Execute this query by selecting Query, Execute or by pressing the F5 key. The Query Pane will split to show the Results Pane, as shown in Figure 27.18.

 TIP

Much of the functionality that is available in the menus is also accessible via the Query Analyzer toolbar. I'll discuss this feature a bit later in the chapter. However, you might want to do a little experimenting to see whether you can locate within the Query Analyzer toolbar some of the functionality I'm asking you to access via the menus (such as the Execute Query option and the Change Database option).

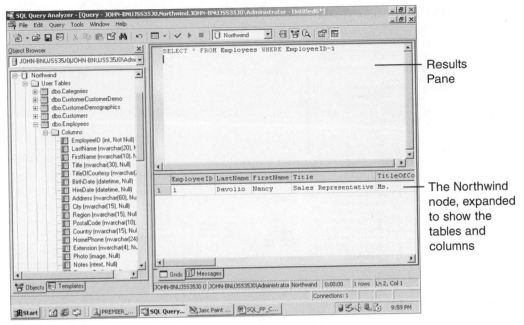

FIGURE 27.18 *When the query is executed, the Results Pane will be displayed.*

5. Now that you have executed a query (albeit a simple one), you can see the information presented in the Display Estimated Execution Plan option. Select this option now from the Query menu, so the Results Pane appears as in Figure 27.19.

6. What does the Estimated Execution Plan tell you? As it turns out, some very useful information—you can view detailed information about the performance ramifications of your query. If you hover your cursor over each of the icons shown in Figure 27.19, a pop-up box will display specific performance specifications for the query, as shown in Figure 27.20.

◆ **Results in Text, Results in Grid, and Results to File.** These options allow you to present the results of your executed query in different forms. In several of the preceding figures, the query results were displayed in grid form. Figure 27.21 illustrates the same query you executed earlier, but with the results in text form.

Use the Results to File option to send your executed query results directly to a file. Prior to the query being executed, you will be prompted to select a location in which to save your file, as shown in Figure 27.22.

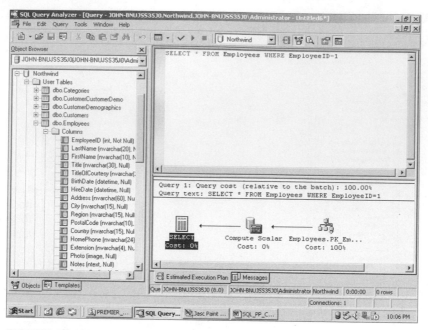

FIGURE 27.19 *The Estimated Execution Plan display.*

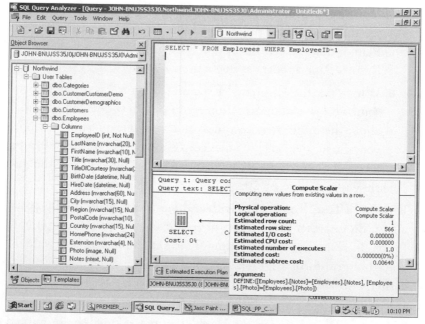

FIGURE 27.20 *The Estimated Execution Plan gives you immediate performance specification information as it relates to your executed query.*

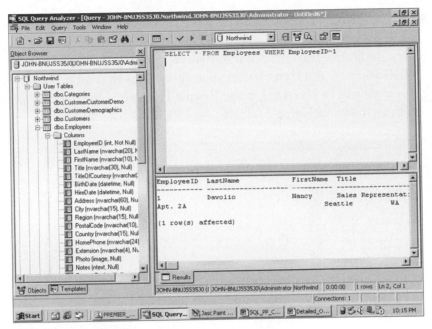

FIGURE 27.21 *Viewing your query results in text form.*

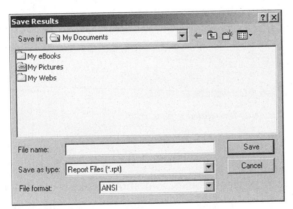

FIGURE 27.22 *Saving your executed query results to a file will allow you to manipulate that information later in a variety of formats.*

◆ **Show Execution Plan, Show Server Trace, and Show Client Statistics.**
These options, like the Execution Plan option described earlier, show
you additional performance information related to your query. Select
these options and then execute your query. Tabs to display these specific
options will be presented in the Results Pane when the query is executed, as shown in Figure 27.23.

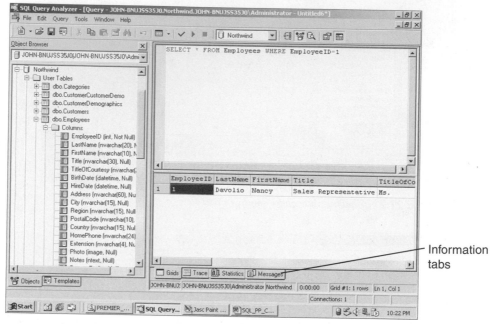

FIGURE 27.23 *Click on the tabs to display the related information.*

The Tools Menu

Although it is beyond the scope of this project, you should take a quick look at
the options in the Tools menu so you at least understand their functions and how
and where to access them.

The Object Search Option

Take a look at the second option in the Tools menu—Object Search.

1. In the Tools menu, select Object Search, New. Your screen should look
   like Figure 27.24.

2. In the Database field, select the sample Northwind database.

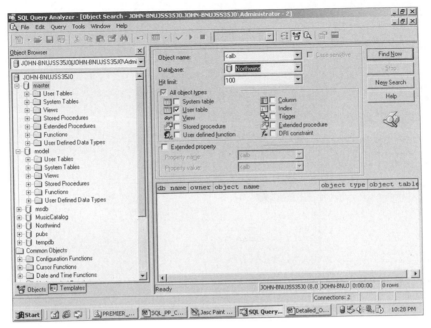

FIGURE 27.24 *The New Object Search window.*

3. Check the User Table option and deselect all other options (if they are selected).

4. Click on the Find Now button. After a few moments, the results of your search will appear, as shown in Figure 27.25.

When your search results are returned, you can access other functionality by returning to the Tools menu, selecting Object Search, and then selecting one of the scripting options, as shown in Figure 27.26.

Your screen should look like Figure 27.26. Take a moment to experiment with some of these scripting options.

1. In the Results Pane (shown in Figure 27.26), select the line that displays information on the Employees table.

2. Right-click and select Script Object to New Window As, Select from the drop-down menu that appears, as shown in Figure 27.27.

3. You should now see a SELECT query template displayed in your Results Pane. Notice how the different columns in the Employees table are provided. If you scroll across the Results Pane, you will also see the rest of the SELECT statement, as shown in Figure 27.28.

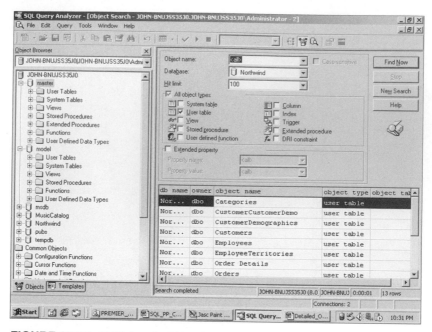

FIGURE 27.25 *Utilizing the Object Search to return all specified values (in this case, all tables within the Northwind sample database).*

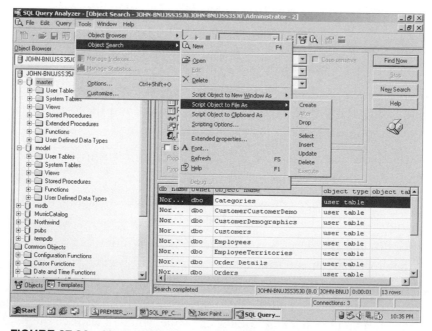

FIGURE 27.26 *After you run an object search, you can utilize advanced SQL functionality on the returned results by selecting a script option.*

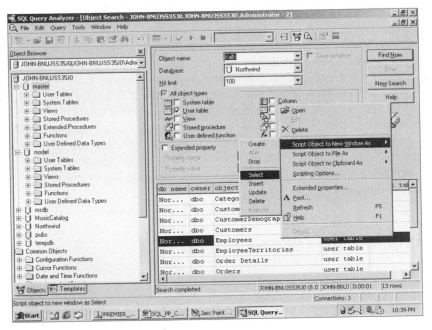

FIGURE 27.27 *Selecting a specific scripting option.*

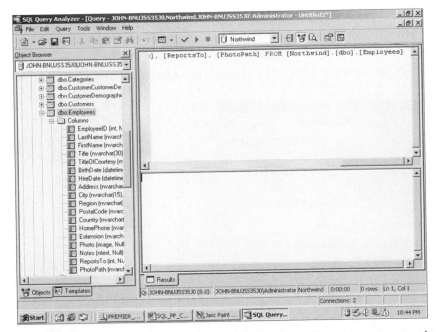

FIGURE 27.28 *The Script Object option allows you to quickly generate query templates.*

TIP

You might have noticed that the Query Analyzer presents redundant functionality. In other words, there are several ways to perform the same general tasks. This is very much on purpose, and it is one of the key design benefits of SQL Server 2000. As you work with the Query Analyzer and generate specific results (not just to queries, but also in preparing certain functions), the application is smart enough to realize that you might want to go one step further and script a query from an object search (as in the exercise you just completed). Be on the lookout for this extended functionality as you work with SQL Server 2000—the next task you want to undertake might be just a single mouse-click away!

Working with the Options Function

The Options function in the Tools menu allows you to configure specific functionality as presented within the entire Query Analyzer. Figure 27.29 highlights the Options dialog box with the various sub-option tabs, which are presented for your customization.

The following is a quick rundown of what each tab represents:

◆ **General.** This tab allows you to customize and configure where your files are stored.

◆ **Editor.** As you work in the Query Pane, you can determine how information appears. Take advantage of the options presented here so you can

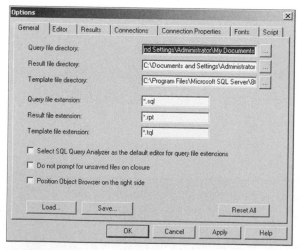

FIGURE 27.29 *The Options dialog box.*

format your query text to make editing that much easier and more applicable to your personal tastes.

◆ **Results.** Use this tab to control how your query results are displayed. Note the options (presented in the Query menu on the Query Analyzer menu bar) to display your query results to grid, text, or file (see Figure 27.30).

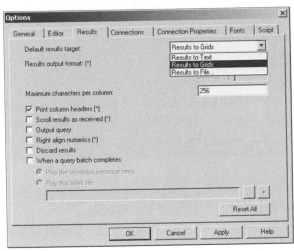

FIGURE 27.30 *Use the Results tab to determine how your query results are displayed.*

◆ **Connections.** You probably won't have much use for this tab because it deals with more advanced settings for connecting to the server.

◆ **Connection Properties.** This tab allows you to determine the specific properties that are set when you log in to SQL Server.

◆ **Fonts.** Use this tab to set the fonts to your specific liking as you work with the Query Analyzer.

◆ **Script.** As you saw in the previous exercise, after you perform an Object Search, you can use the Script tab to set specific options with regard to outputting objects as scripts.

 TIP

As noted above, you can access most of the functionality presented within the Options dialog box (and its related tabs) from other areas of the Query Analyzer. However, the Options dialog box presents many of these functional options in one place, so take advantage of the quick access offered by the Options dialog box.

Using the Query Analyzer Toolbar

The Query Analyzer toolbar provides quick access to a wide variety of functionality, as shown in Figure 27.31.

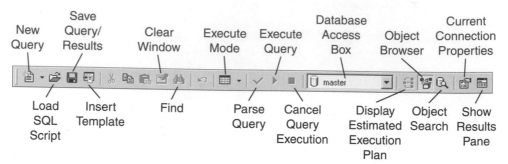

FIGURE 27.31 *The Query Analyzer toolbar gives you access to a wide range of functionality.*

As you work with the Query Analyzer, be sure to take advantage of the quick access to certain functions that the toolbar affords you. Although how you access certain functionalities is sometimes a matter of preference, you would be hard-pressed to argue why it is faster or easier to select an option from a menu than to click on a toolbar icon. This quick access is why toolbars were invented; so take advantage of it!

Up to this point, you've looked at the general working environment of SQL Server 2000, including the Enterprise Manager and the Query Analyzer. Really, the only thing I haven't touched on is undoubtedly the most important component of any database—the data! For the rest of this chapter, you will work with the four basic T-SQL statements, which will prove the foundation of all the data manipulation you perform in SQL Server. These four T-SQL statements are

- ◆ SELECT
- ◆ INSERT
- ◆ UPDATE
- ◆ DELETE

Essentials of Data Retrieval: The SELECT Statement

Before you can really start to insert, update, delete, or otherwise manipulate data (by "manipulate data," I mean change its structure within the database), you should familiarize yourself with the methods and tools of the most basic (yet probably most used) T-SQL statement—the SELECT statement.

In all of the sections of this chapter that discuss the four basic T-SQL statements, I will start with a simple example of the statement being discussed, and then move into more complex illustrations of its functionality (in terms of the actual statement syntax, as well as the SQL Server tools you will use to work with the statement).

The Return All Rows Option

Consider the following basic SELECT example:

1. Open the Enterprise Manager, expand the Databases node, and select the CDShop database. Your screen should look like Figure 27.32.

2. Return all rows of the Catalog table by selecting it, right-clicking, and then selecting Open Table, Return All Rows from the drop-down menu that appears, as shown in Figure 27.33.

   Your screen should now appear as in Figure 27.34. Take a moment to review the structure of this simple table and the type of data it contains.

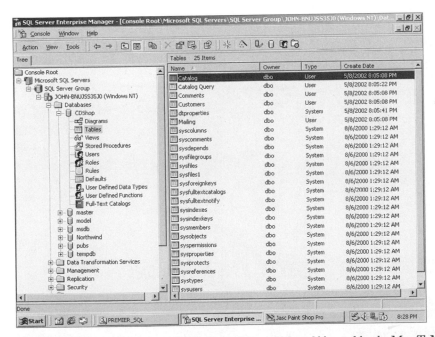

FIGURE 27.32 *The fictitious CDShop database, which could be used by the MuseToMusic company.*

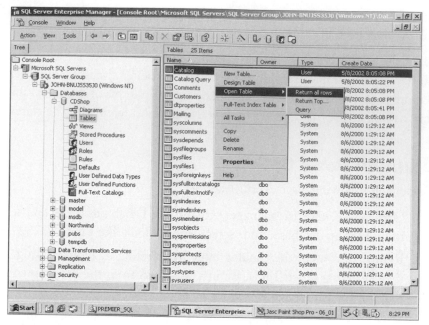

FIGURE 27.33 *Return all rows to view the contents of the Catalog table.*

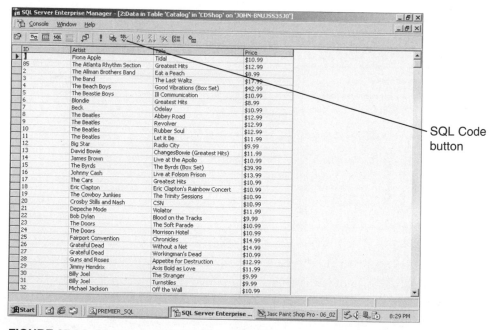

SQL Code button

FIGURE 27.34 *The Catalog table contains general information for a fictitious music store's catalog.*

3. By returning all rows, you have actually run a SELECT query on the Catalog table. You can view the SELECT statement that was used by clicking on the Show/Hide SQL Pane button on the toolbar (see Figure 27.35). Click on this button now, and your screen should appear as in Figure 27.36.

FIGURE 27.35 *The Show/Hide SQL Pane button.*

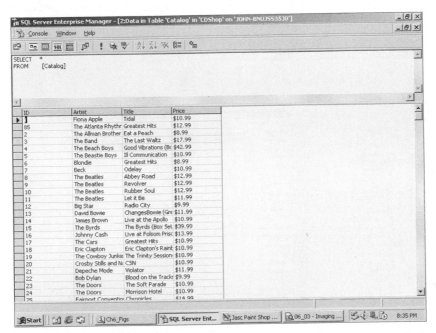

FIGURE 27.36 *You can easily view the actual T-SQL query that was automatically generated when you returned all rows of your table data.*

The Return Top Option

Pretty easy, right? Although you haven't generated any SQL queries on your own, the tools within the Enterprise Manager allow you to do this automatically. Take a look now at another example of how you can generate SELECT queries automatically.

1. If you haven't already done so, close the query you just ran in the previous example by pressing Ctrl+F4.

2. As you did earlier, select the Catalog table. This time, when you right-click to display the drop-down menu, select the Return Top option, as shown in Figure 27.37.

3. You will be presented immediately with the dialog box shown in Figure 27.38, asking you the maximum number of rows to return from the selected table. For this example, enter 20 in this dialog box.

4. Click on OK, and the first 20 rows of data from the Catalog table will be returned. As you did in the previous example, click on the SQL button on the toolbar to see the actual query syntax that was used to generate this data result. Your screen should now look like Figure 27.39.

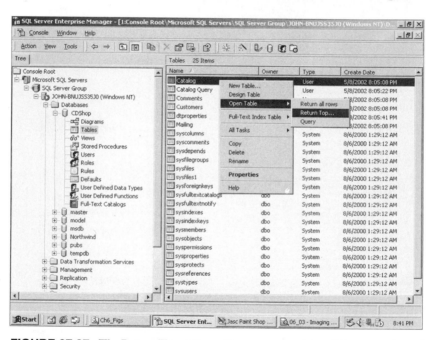

FIGURE 27.37 *The Return Top option will present you with a different result set than the Return All Rows option did.*

FIGURE 27.38 *You can specify the maximum number of rows you want to return in your data result set.*

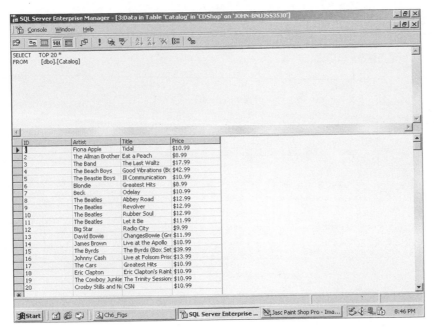

FIGURE 27.39 *Note the difference in this* SELECT *query, compared to the one you executed in the previous example.*

The Query Option

Before I go into a more detailed explanation of the SELECT statement, it is worth noting the other option on the pop-up menu you saw illustrated in Figures 27.32 and 27.36—the Query option. Take a quick look at that option, too.

1. If you haven't already done so, close the query you just ran by pressing Ctrl+F4 so you are returned to the Enterprise Manager.

2. Select the Catalog table, right-click, and this time select Open Table, Query. Your screen will look like Figure 27.40.

3. In the Table window, select the Artist and Title options. As you select each column in the Table window, notice how the SELECT statement is automatically generated in the Query Pane, as shown in Figure 27.41.

4. Click the Execute Query icon on the toolbar to execute your query (see Figure 27.42). You will see, in the Results Pane, the data that is generated from this custom SQL statement, as shown in Figure 27.43.

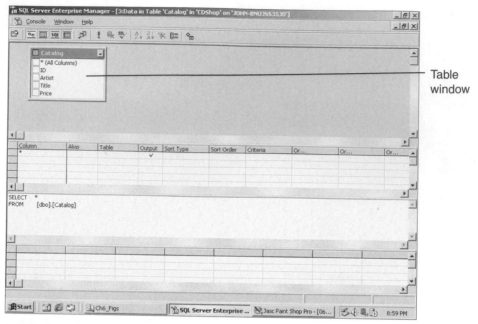

FIGURE 27.40 *The Query option allows you to customize your SELECT query automatically.*

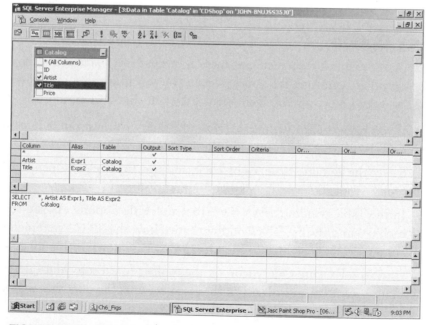

FIGURE 27.41 *When the SELECT query is executed, the Query Pane is updated automatically to reflect your choices of information to return.*

FIGURE 27.42 *The Execute Query button.*

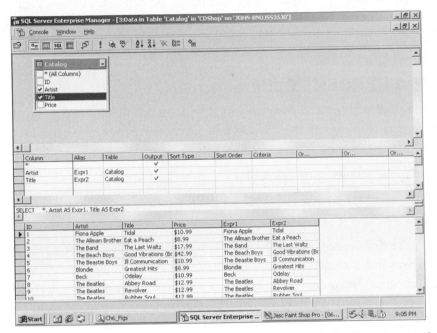

FIGURE 27.43 *Depending on what columns you have selected, the SQL statement that is automatically built will differ.*

Understanding the SELECT Statement Syntax

All of the examples in the previous three sections utilized a basic form of the SELECT syntax. However, to customize and gain greater control over the data sets that are returned as a result of your executed queries, you should become familiar with the additional components of the SELECT syntax. (These components are in addition to the basic SQL syntax that you've seen so far—or specifically, SELECT * FROM.)

A basic SELECT query might look like the following code (or what you have seen so far in this chapter):

```
SELECT * FROM Catalog
```

In this example, all rows from the Catalog table of the CDShop sample database would be returned. This is the essential, basic SELECT syntax.

However, there are far more specific qualifiers you can place within your SELECT queries. The next several sections will give you examples of this additional syntax and its effect on the resulting data sets when you execute the query.

The TOP *n* PERCENT Option

In a previous section, you were presented with an example of the TOP *n* PERCENT option when you opened the Catalog table in the Enterprise Manager and chose the Return Top option.

Consider the following two examples:

```
SELECT TOP 20 * FROM Catalog
SELECT TOP 20 PERCENT * FROM CATALOG
```

What's the difference between the two examples? In the first example, the PERCENT option was not included, so when executed, the query would return literally the top 20 records—no more and no less. However, in the second example, the top 20 *percent* of the records are returned, which may or may not yield the same result as the first query (depending, of course, on the number of actual records in the table that is being queried).

The (Column1, Column2, ...) Option

In the examples in the previous section (as well as most of the other examples so far in this chapter), you have no doubt noticed the use of the * qualifier, as in SELECT * FROM Catalog. When you use the * qualifier, this instructs SQL Server to return all the records in the table that match any additional criteria you have specified. (In the example I just listed, no additional criteria are given, so every record in the Catalog table is returned when this query is executed.)

This is fine if you want to return all rows of data. However, you should think about the performance consequences and what you are really looking for in your returned data before you just use the basic SELECT * FROM syntax. Depending on the size of your tables, the "give me all the records in the table" approach can put an unnecessary strain on your server processor. In addition (and more important- ly), why bother returning all the records (or all the columns for every record) if you don't really need that information?

This is where specifying selected columns to return really comes into play. Take a look at the following example:

```
SELECT Title, Artist FROM Catalog
```

You can immediately see that I do not use the * qualifier in this query. When it is executed, only the Title and Artist columns from the Catalog table will be returned. Again, while you can always return all records by using *, you should consider only returning the specific columns you're interested in seeing.

The WHERE Clause

An additional method of limiting the number of records returned from your SELECT queries is to include a WHERE clause. Consider the following example:

```
SELECT Title, Artist FROM Catalog WHERE ID > 5
```

In this example, I have specified the two columns for which I'm interested in seeing data (Title and Artist). However, I have also added the WHERE clause because I only want to return the records where the ID field has a value greater than 5 (again, with just the Title and Artist columns present).

In short, the WHERE clause is another way of specifying the data you want your query to return. Note that in this example, I used the > operator. In plain English, you could read this WHERE clause as "where the ID field has a value greater than 5." However (and this is where you can really start to see the power of SQL) you can mix and match the various available operators to make some very specific queries. By utilizing the AND option in conjunction with the WHERE clause, you can get really specific. Consider the following example:

```
SELECT Title, Artist FROM Catalog WHERE ID > 5 AND Artist = 'Beatles'
AND WHERE TITLE <> 'Abbey Road'
```

The ORDER BY Clause

The ORDER BY clause allows yet another method of sorting your query results. This clause is particularly useful when you want to see data returned in an ascending or descending order (for which you use the ASC or DESC qualifier, as you'll see in a moment). You can also use the TOP qualifier (as you've already seen) to return the top percentage or number of items from your query.

Take a look at the following example:

```
SELECT Title, Artist FROM Catalog WHERE Price > $12.99 ORDER BY Artist DESC
```

In this example, all of the records with a price greater than $12.99 are returned (with, specifically, the value for the Title column returned). Then, the records that match the criteria are sorted by the value of the Artist column, in a descending order (Z to A). Note that if the query were changed to utilize the ASC qualifier, the returned records would be sorted in an A to Z order.

 NOTE

The DESC and ASC qualifiers can work with numerical as well as text data.

Generating SELECT Queries Using the Query Analyzer

Now that you have an idea of the general syntax and components of the SELECT statement, I want you to see how you can use this via the Query Analyzer.

1. If you haven't done so already, open the Query Analyzer either from the Enterprise Manager or from the Windows Start menu (Start, Programs, Microsoft SQL Server, Query Analyzer).

2. In the Query Pane, enter the code exactly as it is shown in Figure 27.44.

3. Once you have entered the T-SQL code, click on the Execute Query button on the Query Analyzer toolbar or press Ctrl+F5. Your screen should appear as in Figure 27.45.

4. This is okay, but why don't you try sorting the results by the Title field? In the Query Pane, enter the code as shown in Figure 27.46.

5. After you have entered the code, execute the query. Your new results should look like Figure 27.47.

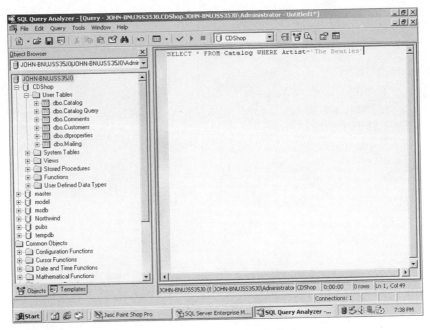

FIGURE 27.44 *This first SELECT query is somewhat basic.*

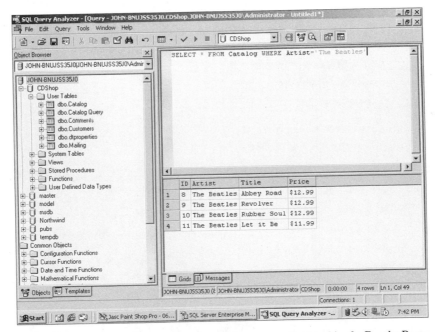

FIGURE 27.45 *The results of your executed query are displayed in the Results Pane.*

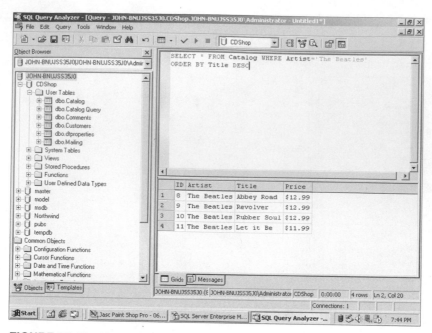

FIGURE 27.46 *Changing the SELECT syntax to order the query results.*

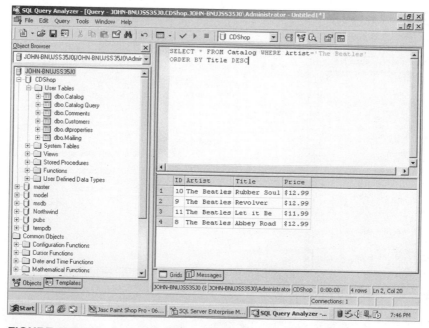

FIGURE 27.47 *Sorting and ordering your query results makes your data more readable and easier to understand.*

6. Before you move on to more exciting queries (utilizing the SELECT statement and others), take a moment and enter the following query, which encompasses all of the qualifiers and statements I've discussed so far. Enter the code as you see it in Figure 27.48.

7. Execute the query. Your screen should look like Figure 27.49.

Again, the SELECT statement is the fundamental SQL statement, and one with which you will become intimately familiar. When you use the SELECT statement in conjunction with other SQL statements, you can create powerful information transactions.

TIP

Notice the error message in Figure 27.48? Syntax errors are very common when working with SQL (as they are in any programming language, including—as I'm sure you've already experienced on your own—HTML). You can do a quick syntax check by clicking on the green checkmark button in the Query Analyzer, also known as the Parse Query button.

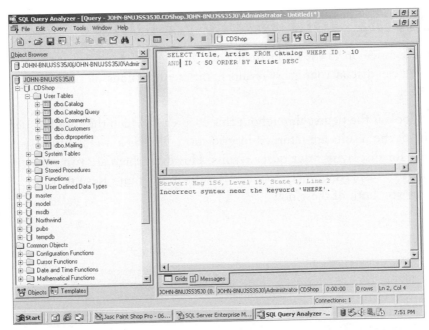

FIGURE 27.48 *A relatively simple SELECT query, but one that is fairly powerful in the type of organization and specificity it brings to the search for information*

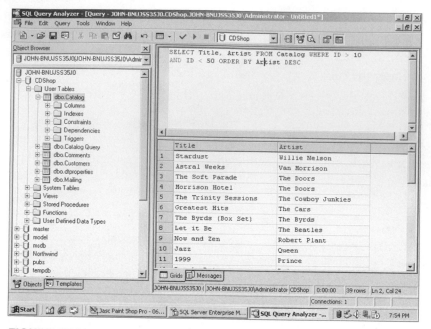

FIGURE 27.49 *Note how the use of the DESC qualifier helped to further sort your data.*

Displaying Your Query Results

Before I move on to the other three basic SQL statements, I want to show you how you can display your query results in different fashions, all through the Query Analyzer.

If you look at the figures throughout this chapter in which the specific queries are executed, the results are returned in grid form. This is a useful and easy-to-read context for displaying your query results. However, there are two other primary methods of displaying query results—Results in Text and Results to File. I want to show you both of these now.

Results in Text

Go back to the query you executed in Figure 27.48 and execute it again, but change a few things about how it's displayed first.

1. Execute the query again, as shown in Figure 27.48. Your screen should once again appear like Figure 27.49.

2. Now change the way the query results are displayed. From the Query menu, select Results in Text, as shown in Figure 27.50.

   Your screen should now appear as in Figure 27.51. Notice how, in the Results Pane, the column names stretch to indicate their actual width in the database table (in this case, the Catalog table).

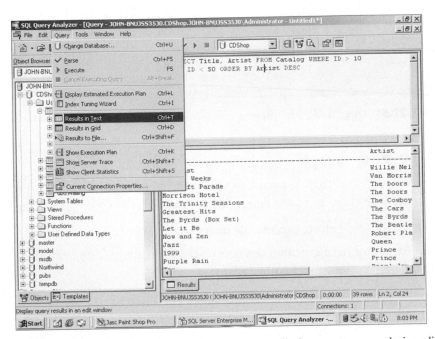

FIGURE 27.50 *Choose the Results in Text option to display your query results in a different fashion.*

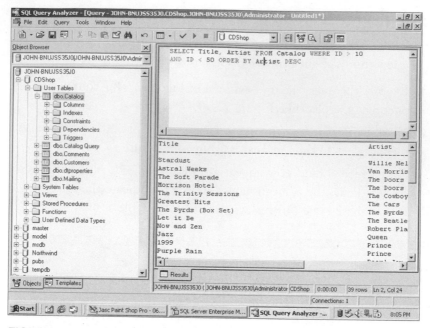

FIGURE 27.51 *Using the Results in Text option helps you visualize the structure of your tables.*

Results to File

Often, you will find that you want to save your query results to a file so you can view or analyze them at a later date. This is easy with the Query Analyzer.

1. As you did before, execute the query that you entered in Figure 27.48.

2. After you have executed the query, select Results to File from the Query menu, as shown in Figure 27.52.

3. Execute the query once again. When you do, you will be presented with the Save Results dialog box, shown in Figure 27.53.

4. Click on Save. Your query results will be saved to the location you specified. You can retrieve the results at a later time by selecting File, Open in the Query Analyzer. You can also open the results in any text file editor (because it is a text file). Figure 27.54 shows the query file that you just saved as it appears in Notepad. Note that the DESC ordering that you applied transfers over to the file. (The exact query results are saved, just as you specified.)

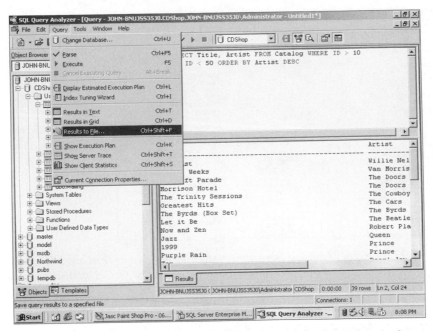

FIGURE 27.52 *The Results to File option lets you save your query results for future analysis.*

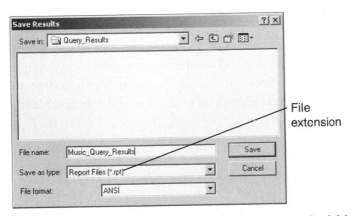

FIGURE 27.53 *Save the query results to a location on your hard drive. Note the file extension (.rpt) for the file you are about to create.*

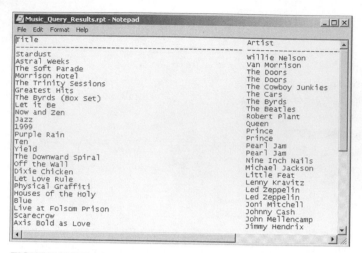

FIGURE 27.54 *Open your saved query files for easy viewing. Saving them also allows you to distribute them in various formats (as simple text files, as attachments or parts of e-mail messages, and so on).*

Building Your Database Using the INSERT Statement

Up to this point, you've seen how to query existing data using the SELECT statement and how to further streamline and organize your results by utilizing the various modifiers with the basic statement. Now I want to move on to the even more exciting INSERT statement, which allows you to build your database tables by—you guessed it—inserting data into them.

Why don't you jump right in by taking a look at a simple example?

1. For this exercise, you will add a new record to the Catalog table of the CDShop database. If it is not already open, open the Query Analyzer and make sure you have the CDShop database selected.

NOTE

It is possible to follow along with this and the rest of the examples in this chapter using any SQL database. You just need to change the column names in the examples because they refer specifically to the fictitious CDShop database.

2. In the Query Pane, enter the code shown in Figure 27.55.

3. Execute the query. If everything works properly, your screen should appear as in Figure 27.56.

   To confirm that your data was inserted into the Catalog table, open the table in the Enterprise Manager and scroll to the bottom of the display. You should see the new record with all the information entered, as shown in Figure 27.57.

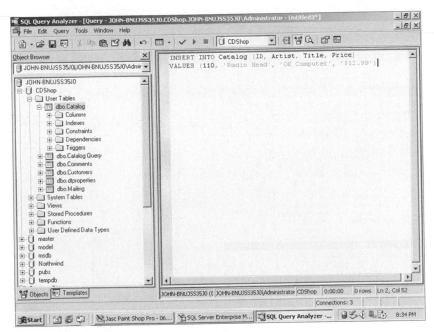

FIGURE 27.55 *This code example highlights the basic syntax of the* INSERT *statement.*

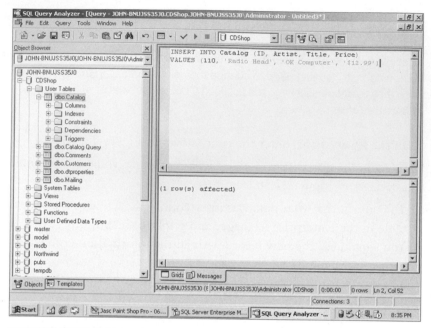

FIGURE 27.56 *This confirmation message lets you know that the query was executed successfully.*

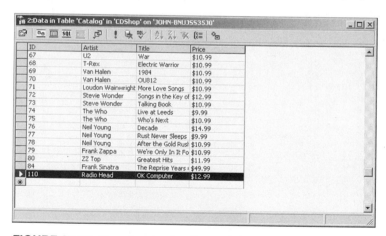

FIGURE 27.57 *Your data has been inserted, just as you specified with the INSERT statement.*

Understanding INSERT Statement Syntax

The syntax of the INSERT statement is generally easy to understand, and it is high-lighted here.

```
INSERT INTO [Tablename]
      [Column1, Column2…etc]
VALUES
      [Expression, Expression,…etc]
```

Pretty easy, right? Generally speaking, it is easy. But consider the following code example:

```
INSERT INTO Customer_Info
(ID, Customer_FirstName, Customer_LastName, Customer_Address1, Customer_Address2,
Customer_City, Customer_State, Cusomter_ZIP, Customer_Phone, Customer_Email)
VALUES
(5, 'Steve', 'Gadd', '123 59th Street', 'Apartment 2', 'New York', 'New York', 10017,
2125551234, 'sgadd@rhythm.com')
```

As you can see, depending on the number of fields for which you might have to enter data (and thus a corresponding value), your INSERT statements can get a little hairy. They are made more difficult because you have to consider the type of data being inserted (text value or numeric) and whether the table allows null values.

This last point is something I want to examine more closely, so let's do that right now!

Working with Null Values and the INSERT Statement

For this section, open the sample Northwind database and, specifically, the Employees table, so you can see what special considerations you must keep in mind when dealing with null values.

1. In the Enterprise Manager, expand the Northwind database and select the Employees table. Right-click and select Properties, as shown in Figure 27.58.

   The Table Properties dialog box for the Employees table will appear, as shown in Figure 27.59. Note how the first three fields (EmployeeID, LastName, and FirstName) do not have the Nulls option checked, which means they do not allow null values to be inserted.

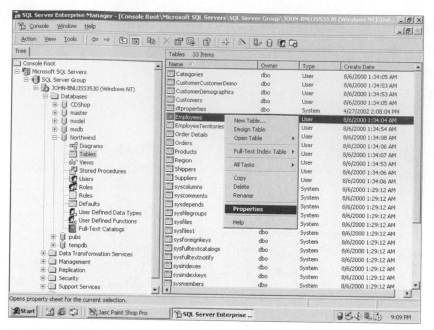

FIGURE 27.58 *Remember that you can access a wide range of functionality via the SQL Server drop-down menus in the Enterprise Manager or the Query Analyzer.*

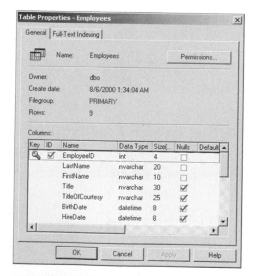

FIGURE 27.59 *The Table Properties dialog box gives you a quick overview of a table's configuration, including whether a specific field allows null values to be inserted.*

2. Close the Table Properties dialog box. To see how some of the fields in the Employees table have null values, return all the rows in the table by again selecting the Employees table, and then selecting Open Table, Return All Rows.

3. Scroll over so the Region column is displayed on your screen, as shown in Figure 27.60.

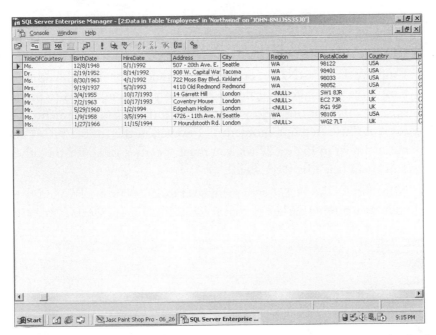

FIGURE 27.60 *Notice how some of the rows of data have <NULL> as a value for the Region column.*

There will be times when you want to allow null values because the corresponding type of information is not critical to your database and information integrity. For example, in the Employees table shown in Figure 27.60, the three values that do not allow null values are, obviously, central and critical information to each employee's record (their name and company identifier). However, the rest of the information gathered about each employee (in other words, the remaining columns in each row of data), while important, are not critical. So in this case, the database designer allowed null values to be inserted into these other fields.

So why worry about all this null business? Well, it becomes critical that you specify a value for those fields in which a null value is not allowed when you are inserting new records into your tables. Consider the following example:

1. With the Northwind database selected, open the Query Analyzer.

2. In the Query Pane, enter the code that you see illustrated in Figure 27.61.

3. Execute the query. Your screen should look like Figure 27.62.

   Why the error message? Again, if you look at the properties for this table (as shown in Figure 27.59), null values are not allowed for the EmployeeID, LastName, or FirstName fields. For this table, the EmployeeID is automatically inserted, so you do not need to provide a specific value for this field when you perform INSERT statements. (You'll see this illustrated in a moment.) However, in the simple INSERT statement shown in Figure 27.61, you must specify a value for the other "no null" field (the FirstName field).

4. Now correct the INSERT statement so it executes properly. Modify the code you entered earlier so that it looks like Figure 27.63.

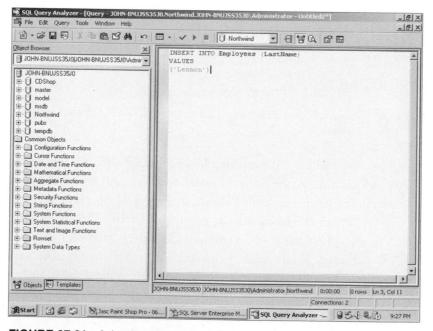

FIGURE 27.61 *A simple INSERT statement that will give complex results in this case.*

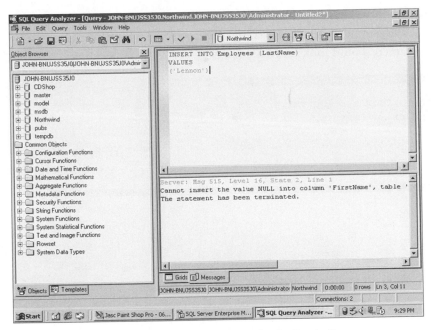

FIGURE 27.62 *Note the error message displayed in the Results Pane.*

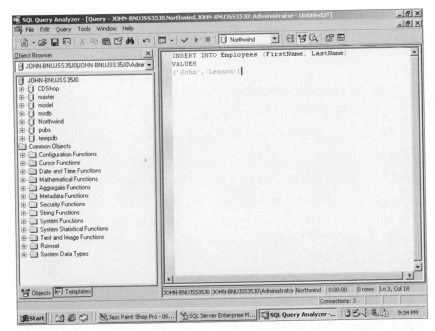

FIGURE 27.63 *In this example, both of the fields (other than the automated EmployeeID field) have been assigned explicit values in the INSERT statement.*

5. Execute the query. You should be given a confirmation message. Return to the Enterprise Manager and return all rows for this table, and your screen should look like Figure 27.64.

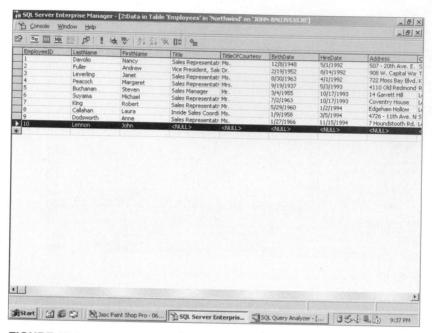

FIGURE 27.64 *Note how <NULL> has been inserted into all fields for which you did not specify a value.*

Remember that you can alter the table in Enterprise Manager to change the specific attributes of each field.

1. In the Enterprise Manager, select the Employees table of the Northwind sample database.

2. Right-click and select Design Table from the drop-down menu.

3. You will see (as shown in Figure 27.65) that the first three fields are set to not allow null values. Try to put a check mark in the Allow Nulls category for the EmployeeID column. Your screen should appear as in Figure 27.66.

 CAUTION

Use caution when changing any table attributes, especially when the table is heavily populated with data. This can adversely affect the integrity (and usefulness) of your entire database and the information it contains.

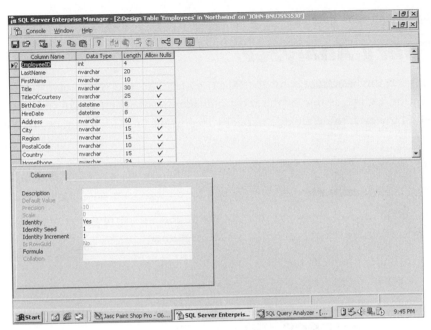

FIGURE 27.65 *Modifying a table's attributes in the Enterprise Manager.*

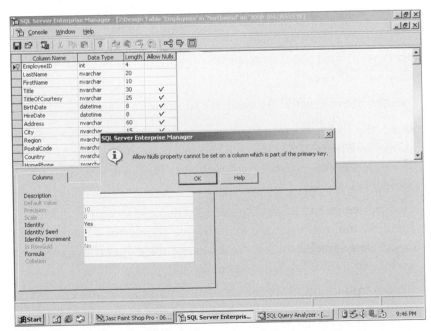

FIGURE 27.66 *You cannot set the Allow Nulls category to yes when the column in question is the table's primary key.*

Generating INSERT Queries Using the Query Analyzer

You've seen the basic syntax for the INSERT statement, and you've investigated the null option (which is one of the most considerations when you're working with INSERT). However, there are other equally important (and useful) issues to consider, such as

◆ Utilizing the DBCC CHECKIDENT command

◆ Working with column constraints

In this section, I will show you these other important attributes while also highlighting some more examples of the INSERT statement.

To begin, take a look at the DBCC CHECKIDENT command, and why you need to worry about it.

Working with the DBCC CHECKIDENT Command

As you insert new records into your database tables, you will find that your automatic identity columns (such as the EmployeeID column in the Employees table of the Northwind sample database) may become disjointed. (They might increase in number beyond what you require, or they might get out of order with the other records in your database.)

What does this mean exactly? As usual, it's time for an example!

1. Open the Query Analyzer and execute the incorrect query that was shown in Figure 27.61. Execute this incorrect query three or four times. (Just keep clicking on the Execute Query button on the Query Analyzer toolbar.)

2. Now correct the syntax of the INSERT statement so that it appears as in Figure 27.63. Execute the query, and you should see a confirmation message in the Query Pane. (You can change the values if you want; you don't have to use "John" and "Lennon.")

3. Return to the Enterprise Manager and return all the rows for the Employees table. Your screen should look like Figure 27.67.

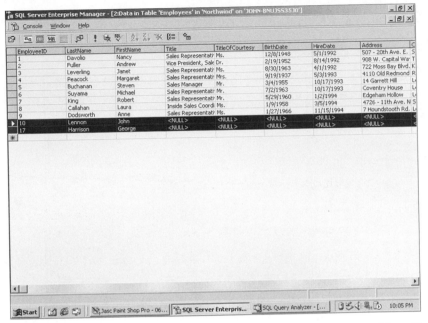

FIGURE 27.67 *Note the value for the EmployeeID field, which has jumped from 10 to 17.*

The type of misnumbering shown in Figure 27.67 is common as you insert, delete, update, and otherwise manipulate the values in your table. The trick is to reset the value so the next record that is entered picks up where the last record in the sequence left off. For example, in Figure 27.67 you ideally would want the next record to be 18—not 22, 27, 45, or whatever other value might be inserted.

To ensure this sequential numbering, you can use the DBCC CHECKIDENT command, which essentially forces the next record inserted to use the highest existing auto-numbered record as a baseline and to increment that baseline by one.

You can see this in action by working through the following example.

1. Return to the Query Analzyer and, with the Northwind sample database selected, enter the code in the Query Pane that you see illustrated in Figure 27.68.

2. Execute the query. You should be presented with a confirmation message in the Results Pane, as shown in Figure 27.69.

3. Now return all records for this table via the Enterprise Manager. As shown in Figure 27.70, the numbering of the EmployeeID column has returned to sequential order.

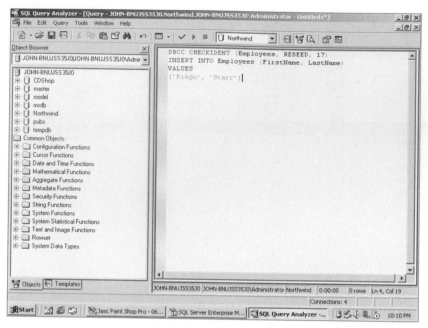

FIGURE 27.68 *Utilizing the* DBCC CHECKIDENT *command will reset the auto-numbering in your table.*

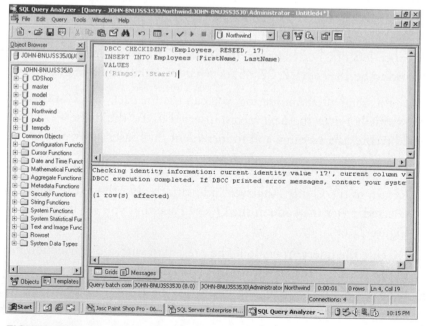

FIGURE 27.69 *Note the specific reference to checking the identify information.*

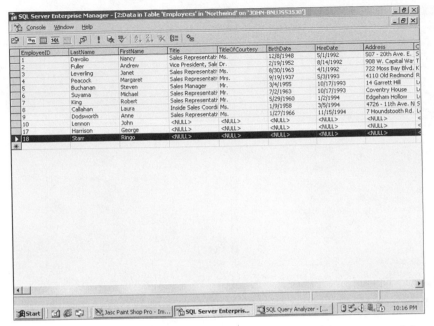

FIGURE 27.70 *The new record is entered with a value of 18 (the next sequential number) in the EmployeeID column.*

Adding Constraints to Your INSERT Statements

By utilizing constraints in your database, you can ensure that the information inserted into your table meets specific requirements. The easy way to do this is via the Enterprise Manager, so take some time now to see how this is done.

1. Select the Employees table of the Northwind sample database. Right-click and select the Design Table option from the drop-down menu that appears.

2. In the Design Table screen that appears, click on the Manage Constraints icon (see Figure 27.71).

FIGURE 27.71 *The Manage Constraints icon.*

3. The Properties dialog box will appear with the Check Constraints tab highlighted, as shown in Figure 27.72.

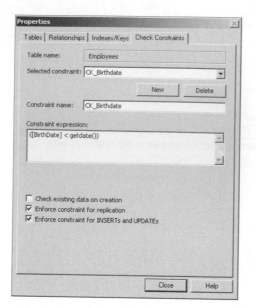

FIGURE 27.72 *You can easily create and modify constraints using the Properties dialog box.*

The various features on the Check Constraints tab are

◆ **Table Name.** This identifies the table to which the constraint will apply.

◆ **Selected Constraint.** You can have several constraints that apply to a table. Use this drop-down menu to select the constraint with which you want to work. (Note that for this table in the Northwind database, there is only one constraint.)

◆ **Constraint Name.** As with all SQL naming conventions, give your constraints names that are indicative of what they refer to.

◆ **Constraint Expression.** This is the essence of the constraint. In this example, the BirthDate field of the Employees table must be less than today's date, which is retrieved utilizing the getdate() function.

◆ **Check Existing Data on Creation, Enforce Constraint for Replication, and Enforce Constraint for INSERTs and UPDATEs.** Finally, the three check boxes at the bottom of the dialog box control how the constraint is applied. Generally, the Enforce Constraint for INSERTs and UPDATEs option is the most important because it ensures that the constraint will be applied any time your data is manipulated by the INSERT or UPDATE statements.

I'm not going to highlight this particular constraint in action in the Employees table. Suffice it to say that if you attempt to insert a value of 5/1/2010 for the BirthDate field in the Employees table, you will receive an error message because that date is greater than today's date... unless this book has achieved a lifespan that far exceeds my expectations!

TIP

As you will see, utilizing constraints is a great way to avoid programming complicated data integrity checks utilizing IF...THEN statements.

Modifying Your Database Using the UPDATE Statement

Once you have data inserted, you will need to allow it to be updated, either by you (as the database administrator) or by end users or customers. You can easily allow modification of data by utilizing the UPDATE statement.

Get your feet wet with a simple example.

1. If it is not open, go ahead and open the Query Analyzer, making sure it is pointing to the Northwind sample database.

2. In the Query Pane, enter the code exactly as it is shown in Figure 27.73.

3. Execute the query. You should see a confirmation message in the Results Pane.

4. Return to the Enterprise Manager and return all rows for the Employees table. For the Ringo Starr record that you created in the previous section, you should now see the Title and TitleOfCourtesy fields completed, as shown in Figure 27.74.

The UPDATE statement is very easy to use, as you can see from this example. Note, however, that you don't have to limit your updates to just one record. Consider the following example:

```
UPDATE Catalog
SET Price='$12.99'
WHERE Artist="The Beatles" AND Title <> "The White Album"
```

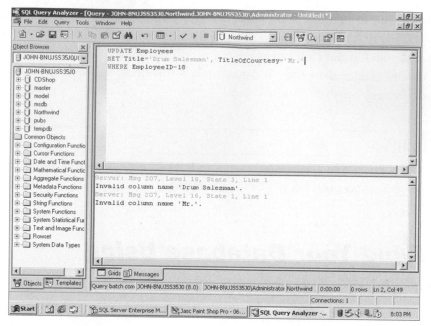

FIGURE 27.73 *The UPDATE statement allows you to modify existing records.*

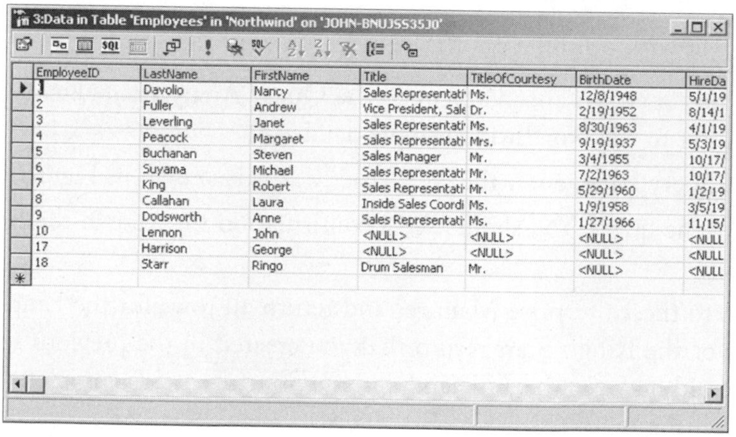

FIGURE 27.74 *The exact record that you specified is updated.*

In this example, all records that have "The Beatles" for a value in the Artist field will have their Price fields updated to $12.99, except for any record in which the Title field is set to "The White Album." If there were multiple rows of data that had "The Beatles" as a value for the Artist field, then the update would be performed multiple times (except for any record that has a Title field value of "The White Album").

Removing Data Using the DELETE Statement

The final basic data-manipulation statement I want to cover in this chapter is the DELETE statement. Its basic syntax is very simple.

```
DELETE
FROM [table_name]
WHERE [some condition…]
```

You can also remove the FROM condition to remove entire tables, such as in the following code:

```
DELETE Employee_Info
```

Take a look at a quick example of this easy (but powerful and potentially dangerous!) statement.

1. Open the Query Analyzer, making sure it is pointing to the Northwind sample database.

2. Enter the code exactly as shown in Figure 27.75.

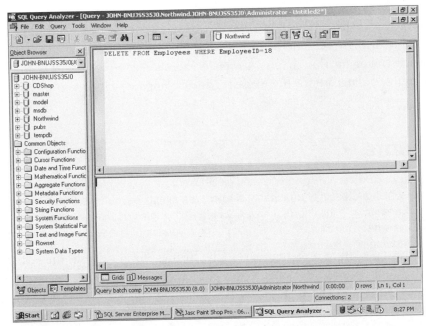

FIGURE 27.75 *Use the DELETE statement with caution because it (obviously) removes information from your database!*

3. Execute the query. You should see a confirmation message in the Results Pane.

4. If you return all rows in the Employees table, you will see that the record with EmployeeID 18 has been removed.

That's about all there is to it. Again, use the DELETE statement with caution because once it's gone, it's gone!

Summary

This chapter covered several issues. First you were presented with a general overview of the functionality and ease of use of the Query Analyzer. You were introduced to the general navigation scheme, including the individual toolbars, menu options, and nomenclature that are used within the application (including the Object Browser, the Query Pane, and the Results Pane). You also were introduced to some of the advanced administration functionality that is presented in the Query Analyzer (such as the Execution Plan), and how you can use this information to fine-tune and manage your query results.

Two other major topics were presented in this chapter as well. First you were presented with a solid overview of the four basic data-manipulation statements available in T-SQL (the SQL Server 2000 version of SQL). You were also shown how to work with these statements in both the Enterprise Manager and the Query Analyzer. But again, this chapter was really intended as a primer for how you will Web-enable a database for the MuseToMusic company, which you will do in the next chapter.

 NOTE

SQL Server 2000 is a very complicated piece of software, and many issues (not the least of which are security and administration) are simply beyond the scope of this book. However, with the information you've learned in this and the previous chapters, as well as what you will learn in the next chapter, you should be well on your way to understanding how you might utilize SQL Server to take your Web site functionality to an entirely new level. If you've been following along with this project and you understand what has been presented, I strongly encourage you to continue to explore the power of SQL Server and the tremendous benefits it can bring to your Web design.

Chapter 28

Web-Enabling Your SQL Server 2000 Database

Despite the bust in the dot com boom, the Internet is as ubiquitous (if not more so) in today's world as it has ever been. However, as exciting as Internet technology is, it is not without its share of very serious concerns for developers, consumers, and organizations (large or small). Ever-present security concerns notwithstanding, there can be significant development issues with taking your data to the Web—not just with SQL Server, but with any application. As I said earlier, although the functionality to accomplish this task (that is, Web-enabling your data) is included in the products you use, it is not always easy to grasp, especially if your Web development skills and experience lean more toward the novice side.

But fear not! The purpose of this chapter is not to turn you into a Web developer; rather, I want to introduce you to some of the important Web concepts and tools that are included with SQL Server 2000 or that you can utilize in conjunction with it. Specifically, I will introduce you to the following topics in this chapter:

◆ First, you will learn how to install, configure, and administer the IIS (*Internet Information Services*) component of Windows. IIS will serve as the foundation for your Web-enabling of SQL Server data, as well as the delivery mechanism for the Web sites you create.

◆ Next, I will present you with an older (but still quite viable) version of Active Server Pages—ASP 3.0. Prior to the .NET framework, ASP 3.0 was one of the most widely used Web development platforms in the industry. Given the complexity and general transition issues from one technology to another, ASP 3.0 continues to be an important Microsoft Web technology despite the move to the .NET platform. Additionally, ASP 3.0, although suffering from limitations which have since been resolved in the .NET platform, is easy to learn and can adequately serve as a quick way to Web-enable some or all of your SQL Server information.

◆ Finally, I will present you with perhaps one of the biggest buzzwords in the industry today—XML. Although it is not really a Web technology per se, XML is often utilized in conjunction with traditional HTML and can be used (powerfully) with IIS and SQL Server.

NOTE

In reading the list of topics you'll work with in this chapter, you might wonder why I am focusing on ASP 3.0 rather than the new .NET platform. In this case the answer is simple: .NET is a complex new development environment to say the least, and it is well beyond the scope of this book. By presenting this additional project on SQL Server, my intention is to show you another level of functionality in your HTML and Web development. I also want to give you a taste of what is possible with some additional software (most notably, SQL Server) and associated technologies (such as XML). Despite the fact that ASP.NET (or ASP 4.0) is the current version, you should still feel comfortable working with and learning from ASP 3.0. Due to the complexity and, quite frankly, the slow acceptance of the still-maturing .NET development platform, ASP 3.0 will remain a viable method of Web-enabling your data.

Installing Internet Information Services (IIS)

More than just a Web server, IIS is really a collection of services aimed at providing full Internet capability to your data, including a wide array of security, encryption, and protocol options. Although a full discussion of the administration and configuration of IIS is beyond the scope and purpose of this book, it is worthwhile (and necessary) for you to have a general overview of the functionality and use of IIS.

 TIP

Even if you aren't the slightest bit interested in SQL, the information about IIS may prove useful as you work with HTML and your Web sites in general. If you've been reading this book in sequential order, you know that I have talked about (and used) IIS extensively as my own Web development environment. If you are using Windows 2000 or XP (and I'm assuming you probably are), I would urge you to consider learning more about IIS because it really does make a nice tool for developing and testing your Web sites (again, regardless of whether or not they use SQL, ASP, or other advanced functionality).

NOTE

Keep in mind that this chapter is intended as a quick primer (as is the entire SQL Server project) on Web-enabling a database. Extensive development and proper long-term administration of SQL Server and IIS can be quite complex. However, if you are interested in taking your HTML development to the next level, I encourage you to further explore these technologies and the exciting new directions they are taking on (literally) a daily basis.

 CAUTION

As was mentioned in earlier chapter, use caution if you are utilizing IIS on a computer that has an "always connected" status to the Web, such as via a cable or other high-speed connection. For these types of machines, you might want to consider a cable modem router or software firewall to guard against outside attacks. You should also stay current on all Windows (and other) security patches, by running Windows Update on at least a monthly basis. Both of these tips apply to your computer security in general, by the way, so it's something to definitely keep in mind.

IIS might already be installed on your development computer. Before you go any further, you should check to see whether IIS is installed. If it isn't, go ahead and install it now.

To check to see whether IIS is installed:

1. From the Start menu, select Programs, Administrative Tools.
2. If you see Internet Services Manager in the list of tools, then IIS is installed and ready for use.

To install IIS:

1. From the Start menu, select Control Panel.
2. Click on Add/Remove Programs.
3. Click on Add/Remove Windows Components.
4. In the Windows Components Wizard dialog box (see Figure 28.1), check the Internet Information Services (IIS) option. You will see a short description of the service in this dialog box. For more detailed information, including what will be installed, click on the Details button (also illustrated in Figure 28.1).

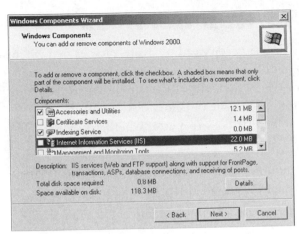

FIGURE 28.1 *You can install IIS and other Windows components via the Windows Components Wizard.*

5. Click on Next to begin the installation process. You might be asked to reboot your computer to complete the installation.

After you have installed IIS, select Programs, Administrative Tools, Internet Services Manager from the Start menu. Your screen should look similar to Figure 28.2.

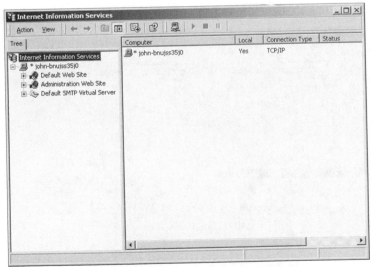

FIGURE 28.2 *The Internet Information Services snap-in administrative tool. I'll discuss how to administer IIS through this screen a bit later in the chapter.*

Administering IIS Web Services

Before you create an actual Web site, you need to create a folder that will become the Web site directory. You might already have a folder on your computer in which you've placed Web pages you've created with, for example, Microsoft FrontPage. You could turn that folder into a Web site directory if you want. However, for this example, just create a new folder. (It doesn't matter whether it has any files in it for this example.)

1. Navigate to your computer's C drive and expand the Inetpub directory, which was created when you installed IIS.

2. In the wwwroot folder, create a new folder and call it HTML_PP.

Now that you have created the basic folder, you can turn it into a Web site via the Internet Services Manager snap-in.

1. If it's not already open, go ahead and open the IIS snap-in tool. From the Start menu, select Programs, Administrative Tools, Internet Services Manager.

2. Right-click on Default Web Site and select New, Site, as shown in Figure 28.3. The first screen of the Web Site Creation Wizard will appear, as shown in Figure 28.4.

3. Click on Next to begin the site creation process.

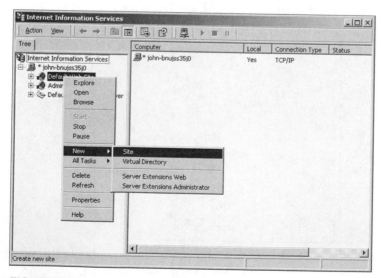

FIGURE 28.3 *Preparing to create a new Web site in the Internet Services Manager snap-in.*

FIGURE 28.4 *The Web Site Creation Wizard offers the quick and dirty method of creating a Web site.*

4. In the next screen, you are asked to enter a description of the Web site. For this example, just enter **HTML_Test** and click on Next.

5. The next screen asks you for IP address and port settings. In the first option, select 127.0.0.1. Leave everything else as it appears and click on Next.

6. Then you are asked to navigate to the Web site home directory. As shown in Figure 28.5, click on the Browse button and navigate to the HTML_PP folder you created earlier. The path to this folder should be C:\Inetpub\wwwroot\HTML_PP.

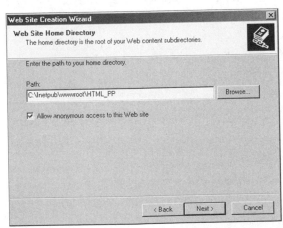

FIGURE 28.5 *Enter the path to your home directory—or in this case, the HTML_PP folder you just created.*

7. Click on Next. In the next screen, leave the default permission settings as they are.

8. Click on Finish at the final step of the Wizard. You should now see HTML_Test showing as an active Web site.

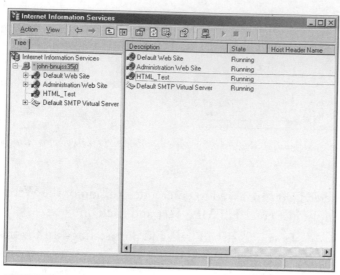

FIGURE 28.6 *Remember that the description (HTML_Test) you enter in the Web Site Creation Wizard is what shows in the Internet Services Manager—not the actual name of the home directory (HTML_PP).*

9. To do a final check on the status of IIS, you should make sure the service is running, along with the World Wide Web Publishing Service. From the Start menu, select Programs, Administrative Tools, Computer Management.

10. Expand the Services and Applications node and click on Services.

11. Scroll through the list of services until you come to IIS Admin Service. The status should be Started, as shown in Figure 28.7. If for some reason it isn't, right-click on IIS Admin Service and select either Start or Restart from the drop-down menu. (I'll talk more about administering IIS a bit later in this chapter.)

12. Scroll down a bit further in the list of services until you see World Wide Web Publishing Service. Check to make sure it is running; if it isn't, follow the same steps as you did for the IIS Admin Service.

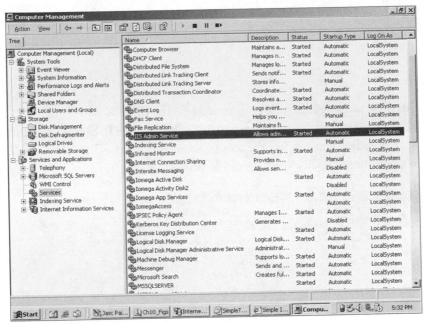

FIGURE 28.7 *Checking the status of IIS and related services via the Computer Management console.*

Testing Your Web Site

Now that you've created a Web site, you need to create a simple Web page to test it and ensure that the IIS is functioning as it should.

If you've created Web pages, you can move them into the HTML_PP site folder and then try accessing them in your Web browser by typing in **http://localhost/HTML_PP/***name_of_your_page*.

> **TIP**
>
> You can also type in 127.0.0.1/HTML_PP/name_of_your_page. Remember that localhost and 127.0.0.1 are the same thing.

If you haven't created a Web page, take a few moments and create a simple Web page using Notepad. The code for this page follows.

```
<HTML>
<TITLE>Simple IIS Test</TITLE>
<BODY>
```

```
<b>This is a test…</b>
<p>
<i>…of the IIS installation and configuration, utilizing the HTML_PP Web site.</i>
</BODY>
</HTML>
```

Save this page as SimpleTest.html in your HTML_PP Web site folder. Then open your Web browser and type **http://127.0.0.1/HTML_PP/SimpleTest.html** (or, as indicated earlier, you can use the localhost term instead of 127.0.0.1: again, they are the same thing). Your screen should look like Figure 28.8.

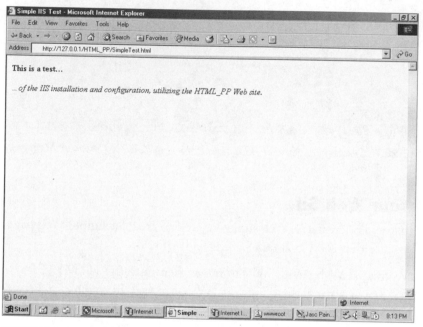

FIGURE 28.8 *Confirming your IIS installation and configuration are working via a simple test Web page.*

General IIS Administration Issues

As I said at the beginning of this chapter, this is not a book about IIS administration or even Windows administration. However, if you want to take the power of SQL Server to another level (and because the Web is so pervasive in our lives), it would behoove you to understand the built-in, essential Windows component that just happens to be IIS.

For right now, since you've installed IIS, you should at least have a general understanding of some of the basic configuration issues. That is the point of this section, so take a moment now and see what the Internet Services Manager snap-in has to offer.

Assigning Specific Web Site Permissions

Because Web site security and general information security are such critical issues in today's world, it makes sense to start the discussion of IIS administration with a look at the Permissions Wizard, which you can use to set permission and security levels for individual Web sites that are administered by IIS.

I want to begin the discussion by setting Web site permissions and taking a look at the newly created HTML_PP Web site.

1. Open the Internet Information Services snap-in, navigate to HTML_PP (or HTML_Test, depending on the description you entered when you created the site), right-click on it, and select All Tasks, Permissions Wizard (see Figure 28.9).

2. Click on Next to move from the opening screen to the Security Settings step. For this example, leave the default setting of Inherit All Security Settings checked and click on Next. If you are an administrator of the machine you are working on, you will see the security message that administrators have full access to files. Leave the default setting checked and click on Next. Your screen should look like Figure 28.10.

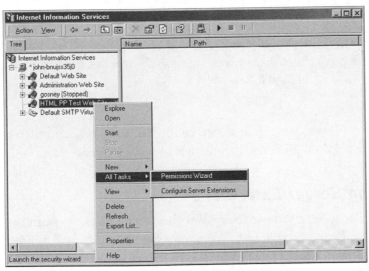

FIGURE 28.9 *Accessing the Web site Permissions Wizard.*

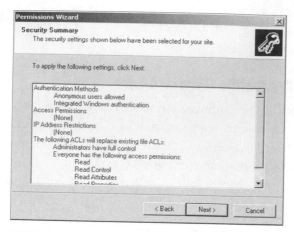

FIGURE 28.10 *Reviewing the security settings prior to applying them to your Web site.*

3. Because you are assigning administrative permission settings to this site, it is very loose in its security structure. (For example, there are no access or IP address restrictions, anonymous access is allowed, everyone has both read and execute permissions, and so on.) If you chose to set specific permission settings in Step 2, you could have made this a more secure site.

 CAUTION

As I noted at the beginning of the chapter, if you are working with IIS on a machine with an "always on" connection status to the Web, you should seriously consider taking some stringent security precautions. As noted in step 3 here, everyone has both read and execute permissions. Obviously, this could lead to some bad situations if a hacker or other mischievous intruder wanted to exploit these permissions to do damage to your machine or the information it contains.

4. Click on Next to see the final step confirmation screen, and then click on Finish to complete the Permissions Wizard process.

Configuring Server Extensions

In direct relation to assigning specific Web site permissions, you can set server extensions so you can create specific Windows groups (such as Administrators, Authors, and Browsers) that have various levels of access on the Web server.

1. As you did in the previous section, right-click on the HTML_Test Web site displayed in the Internet Information Services snap-in. Then select All Tasks, Configure Server Extensions.

2. Click on Next. On the next step of the Wizard, click on the What Permissions Do Users in Each Group Have? button to see a general overview of these permissions levels, as illustrated in Figure 28.11.

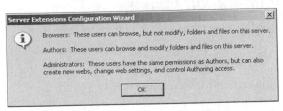

FIGURE 28.11 *Reviewing the general permission levels for the server extensions.*

3. Click on OK to close this dialog box, and then click on Next to view the Access Control step of the Wizard. As you can see in Figure 28.12, you can assign specific Windows groups or user accounts to have administrative rights to the Web server.

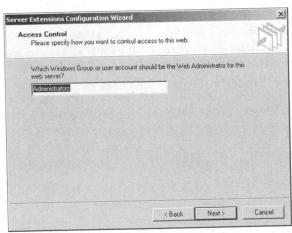

FIGURE 28.12 *Indicating specific Windows groups or users who will have administrative rights.*

4. Leave this option as Administrators for now and click on Next. You should be presented with options to configure the mail server. Note that you can enter specific e-mail addresses for different functionalities of the Web site, such as specifying the e-mail address that should receive problem requests from users.

5. Click on Next to reach the final stage of the Wizard. Depending on the number of files in your Web server, the configuration process can take quite a long time. If you want, click on Finish to apply the settings. Because you really haven't made any changes, you can click on Cancel—I just wanted to show you this Wizard's functionality.

General Web Site Configuration Issues

IIS allows you to assign and configure several individual properties for your Web sites. From the delivery of custom error messages to general directory security, the Properties configuration abilities provide you with powerful, easy-to-use tools to batten down the hatches on your individual Web sites.

To repeat my broken-record refrain, this book is not about IIS and Web development; however, as with other issues presented here, you should become familiar with what is possible with the Web site properties. So take some time to investigate the specific properties you can set for the HTML_PP Web site.

 TIP

Microsoft has taken quite a bit of heat over the "inherent" security problems in IIS, at least as it is presented out of the box. I'm sure you have noticed that, upon initial configuration, there are lots of potential security holes in the initial values that are set in IIS. To help address these issues, Microsoft has released a tool (IIS Lockdown Tool) that examines what is currently in place regarding your IIS installation, and then makes changes to tighten up the security level. While this is not a substitute for the other security warnings in this chapter (routers, firewall, running Windows Update), it could (should) be used in conjunction with these other tools to help keep your computer running IIS as securely as possible. For more information on the IIS Lockdown Tool, see http://www.Microsoft.com/technet/treeview/default.asp?url=/technet/security/tools/tools/locktool.asp.

1. In the Internet Services Manager snap-in, select the HTML_PP Web site, right-click on it, and select Properties, as shown in Figure 28.13.

2. The HTML_PP Properties dialog box will be displayed, along with many tabs (such as Directory Security and HTTP Headers) that allow you to configure and customize specific functionality of the Web site, as shown in Figure 28.14. You can (and should) take time at some point to

review the options on each tab, but I have presented a brief overview of the functionalities in the following list.

◆ **Directory Security.** On this tab you can set anonymous access and authentication control, provide for specific IP address and domain name restrictions, and configure secure communications (such as SSL and server certificates).

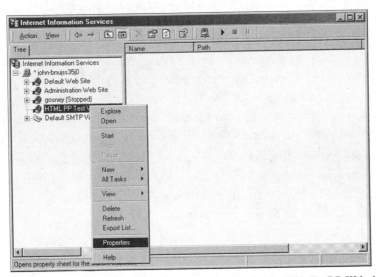

FIGURE 28.13 *Accessing the specific properties for the HTML_PP Web site.*

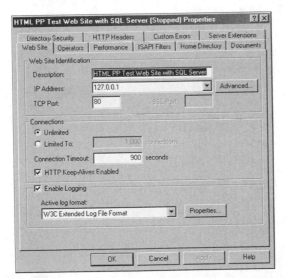

FIGURE 28.14 *The various tabs of the HTML_PP Web site properties.*

◆ **HTTP Headers.** Use this tab to assign specific content expiration dates, create customized HTTP headers to further streamline your site content, provide content ratings so users know the type of content your site provides, and configure individual MIME types your Web server can distribute to Web browsers.

◆ **Custom Errors.** This very useful feature allows you to set specific Web pages and associated messages that will be displayed when an error occurs on your site. For example, instead of just presenting a user with an Unauthorized Access error message, you can edit the message to provide specific help for why they cannot log in, as well as contact information (perhaps a phone number and e-mail address) for someone they can call for help. The tab is particularly neat because it allows you to edit error messages and it gives you a description of what each error is, as well as its associated error code (see Figure 28.15).

◆ **Server Extensions.** I discussed this option in the previous section. You can access it by selecting a specific Web site in the Internet Services Manager snap-in, and then right-clicking and selecting All Tasks, Configure Server Extensions.

◆ **Web Site.** This tab provides for general configuration of the Web site identification (IP address, TCP port, and so on), the number of concurrent connections to the site, and enabling logging.

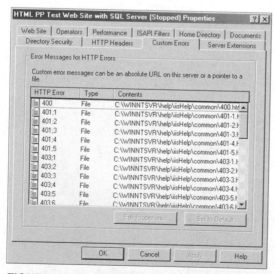

FIGURE 28.15 *The Custom Errors tab allows you to provide site visitors with far more useful information regarding specific errors they might encounter on your site.*

◆ **Operators.** Just as you do in the Web Server Extensions configuration, you can assign specific operator privileges to specific Windows user accounts. Use this tab to add and edit such accounts.

◆ **Performance.** You can set general performance-tuning options with this tab, including bandwidth and process throttling to better maximize available resources.

◆ **ISAPI Filters.** ISAPI filters allow for additional Web site functionality and are beyond the scope of this discussion. Nevertheless, if you need to work with them, you can add specific filters to your Web site on this tab.

◆ **Home Directory.** Use this tab to set general information about the home directory for the site, including the local path (for the HTML_Test site, it should be c:\Inetpub\wwwroot\HTML_Test), the starting-point Web page, permission settings, and so on. This is the path you put in when you created the Web site earlier in the chapter.

◆ **Documents.** Finally, the Documents tab allows you to specify which types of documents will be served (and thus accessible) by your Web site. For example, you might include .htm, .asp, and .aspx (for the .NET framework) in this list of accessible documents. You should leave the Enable Default Document option checked on this tab—it is checked by default when you create a new site (see Figure 28.16).

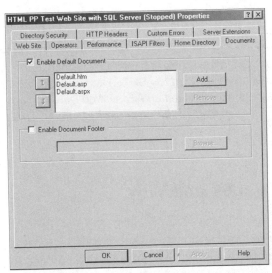

FIGURE 28.16 *Leave the Enable Default Document option checked.*

Working with Active Server Pages 3.0

Prior to the introduction of the .NET framework, ASP 3.0 was the prime method of Web-enabling database (Access and SQL Server) information, as well as providing other advanced Web functionality to otherwise static HTML pages. Deceptively simple to use and with native support in a variety of popular Web development applications such as FrontPage, ASP (in its pre-.NET incarnations) allowed a new level of Web development.

ASP was so widely adopted, in fact, that the transition from ASP 3.0 to ASP.NET (or ASP 4.0) has been a slow process, particularly for organizations with extensive 3.0 applications, because the general framework of the .NET platform is radically different than ASP 3.0.

Despite a bevy of problems, including the infamous "spaghetti code" issue (code that is overly long and convoluted), ASP 3.0 continues to be a viable option for Web-enabling SQL Server data. Of course, the Microsoft PR juggernaut would have you think otherwise—that continuing to use 3.0 is just short of blasphemy. But if you want to take your SQL Server data to the Web quickly, then 3.0 might be the way to go.

This section will provide a brief look at ASP 3.0 and what is involved in using it, and will then provide a quick example of Web-enabling SQL Server data via an ASP Web page.

 NOTE

A full discussion of ASP 3.0 is far beyond the scope and intent of this book. However, there are literally hundreds of great books devoted to ASP 3.0 and its associated components. Good places to start are *ASP 3.0 Fast and Easy Web Development* (Premier Press, 2000) and *ASP Programming for the Absolute Beginner* (Premier Press, 2002).

What Are Active Server Pages and Why Should You Use Them?

In the old days, it was difficult to create interactive Web pages that allowed users to submit information and get an immediate response, for example. Moreover, getting a Web page to interact with a back-end database was not for the novice or the weak of heart. So when Microsoft introduced ASP in 1996, suddenly developers of all kinds (not just Web developers) could harness the ever-growing power and general "Hey, isn't this cool?!" nature of the Web to bring a new level of functionality to their information.

In and of itself, ASP is not a programming language; rather, it is a mechanism for integrating scripting languages (such as VBScript and JavaScript) into otherwise static HTML pages. Additionally, ASP provides objects and components that allow extended functionality, such as accessing databases and manipulating files.

Generally, ASP 3.0 uses VBScript (short for Visual Basic Script) as its primary scripting language. For a beginner, VBScript is very easy to learn and offers significant ability to enhance a Web site and the data that interacts with it. However, for the seasoned programmer, the available functions in VBScript and ASP 3.0 can be very limiting. To get around these limitations, the aforementioned spaghetti code often comes into play, resulting in pages that are difficult to read and difficult to update or change at a later date, when new functionality is required.

Still, as I said earlier, you can utilize ASP 3.0 to bring your SQL Server data to the Web. Now I want to take you through a few examples of how this can be done. In the process, you will gain a better understanding of IIS, VBScript, ASP, and general Web page/database interaction.

A SQL Server/ASP 3.0 Example

The first step in utilizing a SQL Server database with an ASP Web page is to establish an ODBC connection to the database. I will begin this simple example by establishing an ODBC connection to the CDShop sample database.

 NOTE

The database you see illustrated in the following sections is an example of a database that could be used for a music store (maybe MuseToMusic, as discussed in the first and third projects?). If you are following along with this material and have access to SQL Server (which I'm assuming you do, if you've gotten this far), you can create your own mini-database at this point. If you want to really follow along, you might create it so that it is "music store related" (that is, follows the same structure of the database you see here, and has the same type of information contained within); however, this is an example of how to use ASP 3.0 to Web-enable your data, so it really doesn't matter what type of database you are using—the principles described here will be the same.

1. From the Start Menu, select Control Panel.

2. Click on Administrative Tools, and then click on the Data Sources (ODBC) icon.

3. In the ODBC Data Source Administrator screen, click on the System DSN tab. Your screen should appear similar to Figure 28.17.

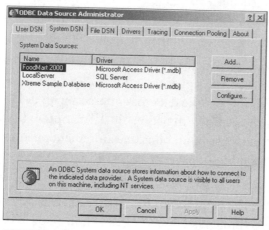

FIGURE 28.17 *The first step in preparing the ODBC connection is to launch the ODBC Data Source Administrator.*

 NOTE

The actual system data source names you see on your own machine will probably vary from what is shown here, of course.

4. Click on the Add button, as shown in Figure 28.17. On the next screen, scroll to the bottom of the list and select the SQL Server option, as shown in Figure 28.18.

5. Click on Finish. You will be presented with the Create a New Data Source to SQL Server screen. You should name the data source something short but descriptive, so it is easy to reference in your code but you still know what it is. Type a brief description of the data source in the Description field. Then select the SQL Server to which you want to connect (see Figure 28.19).

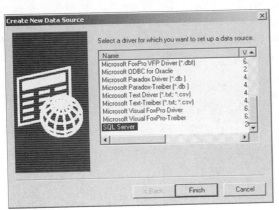

FIGURE 28.18 *If you are not familiar with ODBC, note the wide variety of data sources to which you can create an ODBC connection (including, of course, a Microsoft Access database).*

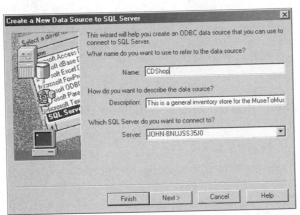

FIGURE 28.19 *Assign a descriptive name as your data source. You will use this name to open the database in ASP.*

 TIP

If you do not see any SQL Server names in the Server drop-down menu shown in Figure 28.19, you can manually enter the name of the SQL Server to which you want to connect. (Again, this entire process assumes you are a system administrator.) The next time you create an ODBC data source, the SQL Server name you entered will appear in the Server drop-down menu.

6. Click on Next to move to the next screen in the data source creation process. For now, leave the login ID authenticity set to Windows NT authentication, as shown in Figure 28.20.

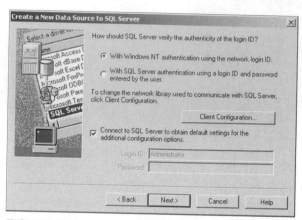

FIGURE 28.20   *SQL Server Authentication uses SQL server accounts (sa), while the Windows NT authentication uses domain user accounts. Unless you specifically created a SQL Server login in Enterprise Manager, leave this option blank.*

7. Click on Next. In this screen, change the default database in the drop-down menu to CDShop. Leave all other options as they are and click on Next.

8. Don't change anything on the last screen; just click on Finish. You will be presented with configuration information for the data source, as shown in Figure 28.21.

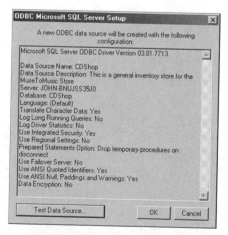

FIGURE 28.21   *All the specifications you established in the Create a New Data Source to SQL Server screens are here for your review.*

9. Click on the Test Data Source button, as shown in Figure 28.21. Assuming you have configured the data source properly, you should be greeted with a message telling you that the test was successful.

10. Click on OK to return to the ODBC Data Source Administrator screen. You should see your new System DSN, CDShop, in the list.

Establishing SQL Server Permissions

Now that you have established a data source, there are a few more steps you must take in the SQL Server Enterprise Manager before you can Web-enable your data using ASP 3.0.

1. Open the SQL Server Enterprise Manager.

2. Expand the Security node, right-click on Logins, and select New Login, as shown in Figure 28.22. The SQL Server Login Properties dialog box will appear.

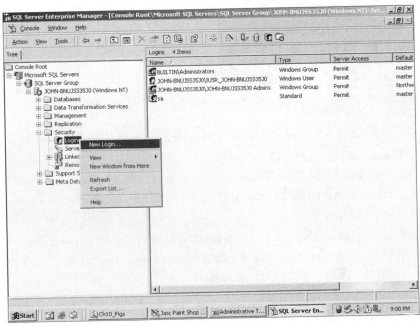

FIGURE 28.22 *To make your SQL Server databases accessible via the Web, you must assign proper permissions.*

3. For this example you want to use Windows authentication with anonymous access, so select your anonymous IUSR account from the list of accounts that appears when you click on the access button (see Figure 28.23). After you do this the Domain field should complete automatically, with Windows Authentication selected. Finally, in the Database field, select CDShop.

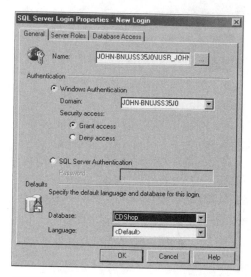

FIGURE 28.23 *Assigning specific login properties to the CDShop database.*

4. Click on the Server Roles tab and select System Administrators.

5. Finally, click on the Database Access tab and select CDShop from the list of databases. The IUSR account will be added as the user, and the public permit database role will be selected automatically, as shown in Figure 28.24.

6. Click on OK. You have now successfully set permissions for the CDShop database. Using the data source name you created, you are now ready to Web-enable this database via ASP 3.0.

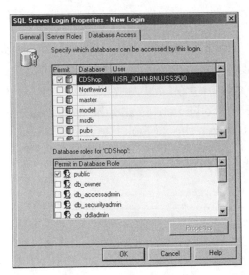

FIGURE 28.24 *Note the different permits you can assign to specific logins.*

Building the ASP 3.0 Data Access Page

It is now time to write the ASP code that will access the CDShop database via a Web page. Open Notepad or another text editor and enter the following code exactly as it appears here.

```
<HTML>
<TITLE>A Sample ASP 3.0 / SQL Server Example </TITLE>
<BODY>
<%
SET TestLoop = Server.CreateObject("ADODB.Recordset")
TestLoop.Open "SELECT * FROM Catalog", "DSN=CDShop"
TestLoop.MoveFirst
DO WHILE NOT TestLoop EOF
Response.Write "<B>" & TestLoop("Artist") & " , " & TestLoop("Title") & "</B>" & "<HR>"
TestLoop.MoveNext
Loop
TestLoop.Close
Set TestLoop=Nothing
%>
</BODY>
</HTML>
```

To test this page, follow these steps:

1. Name the page Test.asp and save it in the HTML_PP Web site folder you created at the beginning of the chapter.

2. Open Internet Explorer and type **http://127.0.0.1/HTML_PP/Test.asp**.

3. Assuming you haven't made any coding errors and the data source is functioning as it should, your screen should look like Figure 28.25.

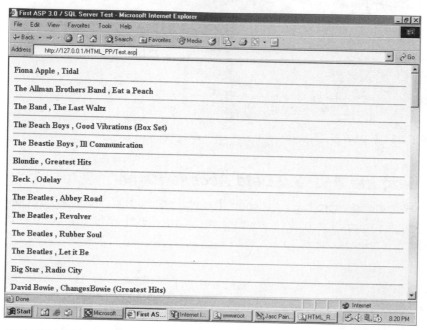

FIGURE 28.25 *The Test.asp page loops through all the first and last names in the Catalog table of the CDShop sample database and displays them on the page.*

Although this is not a book on VBScript, it is worth mentioning some of the basics of what happened in the preceding code sample.

◆ First, an ActiveX Data Object (ADO) connection was established and given the name TestLoop.

```
SET TestLoop = Server.CreateObject("ADODB.Recordset")
```

◆ The next line called this connection and executed a simple SQL SELECT statement. (Note the reference to the CDShop system DSN so the connection knows which data source [and thus, database] to query.)

◆ Next, a simple `DO WHILE` loop was executed. This loop was designed to loop through each record in the returned record set (the data returned via the SQL statement) until the last file is reached. This is signified by the line

```
DO WHILE NOT TestLoop EOF
```

which basically means "do this operation while the `TestLoop` connection has not yet reached the end of the file (EOF)."

◆ For each iteration of the loop, the `Response` object wrote the data returned to the screen. In this case, first and last names of the employees were displayed on the screen. Note that `Artist` and `Title` are the actual field names in the Catalog table of the CDShop database

◆ The loop was repeated until the end of the file was reached. At that point, the `TestLoop` connection was closed.

This is a very simple example, but if you have it working properly on your system, you have achieved some significant goals, including properly installing IIS, properly establishing a system DSN, setting the proper permissions levels on a SQL database so it can be queried via the Web, and using ASP 3.0 for the first time.

SQL Server and XML

XML (*Extensible Markup Language*) remains one of the hot topics in the computing field. Essentially, it allows open, cross-platform sharing of data (or so it promises). XML is often thought of as pure Web technology, but this is not actually true. Although it can be (and often is) used in conjunction with the familiar hypertext transfer protocol (HTTP), XML can (and does) stand on its own apart from the Web.

Although even a somewhat limited discussion of XML is beyond the scope of this book, you should still familiarize yourself with some of the basic syntax issues and especially how it is natively supported in SQL Server. (XML also plays a large role in the foundations of the .NET infrastructure.)

The best way to illustrate this is with an example of how SQL Server supports XML.

1. From the Start menu, select Programs, Microsoft SQL Server, Configure SQL XML Support in IIS. The familiar IIS Management snap-in will appear; however, note in Figure 28.26 that you are working with a virtual directory.

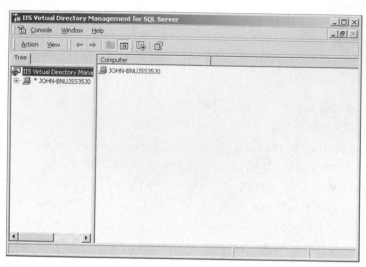

FIGURE 28.26 *Virtual directories allow you a more secure method of interacting with your back-end data source.*

2. Expand the Server node, select Default Web Site, and right-click on it. From the drop-down menu that appears select New, Virtual Directory, as shown in Figure 28.27.

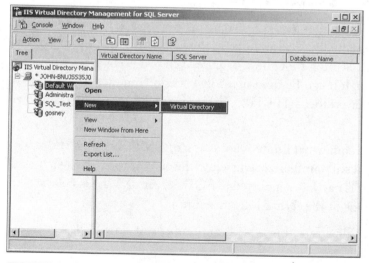

FIGURE 28.27 *Preparing to create the virtual directory under the Default Web site.*

3. In the screen that appears, make sure the General tab is selected. In the space provided for a virtual directory name, enter **HTML_PP**. In the local path section of the screen, navigate to the HTML_PP folder you created earlier in this chapter. The path should be similar to C:\Inetpub\wwwroot\HTML_PP.

4. Click on the Security tab and select the Use Windows Integrated Authentication method of authentication. As I noted in an earlier example, you can use specific credentials for which you can assign specific user permission accounts in SQL Server. However, for this example, you'll just use simple anonymous access via the IUSR account, which you already added to the CDShop database in a previous example.

5. Next, click on the Data Source tab. Select the name of your SQL Server in the first box. (Select Local if that is the only option in the list.) In the Database section, select CDShop from the drop-down menu.

6. Now click on the Settings tab and make sure the first two options are selected, as shown in Figure 28.28.

7. Click on Apply. You will return to the IIS Management snap-in. You should see your virtual directory in the right pane of the window, as shown in Figure 28.29.

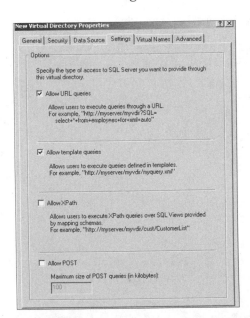

FIGURE 28.28 *Each of these options can be utilized via XML data access in SQL Server.*

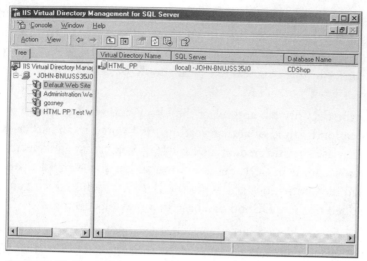

FIGURE 28.29 *Select the virtual directory in question, and then scroll to the right to see specific information or permissions that are assigned to it.*

8. You are now ready to try out your XML access within Internet Explorer. Open IE and enter **http://localhost/HTML_PP?sql=SELECT Artist from Catalog for xml auto &root=ID**. Your screen should look like Figure 28.30.

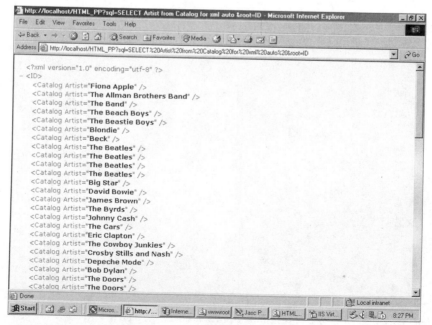

FIGURE 28.30 *Your first XML data retrieval via SQL Server.*

If you receive errors, especially those indicating that you may not have permission to execute the query or access the virtual directory you have created, follow these steps:

◆ First check to make sure the properties of the SQL_PP virtual directory you created within the IIS Manager are set properly. (Select the name of the directory, right-click on it, and select Properties.) When the Properties dialog box opens for the SQL_PP directory, click on the Security tab and make sure you have enabled Windows authentication, as shown in Figure 28.31.

◆ In the SQL Server Enterprise Manager, make sure you have established the correct permissions for the CDShop database. You can follow the directions in the "Establishing SQL Server Permissions" section to make sure you establish (for this example) the IUSR anonymous login for the CDShop database. (If you've already worked through that section and had success with the ASP 3.0 example, then it should be fine.)

◆ Finally, make sure you have entered the URL exactly as shown.

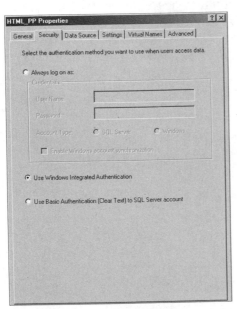

FIGURE 28.31 *Note the different types of authentication that are possible.*

Summary

Web-enabling your data is serious business in terms of what it can bring to your company as well as the significant technical administration issues. With regard to the second point, this chapter has only scratched the surface in showing you the configuration possibilities with some powerful software tools, most notably Internet Information Services and SQL Server. Although this chapter showed you how to configure these tools quickly and how (via the ASP and XML code examples) you can integrate SQL data with the Web, you should still use extreme caution before you work with either of these tools with live, potentially sensitive data. As is evident in the news nearly every day, unauthorized attacks on unprotected Web servers (and database servers) can lead to, at best, embarrassment to the administrators of a company and, at worst, loss or corruption of critical data (not to mention potentially costing the people who administer the technology their jobs). All of this is not meant to dissuade you from exploring and learning more about these powerful tools and the benefits they can bring to your Web site design. However, keep in mind the complexity of these software applications and the power they contain—and how that power can be corrupted if it is put into the wrong hands.

PART III

Appendix

Appendix A

Fundamentals of Process Planning and Database Design

Planning. Depending on what side of the project fence you sit on, this word is either a blessing or a curse. If you are the type of person who likes to sit down and start working (as is the case with many programmers), then you might be put off—indeed, maybe even offended—by the concept of a plan. Although you might appreciate and even welcome the idea that a logical plan will lead to a functioning product, you don't want to be burdened by extensive paperwork and meetings or terms like "stakeholders," "change control management," or "business continuity plan."

However, if you are a business manager (many IT managers and developers are asked to play this role too), then you will recognize immediately the value of a well-designed plan, which can save you many headaches and resources (both in manpower and time) when you need to make changes later in the project (either pre- or post-implementation).

The good news is that successful database design and planning, and how they carry over to an entire application or project design and planning, don't have to be difficult or time-consuming. However, it is absolutely critical that you consider both of these important issues before you commit lots of manpower or money to any database-centered project.

Before you start getting heavily involved in your application development, you should think about a central question: Does the application I'm developing drive a process, or does the process drive my application development? Generally speaking, if you answer this question by stating that your solution is being used to facilitate a process (and not vice versa), then you are in good shape. Although there might be situations in which an IT solution emerges before a defined business process, this should be the exception rather than the rule. Why? Because if this is the case, it is a clear warning that the overriding business goals and objectives are not well defined, and no IT solution—no matter how elegantly designed—will remedy this situation. Therefore, a successful plan becomes even more critical to your ultimate success.

Developing a Process Plan

As I've said, a functional, useful project plan doesn't have to be difficult or overly time-consuming as long as you recognize and address some central points before you dive headfirst into your database project. The following several sections detail such a process plan (or process template, as I like to call it).

> **TIP**
>
> There are several project/process management software applications on the market. Certainly, one of the most useful and popular is Microsoft Project. In addition to offering functionality that integrates with project management methodology and terminology, Project integrates with other applications in the Office suite. You can even Web-enable many of its features; for example, you can take a project timeline or project chart and save it as a Web page, complete with hyperlinks and other functionality.

A typical application development template or process template will consist of the components described in the individual sections of this chapter.

Identifying the Work to be Performed

This opening section of your plan should outline the following information:

◆ **What needs to be done?** This can be a general description of work to be performed, individuals requesting the work, general project background, and so on. It does not have to be overly specific because the goal is not to provide the history of the company or the evolution of the project. However, be sure to provide enough details that this early section can serve as a kind of project preamble, keeping everyone focused on the reason for developing the application in the first place. (This will be an important goal as you get deeper into the development process.)

◆ **Who will develop the application?** This should be a listing of all the developers charged with building the application.

◆ **Who are the project stakeholders?** This section should describe the individuals or groups who have a stake in seeing the project carried to a successful completion. Although you will have listed the IT development team when you answered the question of who will develop the application, it is critical you consider the IT team and developers as central stakeholders.

Again, this section should clearly and concisely define the history and reasons for the project, the people who will be charged with completing the work, and the project stakeholders.

Statement of Current Situation

Similar in concept to what you will define in the first section of your plan, the statement of current situation describes the business' need to have an IT solution implemented. You need to address two basic questions here.

◆ **Where will the system be implemented?** On what server/physical location will the system be developed? What issues (geographical location, cost, available resources, and so on) need to be considered so that the physical location of the application (in regard to both hardware and traditional physical constraints, such as office, resources, and so on) does not hinder the success of the project?

◆ **Why will the system be implemented?** This section should provide a general rationale for developing the system. It can build on the project history that you outlined in the first section of the process template. Why does a system need to be developed, as opposed to continuing with the status quo or using, for example, a paper-based, non-electronic system?

The intent here is to ensure that you, as a system developer or IT manager, are not reinventing the wheel with existing systems, and that you are not over-complicating a process that could easily (and just as effectively) be accomplished without large-scale system development.

Defining the Requirements

Too many IT projects, both large and small, fail to ask what might seem like an obvious question: What does the system have to do to be considered a success?

And how does it need to do it? This section of your plan should answer the following requirement definitions:

- **What are the *functional* requirements of the system?** The bread and butter of your process plan, this section should list all major functionalities that the system must facilitate. Note that I used the phrase "major functionality." In this section you can say, for example, that a system needs to facilitate group scheduling (as opposed to going into minute detail, such as saying that the system must track Mr. Jones' schedule in conjunction with Mr. Smith's calendar, but only on Tuesdays and Thursdays). I am not discounting this type of functional planning, but you can address it in your system process flowchart, which I will describe in a later section of the template.

- **What are the *performance* requirements of the system?** This section should answer the question of speed, again at a general level. How quickly must system information be obtained? What processes are dependent on the system processes? This might be more of an issue in certain systems because some users might not have a problem with waiting until the next morning for the results of a process that runs overnight. However, this time delay might be unacceptable in other systems (or other business processes), so speed is critical.

- **What are the *informational* requirements of the system?** What unique information will the system store and/or manipulate?

- **What are the *maintainability* requirements of the system?** This section should address such issues as how the system workload will be verified and analyzed? Who will be responsible for maintaining the system on a regular basis (in other words, archiving data, running reports, and so on)?

 CAUTION

Do not underestimate the importance of this section. Although I have mentioned that you can be somewhat general in your wording, you should not interpret this to say that you don't have to be complete in your descriptions. You should clearly identify all of these requirements before you begin any work, especially with regard to how they will influence or impact other business processes.

Pre-Implementation Change Management

If the current process needs to be altered in any way prior to system development, this section should describe the changes required and the methods for facilitating these changes. This is another critical early planning section, and it should help you uncover or identify existing business processes that are dependent on (or that can potentially benefit from) the development of the new system.

Vendor Requirements

By vendor requirements, I am referring specifically to any software or hardware outside of the standard application development toolset that will be integrated into the system. For example, if part of your solution is Web-based, and you want to utilize a third-party ActiveX control, what specific requirements does such a control have? Specific requirements can range from general documentation, to how the component functions, to security measures that must be implemented to ensure that the component functions properly.

◆ **What are the specific vendor requirements?** If any third-party component or software (such as development tools, browsers, or plug-ins outside of the regular development platform) is used within the system, list the component, a brief description of it, and relevant technical contact information for that component (such as the company telephone number, fax number, contact person, and knowledge base articles that reference the component).

◆ **With what regulations, policies, and procedures must the final application comply?** Certain applications might require compliance with specific university, government, or federal regulations. (For example, an application used to store data for the FDA might require the ability to print specific data reports on a regular basis.) If so, what are those requirements and how will the system functionality allow for compliance?

Design (Logical and Physical)

In this section your project plan should include the typical programming flow-charts that clearly outline and describe both general and specific system process and requirements. (You'll recall from the "Defining the Requirements" section that I mentioned there would be a place for the details—this is the section.)

◆ **System overview diagram.** This should include a typical system flow-chart that outlines all specific processes

◆ **Functional overview of the system.** What is the system's software inventory? In other words, you should list all software, including the operating system, database engine, scripting language, and so on, that comprises the system.

◆ **Data description.** What kind of data is the system collecting and storing? Is the data numeric or text? Is the system storing images? This section should define, concisely yet as completely as possible, the types of information the system will store and manipulate.

System Security

Security is a critical topic, even more so in our post-9/11 world. That said, you should consider security from the beginning of your project development. Too often, developers (even experienced ones) think security is an issue that can wait until a system is live (in other words, when it is in production and vulnerable to attack). Of course, in reality the time to begin thinking about and planning for security is early in the development process, so that your security issues are properly integrated from the beginning with all system processes. Some issues to consider follow.

◆ **What types of security must the system employ?** This should describe the security model for the system in general. Who has access? How is additional access granted? Who is the administrator for access rights?

◆ **What is the system's security structure?** What type of security mechanisms does the system employ (in other words, encryption certificates, biometric devices, and so on)?

Documenting the System Code

Put simply, an effective, well-designed system is a well-documented system. For many programmers and developers, writing system documentation is akin to having each hair on their body individually removed with a pair of tweezers—it just isn't a task they relish. Still, it is important on so many levels to have properly documented system code. Because personnel changes inevitably occur in any organization, you do not want to be suddenly responsible for a system you didn't design and that has no documentation. Take time to document your system code—you won't regret it.

Testing the System

Although there are developers who like to do things on the fly, it is the foolish developer who puts a system into production without proper testing (or worse, who makes post-implementation changes to a production system without proper testing—more on that point later).

Although effective system trainers are an invaluable commodity to any organization (in terms of presenting the training and developing it), they usually come at a price. Regardless of whether you have someone develop your system training or you do it yourself, you should consider the following issues with regard to training:

♦ How many beta cycles will be performed?

♦ How will test results be analyzed?

♦ How will the actual testing be conducted? (This includes the use of focus groups to gather input prior to testing and other pre-implementation issues.)

♦ How will results of testing be documented for use in future system development and/or post-implementation change control?

Operational Support

Closely related to training (which will be described later in this chapter), you need to consider in your process plan how you will support the system once it is in production. Again, the support resources you have at your disposal might vary tremendously depending on the size of your organization. Perhaps you work for a global company that has a tiered support help desk, with a centralized phone support desk, online support, and so on. Or maybe you are at the other end of the spectrum, where you (and perhaps one other person) are the sole support team. (If this is you, fear not—you are not alone!) Whatever support situation you find yourself in, you need to consider the following operational support issues:

♦ **User manuals.** If the system requires user manuals, how will these be constructed, and by whom? Will they be presented in hard copy, electronic format, or both?

♦ **Operational manuals.** An operations manual will be prepared regardless of whether the support individual is within your central IT support office or is a non-IT employee of your organization. This manual should describe all key system functionality and how to operate the system, including—but not limited to—general troubleshooting, running of reports, entry and retrieval of data, and so on. Obviously, the level of complexity of such a manual will vary depending on the complexity of the system and the level of technical expertise within your organization.

Business Continuity Plan

After the tragedy of the 9/11 terrorist attacks, businesses of all sizes began to take another look at their existing continuity plans by asking the central question: What would happen if a disaster occurred of such a scale that it completely wiped out the company's information infrastructure? While we all pray that a disaster of the 9/11 magnitude will never occur again anywhere in the world, lesser events such as fire, flood, and theft can occur with equally debilitating results in terms of a company's information assets. That said, a strong business continuity plan is an absolute must, and it should address the following issues:

◆ **What is the general description of the business continuity plan?** In the event of a system failure, what is the continuity plan to ensure that work can continue? This can be a general outline with specifics to follow.

◆ **What is the disaster recovery model?** In the event of catastrophic system failure, what is the process for bringing the system back online and ensuring no loss of data and/or data integrity?

◆ **What is the system backup process?** How are the system and the data it contains backed up on a regular basis? Where are the copies of the system and/or data kept? (Off site? In a different location within the building?)

System Training

A system is only as good as the people who use it. With that in mind, proper training is a critical element to any successful system rollout. When thinking about your training components, you should keep the following issues in mind and be prepared to address them before you put the seal of completion on any project.

◆ **What training is required for the system?** This should include training for the users and additional members of your technology staff when applicable as part of the cross-training initiative within the department. This ensures that when personnel changes occur, essential operational knowledge of a system doesn't walk out the door in the hands of only one employee.

◆ **How will training be conducted?** Will an instructor lead the training? Will online training be provided? Will additional materials be required, such as training manuals for users?

◆ **Who will lead the training?** Which individuals and/or departments will be responsible for leading the training?

◆ **How will training materials be prepared, and who will prepare them?** If training materials are required, specify the costs of producing and/or purchasing these materials, and who will be responsible for covering these costs (including information such as department and account number).

Post-Implementation Change Control

So you have a well-designed system in place. You've documented the system, performed the testing, given great training. Now, six months post-implementation, you need to make some changes. How do you do it?

When thinking of post-implementation change control, you must try to remember that a system being changed is a system that needs to go through this entire process to some degree one more time, no matter how well it was designed initially. Two important issues need to be considered when planning for post-implementation change control.

◆ How will requests for changes or revisions to the system be solicited, and how often?

◆ How will changes be implemented?

 CAUTION

Depending on the scope of the post-implementation changes, you might need to prepare a second project template because all issues within the template (from system requirements to security) might need to be re-evaluated and changed or updated to reflect the post-implementation changes.

Retaining Records

Related to so many other topics in your process plan (such as security and business continuity), you must also consider the issue of record retention early in the planning stages.

What types of records should you retain? Generally speaking, the following list is a good place to begin as your consider the requirements for your own project.

- ◆ **System code.** You should store a hard copy of all system code with the signed, approved copy of this document.

- ◆ **Training materials.** This includes electronic master copies of all training materials that are developed.

- ◆ **Change control documentation.** Any requests for changes or revisions to the system must be in writing. You should also retain these change-control request forms with the previously listed items.

- ◆ **Development notes.** This includes any meeting notes, e-mail, or other annotated conversations relevant to system development.

- ◆ **Testing results.** This includes focus group results, survey forms and their corresponding results, and so on.

- ◆ **Post-implementation periodic reviews.** These are described in the following section.

Post-Implementation Periodic Reviews

The Byrds once sang (taking from a famous Biblical passage in Ecclesiastes) to everything there is a season. Such is the case with technology and the applications you develop. Although it is true that you might build an application that will be used for many years, even the best systems are forced to change due to various technical and non-technical forces (such as market issues) acting upon them.

To anticipate these changes, you need to have a system of periodic post-implementation review. Normally, this will consist of a group of key system stakeholders (including users and developers of the system, as well as process managers) who meet on a regular basis to discuss the state of the system. It also includes any comments and feedback given about the system, as well as considerations of technological and business process advancements that might need to be integrated into the system for it to function and meet the business' needs more efficiently. You should answer the following questions with regard to your planning for post-implementation periodic reviews.

- ◆ How/when will the system be periodically reviewed? (Annually? Semi-annually? Quarterly?)

- ◆ Who will participate in these review sessions?

◆ Who will organize the review sessions?

◆ Who (or what process) will be responsible for deciding which changes will be implemented, and thus following the post-implementation change control procedures?

Project Timeline

I'm not a project manager, but I have had the great fortune of working with some very talented project managers. They are an intense group of people; you can normally spot them wandering the halls of an organization with their supplies of Post-It notes, markers, long sheets of paper that have been taped together to represent an entire project, computer printouts… the list goes on. Great project managers represent a combination of business savvy, can-do spirit, and an ability to inspire people on the project team to get things done correctly and on time.

If you have the resources to bring on a project manager specifically for your application development, I highly recommend it because being a great project manager is a full-time job. However, if you have to tackle this role on your own, you should try, at the very least, to set timelines for all of the different sections in your project template (such as when testing will begin and end, and how long each beta cycle will last).

CAUTION

Sometimes even the smallest projects can appear daunting, especially if resources such as manpower and money are tight, if there are strong or conflicting personalities on the project team, or if the existing business environment is negative (for example, if the situation has decayed to such a state that an IT solution must be implemented quickly). Again, if you have access to a professional project manager, you should definitely consider this person a tremendous asset to your entire application development process. However, if you have to do this on your own, even developing a simple timeline, taking each step one at a time, and trying to achieve the deadlines you set for yourself and your team is better than having no project timeline or plan at all.

Project Plan Approval

Last but certainly not least is getting all stakeholder signatures on the final project plan. Do not overlook this critical step, and avoid the temptation to just forge ahead with the project despite not having a completed plan or all of the signatures.

You can think of a signed project plan as a contract in which all parties agree to a certain goal (the implemented application solution) and agree upon the path to achieve it (in other words, the project plan and all the resources—monetary and manpower—that are required to get the job done). There are many things you wouldn't consider doing without a contract (such as getting a loan or contracting to build a house), and your application development should be no different, regardless of the project's size.

Essential Database Design Considerations

Ideally, if you have a well-defined process plan (as defined in the preceding sections), then most of your database design considerations will take care of themselves. Specifically, you will know the system requirements, the data to be recorded, the business objectives the system is to facilitate, and so on.

Again, this is why a well-designed project plan is so critical to your SQL Server application solution initiatives. Databases should, by default, be designed not just to store data, but to store it in a way that is indicative of larger company processes. (In other words, the data should be entered in the same order or fashion as it is used and manipulated within the company.) Moreover, databases should allow information to be extracted, reviewed, and analyzed, because the information is one of the precious commodities of any company, large or small.

As you might guess, database design is a huge topic and includes quite a bit of conceptual theory (in other words, the waters can get very muddy very fast). However, I want to introduce you to some key terms with regard to database design.

Normalizing Your Database

"Normalization" is a loaded term in database design. Everyone wants to have a normalized database, but not everyone understands exactly what this means. (Quite frankly, I would include myself in this group.) To be fair, this is a confusing and sometimes highly theoretical issue that is difficult to grasp for even the most experienced developers. Still, there are some things that you can watch out for in your database design and, in turn, practically apply to your own SQL Server solutions.

With regard to normalization, there are stages of normal form. Ideally, your database should aspire to be normalized to the third normal form (3NF). Although there are normal forms beyond the first three, they are very conceptual and theoretical and not really necessary to having a well-designed, functional database solution.

First Normal Form (1NF)

To achieve first normal form within a database, you need to remove any repeating groups of information.

As with all issues of normalization, you should consider what effect this removal or moving out (to a different database table) of data has on the speed and efficiency of your database to return data results. If your database is relatively small or the types of data you are collecting repeat, but only in sporadic fashion (such as a CustomerInfo table where three or four customers might have the same last name), it probably wouldn't make sense to move that information out to a different table. But consider the Table A.1, which shows an excerpt from a table called MusicOrders.

Table A.1 MusicOrders

Record Number	OrderID	CustomerID	ItemOrdered	Item Price
1	124	1123	Let it Be	$11.99
2	531	4321	Let it Be	$11.99
3	871	4881	Let it Be	$11.99
4	351	9183	The Wall	$19.99
5	912	7312	Aja	$10.99

For illustrative purposes, assume that this table actually contains hundreds of records and that the Beatles CD, *Let It Be* has been ordered 30 or 40 times (and thus is entered 30 or 40 times individually in the table).

In this case, the table can be normalized to the first normal form by having the ItemOrdered data moved out to a separate table (perhaps called ItemsOrdered), and then linked backed to this table via the OrderID column. (In this case,

OrderID would be the primary key of the MusicOrders table.) Additionally, the CustomerID field could be repeated quite often (assuming that some customers are repeat customers), so that column would probably also be moved out to its own table. (You could call this table CustomerInfo, for example, and it could include not only the CustomerID field, but also the name, address, phone number, and e-mail address of the customer in question.)

So to achieve first normal form (1NF), you could split this table into three different tables (MusicOrders, ItemsOrdered, and CustomerInfo). Incidentally, in Table A.1, the OrderID would be the primary key of the table, which would in turn be linked to information in the other two tables.

Second Normal Form (2NF)

Second normal form becomes a bit more complicated. To achieve second normal form, you must meet the requirements of the first normal form and each column within the table must depend on the whole primary key.

 NOTE

Normalization from one form to the next is a cumulative process. In other words, to achieve fourth normal form (4NF) a database must meet the requirements of the first three normal forms. You can't have a database that achieves, for example, third normal form without achieving second or first normal form.

What does this mean? Put simply, if you look at Table A.1, you need to ask yourself, "Can I locate any of this information without relying on the primary key?" (Again, in the case of that table, the primary key is the OrderID column.) The answer in this case is no. Because each row of data represents a specific order that is linked to the OrderID (or the whole key, in this case), this table would achieve second normal form (assuming you split it out into three tables, as described in the preceding section).

To clarify this issue of second normal form and reliance on the whole key, consider Table A.2.

Table A.2 Customer Information

Record Number	FirstName	MiddleName	LastName
1	John	W	Burns
2	William	E	Smith
3	Robert	B	Townshend

There is no primary key identified in this table, and it would be possible to locate information (first name, middle name, and last name) at random, without having to rely on any whole key identifier. Put simply, none of these records are unique to a specific identifier, as compared to Table A.1, in which each row of data (and the individual columns contained therein) was linked to a whole unique identifier. Therefore, this table would not achieve second normal form.

Third Normal Form (3NF)

Third normal form might ironically be the easiest of the three to understand. (At the very least, it is simpler to understand than second normal form.) Take a look at Table A.3.

Table A.3 Order Quantity

Record Number	OrderID	Price	Quantity	Total Price
1	123	11.00	4	$44.00
2	473	15.00	2	$30.00
3	811	5.00	10	$50.00

To achieve third normal form, no column in the table can be dependent on another column within the table that is not defined as a key, and no data can be derived from other data stored in the table.

Table A.3, then, does not meet the third normal form. Why?

◆ The TotalPrice column is dependent on two columns—Price and Quantity.

◆ The TotalPrice column is derived from the same two columns.

Other Preliminary Database Design Issues

Normalization is the key concept I wanted to present you with here. However, consider the following points as important preliminary issues.

◆ **Consider denormalization.** As I indicated in the preceding section, there are times when not meeting a certain normal form (in that example, the third normal form) can actually be a good thing because it can bring performance enhancement to your database functioning. Although as a general rule you should strive toward normalization, this is not always the case.

◆ **Work with relationships.** Relationships are links between tables and the records they contain. Such relationships can be one-to-one, one-to-many, or many-to-many. It is through relationships that the real power of a relational database system comes into full view.

◆ **Diagramming your databases.** A central component of good database design (and good database administration) is knowing how to diagram your databases and in turn read and interpret those diagrams.

◆ **OLTP and OLAP.** Short for *Online Transaction Processing* and *Online Analytical Processing*, these two methods of manipulating data involve the fashion in which information is updated within a database (either instantaneously or after a delay), and the expected effects on normalization and other areas of database design that this process involves.

Summary

This appendix presented you with some critical planning and design advice with regard to your overall project/application design plan and database design theory. You were introduced to a 17-step application design planning template, and each section was described and discussed in relation to the entire development process. Then, you were presented with the key element of database design—normalization—and given examples and illustrations of the three normal forms (1NF, 2NF, and 3NF) that most database applications seek to achieve. Finally, you were briefly introduced to other database design considerations.

Index

Symbols

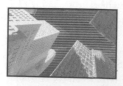